Cuban Catholics in the United States, 1960–1980

D1525437

LATINO PERSPECTIVES

Gilberto Cárdenas, series editor

INSTITUTE *for*

Latino Studies

UNIVERSITY OF NOTRE DAME

The Institute for Latino Studies, in keeping with the distinctive mission, values, and traditions of the University of Notre Dame, promotes understanding and appreciation of the social, cultural, and religious life of U.S. Latinos through advancing research, expanding knowledge, and strengthening community.

CUBAN CATHOLICS
IN THE
UNITED STATES,
1960–1980

Exile and Integration

GERALD E. POYO

University of Notre Dame Press
Notre Dame, Indiana

Manufactured in the United States of America

Library of Congress Cataloging-in-Publication Data

Poyo, Gerald Eugene, 1950–
   Cuban Catholics in the United States, 1960-1980 : exile and integration /
Gerald E. Poyo.
      p. cm. — (Latino perspectives)
   Includes bibliographical references and index.
   ISBN-13: 978-0-268-03832-8 (cloth : alk. paper)
   ISBN-10: 0-268-03832-5 (cloth : alk. paper)
   ISBN-13: 978-0-268-03833-5 (pbk. : alk. paper)
   ISBN-10: 0-268-03833-3 (pbk. : alk. paper)
   1. Cuban American Catholics—History—20th century.   I. Title.
   BX1407.C83P69 2007
   282'.73089687291—dc22
                              2007025335

∞ *The paper in this book meets the guidelines for permanence and durability
of the Committee on Production Guidelines for Book Longevity of the Council
on Library Resources.*

TO MIRYAM

CONTENTS

ACKNOWLEDGMENTS

After completing in 1989 a monograph on the nineteenth-century Cuban communities in the United States, I knew my next project needed to focus in some way on the post-1959 Cuban exile experience. During the previous decade I had spent considerable time in Cuba, where most of the records of the nineteenth century's exile experience are available, but now research time would be spent mostly in south Florida, a dramatic change to be sure. Though quite radically different settings, research experiences in both places proved fruitful and genuinely satisfying. I have learned about the history of Cuban exiles and immigration, as well as about the Cuban people themselves, on both sides of the Florida Straits and could not have contributed what I have without the use of libraries and archives in Miami and Havana, not to mention without the help of knowledgeable scholars, librarians, and archivists in these two cities. Access to research materials, scholars, and everyday people on both sides of the Straits of Florida is necessary to write the history of Cuba and its relations with the United States. It is my hope that academic and educational interaction continues and brings the two alienated peoples closer together.

The idea for this volume coincided with my acceptance of a teaching position at Florida International University (FIU) in Miami in fall 1990. Lisandro Pérez, sociologist at FIU and leading academic figure in building FIU's Cuban and Cuban-American program, encouraged this project, as did Mark Szuchman, history department head at the time. With the support of both, FIU generously provided resources to complement a National Endowment for the Humanities Fellowship during January–June 1991, facilitating my first explorations into the topic. For a variety of personal reasons that led me to take a teaching post at St. Mary's University in San Antonio, the project lost priority to several other research initiatives and did not revive until 1998, when I received a six-month Rockefeller Humanities Fellowship at FIU's Cuban Research Institute (CRI). Lisandro and Uva de Aragon, CRI director and associate director respectively, as well as their staff, helped me in countless ways that I deeply appreciate.

Another opportunity to advance the project presented itself during the period from August 2000 to May 2002, when I held visiting appointments at the Institute of Latino Studies (ILS) and the history department at the University of Notre Dame, which provided two years of virtually uninterrupted research. Facilitated by Gilberto Cardenas and Allert Brown-Gort, ILS director and associate director respectively, I completed the research and began to write. I appreciate the support and encouragement of these colleagues, as well as of the ILS staff, especially Caroline Domingo, who took a speical interest in the project, kept in touch when I returned to St. Mary's, and encouraged me to send the manuscript to the University of Notre Dame Press. A final financial contribution for this project came from a research grant from Recovering the Hispanic Religious Thought Project at the University of Houston, headed by Nicolás Kanellos.

Over the years, administrative decisions at St. Mary's University by President Charles Cotrell; Vice President for Academic Affairs David Manuel; Deans Rev. Charles Miller, Anthony Kaufmann, and Janet Dizinno; and history department chair Daniel Bjork gave me the opportunity to take full advantage of the various research opportunities. Moreover, faculty development grants from the Office of the Vice President for Academic Affairs of St. Mary's University made possible additional research travel to south Florida during two summers. Certainly, this book would not have been written without the financial and logistical support of these various institutions and their leaders.

Many other colleagues also contributed to the development of this book. Tim Matovina, director of the Cushwa Center for the Study of American Catholicism, University of Notre Dame, provided abundant guidance and input on the manuscript. Tim's vast knowledge of Catholic history and theology helped me navigate fields I knew little about; his challenging and critical readings of chapters kept me rethinking and revising; his keen editorial skills caught many problems that improved the manuscript. The book profited dramatically from his numerous readings and suggestions, though I did not always take his advice, and any deficiencies are my own.

Marifeli Pérez-Stable and José (Manolín) Hernández read at least one draft of the first chapter and offered important comments that helped me rethink aspects of Cuba's history of the 1940s and 1950s. Manolín also made available materials from his personal collections and discussed his own experiences as a Catholic activist. Likewise, Salvador Miranda, another committed Catholic of the era and assistant director for collections management at FIU's library provided material from his personal collection, especially extensive newspaper clippings on Cuban Catholicism of the late 1950s. His willingness to speak with me about his background, including his memories of prominent Catholic personalities, involvement with Agrupación Católica Universitaria and his participation in the Bay of Pigs invasion revealed important contextual frames and research clues. Anthony Suárez, a former employee of the archdiocese of Miami and doctoral student at University of Notre Dame, introduced me to numerous people who also helped contextualize the story.

This book naturally owes a great deal to archives and libraries and of course their staffs. The Cuban Heritage Collection at the University of Miami's Otto G. Richter Library, under the direction of Esperanza B. de Varona, provided the critical mass of research material for this project. The library's archives and newspaper collection is an extraordinary body of source material for the study of Cuban exiles. I must also acknowledge Lesbia de Varona and Gladys Ramos who helped in many ways whenever I visited the library. FIU's library helped a great deal, especially with a complete collection of the Franciscan magazine *La Quincena* in its special collections. Besides its remarkable general Catholic history holdings, the University of Notre Dame library contains much difficult-to-find material on Cuban Catholicism and a complete microfilm of the important Archdiocese of Miami newspaper, *The Voice*. Belén school's collection of José Ignacio Lasaga's papers provided important data, as did the library at the Southeast Pastoral Institute in Miami. Brief conversations with Araceli Cantero at the Archdiocese of Miami provided several important research directions, as did conversations with archivists regarding State Department and Central Intelligence Agency sources at the National Archives, College Park, Maryland.

The work of producing a book is always a complex process involving many people. I want to thank the staff of the University of Notre Dame Press, including Rebecca DeBoer (managing editor), Lowell Francis (acquisitions), Margaret Gloster (book design), and Katherine Pitts (marketing), for making the process relatively easy. Thanks also to copy editor Beth Wright who improved the manuscript and José M. Cabrera whose artistic digital redesign of the mural at the Shrine of Nuestra Señora de la Caridad del Cobre in Miami appears on the book cover. I also appreciate very much Noel and Sonia Poyo and Miryam Bujanda for suggesting a "book indexing party" that turned an always tedious task into a family affair.

Family offered important support on many other fronts. My father, Sergio, and uncle José Poyo, shared their memories of life in Cuba in the late 1930s and their days at Colegio Belén. My uncle Jorge Poyo, a resident of Miami, kept a close eye on the press and other sources of interest to this project. His many mailings contributed to my understanding of south Florida Cubans. Over the years they all encouraged my interest in Cuban history. Though my father passed away before seeing the completed book, he read early drafts of the manuscript which to my great satisfaction he liked very much.

My spouse, Miryam Bujanda, to whom this book is dedicated, was an unfailing companion throughout this project. Her support for what I do, her encouragement, and most of all her enthusiasm for writing and literature helped me keep my perspective when, as often happens, one wonders if the goal is even in sight. She is always an inspiration in so many ways.

ABBREVIATIONS

ACU	Agrupación Católica Universitaria
ASH	Asociación Sacerdotal Hispana
CANF	Cuban American National Foundation
CCAS	Comité Coordinador del Apostolado Seglar
CCD	Confraternity of Christian Doctrine
CELAM	Consejo Episcopal Latinamericano
CHC	Centro Hispano Católico
CICOP	Catholic Inter-American Cooperation Program
CLASC	Confederación Latino Americano de Sindicalistas Cristianos
CNPC	Cuban National Planning Council
COCCE	Comité de organizaciones Católicos Cubanos del Exilio
CRC	Consejo Revolucionario Cubano
CRECED	Comunidades de Reflexión Eclesial Cubana en la Diáspora
CRP	Cuban Refugee Program
CTC	Confederacion de Trobajadores Cubanos
CYO	Catholic Youth Organization
DRE	Directorio Revolucionario Estudiantil del MRR
ENEC	Encuentro Nacional Eclesial Cubano
EPC	Equipo de Pastoral de Conjunto
FEU	Federación Estudiantil Universitario
FJC	La Federación de la Juventud Cubana
FON	Frente Obrero Nacional

FRD	Frente Revolucionario Democrático
IAISF	Inter-American Institute for Social Formation
IEC	Instituto de Estudios Cubanos
INRA	Instituto Nacional de Reforma Agraria
ISA	Institute of Social Action
JEC	Juventud Estudiantil Católica
JOC	Juventud Obrera Católica
JPC	Junta Patriótica Cubana
JUC	Juventud Universitaria Católica
MDC	Movimiento Democrático Cristiano
MFC	Movimiento Familiar Cristiano
MRP	Movimiento Revolucionario del Pueblo
MRR	Movimiento de Recuperación Revolucionaria
OAS	Organization of American States
OCSHA	Obra de Cooperación Sacerdotal Hispanoamericana
PREC	Primera Reunión de Estudios Cubanos
RECE	Representación Cubana del Exilio
SALAD	Spanish American League against Discrimination
SEPI	Southeast Pastoral Institute
STC	Solidaridad de Trabajadores Cubanos
TACC	Truth About Cuba Committee
UCE	Unión de Cubanos en el Exilio
UFW	United Farm Workers
USCC	United States Catholic Conference

INTRODUCTION

The flight of tens of thousands of Cubans during the 1960s from a radical revolution that eventually became an orthodox Marxist state along Soviet lines produced militant nationalist communities abroad dedicated to an eventual return. These refugees followed a long tradition of political exile in Cuban history. Throughout the island's turbulent history highly politicized populations have fled political repression but more often than not remained engaged with the destiny of their homeland. Cubans departed with strong national feelings and deep connections to their *patria* that influenced community and family life, institutions, and attitudes characterized by a powerful sense of exile identity. Certainly not all Cubans yearned for their homeland in the same way during all periods, but the phenomenon has been present throughout with differing degrees of intensity.[1]

In 1992, a wide cross-section of Cuban Catholics representing religious and laity, diverse generations, and competing political perspectives met in St. Augustine, Florida, and issued a document known as CRECED.[2] Catholic leaders described themselves "as essentially exiles and not mere immigrants of an economic kind" and interpreted their overall experience as similar to the biblical Babylonian exile.[3] Central to this affirmation of exile was the idea of return. "The great prophets of the exile . . . devoted a great deal of their activity to preparing for the return with programs and slogans that would help the restoration of the dispersed of Israel as the People of God returned to the promised-land." Though the time had not yet arrived for Cubans to return home, "we would be remiss in our duty if we did not begin, right now, to prepare with prayer and concrete plans."[4] "The spiritual climate of the Babylonian exile," they declared, "is the yearning for the fatherland, both bitter and sweet at once; together with it, as the years go by, the urgency of preparing for return is a part of that climate."[5] Any thought of return, of course, required maintaining a genuine sense of Cuban identity and nationality. "We have been in exile for over thirty years and we have not forgotten or set aside the Cuban issue," and this should continue as a pastoral challenge; to form "men and women with a Christian outlook on life, capable of sacrificing themselves to rebuild a nation as envisioned by the Apostle of our Independence, José Martí."[6]

1

These characteristics so clearly articulated in the early 1990s in fact emerged and developed during the first twenty years of exile, a period now often referred to in the Miami Cuban community as the "historical exile." Their powerful sense of exile and desire for return, even as they established a formidable economic, political, and sociocultural presence in Florida and other states quickly defined the Cuban community in the United States. This is a story of the Cuban-born exile generation of the 1960s and 1970s: those arriving as already formed adults, young adults who completed their maturation in exile, and adolescents and children whose formation occurred outside Cuba. They all struggled over time to translate their exile and emerging ethnic realities into coherent actions that would honor their commitment to their homeland while facilitating their integration into other societies. This book explores their exile from Cuba and their integration into the United States, mostly in south Florida but also in other places, and considers the relationships between exilic and ethnic identities and the place of Cubans in the broader society.

Unlike immigrants who arrived without any intention of ever returning home, Cuban refugees in the 1960s and 1970s more often than not remained engaged with their island nation, intent eventually on reclaiming losses and redressing grievances. Since loss of culture also meant disintegration of traditional identity and claim on the homeland, exiles did what they could to retain and cultivate their way of life. This psychological orientation informed almost everything in their daily activities, giving their preoccupation with return at least equal if not more importance than strategies of integration. At the same time Cubans evolved an ethnic identity through which they engaged North American society. Though Cubans rejected the idea of assimilation, reflecting the conviction that their situation was temporary and that they would eventually return home, they had to contend with the reality of integrating into new societies. For Cubans, assimilation meant turning their back on their heritage while integration sought ways of adjusting without losing their Cubanness. Exile and integration remained distinct ideas for Cubans, but they inevitably influenced each other.

Cuban Catholics lived within a larger Cuban community imbued with a strong secular tradition, but the interest here is to examine the particularly Catholic influences that affected their thinking and action during this era of dramatic change in their country, church, and the world.[7] Though a diverse population, Cuban Catholics usually remained tied to their religious traditions, which invested their disrupted lives with a measure of coherence. Catholics sought direction from their church, theology, and leadership, as well as their own consciences, as they tried to make sense of the significant changes in Catholic thought emanating from the Second Vatican Council (1962–1965) and papal encyclicals of the 1960s and 1970s. Cuban refugees rarely came to the same conclusions about their obligations as exiles to their land of origin or their adopted homes, but most practicing Catholics did take seriously the tenets of their faith in the Catholic Action tradition of "seeing, judging, and acting." They routinely looked to the principles of their faith to determine the best options in their new environment, though they did not always agree with their church nor even act in unison.

While Catholics represent only a small slice of the Cuban exile story, they offer a microcosm through which to explore in some detail and understand many of the themes relevant to the exile experience generally. Initially conceived as a study of the Cuban community in south Florida, in time the examination narrowed to Catholics when it became evident that one version of the exile story could be told in considerable detail from their point of view. Though most Cuban refugees may have been nominally Catholic, only a small segment practiced their religion on a regular basis and lived their lives in relation to Catholic faith and tradition. This book is mostly about them, though the voices of others who shared the journey also appear.

"Catholics" in this book refers to those serious practitioners of their religion whose thought and action were informed by the spiritual inspirations and theological teachings of their faith. Obviously, to what extent an individual was motivated by faith, or other considerations such as class interest and personal ambition, is not always easy to discern, and certainly all these elements existed. For this reason, in identifying Cuban Catholics, determining the content of their hearts was less a concern than simply identifying whether their actions responded to some commitment to Catholic ideals and whether they seemed to live their everyday lives within the general context of their religion. Many of the voices that appear here are confessional Catholics, people who projected their faith in their writings, speeches, and other communications, who grappled with Catholic thought and attempted to live by its principles. Others are nominal or lapsed

Catholics, though influenced by its traditions. Still others are people not identified as Catholics at all but who operated within the political and social circles here considered. According to estimates, perhaps only 5 to 10 percent of Cubans fell into the category of practicing Roman Catholics in the 1950s. A significant percentage of these, however, fled the island during the 1960s, concentrating the island's Catholics in a relatively few cities, especially influencing Miami. Some have suggested that in Miami, the largest and most important exile community, Catholicism had a greater influence on Cubans after they left home than when they lived in Cuba.

This book examines all these facets among Catholics mostly in south Florida, though Cubans across the United States, Latin America, and Europe also enter the story. The personal papers of exiles, newspapers, books and pamphlets, government archives, and personal interviews provide the historical data for this book. Though future studies need to explore sources neglected here, including parish records, the archives of the apostolic movements, the personal papers of the many actors included here, and archdiocese of Miami archives, this project does provide a step toward a history of Cuban exile Catholics that engages the many critical themes necessary for understanding their place in United States immigration and ethnic history. The themes, woven throughout this narrative, which spans the 1960s and 1970s, include their life at home before departing; the causes, motivations, and manner of their exodus; their resettlement and creation of exile identity and community, and ultimately their adjustment to and integration into their new society.

The conventional wisdom about Cubans in the United States holds that they are conservative and staunchly hard-line exiles obsessively preoccupied with overthrowing the Castro regime using all available means. The majority did become convinced Cold Warriors, routinely reaffirming the church's traditional anti-communist teachings and suspicious of those who persisted in supporting revolutionary politics in Latin America and the United States. Cuban Catholics did indeed participate in developing and maintaining numerous strategies for trying to dislodge the regime in Cuba, including organizing armed incursions to establish guerrilla operations on the island, international diplomacy and propaganda, and lobbying in Washington, DC. Religion often played an influential role in justifying and sustaining hard-line attitudes among Cuban Catholics.[8]

The story, however, is more diverse and complex. It is also the case that a significant minority of exile Catholics revealed pragmatic sensibilities, advocating dialogue and advancing diverse options to difficult problems. Catholicism of the 1960s and 1970s spoke to many aspects of the exile reality and for some provided the logic for pragmatism and openness that eventually carved its place in the hearts of a significant Catholic exile sector. This study explores the evolving attitudes and debates that framed the exile journey to secure a return home. As Cuban-American theologian Fernando Segovia has noted, "The human world . . . forged in exile is . . . a world of pessimism, where evil is seen as reigning largely undisturbed." At the same time, exile also included "a world of optimism, where deliberate measures to disturb evil are nonetheless constantly planned and undertaken—despite the known odds, the meager hopes for victory, and the ever-present conviction that any victory or disturbance is in the end but apparent and short-lived." "Such a world," Segovia suggests, "is beyond reformation and crying for reformation, beyond justice and well-being and in dire need of them, fatefully resigned and yet outright defiant . . . a world of profound ambiguity, with a logical discourse that goes back and forth endlessly."[9] Perhaps pessimism encouraged a hardened intransigence while optimism birthed a vision of what might yet be.

Exile identity not only influenced attitudes about the homeland but also provided Cubans with a foundation for an ethnic consciousness focused on maintaining national identity and culture as they integrated into the United States. Cubans arriving in south Florida during the 1960s created a self-sustaining community with remarkable economic, cultural, and political autonomy from the dominant society.[10] Cubans established a strong foothold in the economic structure of south Florida, influenced its cultural environment, and established political dominance.[11] They created institutions and cultural traditions that reflected and reinforced their exile and ethnic realities, and Catholics utilized their faith to guide family and community through these turbulent times.[12]

Ethnic consciousness also manifested itself among Cuban Catholics in relation to other Hispanic ethnic groups in the United States, especially Mexican Americans and Puerto Ricans. Historically, the United States society's attitude toward Latinos was ambivalent at best and brutally racist and segregationist at worst. Despite the rhetoric of the melting pot and the "Americanization" programs of the 1920s and 1930s, Euro-Americans did not welcome Latinos on equal terms. Certainly racial concerns about what was generally considered a nonwhite population fueled Euro-American animosity toward these "alien" people. The history of race and slavery in the

United States promoted segregation and separateness toward non-European minorities, provoking them eventually to an affirmative and sometimes militant embrace of ethnic and minority perspectives. Added to this, the constant arrival of Hispanic immigrants maintained ethnic communities in touch with their cultures of origin and even broadened their territorial reach, giving them the possibility of maintaining an ongoing ethnic world even after several generations had grown up in the United States.

With the Civil Rights Movement and immigration reform of the 1960s, as political barriers dropped and even more immigrants arrived, Latinos became more integrated into society at the same time that they reaffirmed their cultures and identities, reinvigorating the traditional cultural expressions of many second- and third-generation U.S. Hispanics. During the 1960s and 1970s this influenced Hispanic Catholics who, rather than seeking integration into a culturally Anglo-American church, sought space for their own forms of worship. They demanded respect for their traditions, language, and religious practices, which the church cautiously accepted within a paradigm of the new pluralism.[13]

This generally familiar story has been told without reference to Cubans, who also participated, though in their own way and with their own rationale. Conventional perceptions that Cubans shared few affinities with Latinos and remained apart from their struggles are here challenged. Cubans, too, consciously rejected the idea of assimilation and insisted on maintaining their language and culture, but not for the same reasons. Except for the initially small percentage of mulattos and blacks, Cubans did not generally experience the racialized exclusion felt by other Latinos in the United States. They did, however, experience a cultural alienation that inspired them to make common cause with other Hispanics. This study reveals the enthusiasm with which Cubans engaged other Latinos and traces their contributions to the national Hispanic Catholic movement of the 1970s. While Cubans generally may not have shared in the radical articulations and activism of the Chicano movement, for example, many Cuban Catholics certainly made common cause with Hispanics in defending cultural traditions and advocating the maintenance of the Spanish language.

Cuban Catholics arriving in the United States in the 1960s became stridently anti-communist in reaction to their experience of displacement and eventually became in their majority aligned with the increasingly conservative Republican Party, but this too is not the entire story. The detailed and nuanced narrative presented here challenges popular perceptions of Cubans as an exclusively insular and homogeneous community of right-wing ideologues. Cubans remained closely aligned with Cuban, Latin American, and Spanish values and traditions, developing diasporic communities that often looked as much to the south as to the north. This contributed to the emergence of international perspectives among Cubans whose exile identity kept them in relation with the Hispanic world outside the United States. This book highlights the avenues of contact and relationship with the world that provoked changing attitudes and perspectives in many Cubans. Cuban Catholics possessed a traditional commitment to the social doctrines of their church that routinely challenged them to think about more than opposing communism. Though interpretations varied, many Cuban Catholics nevertheless remained cognizant of the importance of social consciousness within the traditions of their faith, necessarily influencing their thinking about a number of issues.

By tracing in some detail the historical trajectory of Catholic personalities and actors, revealing their ideas and aspirations, and analyzing the meaning of their actions, this book aims to further the goal of writing the history of Cubans as exiles while also exploring their place in the broader landscape of U.S. history during the 1960s and 1970s. Without losing sight of Cuban exiles as a heterogeneous population with divergent views and experiences, the fundamental intent is to explore how one group—Catholics—coped with exile, maintained a commitment to their homeland, integrated into a new society, and transformed over time, guided by their church and faith.

Chapter One

REFORM AND REVOLUTION

I wish only to insist that Catholics are generally disposed to second all government actions that promote the public good and harmonize our personal rights with those of our neighbors, in a climate of justice and social charity.

—Bishop Evelio Díaz (1959)

Thousands of Catholic activists fleeing the communist Revolution in Cuba arrived in south Florida during 1960 and 1961. Confused and disoriented by events in Cuba during the first two years of the Revolution, they acted with anger and determination to stop the communization of their homeland. Scenarios they could never have imagined overtook the Revolution; Fidel Castro had gone from characterizing Catholics as important contributors to the revolutionary victory to reactionaries and fascists working for the interests of the United States. The revolutionary leader convinced the Cuban people and international observers especially in Latin America and Europe that Catholics, particularly priests and the church hierarchy, opposed the interests of workers and campesinos, of the Revolution itself.

8

Economic dependency on the United States, political instability and violence, and social stratification characterized Cuba in the 1950s. During its first thirty years of independence, Cuba existed as a virtual protectorate of the United States. Forced to accept an article to the Cuban constitution drawn up by the U.S. Congress known as the Platt Amendment, which ensured U.S. control and protected U.S. interests, Cubans struggled to create a viable nation-state. In 1933, a revolt against President Gerardo Machado, an elected president turned dictator during the 1920s, initiated the unraveling of the old "Plattist" republic created under the watchful eye of the United States. The insurrection against Machado swept away the political elites that had arisen on their reputations as veterans of the independence wars, initiating realignments in Cuban political and socioeconomic life. The political environment became more complex, as the military, led by Fulgencio Batista, intellectuals, student leaders, labor activists, and the ideological left and influenced by democratic socialism and communism, vied for political power throughout the 1930s. Batista's authoritarian rule guaranteed a measure of political stability and brought some social reform—particularly to the urban working classes during the 1930s—leading to the writing of a new constitution in 1940.

The new governing document established democracy, provided universal suffrage, and offered a blueprint for reforming Cuban society. It included many socially conscious provisions and, while ensuring the primacy of private property, gave the state ample authority to intervene in Cuba's socioeconomic system.[1] The document reflected a genuinely reformist instinct among Cuba's political classes, many of whom had gained their training in the revolutionary climate and movements of the 1930s. They embraced social democratic precepts, generally exhibited secular sensibilities and did not hesitate to engage in alliances with communists if it suited their political strategies.

During the 1940s Cubans elected three presidents under the new reformist constitution. This string of successful electoral experiences augured well for Cuban democracy, but unfortunately corruption in the government and a lack of concrete social reform, especially in the rural areas, led to considerable popular disenchantment with the system. Reading this as an opportunity, Batista secretly returned to Cuba from his home in south Florida and staged a military coup in March 1952, gaining the recognition of the United States. For the next six years, he ruled Cuba in caudillo fashion,

rewarding his friends and killing, imprisoning, or exiling his enemies, leading to dissent and revolutionary action against his government. Though
Catholics were among those backing Batista, an even larger number opposed the dictator and embraced change.

For thirty years Catholic activists and intellectuals had worked hard to
advance a vision of their nation founded on the moral tenets of their faith
and social justice. Before the Revolution, Catholic leaders encouraged the
faithful to be socially aware, and they combined an impulse for change
rooted in the traditional papal social encyclicals with the activism of Spanish
Catholic Action. This predisposed large numbers of Catholics to support
the civic, reformist, or revolutionary movements against Fulgencio Batista
in the 1950s. To be sure, some Catholics were conservatives, but the reform-
minded constituted the majority among activists and perhaps among those
practicing their faith. This majority felt frustrated and then outraged by the
turn of events during the 1950s.

Like the great majority of Cubans, Catholics celebrated the triumph of
the Revolution on January 1, 1959, and felt satisfaction about the role they
had played. They believed a new moment had arrived for Cuba, a time for
cleansing, reform, and a continuing opportunity for spreading the Catholic
faith and its social doctrines. Catholic social activists believed that the
Revolution provided Cuba with the historical opportunity for moving from
theoretical and theological ideas about change to practical action. At the
same time, Catholics appealed to their traditions in resisting the communist Revolution, which seemed to appear out of nowhere to replace what
they considered was a Christian-inspired humanist movement aimed at
political and socioeconomic reform in Cuba.

As the Revolution became increasingly radical after mid-1959, the
Catholic Church, including hierarchy, clergy, and laity, represented the only
organized group in the least bit capable of contesting the new government's
policies. The church, its school system, and well-developed lay apostolic
movements, led by educated and dedicated militants with access to the
press, offered a competing vision for Cuban society and culture. While
Catholics supported the overthrow of Batista, they also naturally opposed
Fidel Castro's communist alternative, but in the end they did not represent
a sufficiently representative or unified social force to effectively oppose the
new regime.

Catholics first publicly challenged the revolutionary government during
late 1959 and organized open opposition during 1960–1961. Traditionally

opposed to involvement in the nation's political affairs, the politically in-experienced church hierarchy was no match for the highly motivated and astute Cuban rebels led by Castro, who subsequently gained the support of well-disciplined communist cadres. Within two years the revolutionary government crushed and silenced the Cuban church. Cubans streamed from the island, mostly to the United States but also to Venezuela, Puerto Rico, Spain, and other places. The mass exodus of Cubans opposed to communism included virtually the entire lay and clerical leadership of Cuba's Catholic community. Most Cuban Catholic activists left their homes with only training, traditions, and experience to use to build a new life.

Catholic Renaissance

Support for the revolutionary movement by important sectors of Cuban Catholicism, including lay leaders, priests, and at least three members of the church hierarchy, reflected a general renaissance in the Cuban church during the 1940s and 1950s. This renewal produced not only growth in the church but also at least two generations of militant laity and religious who, inspired by the moral and social teachings of their faith, took Catholic concerns into the arena of public policy discourse. This revitalization of Catholicism mainly among Cuba's middle classes during the first half of the twentieth century for the first time inspired them to become involved as Catholics in the nation's civic and political life. Cuba's economic and political elites had always been predominantly although only nominally Catholic and certainly had never governed as Catholics, in a confessional way inspired by the ideological and theological tenets of their religion. The church especially made its influence felt after 1940 when the Catholic Action movements took their ideas into the public and political arena and in the 1950s became actors in their own right opposing the Batista dictator-ship and supporting change.

The Catholic prominence in Cuba at the time of the Revolution may seem surprising, since Catholicism played a relatively marginal role in Cuban history, especially when compared to the church in Mexico and many other Latin American nations. In Cuba the Catholic Church had never developed as a powerful institution during the eighteenth and nineteenth centuries, nor did orthodox Catholicism become deeply rooted among the Cuban people; the faith remained mostly limited to the upper and middle classes.

Part of this phenomenon had to do with the popular following enjoyed by African-origin religious traditions like Santería that had connections to Catholicism but maintained their independent identity and expressions. The Cuban church's consistent identification with Spain and its rulers also troubled and alienated Cubans. Led by Spanish clerics, the church in Cuba remained faithful to Spain and openly opposed the various separatist movements during the final half of the nineteenth century. During the occupation of Cuba by the United States (1898–1902), the Cuban church found itself deeply isolated and marginalized by the North American ruling authorities, who immediately implemented a separation of church and state that was confirmed by the new Cuban constitution. With little backing from Cubans as well as a concrete loss of financial and moral support from the state after the departure of the Spanish, the church faced the challenge of re-creating itself. It accomplished this re-creation during the next half century.[2]

The church's emergence to a new position of respectability in Cuba proceeded slowly and steadily after independence and never reached its full potential before the outbreak of the Cuban Revolution. Still rooted in Cuba's white upper and middle classes, and strengthened by an influx of Spanish immigrants during the first twenty years of the century, the church developed institutionally, led increasingly by Cuban clerics but with the indispensable help of a large number of foreign religious, especially Spaniards. With the cessation of Spanish rule the authority to name Cuban bishops shifted away from the Spanish monarch to the pope, resulting in the appointment of Cubans. The church included two archdioceses (Havana and Santiago de Cuba) and four dioceses, and in 1946, for the first time, the pope named a Cuban Cardinal, the Archbishop of Havana, Manuel Arteaga.[3]

The establishment of a network of quality Catholic schools run by a variety of religious orders and the promotion of lay movements that recruited directly from the schools produced new generations of instructed and deeply committed Catholics who brought life to the church perhaps like never before in Cuba's history.[4] Certainly this growth in the first instance must be credited to the Catholic schools, which grew dramatically in the early twentieth century. Jesuits, Franciscans, the Christian Brothers (La Salle Brothers), Augustinians, Salesians, Dominicans, Marists, Ursuline Sisters, Sisters of Charity, Sisters of the Sacred Heart, and perhaps a dozen additional orders established schools in Cuba.[5] Many of the religious came from abroad, including Spain, France, the United States, and other countries. Cubans with sufficient resources, even those not disposed toward Catholicism, enrolled their children in Catholic schools. The schools did recruit a limited number from the urban working classes, but they failed altogether to influence Cuba's rural sectors.

Though many of the schools offered a limited number of scholarships for the poor, the Catholic school system became the educators of Cuba's middle and upper classes, reaffirming the church's traditional relationship to the established classes. Those Cuban poor, including the majority population of color, who studied at all, attended the terribly underfunded and secular public school system. Catholic education focused exclusively on primary and secondary school education until 1946, when Father Lorenzo Spirali, an Italian immigrant to the United States ordained in Philadelphia and sent to pastor in Cuba in 1926, promoted the idea of a Catholic university. He encouraged his Augustinian community in Philadelphia to sponsor the effort and founded Villanueva University. During the next decade, Villanueva University became the center of Catholic intellectual life on the island.[6]

In a society with strong secular traditions like Cuba, Catholic lay movements provided the vehicle for keeping Cuban youth graduating from Catholic schools linked to their faith beyond Sunday Mass. With the establishment of Villanueva, students could continue at a Catholic university, but most still went to the University of Havana, which was free and more prestigious. Whether they went directly into the job market or on to the state university, young Catholics were encouraged to join lay movements. The church embraced the Catholic Action model, which, during the first forty years of the twentieth century, the church in Europe and Latin America promoted as a way of broadening its impact on society.[7] As early as 1919, at a Eucharistic Congress in the diocese of Havana, the church encouraged Catholic men to become more involved with the church. "In order to frankly initiate Catholic action among us, for it remains in diapers," declared a church circular published in 1922, "unanimously we recognize the need to establish men's organizations." The document called on each ordinary on the island to consult with their priests to establish a network of lay organizations in large and small communities alike. In the same document the bishops also called for the creation of Catholic youth organizations, especially for those educated in Catholic schools, in order to maintain and strengthen their faith and religious training after leaving school. They called on Catholic schools to establish alumni associations and to create centers where they could meet and establish a *segundo hogar* (second home).[8]

These exhortations by the church hierarchy bore fruit before the end of the decade. In 1927, French-born Brother Augustín Victorino and a young university leader, Jorge Hyatt, organized Catholic youth, mostly graduates of private Catholic schools, hoping to provide students with a continuing relationship to the church and Catholicism as they entered the secular world of universities and professional life. Brother Victorino was one of fifteen French and Canadian religious of the Christian Brothers Congregation (also known as La Salle Brothers) who arrived in 1905 to establish Colegio La Salle. The French Brother's vision included forming a new generation of Cubans instructed in Catholic thought, convictions, and action.

Chapters opened all across the island, and the movement soon formalized into Federación de la Juventud Cubana (FJC), headquartered at La Salle. At the University of Havana students of the Federación formed the Club Universitario Católico in 1928. The FJC also launched a journal, *Revista Juventud Católica Cubana,* and established several night schools for workers.[9] In 1929, Jesuit priest Antonio Rivas and Dr. Valentin Arenas, a lawyer and notary from Sagua La Grande, brought together numerous lay organizations that had formed locally across the island into the Asociación de Caballeros Católicos de Cuba. Initially founded by some five hundred men, within fifteen years the organization had some six thousand members and 112 local chapters. It published a monthly bulletin; founded centers for religious education, schools for workers, model farms, free clinics, education scholarships for the underprivileged, social services, and libraries; and hosted conferences. Its primary goal was to establish a Christian social order in Cuba and to disseminate Catholic traditions.[10]

Congregations dedicated to Mary also formed and played an important role in spreading the faith throughout the 1930s and 1940s. Perhaps the most important was Agrupación Católica Universitaria (ACU) formed officially in 1928 by Father Felipe Rey de Castro, S.J., a Spanish priest from Galicia who worked as a prefect at Colegio Nuestra Señora de Belén operated by the Jesuits, perhaps the most prestigious private school on the island. ACU provided a place where university students of Catholic backgrounds could gather to cultivate their spiritual and religious life as they continued their education. Rey de Castro molded a highly devout, educated, and disciplined cadre of youth who entered the professional classes, hoping eventually to infuse Christian values and culture into the country's political, social, and economic life. To create a presence and provide students with a place to meet, ACU established a house near the University of Havana campus that included a study area, library, mimeograph machines, and a chapel.[11]

By the end of the 1930s, church activities had expanded considerably in Cuba, led by organizations like ACU and the FJC, inspiring the church hierarchy to do more. In January 1941, at a Eucharistic Congress in Camaguey the bishops announced the official formation of Cuban Catholic Action and by that June published the organizing statutes. In traditional Catholic Action fashion, the movement included four sections: men, young men, women, and young women. The already established lay organizations provided cadres with leadership skills and experience. The Caballeros Católicos became part of the La Rama de Hombres de Acción Católica; divided by gender, the FJC became the young men's and young women's sections of Catholic Action. The archbishop himself took charge of organizing the section for adult women. He also announced that every parish on the island should form chapters of Catholic Action, and by 1954 some 26,000 members worked to "rechristianize the family and society." Other specialized Catholic Action groups formed, including Juventud Estudiantil Católica (JEC), Juventud Universitaria Católica (JUC) and Juventud Obrera Católica (JOC).[12]

The institutional church and the lay movements increased their visibility in Cuban society through a variety of publications. The archdiocese of Havana, for example, published its *Boletín Eclesiástico.* Many of the religious orders, especially the Jesuits, Franciscans, Paulists, and Christian Brothers, published journals or small newsletters. Most of the daily or weekly newspapers contained religion sections, including *Diario de la Marina, El Mundo, La Prensa,* and *El País,* which commented on the issues of the day.[13] By the 1940s and 1950s Catholics in Cuba had established a firm institutional base, and Catholicism had taken firm root, especially among the middle and upper classes on the island.

Social Catholicism

Despite the instinctively conservative, pastoral, and predominantly class-based nature of Cuban Catholicism, reformist and even radical currents of

Catholic thinking emerged in the 1930s and 1940s. New generations of Catholic leaders and intellectuals, inspired by the social doctrines of the church, moved beyond the traditional pastoral focus of their faith to engage Cuba's pressing civic problems. Catholic Action's fervor in promoting education and evangelizing among Cuba's middle classes took on temporal concerns, as they responded to the daily socioeconomic and political realities of their nation. Catholics developed a mission beyond spiritual and pastoral matters, embracing an activist stance with regard to the social and moral issues.

In the first half of the century, secular thinking dominated Cuban politics. Nationalist, social democratic, and communist ideologies increasingly influenced political culture and naturally advocated solutions to human problems not much connected to Catholic thought.[14] Living in this time of high-minded revolutionary rhetoric, considerable social reform, but obvious intractable social and economic inequalities, many Catholics explored more closely what their faith had to say about the socioeconomic issues of the day. Their primary sources of inspiration in this regard were the social doctrines outlined in the papal encyclicals *Rerum Novarum* (1891) and *Quadragesimo Anno* (1931). These encyclicals offered official Catholic teachings about the application of faith to matters of social concern. Published in response to the exploitative nature of liberal capitalism and the rise of socialism during the nineteenth and early twentieth centuries, the encyclicals advocated reform capitalist solutions to deepening social tensions and divisions in Europe. The popes viewed liberal capitalism as an inherently exploitive system that overemphasized individualism to the detriment of the common good, causing dissention and radicalism among the working classes. At the same time, they viewed socialism as contrary to natural law, traditional ideas of hierarchy and authority, and an even greater threat to society and the common good. Catholic social thought condemned totalitarian socialist systems of the right and the left that repressed the individual and sinned against human dignity.

To ensure the survival of a capitalist order, the pope urged structural reforms aimed at relieving exploitation and poverty. Charity no longer sufficed; structural changes ensuring social justice were necessary. This could be accomplished through a new ethic encouraging a moral obligation to justice, along with state action and corporate social forms in the tradition of the medieval guilds. According to the encyclicals, associations that encouraged capitalist-worker cooperation within a decentralized capitalist system guided by a benevolent state could ensure social justice for all. Beyond these broad theological guidelines emphasizing the need to remain concerned about social justice, the encyclicals had little to say about specific political and socioeconomic organization. Human society could never be perfect, but through spiritual renovation individuals would naturally come to recognize the imperative for social justice and work to improve social conditions and the common good. Evangelization and conversion, Catholic education, and the dissemination of the social teachings provided the method for advancing social justice. The encyclicals succeeded in inserting concern about humanity's temporal condition on earth into the heart of Catholic theology. Though not binding on the faithful, they produced considerable debate and reflection, despite the well-established church tradition of generally supporting the status quo in socioeconomic matters.[15]

Until the 1930s, Cuban Catholics had not spent much time in serious reflection and analysis about the meaning of the social encyclicals, but this changed during the next two decades. For the first time since the early nineteenth century, Catholic intellectuals contributed to the public discourse about Cuba's socioeconomic and political future. ACU-trained Catholics became some of the most active under the guidance of Father Rey de Castro, who believed that normal Catholic education did not sufficiently form individuals to live their faith daily. He emphasized teaching students to be responsible for themselves and to control their passions through learning the spiritual exercises of St. Ignatius, which emphasized frequent retreats and solitary reflection and prayer. If the solution to humankind's problems was conversion to Christ, as Rey de Castro believed, it had to be accomplished individual by individual and through organizations like ACU that provided a supportive and giving environment to its members. The people could not be converted en masse, he believed, they had to be approached by an elite group of highly spiritual and dedicated Christians interested in changing the world for Christ. Though inspired by Catholic Action and the social encyclicals, Rey de Castro also felt that effective Catholic social action could only stem from people truly dedicated to God. With this emphasis on spiritual growth and education, over the years ACU members did well at the university and went on to professional careers in all areas of Cuban life. Members pursued their professional interests and established a variety of study groups to encourage growth in their fields. In time a *círculo social* formed to study social theory and problems, as did study groups in medicine, law, and commerce. Also a magazine, *Esto Vir,* was published for the membership, which focused on Catholic perspectives on concerns of the day.[16]

Among Rey de Castro's disciples was José Ignacio Lasaga, perhaps the most important Cuban Catholic intellectual of his generation. A 1931 graduate of Colegio Bélen, who participated in some of the student movements against Dictator Gerardo Machado, Lasaga dedicated much of his time during the 1930s to ACU activities. At twenty-two he became president of ACU, a position he held for three years, during which he founded and edited the organization's internal bulletin, *Esto Vir.* In that time of national turmoil, he—like the bishops—turned his attention to the social challenges that needed to be confronted. In an article written for *Esto Vir,* Lasaga observed that "in these days of ideological disorientation, few Catholics are familiar with the social doctrines of the Church." "For many," he noted, "this doctrine is simply Christian charity, a Christian Charity only superficially understood, without real application, or concrete solutions." Resolving social problems boiled down to calls for the rich to be more giving and live more moderately and for the poor to be prudent and resigned to their situation. Fortunately, he noted, the popes had recognized the need for change and through their social encyclicals had charted a path for significant social reforms that avoided individualism, materialism, and socialism.

Lasaga advocated supporting unions, creating cooperation between committees of workers and capitalists, promoting credit and savings institutions, worker insurance, worker compensation based on the needs of workers as well as the profitability of businesses, involving workers as owners of businesses, prohibiting child labor, regulating the workday, and building a corporatist society capable of implementing these ideas. At the same time, he noted, Catholic social doctrine should be flexible and capable of changing its ideas over time, depending on circumstances—"an art, adaptable to the needs of the times."[17]

Lasaga's reference to corporatism reflected the ideological influences of Spanish Catholicism during the 1930s and 1940s, which identified itself with right-wing parties, including the Spanish Falange led by José Antonio Primo de Rivera, and then General Francisco Franco's assault on the communist- and socialist-dominated Spanish Republic in 1936. Unlike

Italy and Germany, where Fascism and Nazism undermined church authority and power, Spanish Falangism under Franco remained in alliance with the church and even evolved an ideology that emphasized many aspects of Catholic social thought. Emphasizing the need for a unified Spanish civilization, revolutionary ethics, authoritarian and corporatist political forms, cultural nationalism or *españolidad* based on Spanish traditions, strong state involvement in economic matters, and a Catholic spiritual dimension that emphasized human dignity and social justice, Primo de Rivera built a strong following among Catholics interested in exploring practical approaches to implementing Catholic social thought.[18] Aspects of this thought, especially authoritarianism and an even stronger Catholic identity, became the heart of Franco's more pragmatic ideological system during the Spanish Civil War and in the 1940s.[19]

The leading Spanish Catholic theorist of corporatism, Jesuit José Joaquín Azpiazu, openly accepted dictatorship as a way of making "the state assist the Church in achieving her most holy goal of the salvation of man to the greatest possible degree possible." Under this system, state power was not designed to establish total control of society, culture, religion, and institutions but to concentrate political power to facilitate the purposes of the general welfare.[20] A professor of sociology and economics at the University of Deusto in Spain, Azpiazu published important studies on Catholic corporatism, including *El Estado Corporativo* (1936) and *El Estado Católico* (1939).[21] A strong Spanish Catholic community in Cuba supported Franco and falangist thought, along with sectors of Cuba's elites led by José Ignacio Rivero, editor of the island's conservative newspaper *Diario de la Marina*. During the 1930s, for example, Rivero sympathized with European Fascism generally and Spanish Falangism in particular, heading one cell of the Falange Española in Cuba.[22] Many in the Cuban church, including members of the hierarchy, priests, and laity, embraced Franco and aspects of falangist thinking, including the authoritarian attitudes and methods outlined in Azpiazu's thought.[23]

The tumultuous political, ideological, and theological debates among Spanish Catholics in the 1930s and 1940s had a dramatic impact on a new generation of Catholics in Cuba and Latin America generally who discovered the church's social thought. Traditional Catholics in Latin America tended to align themselves with conservative parties interested in the status quo and certainly not overly concerned with the social teachings of the church.

Falangists broke with traditional Catholics, emphasized the social doctrines, and sought support among the working classes. In Cuba, a Jesuit priest Manuel Foyaca, spiritual counselor of Catholic Action and social science teacher at Colegio Belén, was the first to successfully gain national attention for raising the social question from a Catholic perspective.

Born on the island, Foyaca trained in Spain and in 1935 became the Jesuits' primary social teaching advocate in Latin America.[24] Foyaca created an especially avid following in Cuba with a book on Catholic socio-economic ideas, a synthesis of the writings of several European Jesuit thinkers, including Azpiazu; Victor Cathrein, a German moral theologian; Narciso Noguer, a Spanish supporter of Catholic worker organizations; and Giuseppe Toniolo, an Italian writer on Catholic social economy.[25] He introduced his ideas in a series of ACU-sponsored lectures, formally published in 1941, which analyzed the fundamental tenets of Catholic social thought and offered ideas about their implementation in Cuba. He lectured at workers' night schools in Havana and other towns and cities, including Cienfuegos and Jovellanos.

Following the guiding principles of the social encyclicals, Foyaca emphasized the church's concern for the country's spiritual and material welfare, declaring that it was not wedded to the status quo and did not represent an obstacle to social reform and a just social order. Foyaca called for the social and economic betterment of Cuba and a readjustment of national life through charity and justice rather than social strife and confrontation. All work, "the natural occupation of honest and diligent men," whether physical, intellectual, or artistic, contributed to the nation and needed to be organized through the cooperation of labor and capital, the two pillars that sustain production and social development. This required upholding private property rights, "in conformity with natural law," but such rights also had to fulfill a "social function." Cuba needed to keep in mind the social obligations of property in both rural and urban settings and implement the agrarian reform promised in the Constitution of 1940. "We believe," he said, "that in making each Cuban a landowner we contribute to social stability." He also noted that profits had a social role and that the fruits of production should be equitably distributed between capital and labor. He advocated the idea of a family wage as a central way of ensuring social justice and the "humanity" of the wage worker.

Foyaca also protested racial discrimination and characterized exaggerated class divisions as anti-Christian. In order to ensure the implementation of these ideas, Foyaca in principle supported corporatist socioeconomic organization and the idea of state intervention in the economy, "to as large extent as may be necessary for the welfare of Cuba." Indeed, the state had the obligation to promote the social welfare of all, but particularly "the needy and the incapacitated.[26] He advocated the nontotalitarian Catholic corporatist vision outlined in Pope Pius XI's encyclical *Quadragesimo Anno* and in the writings of Azpiazu.

Though criticized by conservatives, Foyaca influenced young Catholics in the 1940s and, with the encouragement of the church hierarchy, inspired the founding of an activist social Christian movement. In establishing Catholic Action in 1941, the bishops specifically charged the men's section with promoting and defending the church's social Christian thought and especially cultivating harmonious relations between capital and labor advocated in *Quadragesimo Anno*. They also named Foyaca as spiritual counselor of men's Catholic Action. In November 1942, Foyaca, Catholic Action leaders, and followers from many Catholic organizations held the first meeting of what became known as the Christian Social Democratic Movement. Meeting at the Teatro Auditorium in Havana, the movement received the full blessings of the Catholic hierarchy and the archbishops of Havana and Santiago, and the bishop of Camaguey attended. Led by its first president, Abel Teurbe Tolón, a national Catholic Action officer, the movement developed an official program and revealed its basic aims and goals: essentially those outlined in Foyaca's thought without the corporatist prescriptions.

The Christian Social Democratic Movement became quite active in the following years, holding street meetings, using trucks with loud speakers to disseminate its message, distributing pamphlets, and the like. The movement also created a press service and found its way to the radio waves by offering a program called "A Sunday Catholic Hour" on station CMQ. In addition, many enthusiasts of the movement offered their services to speak at all kinds of events, and Azpiazu even traveled from Spain to give lectures on Catholic social doctrine. The leading conservative newspaper in Cuba, *Diario de la Marina,* commended the movement as the most adequate reply to communism, while the communist newspaper *Hoy* called the movement "fascist and falangist."[27]

Despite the enthusiasm among Cuban Catholics for Foyaca's thought, including his call for greater social justice following the teachings of the faith, most did not embrace the corporatist approach. Perhaps aware of this, Foyaca's keynote speech at the inaugural meeting of the Christian Social

Democratic Movement avoided mentioning corporatism, simply noting that the state "is the agent of the common good; it watches over the interests of the collective."[28] Cuban reluctance to embrace corporatism did not represent a rejection of state involvement in regulating the economy and promoting social justice, mainstream ideas institutionalized in the Constitution of 1940. Instead, Cuban resistance to Catholic corporatist formulations had more to do with corporatism's fundamentally theocratic and authoritarian vision of political organization.

In fact, a theological split developed among clergy and activist laity. While the Spanish Jesuits at Belén school embraced Foyaca and Spanish Catholic traditions, other Cuban Catholics preferred the ideas of French philosopher and theologian Jacques Maritain, who offered an alternative view. Maritain developed his ideas in the midst of the emerging European crisis of the 1930s. Calling his ideas "integral humanism," Maritain advocated a "New Christiandom," inspired by the social encyclicals that recognized humanity's need for not only spiritual salvation but a dignified life on earth. He outlined this concept in *Problemas espirituales y temporatles de una Nueva Cristiandad*, published originally in Madrid in 1935.[29] Disturbed by the tendency among some Catholics, especially in Italy and Spain during the 1930s and 1940s, to support authoritarianism, Maritain insisted on democratic frameworks for social change. Opposed to socialism (fascist as well as communist) and liberalism, Maritain promoted a Christian Democratic movement—based on religious values and framed in participatory principles—as an alternative political vision. Maritain believed that this New Christiandom had to be pluralistic, committed to social justice, and in touch with the secular world. This included religious freedom and political action based on the values of the gospel.[30]

A Catholic student generation in Latin America, exemplified by Chile's Eduardo Frei and Venezuela's Rafael Caldera, admired Maritain and embraced Christian Democracy as well-suited for their reality. They credited Maritain as a critical influence in their thinking. In the 1930s and 1940s, young Catholics grew impatient with Latin America's elites who simply ignored the social encyclicals, as well as with the authoritarianism of the Italian- and Spanish-inspired corporatist Catholic movements. The obvious contradictions between the social encyclicals and traditional Catholic politics led to a great deal of turbulence in Catholic movements, including splits and the emergence of reformist Christian Democratic parties. In

Chile, for example, the Falange Party, founded by Frei and others in 1935 and influenced by the papal social encyclicals and corporatist Catholic thinking, transformed into a postwar Christian Democratic Party.[31] These movements tended to be reformist on the socioeconomic front, supporting effective state intervention in the economy, but opposed to authoritarian and dictatorial regimes. They sometimes cooperated with socialist and communist movements in underground opposition to dictatorships and even in electoral politics. In 1949, a Latin American Christian Democratic organization formed to encourage collaboration among the various parties in the region. The organization defined Christian Democracy as a movement dedicated to democracy, pluralist and participative human rights, and cultural, political, social, and economic structures that promoted the full development of the whole person.[32]

Cuban supporters of Maritain represented a new generation in their twenties initially influenced by Foyaca who also looked to the French theologian for inspiration. While Spanish and Cuban Jesuits especially viewed Maritain with great suspicion for his support of the Republic during the Spanish Civil War, French Christian Brothers (founders of Havana's La Salle School) as well as the many Basque Franciscans in Cuba embraced his thought. In general, a new generation of Cuban Catholic lay leaders embraced Maritain, whose ideas seemed in line with Cuba's Constitution of 1940, a document with clear republican and social democratic principles that most Cubans viewed as progressive and perfectly capable, if fully implemented, of addressing many of the nation's social problems.[33]

Maritain's thought inspired a group of Catholics, led by Andrés Valdespino, Rubén D. Rumbaut, Angel del Cerro, and a host of others, to organize the Humanist Movement of Cuba in December 1950. Ideological, pre-political, and strictly nonconfessional, the Humanist Movement drew together people of various philosophical and religious traditions in support of socioeconomic reform. In some ways, this movement represented evidence of Catholicism's growing influence within Cuba's traditionally secular socioeconomic thinking. The organization held continuous and intense meetings with Cuba's leading intellectuals. It also published a newspaper (*Baraguá*), bulletins, and doctrinal sheets, and sponsored a radio show, "For Cuba That Suffers" (*Para Cuba que Sufre*). Many of the members of the first revolutionary government in January 1959 came from the ranks of this movement or were inspired by its ideas.[34]

Established to "translate into action the principles that inspire social Catholicism," the Humanist Movement advocated for urgently needed reforms but warned that these concerns were universal problems that, in the end, also had to be thought of in global terms and through democratic means. The solutions to human problems required both just structures and systems and the spiritual progress of each individual. "Perfecting the human person," they noted, "is the basis for perfecting the societies they live in." The creation of a harmonious society required growth in human spirituality along with the implementation of just political, juridical, economic, and social formulas consistent within the contexts of particular historical moments. This was the integral humanism necessary for human happiness. "The role of civil society," they noted, "is, first, to help men find their personal destiny, and then provide them with the means to find welfare and become more perfect." Individuals had to become conscious of their transcendent purpose and then contribute to the common good, though this demanded great sacrifice. The Humanist Movement insisted that Cuba passionately needed people committed to the common good, a passion that could become the vision for a future world.

As a practical matter the Humanist Movement called for the implementation of policies to promote effective democracy, reject totalitarianism, expand education, decentralize public administration, strengthen municipal life, enact agrarian reform and agricultural development, and strengthen workers' rights by facilitating their acquisition of property and a sound economic base. The key to attaining these goals was the transformation of individual and state capitalism into "economic humanism," a system that would favor the moral dimension over the desire for wealth, favor distribution over production, favor work over capital, and exchange traditional private enterprise for a communal system in which all would participate in the ownership, running, and production of enterprises. Finally, in order to promote these ideas across the world, the Humanist Movement needed an international dimension.[35]

The movement's president, Rumbaut, a medical doctor and psychiatrist, national leader of FJC during the 1940s, and editor of its Catholic journal *Juventud,* believed that humanism offered an alternative to the great confrontation between liberal capitalism and communism.[36] "Capitalism is," he wrote, "the predominance of capital and the primacy of money over humanity," while communism is "the predominance of the collective, that is, the primacy of the State (the political form of the collective) over humanity." In both systems he said, "the human person is corralled."[37] Maritain's integral humanism offered a powerful ideological rationale for a political and socioeconomic system that was neither liberal capitalist nor communist, standing apart from the two contending forces of the Cold War in the 1950s and 1960s.

For Cerro, president of FJC during 1954 and 1955, high school teacher, theatre and film professor at Villanueva University (from where he graduated), a columnist for *Prensa Libre*, and great admirer of Maritain, integral humanism was a fundamental text of "modern Catholicism."[38] In the article "In Search of a Third Position," Cerro argued that a false dichotomy existed in popular perception, viewing materialist or immanent-based philosophies as inherently more interested in resolving human problems than spiritual and transcendent philosophies, seen as mostly concerned with questions of the afterlife. Maritain's work, Cerro suggested, demonstrated that spiritual people could also practice a "sincere and progressive humanism." Indeed, integral humanism was the merging of humankind's transcendent nature with their need to be human and live in a just and harmonious society.[39]

Of this same group, Valdespino, professor of civil law at the University of Havana who served as president of the Havana diocesan council of Catholic Action during 1947–1949 and as national president during 1950–1953, was perhaps the clearest voice, translating these ideas into concrete language for the general public. He perhaps more than others offered the public the most comprehensible articulation of what Cuba's "new Catholicism" was all about. Valdespino had a long tradition throughout the 1950s of speaking forthrightly about the need for significant reforms to eliminate poverty (*la miseria*). Like Rumbaut, relying on the basic tenets of Catholic social teaching, he noted that there would always be rich and poor, but the church had to work to ensure that outright misery was eliminated. "Human dignity," he argued "requires that we all have the right to enjoy a minimum of material comfort capable not only of satisfying our most urgent needs but capable of providing a decent, dignified and respectable existence. Anything to the contrary is misery, the absence of the essential elements necessary for minimal personal and social decorum. And it is this that should not and cannot be tolerated: the misery of some in the face of the excesses of others." He reminded his readers that the central point in

Catholic social teaching was the struggle for a more equitable distribution of resources; the church opposed the concentration of wealth in the hands of the few. He acknowledged that the Cuban Constitution of 1940 provided all the necessary legal tools for distribution of wealth and advancing social justice, but that the political and moral will to legislate the required measures did not yet exist. "We do not see," he declared, "that the leaders of our society possess a sufficiently serious preoccupation to lead toward a moral economic and social order more in line with the principles of a true Christianity."[40] Valdespino believed that creating a new, more equitable economic and social order was one of Catholicism's central imperatives in the mid-twentieth century, not only in Cuba but also throughout Latin America.

This generation of Catholics developed an interest not only in the intellectual challenges of searching for the relationship between their faith and the national welfare but also in concretely influencing society. By the 1940s Catholic voices joined in the national debates over Cuba's future, often focusing on the need for social reform promised in the Cuban constitution of 1940, though frequently articulated even before. Though the church maintained a firm belief that its role was essentially spiritual and moral, and not political, it did encourage raising matters of moral concern publicly. As early as 1914, for example, in a circular titled "Precarious Situation of the Workers," the ecclesiastic governor of Havana congratulated the diocese for "the generosity and selflessness with which you contributed financially to alleviate misery and attended to the most urgent necessities of those victims of misery who wait for your humble contributions with gratitude."[41] Similar issues of social concern were discussed in a Eucharistic Congress in 1919, whose concluding document included an exhortation to the church to become more involved with the needs of the working classes, constituting the largest segment of Cuban society. "So that they do not fall into, or continue with, disbelief, disagreement or prejudice toward the church," the bishops noted, "we should quickly approach them, teach them, and organize them." The bishops asked Catholic organizations not only to form good Catholics but to promote mutual aid and establish consumer cooperatives.[42]

In the early 1930s, economic depression and revolution led to the rise and fall of various governments, transforming Cuba's political system and bringing workers' issues to the forefront of national discussion. During

1933 and 1934, dozens of strikes shook the nation, including three general strikes of more than 200,000 workers. A communist-controlled, though officially unrecognized, labor federation, the CNOC (Confederación Nacional Obrera Cubana), came on the scene.[43] Watching the increasing tensions and class confrontations, the bishops again turned their attention to the social question in Cuba. A pastoral titled "The Problem of the Worker," issued on August 20, 1933, in the midst of considerable political and social conflict and violence, described the difficult problems faced by Cuba's working classes and encouraged workers to demand their rights, including social legislation that would improve their conditions and provide them with the right of negotiation and arbitration. "Workers," the pastoral declared, "you are justified in making these demands, against an abomination which is in open conflict with the sound and sublime principles of the most sound Christian morality, and in consequence, with the dignity and decorum of mankind."

The pastoral also addressed capitalists (*patronos*), asking whether they had met their own Christian obligations. Reflecting the paternalistic nature of Catholic social thought, the bishops asked capitalists if they had ever inquired whether their workers lived an honest and moral existence. Were they themselves models of Christian living that would keep their workers satisfied and loyal? They counseled capitalists and workers to create relationships based on mutual love and to rely on the law of God and the charity of Christ. This was the formula for overcoming Cuba's social problems. Almost two months later, another pastoral, "Problems of the Moment," offered a detailed and condemnatory description of Cuba's social conditions, urging that they be attended to and warning that "for their part, the proletariat is already in disciplined formation, with a combative attitude, not asking but demanding, confident in the justice of their grievances and in the necessity of force."[44]

Though labor and political activism in Cuban society during the 1930s did lead to some improvements for workers, particularly in urban areas, a comprehensive offensive against Cuba's social ills certainly did not materialize. Nevertheless, church concerns regarding the country's social reality did translate into increased activities by Catholic Action movements in the traditional work of Catholic charity in Havana's worst slums. Perhaps among the poorest barrios was Las Yaguas (palm tree cuttings), where some two thousand people, mostly of color ("although there are also a good number of white Cubans, Spaniards and an occasional Syrian"), lived generally in family units, in some five hundred houses made of *yaguas,* used lumber, and discarded tin. The residents usually obtained the *yaguas* from the Cuban Land and Leaf Tobacco Company, close to the neighborhood, which used them to cover the tobacco leaf during transport. People could buy the old lumber at nearby yards for a few cents, and they scavenged the tin at a nearby garbage dump. The house interiors usually included just a few old pieces of furniture, a few boxes to sit on, perhaps a table, and one or two old used mattresses. Only three water faucets serviced the entire neighborhood, approximately seven hundred people per faucet.

This barrio drew the attention of social activists, beginning with the work of communist leader Juan Marinello, who for a time organized a group of professors to teach in the neighborhood. Among Catholics, ACU began working with the poor shortly after its foundation, establishing a night school for workers at Reina Church in Havana in 1931. Members offered classes in religion, math, Spanish grammar, English, civics, typing, and drawing to some 130 workers. That same year, three members began monthly visits to the Rincón leper hospital, and by the end of the year nineteen had entered this ministry. In Las Yaguas ACU built a school that taught a variety of courses, including catechism, accounting, writing, reading, and sewing. Eight- and nine-year-old children attended in the morning; those ages ten to fourteen attended in the afternoon; and children who worked and adults attended at night. Twenty-one teachers taught some two hundred students, and according to the report many more would have attended, except that "the terrible problem of having to find food prevented many from going to school with more constancy."

ACU also established a medical clinic run by a group of doctors and medical students, who were accompanied by a priest "so that people would become used to seeing ministers of spiritual and physical health and not just a messenger of death whose only function was to administer extreme unction once the sick lost consciousness." Though the parish church of Jesús del Monte was nearby, ACU built a chapel in the barrio. A small shop of used clothes stocked by ACU donations provided residents with needed items; films from the Bélen School were shown; and religious activities of all kinds were held, especially during Easter and Christmas seasons.[45] In addition to this work in Las Yaguas, ACU expanded into other needy neighborhoods in Havana, including one called "Cuevas del Humo" (Caves of

Smoke). Catholic youth from other organizations also worked in a variety of settings, from hospitals and asylums of different kinds to the private homes of the poor and prisons. They supported the work of St. Vincent de Paul, established schools for the poor, and organized drives to acquire food and clothes for the poor.[46] While this work did not offer structural solutions to Cuba's social conditions, it did certainly contribute to raising consciousness among many middle- and upper-class Catholics regarding the needs of Cuba's poor.

In 1953, the national junta of Catholic Action published a catalog detailing Catholic social work in Cuba. Interested in showing concretely the substantial commitment of Cuban Catholicism to alleviating the country's social problems, the catalog identified some 255 Catholic social work organizations dedicated to that work, composed of seventy-two schools, fifty-two asylums, thirty-three hospitals, and fifty-six other institutions of various kinds aimed at helping the poor. At the same time, however, the introduction to the catalog, written by Catholic Action activist Felipe Zapata, noted that this work reflected traditional Catholic charitable instincts based on the evangelical texts rather than the structural reforms called for by papal encyclicals, especially *Rerum Novarum* and *Quadragesimo Anno*. Without diminishing the value of the work already done, Zapata wrote that "a grave deficiency exists, very evident and deplorable, when in a country of nearly six million inhabitants, we find only twenty-one projects of a class or mutualist character." Zapata urged Catholics to promote cooperatives and mutualist organizations among the working classes, especially since secular-oriented unions had already largely established themselves among urban workers.

Zapata also lamented the lack of attention to the rural areas, where most of Cuba's poor lived. More than half of the Catholic activities cited in the catalog were in Havana and Marianao, a town just west of Havana, and the rest were in thirty-five other municipalities. Cuban social organizations were not present in more than 75 percent of Cuba's municipalities, much less in the rural sectors of the country. "Christ would come to evangelize the poor. And we only evangelize the fortunate sons of the wealthiest cities. This is the great deficiency, the enormous fatal void that we should recognize in all its horror, so that, in recognizing it, our spirit is moved to remedy this abandon and neglect." Cuba's rural areas needed attention, Zapata concluded, and, in a not-so-veiled reference to the work of communists, he noted: "Let us not permit that those who have already won the urban pro-letariat, because of our negligence and laziness, also be allowed to win over the rural poor."[47] The introduction to this catalog reflected the recognition among Cuban Catholic intellectuals, as well as many other intellectual traditions, that Cuba's problems required reform and structural solutions, not only works of charity.

This spirit of reform and social change became an important dimension of Catholicism in Cuba in the late 1940s and 1950s, and Catholic voices became prominent in the discussion of agrarian reform and the problems of the urban poor. The bishops especially encouraged evangelization among the working classes and endorsed the creation in 1946 by Catholic Action of Orientación Obrera. Headed by a University of Havana law student, José de Jesus Plana, the new organization affiliated the next year with Juventud Obrera Católica (JOC), an international movement. Founded in 1924 in Belgium by Father José Cardjin to spread Catholicism among Europe's working classes and to struggle for improvements in their material conditions, JOC spread to Latin America. With the guidance of Costa Rican priest José Vicente Salazar, JOC initiated the expansion of Catholicism in Cuba beyond the middle and upper classes. In 1947 JOC attracted some ten thousand workers to a celebration at the National Amphitheater in Havana, marking the organization's inaugural entrance into working-class evangelization. Three years later, *JOC Femenina* appeared, headed by Lydia Maribona, focusing on office and factory workers and domestics.[48]

An important aspect of JOC's work included disseminating Catholic social teachings, which became a central topic of concern in its official publication, *Juventud Obrera*. The magazine, for example, published an overview of Catholic social thought by Lasaga, by now a well-known and respected Catholic thinker, psychologist, and leader of Catholic Action. His article began with the fundamental observation that humankind has a body and a soul, "and, as such, has corporal and spiritual needs, which constitute the fundamental aspects of essential rights." Economic security was an essential part of those rights, which he articulated as seven basic principles, including the right to work, the right to a just salary, the right to social security benefits (medical, unemployment, accident, and old age), the right to social assistance from private and state sources, the right to organize associations and unions without undue interference from the capitalists or the state, the right to own property in a widely distributed land tenure system, and the need to cultivate a spirit of charity, understood not as *limosna* but rather as love of God and neighbor. Lasaga noted that "Charity takes us necessarily to the idea of fraternity among men: my black brother, my white brother, my working-class brother, my capitalist brother; my brother who lives in the city, my brother who lives in rural areas; my compatriot brother; my foreign brother, my brother who thinks like I do; my brother who thinks otherwise." To the extent Cubans live in this way, Lasaga concluded, "we will march toward a happier world and toward a society more in conformity with the Christian ideal."[49]

In the 1940s and 1950s, Catholics also recognized the importance of paying attention to Cuba's rural working class, the campesinos. Although they were not successful in establishing Catholic Action organizations like JOC among the campesinos, they certainly initiated efforts. In 1945, Enrique Cano urged Catholic activists to focus on the countryside, where their compatriots lived in worse conditions than even urban workers. "We need young people willing to sacrifice . . . willing to valiantly enter the Cuban countryside," he declared. Sometime later, Father Julián de Bastarrica reported on Catholic Action activities among campesinos, but this work did not progress very quickly.[50] In mid May 1951, Havana's Archbishop Arteaga sponsored the Cuban church's first *semana social,* which focused on Cuba's agrarian problems at Colegio Belén. Organized by Catholic Action leaders, including Julio Morales Gómez, Tolón, Foyaca, and Miguel Suárez, the conferences included many of the Catholic leaders interested in issues of agrarian reform.[51]

Catholics remained concerned throughout the decade. In 1958, for example, ACU published a study, *¿Por qué reforma agraria?,* that again highlighted the disconcerting agrarian situation in the country. The authors noted that "Christian doctrine obligates man to comply with the social function, not only with regards to material wealth, but also in the use of one's talents and energy." Carrying out this project represented nothing more than their duty as Catholics. The study revealed in stark statistical terms the dismal conditions faced by Cuba's rural population. Though the authors did not offer a specific agrarian reform program, they did state categorically that the time had arrived for the nation to stop being the "private feudal estate of the few powerful." At the same time, they ended on an optimistic note by saying that within a few years Cuba would no longer be the property of a few but instead the nation for all Cuban citizens, and that

Catholicism would play an important role in transforming the country. Among the authors of the pamphlet was Melchor Gastón, president of the Catholic Businessmen's League, who himself was a hacendado who shared his profits with his workers. He funded the production of *¿Por qué reforma agraria?* as well as a work by JOC priest Salvador de Freixedo, which in human terms detailed the severe social injustices in Cuban society.[52] Freixedo's publication was composed of a series of forty anecdotes from everyday life in Havana that demonstrated the hard realities of economic exploitation and racism. Angel del Cerro noted that "[Freixedo's] intention, using the dagger of denunciation, is none other than to remove from the pontifical texts about social justice the façade of measured words in which they are wrapped."[53]

Politics and Revolution

Just as Catholics felt the need to express their thoughts and perspectives about the nation's social problems, they inevitably became interested in politics itself as a way of implementing their ideas in Cuban national life. Though Catholics participated in the political system, they had rarely engaged politics as an identifiable political constituency. In the 1940s, the hierarchy encouraged Catholics to openly engage politics as a way of counteracting the secular ideologies that dominated Cuban politics, including liberalism, socialism, and communism. As Cuba's elected leaders gathered in assembly to write a new constitution in early 1940, the bishops, among other things, called for the delegates to formulate laws that would harmonize relations between capital and labor. "Every one knows," their letter noted, "the hard and miserable existence of a great portion of the men who have to earn a living with the sweat of their brow and the strength of their arms." The large number of workers joining radical parties that advocated class struggle did so because they felt abandoned and unprotected. Workers, the bishops reasoned, would willingly move from supporting ideas of class struggle to cooperation if society protected their legitimate aspirations and rights. The principles for a constitutional and legislative agenda that could satisfy proletarian aspirations could be found, the bishops argued, in the papal encyclicals. "Inspired by the doctrines of these important documents," they concluded, "it will be necessary to affirm the standards of social justice that will promote peace between capitalism and labor."[54]

In the first election after the promulgation of the Constitution in 1940, Batista won with a coalition that included the Communist Party, and, two years later, he appointed two communists to his cabinet, Juan Marinello and Carlos Rafael Rodríguez. Though the Communist Party advocated a relatively moderate political agenda—participating in the writing of the Cuban Constitution of 1940, promoting labor interests, calling for racial equality and women's rights, and urging nationalization of strategic industries—they nevertheless alienated Catholics when they led a political initiative against private education during the constitutional assembly in 1940.[55] Reacting immediately, the Knights of Columbus, ACU, and others, organized a series of roundtable discussions on the radio known as "Pro Patria y Reafirmación Nacional," in which they defended freedom of religion and private Catholic education. The issue remained contentious even after the implementation of the Constitution, when communist leader Marinello, heading up a Committee on Private Schools in the Ministry of Education, proposed measures to regulate private school education. Catholics again responded with a movement known as Por la Patria y por la Escuela, led by ACU member Angel Fernández Varela, which organized a mass meeting at the National Theatre on May 25, 1941, effectively blocking Marinello's plans. One result was the establishment of the Confederation of Catholic Schools, which henceforth defended the interests of Catholic schools in Cuba.[56]

In addition to the democratization of Cuban political life and defense of private education that encouraged Catholics to test the waters of political activism, other concerns about social matters and political corruption inspired Catholics to greater involvement. The new political system, which began propitiously enough with two legitimate elections in 1940 and 1944, soon found itself tainted by an outbreak of political gangsterism, political opportunism, and corruption in public office, while attention to the social principles that inspired the Constitution of 1940 dwindled to almost nothing. The Constitution had represented the culmination of the Revolution of 1933, offering a social democratic model for Cuba that allowed for agrarian reform, labor legislation, and employment rights.[57] Nevertheless, politicians enacted few concrete social measures encouraging some Catholics to enter the political arena, a controversial proposition at the time but one whose time had come.

Among the most active were members of the ACU. Initially the organization's founder and spiritual leader, Father Rey de Castro, had opposed the participation of ACU members in political affairs, but in the 1940s he changed his mind and spoke of Catholic responsibilities to take Christian values into public life. "Those with a political vocation should follow their calling," he counseled the ACU activists. The first to take up the challenge was Fernández Varela, who successfully ran for legislative representative from Havana in 1946. Shortly thereafter ACU members formed a movement called Acción Cubana to support Catholics in the political parties, eventually intending to form their own party. Connected to this movement, but effectively independent, was a Catholic student organization known as Pro-Dignidad Estudiantil, also founded by ACU student activists, including José Ignacio Rasco, Valentín Arenas, Manuel Artime, and others. They engaged student politics at the University of Havana, opposing the Federación Estudiantil Universitario (FEU), the main student organization.

ACU and other official Catholic organizations remained active until March 1952, when—just three months before Cuba's next presidential election—former president and presidential candidate Fulgencio Batista went to the barracks at Camp Columbia, Cuba's military headquarters, and convinced the military to support a coup, dramatically altering Cuba's political landscape.[58] The disruption of the political process by the coup launched Cuba down a path of confrontation and violence. Batista ruled with an iron hand, intimidating, imprisoning, and assassinating his opponents whenever necessary.

During the next seven years, Batista alienated almost every sector of Cuban society, leading to an insurrectionary movement that included a diversity of thought from which a young Jesuit-trained attorney, Fidel Castro, emerged as the most visible and articulate leader. Though Catholics and others raised their voices against Batista, Castro eventually represented the greatest threat to the military government and elicited the greatest response from the Cuban people. On July 26, 1953, Castro and a group of followers, including his brother Raul, assaulted the Moncada military barracks outside of Santiago de Cuba. This poorly planned attack failed miserably but captured the attention of many Cubans who agreed that only armed force could dislodge Batista from power. After the assault, Batista's troops tracked down the remnants of the rebel group, killing many and capturing others, including Castro, who went to prison for a time before receiving an amnesty.

He went to Mexico and reorganized his movement, and in 1956 he returned to continue his fight in the Sierra Maestra. In addition to building a
rebel army in the mountains and engaging Batista's military, Castro directed
the activities of his 26th of July Movement, which also gained adherents
in the cities, including among many Catholics. Castro espoused ideas few
Cubans could dispute.

In his political manifesto, "History Will Absolve Me," originally developed
as a defense at his trial in 1953 and later revised in prison, Castro called for
a return to democratic government under the terms of the Constitution of
1940. Besides tyranny, Castro condemned Cuba's socioeconomic situation,
calling for immediate action in favor of agrarian reform, industrialization,
reducing unemployment, and improving housing, public education, health,
and general welfare. He quoted thinkers such as St. Thomas Aquinas, Jean
Jacques Rousseau, Martin Luther, Thomas Paine, and José Martí, and he
cited the American Declaration of Independence and the French Revolution's Declaration of the Rights of Man. Castro also alluded to foreign
policy issues calling for Cuba's alignment with the democratic governments
of the continent and extending asylum to the persecuted. Young, idealistic,
and willing to stand up to Batista, Castro represented a new generation
with a vision that most Cubans considered appropriate for the times.[59]

During the Batista years in the 1950s, Cuban Catholic opinion was far
from homogeneous. Catholic individuals, organizations, and the hierarchy
all grappled with the political crisis in Cuba in a variety of ways, having to
take into account Catholic moral thought and traditional concerns about
involvement in political matters. Many Catholics supported Batista and
served his government, but most opposed him, working in a variety of
ways, including seeking a peaceful transition to constitutional normality by
pressing for elections, pressuring the government to resign, and backing
revolutionary armed action.[60] Different sectors of Cuban Catholicism embraced differing strategies, but many important leaders expressed their outrage about the coup from the outset.

The Catholic journal *Juventud* declared that the coup constituted "a
backward movement in our history," as did the official organ of the JOC,
which called on the usurper government to return the country to its constitutional process. The Franciscan journal edited by Father Ignacio Biaín,
Semanario Católico (which later became *La Quincena*), declared that "the
reasons presented by the coup leaders do not justify such drastic action"

and that it was an illusion "to think that public vices can be corrected over night through the vehicle of a military coup."[61] Just a week after the coup, Franciscan priest Julián de Bastarrica openly condemned Batista from the pulpit of San Antonio de Padua Church. Lay leaders Valdespino and Marta Moré, presidents of the men's and women's sections of Catholic Action, also protested in the popular magazine *Bohemia.* José Ignacio Rasco, Manuel Artime, Amalio Fiallo, and others founded the Partido de Liberación Radical, an organization of Christian Democratic inspiration opposed to Batista that advocated elections and a return to democratic procedure.[62] Angel del Cerro condemned the coup at a Havana archdiocese gathering of JUC, an organization that also took part in a public swearing of loyalty to the Constitution at the University of Havana, as did Rubén Rumbaut, who became a leader of Movimiento Nacional Revolucionario, founded by a University of Havana professor, Rafael García Barcena, in May 1952 in response to the coup. Within three months after the coup, military authorities violently broke up a public demonstration by Catholics in Guanajay organized by Fiallo, the first of many confrontations with the government.[63]

As general opposition to the Batista government grew in Cuba throughout the decade, Catholic organizations also spoke up and made their positions clear. Among the first was JOC, whose members took a central role in a banking strike during September 1955. Led by bank worker Reinol González, secretary general of JOC, and supported by the organization's spiritual counselor, Father Enrique Oslé, the strike lasted thirteen days before government repression, which included arrest of the leadership and a takeover of JOC headquarters, brought the action to an end. Later, JOC leaders González and Planas participated in the Frente Obrero Nacional (FON), the labor arm of the 26th of July Movement founded by the revolutionary leader Frank País. They helped organize an ill-fated FON general strike in April 1958, which resulted in increased repression and the flight of JOC leaders from the island.[64] González, Planas, and many others, including spiritual counselors Fathers Oslé and Freixedo, went into exile, where they continued to oppose Batista.[65] Other Catholic organizations also expressed their opposition. During 1957, representatives of a variety of secular and religious organizations met to create a Movement of Civic Institutions that hoped to find a peaceful solution to the political crisis. This broad coalition of forces, including the FJC, ACU, and Knights of Columbus, called for a provisional government as a first step toward returning to normal constitutional rule. In February 1958, the men's section of Catholic Action officially condemned the government, calling for the reestablishment of constitutional rule.[66]

For practicing Catholics, participating in a revolutionary option required the existence of certain conditions. By 1957, when Castro established himself in the Sierra Maestra, many Catholics felt sure the conditions had been met, an interpretation confirmed by Lasaga, also a leading authority in Cuba on ecclesiastical legal issues: "The necessary conditions to legitimize armed resistance against a usurper and tyrannical government now exist in Cuba." Referring to the specific requirements of Catholic moral teachings on the subject, Lasaga pointed to the total lack of justification for the coup itself, the extraordinarily repressive and violent nature of the regime, the exhaustion of all realistic possibilities of a peaceful transition, the probability that a new government would be an improvement over the existing one, and the real probability that a revolutionary movement would succeed. From many Catholics' point of view, church teachings certainly justified their involvement in armed action against the Batista government as long as their individual actions avoided terrorism, assassinations, and other morally unacceptable forms of resistance.[67] While official Catholic organizations had to avoid overt political partisanship, individual Catholics followed their conscience.

As the insurrection grew and gained a strong popular backing, Catholics increasingly participated. Hundreds of Catholics joined many of the student and worker revolutionary organizations that confronted the government, including the 26th of July Movement. Catholic Action militants, like president of the youth section Antonio Fernández and former president of the organization in Santiago de Cuba Enrique Cantero, took the lead. Catholics participated in the clandestine activities of dozens of organizations; many were later killed, including José A. Echeverría, member of the Knights of Columbus and student leader at the University of Havana. Numerous ACU and Catholic Action militants also died in the struggle.[68]

Important sectors of the clergy supported insurrectionary activities. When Castro's small surviving group first managed to reach the Sierra Maestra, after almost being wiped out in an ambush on landing, Father Antonio Albiza, pastor in Manzanillo, became the principal contact for communication with the isolated rebels. As the rebel army formed in the mountains and divided up into separate fronts, Catholic priests volunteered to join them as chaplains. Fathers Guillermo Sardiñas, Antonio Rivas, and Manzanedo joined the fronts directed by Fidel Castro, Raul Castro, and Juan Almeida respectively. Catholic priests also worked with the civic resistance in the cities. In late 1956, authorities arrested Father Ramón O'Farrill for hiding eight young revolutionaries. When he refused to turn them in, he was tortured, leaving prison with a bloodied head and broken ribs. Fathers Rivas (before he went to the Sierra), Francisco Beristain, and Jorge Bez Chabebe (treasurer of the 26th of July Movement) became important contacts for the Civic Resistance in Santiago de Cuba. On his radio show Bez Chabebe often sent coded messages to the rebels imbedded in his prayers and talks. In Havana Father Eduardo Boza Masvidal at Caridad Church sympathized with and supported insurrectionary activity, in the parish bulletin voicing opposition to the government's violence.[69]

In expressing their opposition to the Batista regime, Catholic organizations initially walked a careful line between speaking up for the moral issues dear to the church and not becoming involved in the country's partisan politics, that is, favoring one political group over another. Nevertheless, by early 1958, most Catholic organizations had condemned the government and asked for its resignation without supporting a particular political alternative except a return to democratic rule, and they encouraged the hierarchy to do the same. A deeply divided Cuban hierarchy, however, remained silent. Though the bishops spoke up against violence by all sides, they did not offer practical political solutions. As violence increased, grassroots Catholics criticized church leaders for their silence and increased their calls for the church to speak against the government, especially in Santiago de Cuba, where the anti-government activity was perhaps strongest. At the insistence of Archbishop Pérez Serantes, who had long urged action by the hierarchy, the bishops met in the final days of February 1958 to consider a collective pastoral asking for a definitive and peaceful solution to the nation's political crisis.

Three members of the group—Archbishop Pérez Serantes of Santiago, Bishops Evelio Díaz of Pinar del Río, and Alberto Martín Villaverde of Matanzas—lobbied for a strong statement demanding Batista's resignation, while two conservative bishops, Carlos Ríu Anglés of Camaguey and Eduardo Martínez Dalmau of Cienfuegos, opposed what they considered church involvement in partisan politics. Counseled by his auxiliary bishop, Alfredo Muller, and conservative secretary Msgr. Raul del Valle,

Msgr. Manuel Arteaga, the cardinal and archbishop of Havana, who was of advanced age and rapidly losing his faculties, fashioned a compromise statement that left the church's position unclear and seemingly intimidated by the regime. Titled "In Favor of Peace" the statement called on all to cease their violence and work together for a government of national unity "that could prepare our country for a return to a normal and peaceful political life."[70]

Observers interpreted the pastoral in different ways; those opposed to Batista said it meant he should step aside in favor of a provisional government, while those supportive of Batista declared that it was simply a call for a new, more inclusive cabinet. Obviously disturbed by the weak statement, Pérez Serantes later clarified that he did not support a cabinet of national unity but rather a new government altogether.[71] In March, Bishop Villaverde went to see Batista and personally suggested that he resign.[72] Later, Bishop Díaz issued a prayer, "For Peace in Cuba," which was widely read as a criticism of the government—including by the government itself.[73]

Despite the mild nature of the collective pastoral, and the absolute failure of a subsequent church initiative to create a credible and viable commission to oversee the creation of a government of national unity, the hierarchy's statement did represent a setback for the government, which had always worked hard to keep the church silent. According to the responses in the press, Cubans understood the pastoral as a critique of the government, especially as the individual bishops broke their silence. Nevertheless, many Catholics remained angry by the timidity of the hierarchy. At the beginning of December 1958, meeting at the offices of the Nuncio, Fathers Manuel Rodríguez Rosas, Manuel Colmena, Angel Gaztelu, and Ignacio Biaín endorsed a strongly worded letter by Father Belarmino García to the bishops criticizing their lack of forthrightness. "The high ecclesiastical dignitaries," they charged, "have publicly shown . . . an inconceivable indifference to the ill-conceived acts of the repressive forces."[74] On Christmas Eve 1958, Pérez Serantes issued another pastoral, titled "Stop the War." He again called for an end to the violence but placed special emphasis on the "obligation of those in power to take steps to find a peaceful solution to the grave problems confronted by the nation."[75]

On January 1, 1959, facing growing opposition from all sectors of Cuban society, Fulgencio Batista fled Cuba. In short order, Fidel Castro, the symbol of the revolutionary struggle and an extraordinarily charismatic figure, took control of the government. Many associated with the Batista regime left the island quickly, and conservatives felt vulnerable given the revolutionary tone of the new government. Those who had hoped for change welcomed these momentous events, including members of the church hierarchy who expressed gratitude and publicly applauded the installation of a new government. On January 3, in a pastoral letter called "New Life," Archbishop Enrique Pérez Serantes of Santiago de Cuba, who had baptized Fidel Castro and personally intervened to save his life in the immediate aftermath of the assault on the Moncada barracks in 1953, struck a positive and supportive note and at the same time called for reforms. Pérez Serantes asked the new leaders to recognize the centrality of God and act with this in mind. He asked that all children be given the benefit of religious instruction; that the family be protected, especially by recognizing the inviolability of marriage and abolishing divorce; that social morality be maintained by restricting pornography and other ills; that social justice be advanced according to Catholic teachings; that honesty in public office and political procedure be demanded; and finally, that the critical problems of Cuba's campesinos be attended to. Certainly, this mix of traditional doctrinal concerns, issues of public morality, and social justice grievances did not coincide exactly with the vast array of perspectives and interests initially represented by the revolutionary movement, but the archbishop's message nevertheless offered a receptive tone at a time of considerable uncertainty and lack of definition.[76]

If not completely clear about what the Revolution represented, Pérez Serantes and many other Catholics were optimistic, at least, that Cuba was about to see an expansion of Catholic influence within the context of a movement for social reform. Castro's Catholic background and Jesuit education and the highly visible symbolism of the *barbudos* (the bearded ones) entering Cuba's cities with crucifixes around their necks led some to perceive that Catholic influence in revolutionary ranks was greater than it was. The Franciscan magazine *La Quincena,* the most influential Catholic news organ in the country, dedicated its January issue to recounting the support of Catholics, including priests, to the struggle against Batista. As Father Ignacio Biaín, editor of *La Quincena* wrote, "The *fidelista* revolution's social doctrine can well be situated within the Social-Christian tradition advocated by the Christian Democratic parties of other nations."[77] During the next months, Catholics expressed optimism that the Revolution would bring change following the Christian social traditions expressed during the previous twenty years.

Despite the general uncertainty regarding what the Revolution would bring, the episcopate initially lent its considerable moral support to the new revolutionary government. By March, the Vatican replaced two conservative members of the hierarchy, Archbishop Cardinal Arteaga and bishop of Cienfuegos Msgr. Martínez Dalmau, with church officials more open to the Revolution. Rome relieved Arteaga of responsibility for day-to-day governance, while Martínez Dalmau, too closely aligned with Batista, found it prudent to leave Cuba. Monseñor Evelio Díaz, bishop of Pinar del Río, became apostolic administrator of the archdiocese of Havana, to administer in the name of Arteaga, until November, when he became archbishop. Arteaga's auxiliary bishop, Alfredo Muller, replaced Martínez Dalmau in Cienfuegos, and Manuel Rodríguez Rosas took Díaz's post in Pinar del Rio. These appointments produced a hierarchy willing to support social change in Cuba. Rodríguez Rosas, who had been among those who signed the letter criticizing the hierarchy for its timid collective pastoral in February 1958, especially embraced the promises of social reform. Bishops Díaz, Pérez Serantes, and Villaverde also expressed support for social reform within this revolutionary situation.[78]

In addition to a new hierarchy with a clear openness to reform, support came from many Catholic quarters during the first six months. On January 25, Catholic Action organized "a meeting of Catholic ratification and revolutionary reaffirmation." The gathering took place on the steps of the national capitol and included a mass in honor of Cuba's patroness, Nuestra Señora de la Caridad del Cobre (Our Lady of Charity), as a thanksgiving for the successful struggle against the tyranny. After a procession with the image from Caridad Church to the capitol accompanied by a large multitude, the Mass was celebrated by well-known guerrilla priest Sardiñas; Fr. Madrigal, former treasurer of the 26th of July Movement; and Fr. O'Farrill, who had been harshly persecuted for his anti-Batista activities. Fr. Eduardo Boza Masvidal, 26th of July Movement supporter, delivered the homily. Numerous personalities attended, including Cardinal Arteaga, the Papal Nuncio Msgr. Luigi Centoz, President Manuel Urrutia, and many members of the diplomatic corps. Boza Masvidal's homily called for a Christian revolution, one like "Christ's first revolution, the evangelical revolution, through which we will have social justice, and respect for the worker, and harmony of the means of production."[79]

JOC expressed strong support for the Revolution at the organization's twelfth-anniversary celebration and called for Christian-inspired social change. Over two thousand attended the event held at the Cathedral plaza, where JOC spiritual advisor, Father Oslé, emphasized the significance of the moment. He believed Catholic social doctrine to be in perfect harmony with the revolutionary project and encouraged the membership to support change. The gathering produced a document that included a comprehensive discussion of the social needs of Cuban workers and asked for legislation to address unemployment, apprenticeship, education, and a variety of other topics.[80] JOC activists González and Plana, now leaders of the Cuban labor federation, helped prepare the 1st of May celebration. Hoping to encourage Cuban workers to build a Christian-inspired labor movement, they invited to the event Emilio Máspero, the leader of the Congreso Latino Americano Social Cristiano (CLASC), an organization of Latin American Christian-oriented unions founded in 1954 in Chile by leaders from twelve countries, including Cuba, who was represented by JOC leader Juan Augusto Woods. Máspero had met Father Oslé in Buenos Aires in 1956 and González at the World Congress of Laity in Rome two years later. An alternative to Marxist, social democratic, and "bread and butter" unionism, CLASC emphasized worker education through the formation of institutes focused on teaching Christian doctrinal formation, sociology, economics, syndicalism, and cooperativism.[81] Máspero supported the Revolution's social goals but reminded the Cuban leadership that their work should encourage "a greater and more effective exercise of human liberties and the construction of a new and just regime" and that the social doctrines of the church should serve as philosophical basis for this project.[82]

Later in the year, in September, JOC also sponsored a *semana de estudios* for priests and religious to encourage them to think about the nation's social problems. Introduced by Bishops Evelio Díaz and Martín Villaverde, the meetings included lectures on the sugar industry labor problems, worker and employer relations, cooperatives and their benefits, teaching the social agenda to the laity, formation of labor leaders, and the work of JOC itself. The final resolution unanimously called for the advancement of social justice through a commitment to Christian doctrines and support of the government's plans for bettering the condition of Cuba's workers, campesinos, and those most in need.[83]

Catholic intellectuals also enthusiastically expressed pro-revolutionary positions throughout these early months. Biaín offered the government uncompromising support in the pages of *La Quincena*. In March, Catholic leader Valentín Arenas wrote that though the Revolution did not have an official ideological definition, its policies were clearly inspired by Christian morality. Already, he noted, honesty in public administration and the elimination of gambling had been achieved. Politically the Revolution had achieved national sovereignty and respect for the human person. Economically and socially, he wrote, the Revolution was radical and just and demonstrated a clear Christian inspiration.[84]

Andrés Valdespino, the vocal Catholic leader of the 1950s, immediately joined the revolutionary government as undersecretary of the Treasury, and embarked on the revolutionary adventure with obvious optimism and enthusiasm. In early 1959, Valdespino published an article noting that although the struggle against the Batista regime was over, the battle was really only beginning. "Oppression was an obstacle to be removed," he noted, "but the Revolution is an ideal to be reached." Now, "with the chains of tyranny broken, the path is open." Cuba's destiny would be defined. "It has been said that this is the hour of reconstruction. But it is to be even more: it is the hour to establish the basis for a definitive liberation. Reconstruction means to rebuild what was previously built. But much more is needed. Cuba needs to construct what has never before been built." He outlined a litany of needed policies, including austerity and honesty in the management of public funds, democratization of the electoral process, abolition of the large landholdings, regulation of foreign capital to ensure the interests of the nation, agrarian reform to elevate the standard of living of the campesinos, reform of Cuba's public school system, and reform of the nation's political economy and credit system. "All of this will not be done in one day," noted Valdespino. "Nor can it be the work of just one administration. But it must begin at some moment. And no moment seems more propitious to embark on the great task of rectifications than this genuinely revolutionary movement which Cuba lives."[85]

As the government initiated its reforms, members of the elite classes raised concerns and opposition, among them many of Cuba's most influential Catholics. In response, in a "Letter to Cuba's Rich," Valdespino lectured the wealthy regarding their obligations to Cuba and their fellow citizens. He acknowledged that many wealthy Cubans had gone beyond their narrow self-interests and embraced the revolutionary process, but he also noted that others had not been able to place the Revolution's moral imperative above their economic interests. To these he addressed his remarks. "Before anything else," he noted, "you have to convince yourselves that it is not hatred for the rich but love for the poor that inspires this social revolution." If the revolution had hurt their interests, he noted, it was not out of spite for the wealthy but to care for the welfare of all social classes. "I sometimes think," he sarcastically noted, "that some of you have come to believe that God created the world and the rest of humanity to put them unconditionally at your service." The article argued for a political economy that was neither capitalist nor communist, but one based on humanist principles, where the wealthy would have a modified role. The Revolution, Valdespino insisted, did not ask for them to accept ruin but sacrifice, that they accept being "a little less rich so the poor can be a little less poor."[86]

The following week turned his attention specifically to Christians who raised their voices against social reform. For those "false Christians" who opposed the Revolution's intention to ensure social justice, Valdespino laid out the many biblical passages that required Christians to engage in good works and watch over the welfare of their fellow human beings. Quoting St. Thomas Aquinas and Popes Leo XIII, Pius XI, and Pius XII, Valdespino also reminded these "Christians" that nothing in Catholic social teaching legitimized an absolute right of private property at the expense of the common good. He sharply rebuked those "false Christians, men of large fortunes who have never preoccupied themselves with the welfare of the people, who have never supported works of collective beneficence, who have spent amassed fortunes on travel and pleasures gained through the sweat and hunger of thousands of unfortunate people," who now, in the name of Christianity, accuse the Revolution of acting against Christian values and ideas. Valdespino asked Christians to replace their selfish spirit "with social justice, love for the poor [and] respect for the dignity of man, which was proclaimed by the Divine Master in the Sermon of the Mount and sealed with His blood in the sacrifice of the Cross."[87]

Finally, Cerro, who took a job as director of the City of Havana's Department of Fine Arts, also spoke publicly of the need for Catholics and the church to become revolutionary. Like Valdespino, Cerro made his sympathies clear and in April 1959 called on Catholics to leave behind the old and accept the revolutionary imperative. He acknowledged a division within the church: not a division of doctrine, but one of social consciousness. He pointed out that throughout the 1950s the church had been split between those who accepted the status quo and those opposed to Batista and the church's traditional conformity. Now Cuba was embarked on a Revolution, and Catholics had to prepare themselves for this historic moment. "Valiantly and honestly," he declared, "the Church must recognize its errors, human errors, and take steps to enter into the renewing force of the revolution." In order to contribute to the revolutionary enterprise, Cerro noted that the church would have to relinquish many of what it considered to be its traditional rights and accept new perspectives. It would have to discontinue favoring its profound links with the established social classes, which were maintained at the expense of the less privileged; furthermore, it would have to alter its policy of educating the nation's wealthy instead of its poor; and finally, it would need to emphasize the importance of Catholic social teachings and concentrate its activities in order to effectively advance a new vision for Cuba. If the church's spiritual influence is necessary to guide the Revolution toward human dignity and liberty, then it cannot be tied to political and social cadavers. "This is the hour of the Resurrection and the light."[88]

During these first months, the public discourse was revolutionary, and the public mood supported substantive if not radical reforms, but up to that moment social and economic reform had been limited to rent controls, the nationalization of the telephone company, import licenses for luxury items, strengthened measures to control tax evasion, confiscation of Batistiano property, and modest land redistributions in the Sierra Maestra and in Pinar del Rio. For the most part, Castro occupied himself with the controversies surrounding the trials and executions of Batistianos and an extended trip to Washington, DC, Canada, and Latin America during April and May. Ten days after Castro's return to Havana, on May 17, the much-awaited agrarian reform law was promulgated in an official ceremony in the Sierra Maestra.[89] With this law, the Revolution began in earnest.

For most Cubans agrarian reform represented the most important symbol of the revolutionary vision. Cubans generally, as well as reformist Catholics interested in the practical applications of the church's social teachings, considered the island's rural inhabitants the most oppressed and in need of immediate attention. The issue had been a point of considerable national debate since the 1940s, and the general consensus seemed to be that the moment to resolve the problem had arrived. During February, March, and April, the government confiscated lands and sugar mills from leading and wealthy supporters of Batista and initiated land distributions in selected areas of the country.[90]

Catholic jurist and ex-senator Manuel Dorta Duque, who had long supported agrarian reform, expressed the Catholic position, saying that private property had a double purpose—to benefit the individual and to advance the collective social welfare. Dorta Duque expressed no concern about the land confiscations and assured an interviewer from *La Quincena* that the private land distributions fell within the principles of Catholic social teaching, though still falling well short of what was needed to abolish the problem of *latifundismo* in Cuba. He called for much broader action, which he assumed would be addressed in the forthcoming agrarian reform law. The simple distribution of land to the campesinos was not sufficient; the state would need to offer credits and technical assistance and encourage cooperatives and associations of small farmers. At the same time, Dorta Duque warned that the reforms should be careful not to seriously hurt the actual production process and that first emphasis should be placed on distributing unutilized or underutilized lands.[91]

The same month, in a joint statement addressing issues of public policy, Cuba's most significant Catholic associations made clear their support for agrarian reform. Agrarian reform was "one of the great promises of the triumphant Revolution," the document noted, and it should permanently resolve the nation's rural problems on the basis of sound legal and economic principles, distribution of land, and support of the new farmers, including education, credit, health care, and technical support.[92]

Already on record before the Revolution as supporting agrarian reform, ACU activists led by Manuel Artime engaged the issue soon after the triumph of the Revolution. In 1957, Artime had worked with the Partido de Liberación Radical, but in the waning days of the insurrection, with the encouragement of his mentor, Father Armando Llorente (spiritual director of the ACU), he joined Castro's Rebel Army under the command of Humberto Sorí Marín and obtained the rank of lieutenant. After Batista's flight, Artime and other ACU activists, including Rogelio González Corzo, organized the Catholic-inspired *comandos rurales* to work among the campesinos.[93] In April and May, with the encouragement of the Sorí Marín, now Minister of Agriculture, Artime and about sixty university students went to the Sierra Maestra mountains. According to one activist, Roberto de Varona, "We departed with everything needed by a soldier on campaign, inspired by an

intense love of God and Country, to be faithful servants of our 'guajiros.'"
The *comandos rurales* worked with campesino families. In the mornings they
provided schooling for the children, and in the afternoons they helped
with the daily work. At night the *comandos* offered adult classes, teaching
the campesinos how to organize cooperatives. They also carried out a census of population, lands, and rural production in the Sierra. In general, the
comandos promoted agrarian reform based on redistribution of property
and support for campesino initiatives to improve their lot.[94]

Catholics, then, fully expected and supported an agrarian reform when
the government announced and formally promulgated the law on May 17
at a formal ceremony in the Sierra Maestra. The new law, consistent with
language specified in the Constitution of 1940, proscribed estates larger
than a thousand acres, except for those plantations with exceptional productivity, in which case the maximum acreage was 3,333. Larger properties
were subject to expropriation, with compensation promised in twenty-year
bonds. This law directly affected only about 10 percent of the farms, but
40 percent of the land holdings. Expropriated lands would either be run as
agricultural cooperatives, to be managed initially by a state organization,
INRA (Instituto Nacional de la Reforma Agraria), created for that purpose
and other reasons, or be distributed in 167-acre plots to individuals. Share-
croppers and renters would have first claim on lands they had previously
worked. Once in the hands of individuals, however, the land could be
resold only to the government, unless otherwise arranged with permission
from the authorities. Foreigners would be prohibited from owning or in-
heriting agricultural lands, and distributed lands could not be divided and
would be forfeited to the state if not placed in production.[95]

Certainly, this law represented a radical threat to the largest landowners,
especially in the sugar sector dominated by U.S. firms, which immediately
protested. Cuba's landholding elites also opposed these measures, and many
appealed to the church. Most of Cuban society at least initially applauded
the reforms, however, as did church leaders, though with some reserva-
tions. Even the conservative *Diario de la Marina,* owned by the prominent
Rivero family and edited by José Ignacio Rivero, a member of ACU, supported the plan, though the newspaper argued that landowners should
be represented in INRA.[96] On May 30, Msgr. Evelio Díaz declared that,
although he had not yet seen the details of the reform law, "I wish only to insist that Catholics are generally disposed to second all government actions

that promote the public good and harmonize our personal rights with those of our neighbors, in a climate of justice and social charity."[97] The next day, he issued a more detailed message on the subject: "We believe that our Agrarian Reform, with its noble purpose, falls fully within the spirit and sense of social Christian justice, so clearly outlined and defined by the Roman Pontiffs, especially Leo XIII in his encyclical Rerum Novarum."[98]

In June, Biaín offered his analysis in a lengthy editorial approved by "Excmo y Rvmo. Eveilio Díaz, Arzobispo de La Habana." Biaín reminded readers of the terrible injustice of the Cuban countryside: "A very large percentage of the *guajiros* live as pariahs in their land, in the midst of latifundios that produced millions. The *guajiro*—see the atrocious statistics, a slap in the face for a civilization that calls itself Christian—lived undernourished, hungry, parasite infested, without the possibility of redemption like a beaten beast." The reform, he noted, through the effective use of the state, offered profound changes to the latifundio system based on the principle of private property. At the same time, Biaín expressed some concern about the power given to INRA, which was retaining control of many of the expropriated lands while arguing that the campesinos were not in a position to use them effectively. He concluded, however, that the state role at this point was warranted, and he expressed confidence that, in time, the Revolution would turn lands over to the campesinos as individual property or as voluntary members of cooperatives.[99]

Catholic leader Lasaga also published an analysis of the reform. On careful analysis, he noted, the agrarian reform law was indeed in conformity with church social doctrine because it favored the distribution of land in the form of private property. On the other hand, like Biaín, he pointed out that the plan gave tremendous authority to INRA across the entire country. With this power INRA could oversee the dismantling of Cuba's latifundio system and create a small farmer class, but it might also use its authority to create an agricultural system controlled directly or indirectly by the state, undermining reliance on private property. He warned his compatriots that the agrarian law could be subverted and pointed out that the Communist Party advocated the collectivization of Cuban agriculture. In July, after some delay, Bishops Villaverde and Pérez Serantes also offered their blessing to the reform law but, seemingly influenced by Lasaga's analysis, reminded Cubans of Catholic social teaching and emphasized the importance of an agrarian system based on private property and not on communist principles of collectivization. Nevertheless, Pérez Serantes expressed confidence that "Dr. Castro, certainly not influenced by Moscovite orientations, knows perfectly well that such an orientation does not at all favor the success of the Revolution."[100]

During the first half of 1959, perhaps most Cuban Catholics supported revolutionary developments, as did important Catholic organizations, intellectuals, and the hierarchy. The evolution of Catholic thinking during the previous twenty years had prepared them to support a process of reform and social change on the island. Initial Catholic support for the agrarian reform project reflected this instinct and desire for reform consistent with the papal encyclicals. On the other hand, Cuba's wealthy Catholic landholding elites opposed the Revolution from the beginning and exerted pressure on the bishops to condemn the law, but the bishops chose instead to lend their voices to the cause of reform. At the same time, though most Catholics clearly supported agrarian reform, they were not naïve about the intentions of radical anti-Catholic sectors within the Revolution, especially communists. Not unanimous about the dangers of communist domination of the Revolution, some Catholics thought communism had to be condemned from the outset, while others believed communism would simply fade away in the face of a Catholic-supported, truly revolutionary movement led by the charismatic, Jesuit-trained Fidel Castro.

By the middle of 1959, it was evident that Archbishop Pérez Serantes's call for "New Life," articulated just days after the revolutionary triumph, was indeed being heeded by the government, but as the process proceeded, Catholics slowly came to realize that the Revolution's new vision for Cuba had little to do with their own ideas articulated throughout the 1940s and the 1950s. As the Revolution initiated its radicalization during 1959, Cuban Catholics believed that their support for the Revolution gave them as much right to promote their vision of Cuba's future as any other sector of Cuban society. During the twentieth century, Catholicism had transformed and emerged as a genuinely legitimate actor in Cuba, committed to political democracy and social reform. Involved for the first time in the heart of public discourse about Cuba's future, Catholics remained determined to be heard and respected within the political process. Shortly, Catholics overwhelmingly broke with the Revolution as it took a communist path.

Chapter Two

BETRAYAL AND DISSENT

The Revolution has been betrayed.
—Andrés Valdespino (1960)

"The Revolution has been betrayed," concluded Andrés Valdespino in November 1960, after arriving in the United States.[1] He and tens of thousands of Catholics fleeing during the 1960s considered the Cuban Revolution a great deception, a sentiment they expressed regularly and with considerable intensity. They experienced this in different ways, depending on their particular concerns, but they all shared the same fundamental belief that the Revolution promised by Fidel Castro had been totally perverted and diverted onto a communist path against the will of most revolutionaries. A broad-based revolution that Castro himself had talked about as "humanist" and "green as the palms" became radicalized and dominated by communist ideology. Overall, Catholics and many others lamented that what they had considered a popular, democratic movement dedicated to social justice and human dignity had been converted into an authoritarian, class-based revolution committed to establishing a totalitarian communist system.

In 1961, Catholic Action exile leader Miguel Suárez, with the help of Rubén and Carmen Rumbaut and others, formed a Comité de Católicos

Cubanos in Miami and published a newsletter, *Información Católica Cubana,* "for the purpose of telling Central and South America and the United States the truth about the situation of the church in Cuba, disseminating our doctrine throughout the Americas, and publicizing the activities of Communism that are now posing a threat to the entire Hemisphere." These Catholic critics viewed religious persecution, nationalization of Catholic schools, searches and interference in churches and convents, detentions of priests and activist Catholics, and efforts by the government to establish a "national church" as totally unwarranted, especially since they too had opposed Batista and backed the Revolution. "Cuban Catholicism," they declared, "seriously criticized liberal capitalism, preached the need for a profound, radical and Christian solution to the social question, and called for a change in social structures. . . . Cuban Catholicism always stood on the side of justice." Nevertheless, the church had been attacked and silenced and its leadership exiled or imprisoned and characterized as "falangist and *franquista.*" The last five presidents of Catholic Action had been forced into exile, and the president of JOC languished in prison. Such a revolution, they argued, could not be considered to be just because it violated the basic requirement of human dignity as defined in Catholic doctrine and betrayed the basic tenets Catholics believed had inspired and fueled the revolutionary movement.[2]

For Christian Democratic leader José Ignacio Rasco, developments simply confirmed what he had always suspected. From his perspective, the Revolution did not represent a betrayal, really, but rather a defeat. Castro's unpredictable actions, desire for power, and attraction to radical ideologies did not surprise Rasco but did represent, he thought, a betrayal of his generation's deepest aspirations.[3] Overall, Catholics believed that the promise of a broad-based movement dedicated to reforming Cuba's political and socioeconomic system had been hijacked by Fidel Castro, leaving them shocked, disappointed, and disoriented. A popular social democratic, humanist, and—for some—Christian revolution took on a radical character with clearly socialistic and authoritarian tendencies.

1959

Despite their initial optimism, in the months following Castro's triumph, many Cubans faced the new reality of a radicalizing revolution with great trepidation. With a rapidity that was hard to believe, in a little more than two years it became a Marxist-Leninist revolution allied with the Soviet Union. At the end of the first year the Revolution remained officially undefined, though its rhetoric became increasingly radical, nationalist, and collectivist. Not until mid-1960 did the government actually initiate a systematic socialization of the economy, but before the end of 1959, many Cubans already believed Cuba was about to undergo a communist revolution. Castro's dictatorial tendencies and phenomenal charisma offered one clue, but other evidence included the emergence of a collectivist and state-centered land reform movement, the growing influence of communists and people with radical instincts, and the shunting aside of the original moderates who formed the first government. Catholics saw Castro's continual call for "revolutionary unity" during 1959 as a thinly veiled discourse of intolerance and conformity.

After Batista's flight from Cuba in the early morning hours of January 1, Dr. Manuel Urrutia, provisional president of the "Cuban Republic in Arms," became the new head of state. He named prominent lawyer José Miró Cardona prime minister, a position called for in the Constitution of 1940. Urrutia had been appointed provisional president by a revolutionary junta of unity formed in Caracas in July 1958, when representatives of the Civic Resistance and Castro's 26th of July Movement agreed to work together. The same junta named Miró Cardona political coordinator and Fidel Castro commander in chief of the revolutionary army.[4] The agreement called for a common strategy to defeat Batista through armed struggle, which would be followed by a provisional government dedicated to reestablishing full constitutional and democratic procedures. The government formed by Urrutia and Miró Cardona included a reputable cast of social democrats and reflected the broad coalition that had defeated Batista, including the urban bourgeoisie and working class, some large landholders, small farmers, and rural workers. Nationalist and clearly reformist, the government reflected Castro's descriptions of his own 26th of July Movement.[5]

Despite the installation of a new government, Castro remained the dominant political figure from the beginning. His control of the rebel army ensured his influence while he developed critical political alliances. During the month of January, Castro occupied himself making speeches, giving interviews, and establishing his incredible popular following, which must have surprised even him. Castro bided his time until early February, when

Miró Cardona, unable to command any authority of his own, resigned and suggested Castro take his place. Just before, the Council of Ministers passed a Fundamental Law essentially abrogating the Constitution of 1940, giving the government full authority to proceed. During the rest of the year, Castro consolidated power and filled his government with loyalists, including many communists, and demanded "revolutionary unity" in the face of growing opposition.[6]

That summer, INRA (Instituto Nacional de Reforma Agraria)—created to implement the agrarian reform program adopted in May—initiated expropriations of lands, a process that accelerated dramatically during the fall and winter months. During two days in late October, INRA expropriated almost 750,000 acres. Land expropriations affected many strong supporters of the Revolution, even Castro's own family, who lost almost 22,000 acres. By November, INRA officials declared quite openly that the purpose of the agrarian reform was to "do away with the men of power . . . do away with vested interests . . . to do away with the families here that thought themselves feudal lords." In April 1960, in a highly symbolic moment the INRA completed the confiscation of the 260,000 acres owned by the United Fruit Company, the very symbol of land concentration and foreign economic domination in Latin America and Cuba. By this time, the state also routinely expropriated smaller Cuban-owned holdings, making clear the Revolution's goal of collectivizing Cuba's rural sector.[7]

These developments alarmed many who objected not only to the arbitrary process of land confiscation without due process or compensation but also to the increasing role of communist cadres in the revolutionary government. In June, Pedro Luís Díaz Lanz, commander of the Cuban Air Force, fled to the United States, condemning communist influences in the government; the following month, Castro forced President Urrutia to resign after he too denounced communists. Concerns about communism surfaced yet again in October, when Huber Matos, a highly respected revolutionary leader and governor of Camaguey Province, resigned, decrying growing communist activities. Furious, Castro personally flew to Camaguey, mobilized the population with a speech, and arrested Matos and almost his entire staff. Tried as a counterrevolutionary, Matos received a twenty-year prison sentence, signaling to dissidents of whatever background what they could expect if they challenged the revolutionary process.[8] In November, Castro reorganized the government and removed the last remnants of independent 26th of July Movement leaders still in the cabinet. He also removed the head of the National Bank, giving the job to "Che" Guevara, among the most radical leaders in the government.[9]

Catholics responded in diverse ways to these developments. One sector remained committed to the Revolution through the middle of 1960, seeking to influence its direction, while others became convinced in late 1959 that communists had already taken control. Still others simply felt confused. Within this complex and unpredictable environment, the church called a National Catholic Congress in Havana for November 27 and 28, 1959, to demonstrate Cubans' commitment to the Catholic faith and their devotion to the Virgen de la Caridad del Cobre, whose image was brought to Havana for the occasion. Immediately, many on the political left, including communists, charged that the Congress amounted to a political power play by the church to intimidate the government. Organizers of the event repeatedly denied the allegations, insisting that the Congress had an exclusively religious purpose.[10] In *La Quincena* Father Biaín declared that "it is not convenient to envelop what is clear with suspicions and rumors: this is a Catholic Congress that will be conducted without political goals of any kind."[11] Just a week before the Congress, Bishop Díaz reiterated this once again in a television interview. The purpose he said is to "give testimony of the Catholic sentiment of a people and give social and collective tribute to God. The specific and concrete purpose is to offer homage to our patroness the Virgin of Charity."[12]

On the day before the Congress's inauguration, Castro addressed the matter. Standing at the University of Havana's main entrance, he questioned the motives of those interested in creating an "unscrupulous confrontation" between "religious and revolutionary sentiment." He denounced those who would use religion to oppose the Revolution, those who "are trying to harm traditional religious sentiment and devotion of our people toward Our Lady of Charity, the Virgin of Sierra Maestra and of all Cubans—the devotion born of the faith of humble fishermen, never of the rich and powerful." He went on to say that Christ looked to the humble, not the powerful, for his followers, and "on the streets, hundreds of people have come to give me religious images and wish me blessings; this is part of the nature of our people." He also expressed enthusiasm for the upcoming Catholic Congress, saying, "the tens of thousands of people gathering there will be praying for Cuba and the revolutionary laws."[13]

Nevertheless, verbal confrontations between the government newspaper, *Revolución,* and the communist organ, *Hoy,* on the one hand, and traditional newspapers like *Diario de la Marina, Avance, Prensa Libre,* and *El Mundo,* on the other, left no doubt about the event's political significance. Hoping to defuse the tensions, an editorial in the country's most popular magazine, *Bohemia,* called on Cubans to be united, insisting that on this historical occasion "not only of national importance, but also of American and universal significance, there cannot be divisions between Cuban Catholics and Revolutionary Cubans."[14] In the meantime, the church hierarchy continued to repeat their insistence that the Congress was a religious and spiritual gathering, having nothing to do with politics.

Catholics from all over Cuba streamed into Havana in the days preceding the Congress. On November 24, at the Shrine of Our Lady of Charity at Cobre, in eastern Cuba, a young man in blue shorts and a white shirt emblazoned with the words "Juventud Católica" received a flaming torch representing the Virgin's light from the president of the men's section of Catholic Action and initiated a run that took the torch across the island to Havana in time for the inauguration of the Congress. Carried by fresh runners along the way, the torch slowly approached Havana, and so did thousands of pilgrims. As Catholics in Havana waited for the torch in the days leading to the Congress, the four sections of Catholic Action celebrated national assemblies; Villanueva University organized sessions to discuss socioeconomic matters; and fifteen hundred inmates at the Príncipe Prison in Havana attended religious meetings. The government expanded bus service, dispatched additional police to provide security, and directed the Ministry of Public Works to help prepare the facilities. The presidential airplane left for Santiago de Cuba to transport the image of the Virgen de la Caridad to Havana.

The event began with a grand procession to the Plaza Cívica departing from the statue of José Martí in Central Park, in the old colonial section of Havana, where the final runner arrived with the torch. At 8:15 p.m., at the corner of Prado and Neptuno streets, the torch bearer raised the flame high and, surrounded by national and religious flags and escorted by police on motorcycles, led the pilgrims forward. The papal nuncio, the bishops of Havana and Matanzas, and the national presidents of Catholic organizations followed the torch bearer. Behind them came the image of the Virgen de la Caridad, on a decorated cart pulled by a tractor. The bishops of Santiago and Cienfuegos flanked the image, followed by representatives of the parishes of Havana and leaders of diverse religious associations. Thousands of believers fell in line and carried torches, together lighting the way. Bands played as the procession made its way toward the Plaza Cívica, while television and radio transmitted images and sounds of the event across the island. Despite rains and a penetrating cold uncommon for Havana, the enthusiasm of the pilgrims did not flag, as half a million faithful carrying thirty thousand torches and two thousand banners moved for six hours like a river down the streets toward the plaza. As the procession arrived at the plaza, people saw another huge statue of a pensive José Martí, overlooking the altar on which the image of the Virgen de la Caridad had been placed and around which stood church leaders. Though the rain picked up and the cold became more intense, no one moved.

Shortly before the arrival of the image of the Virgen de la Caridad at 1 a.m., Fidel Castro, accompanied by President Osvaldo Dorticós, who replaced Urrutia, and other *comandantes* and government officials, arrived at the plaza. Greeted by his mother and sisters and the church leadership and with shouts of support from the crowd, Castro sat as one more observer. As the last of the faithful arrived at 2 a.m., the program scheduled for midnight began, but because of the late hour, Archbishop of Santiago Pérez Serantes, the main celebrant, limited worship to a brief prayer service asking the Virgin for peace, justice, faith, and salvation. He also thanked Cubans for their strength and firmness and the government for facilitating the event. Archbishop of Havana Evelio Díaz then offered homage to the Virgin. In the final act of the evening, Pope John XXIII broadcast a message live from Rome, and as he imparted his closing benediction, the people knelt and lowered their heads, and then, one commentator reported, "as the one million faithful Cubans raised their heads, the stars in the sky did not shine, but each soul was a sun that lit the paths of the nation."[15]

The National Congress ended later that day, Sunday, at the Plenary Assembly of Cuban Catholic Action held at the Tropical Stadium. Though the hierarchy had denied any political intent, the speeches at the plenary assembly were clearly understood within the context of the obvious political tensions that had emerged during the year. On the one hand, the speakers focused on the meaning of the main themes of charity and justice, fraternity, and love of country within the Catholic tradition, but, on the other, in clear and unequivocal language, speakers criticized materialist thinking, especially Marxism and communism.

The first speaker, José Ignacio Lasaga, emphasized the centrality of charity and social justice, which he described as the two foundational concepts of the social order. When effectively embraced, he said, the right to work, a just salary, and an equitable distribution of property would be a reality, but he warned that people had to be free in order to reach this goal. "Man," he noted, "was not born to be a slave of another man, an enterprise, an organization, a party, or a State." Charity and justice are of no consequence without freedom, a necessary condition for spiritual growth. That is why "Catholic thought opposes communist and Marxist doctrines, and in general all ideas that promote the subordination of the human being to a totalitarian State." He concluded with a slogan: "Totalitarian State, no!; Social Justice, yes! Redemption of the Worker and Campesino, yes!; Communism, no!"[16]

The next two speakers, Catholic Action leaders Clara Lucas Azcona and Mateo Jover, also emphasized the evils of totalitarian systems of the right or left. Closing the plenary, as well as the Congress, Msgr. Martín Villaverde insisted that the idea of God had to be maintained because without God the only real reason for love among people was removed. Humanity had to choose between God and materialism, and the Congress had met to tell the world that Cuba had chosen God, that Cubans had chosen to embrace love and *patria* to avoid the divisions and hatreds advocated by those who rejected God. This Congress, he concluded was "a shout for faith and love . . . that does not die in the world, that does not die in Cuba, but on the contrary revives each moment with greater strength."[17] Though certainly not openly political in advocating particular policy prescriptions, the speeches did make clear that Catholics supported social reform consistent with Christian social teachings and at the same time vehemently opposed the materialist prescriptions of communism. Late that afternoon, a multitude accompanied the image of the Virgin to the airport for the return trip to the sanctuary at Cobre.

Catholic Resistance

The anti-communism expressed by Catholics at the Congress reflected not only the traditional theological attitude of the church but the real concrete fear that communists had indeed taken charge of many aspects of the Revolution. Even before radicals emerged to take prominent positions in the government, Catholics warned of the dangers communism presented in an inherently unstable revolutionary situation. With the fall of Batista, Catholics expected to engage in civic dialogue and participate in public policy discussions about the revolutionary process, but growing government intolerance and insistence on absolute conformity beginning in the latter half of 1959 caused many to openly oppose the government. At the same time many in the government, no doubt including Castro himself, interpreted the Congress as a show of force by Catholics who articulated the limits of their support for Castro's brand of unity.

As a new year opened, the tensions between the government and Catholics spilled into the public arena, initiating an anti-Catholic discourse led by Castro himself that became increasingly virulent throughout the year. This led to political confrontations and a government assault on Catholic dissidents and the church itself. In a speech at the first national congress of socialist youth in April, communist leader and recently named rector of the University of Havana Juan Marinello warned Catholics that their efforts to resist the Revolution would be met with force. "Catholics have nothing to fear from the socialist party or socialist youth," Marinello declared, "so long as they remain in their temples adoring their images." "But," he warned, "should they leave their temples to make counterrevolution, they will find us fighting them on the front lines, not for being Catholics but for being counterrevolutionaries."

Catholic Action responded angrily, declaring Marinello's speech not only insulting to Catholics but also an open assault on the right of free expression guaranteed by the Cuban constitution. It denounced Marinellos's attack on Catholics as unwarranted and charged that his comments conspired against citizens' constitutional rights to freedom of expression, religion, education, and peaceful association and the right to demonstrate. These rights had already been publicly proclaimed and confirmed by the Revolution itself but were now threatened. At the same time, Catholic Action made clear its support for the principles that inspired the Cuban Revolution, including social justice, national sovereignty, public morality, and all measures aimed at eliminating hunger, misery, and class exploitation through the equitable distribution of resources, but this did not mean accepting communism. "The Church," Catholic Action pointed out, "does not condemn communism to defend the privileges of the few and social injustice; it condemns it for its atheism and materialism that negates spiritual values and morals." On the eve of Easter, in the midst of all this controversy, Archbishop Díaz called on Cubans to join in fervently celebrating Holy Week, in order to publicly confess to Christ, "even as the hour of sacrifice arrives, so indispensable for Christian life."[18]

Catholic dissidents opposed to Castro expressed their concerns during spring 1960, though ACU activists led by Manuel Artime became suspicious of Castro's intentions much earlier. Artime represented those in ACU committed to land reform as defined by Catholic doctrine and outlined in the reform law enacted in May 1959. Nevertheless, as early as April, ACU members already complained of troublesome developments. The new library at the military headquarters, for example, included mostly Marxist texts, and the government cancelled an ACU literacy program for soldiers at Managua military camp near Havana. Others had also expressed concerns. In February, JOC activist and *La Quincena* columnist Rodolfo Riesgo denounced ongoing efforts by communists to forcibly take control of trade unions associated with the national labor federation. Riesgo wrote that from the very "day of liberation," communists initiated efforts to impose their leaders on the unions, but he remained confident that the Revolution would block them. "Communism persists, true, but it will be confronted by the unanimous repudiation of all who are conscious of the purity of our Revolution."[19]

With the encouragement of the Catholic Minister of Agriculture, Humberto Sorí Marín, ACU volunteers (*comandos rurales*) from Villanueva and Havana universities took jobs with INRA. Artime became chief of one of the agricultural zones but soon concluded that INRA's goal was actually to nationalize the agricultural system and create state farms or highly centralized and controlled cooperatives.[20] Artime still thought that Castro and his inner circle would at the most opportune moment block the communists, but his hopes dissolved at a meeting in November 1959, in which INRA's director characterized the institution as an independent shadow government. At the meeting, Castro himself outlined a radical plan to establish government control over agriculture, banking and finance, and eventually the entire urban economy.[21] The next month, Artime and two colleagues, Rogelio González Corzo and Carlos Rodríguez Santana, resigned their positions in INRA and organized the Movimiento de Recuperación Revolucionaria (MRR).[22]

MRR emerged initially from a coalition of Catholics who had been members of Legión de Acción Revolucionaria, which had struggled against

Batista, and the *comandos rurales,* on the one hand, and a group of dis-
gruntled rebel army officers, on the other. In January, they published their
ideario, or political testament, stating their goals to overthrow Fidel Castro,
defeat communism, and fight for the ideology of Christ. According to their
political program MRR sought to defeat this emergent communist system
and institute a democracy that respected "rights, order, justice and decorum," while eliminating "misery, economic slavery, and political oppression."
MRRistas believed that Cuba's failed efforts at civic life stemmed from a
lack of men with a well-formed ideology, from a total indifference by those
most prepared to govern, and from a crisis in idealism. "Our struggle then,"
they declared, "is not revolution, but a holy war, a real Crusade, for today
and for always, for Cuba and for the world."[23]

In time, events confirmed Artime's worst fears as well as Lasaga's warning that INRA might be used to nationalize the agricultural sector. By May
1960, INRA controlled directly more than five hundred farms, including
more than two million acres. Most lands occupied by INRA throughout the
year became state-owned farms, as did the cooperatives, which never really
got off the ground. During the next two years, INRA continued to acquire
lands, but by now only about a quarter were gained through agrarian reform law stipulations, while more than 50 percent represented outright na-
tionalizations of lands belonging to opponents of the Revolution. By spring
1961, the state controlled perhaps a third of Cuba's agricultural sector,
operating 266 state farms, which covered more than five million acres,
defining the future of Cuba's agricultural sector. The government honored
private land distributions made to campesinos during 1959 and 1960, but
few distributions of this kind continued.[24]

While Artime and his colleagues focused their energies on the issue of
land reform, Christian Democrats worked for the creation of a democratic
political system, calling for elections at the earliest possible moment. Mostly
young, under forty, without much political experience, and not connected
to the old political groups tied to the struggle against Machado (the Generation of 1930), this new generation of mostly middle-class Catholics had
been among those in the 1950s promoting the idea of a stronger Christian
presence in Cuban life and society. Their leader, José Ignacio Rasco, intellectual and professor of history and philosophy at Villanueva University,
advocated the reform agenda articulated by many of his Latin American
Christian Democratic colleagues. As a Catholic, Rasco believed deeply in

the relationship between freedom and salvation. "For Christianity, the search for God is a daily activity, which must be free. Without freedom we can never *be*." This freedom involved a political dimension, which Rasco believed could not be compromised. "Men and nations that have enjoyed [the] benefits [of freedom] remain committed with incomparable tenacity," he noted.[25]

Immediately after the revolutionary triumph Rasco and his colleagues lobbied for a return to civil society and a multiparty system as quickly as possible.[26] Having studied with Castro at the Belén School, Rasco distrusted his former classmate, considering him deeply influenced by Marxist thinking.[27] From the moment of his arrival in Havana, Castro hedged on elections, confirming what Rasco, at least, expected. On January 9, 1959, Castro announced that elections would be delayed for at least fifteen months, a statement supported by the new president, Urrutia. On February 23, Castro again pushed elections aside, saying, "It is in the public interest that elections are delayed till political parties are fully developed and their programs are clearly defined."[28] In mid-March, Castro extended the delay for two years to enable effective opposition to develop.[29] Finally, in late April, in a speech to the United Nations, Castro spoke about delaying elections for as long as four years while the government implemented sweeping land reform and social and economic development projects.[30] Equally troubling, the government issued a decree abolishing political parties and dismissing the idea of creating some kind of provisional legislative body. The government felt that at this point partisan politics was not useful; the constitution had to be reformed, and the nation had to be purged of its corrupt elements.[31] In the meantime, government would be conducted by decree.

Rasco protested in the press frequently and, during late summer 1959 in a series of articles in the newspaper *Información*, systematically criticized aspects of the revolutionary process. He wondered why the preamble of the Fundamental Law did not mention God, as found in the Constitution of 1940, and called on the Council of Ministers to rectify this "oversight." Rasco also warned against Castro's extraordinary charisma, stressing that the Revolution could not rely indefinitely on the relationship of the leader with the masses, devoid of constitutional procedures and an independent judicial system. He called for the reestablishment of the Constitution of 1940 and fair elections. Rasco also criticized the state-dominated approach to agrarian reform, arguing that the solution to excessive individualism was not to fall into the excesses of socialism. He called for an agrarian reform that dismantled "latifundio privado" but not in exchange for "latifundio estatal."[32]

By October, Rasco and his associates viewed the Revolution as deeply influenced by communists and began traveling the island seeking to organize a formal party. In December, these activists, encouraged by Foyaca, organized the Movimiento Democrático Cristiano (MDC) as an "essentially democratic" group that "rejects any coexistence with communist or pro-communist elements, since it knows perfectly well that there cannot be conciliation or understanding between Marxist materialism and Christian idealism."[33] They modeled their movement after the Latin American Christian Democratic parties, similar to those emerging to prominence in Chile and Venezuela. This prompted Castro's reaction in early January on a television program "Before the Press," charging that MDC represented large landowners, old-style politicians, and financiers. The premier is "misinformed in this regard," Rasco responded, denying that the movement was associated with landed interests or right-wing politics. Another MDC leader, Enrique Villarreal also denied Castro's charges, saying that the group was not "counterrevolutionary" and supported the Revolution's goal of social justice.[34]

Besides the government's criticisms, MDC also earned attacks by Catholics and other Christians still supporting the idea of revolutionary unity. In early 1960, Biaín, for example, said that the Revolution embodied Christian Democratic ideals and rejected the idea that all radical social movements were necessarily "socialist" (meaning "communist"). The Cuban Revolution was, he insisted, Christian. He warned that any new Christian Democratic party should embrace the Revolution, including anti-imperialism, the destruction of unjust systems, and the advancement of a more communal order, not the privileges of the Catholic middle class. Biaín criticized MDC for failing to offer clear unequivocal support for the Revolution, causing suspicions regarding its intentions, and he hoped that the movement would extend a hand of support instead of taking a confrontational posture.[35]

Another Catholic supporter of the Revolution agreed that a Christian party was certainly legitimate, and he pointed to the Christian Democratic experience in Europe but noted that the "current revolutionary government is advancing a program consistent with the Church's social doctrines and we think that the correct posture is to support the revolution, making a Christian political party unnecessary." Instead of protesting, Catholics should work to spread progressive ideas among the working classes, encourage Catholic schools to form militant Catholic cadres, and expand the progressive Catholic press like *La Quincena* and *Juventud Obrera*.[36]

Despite this criticism, MDC confronted the government, declaring that only free elections could legitimize and consolidate the Revolution. On April 13, MDC issued a severe condemnation of the Cuban government in *Información* signed by Rasco and Villarreal, president and secretary general, respectively. "The Christian Democratic Movement formally requests the Revolutionary Government to set a date for terminating its provisional rule," the document stated. "After almost a year and a half of the revolutionary triumph," it continued, "the government has not announced the limits of its provisional rule and when and how public life will begin to move towards what theorists of modern Public Law call a State of Law, whose first steps is the full installation of a constitutional regime."[37] The government responded with orders to arrest the two, but they found refuge in foreign embassies and left the country. Shortly thereafter, the remaining MDC leaders in Cuba, announcing that conditions for legal political activism did not exist, suspended their activities as an organized movement, destroyed its membership lists, and initiated underground resistance.[38] While several other top MDC leaders also left the country and formed an exile executive to support clandestine activities, Enrique Ros became national coordinator and worked with others to structure the underground organization. Throughout the summer the MDC underground expanded across the island and established contacts with well-known priest Eduardo Boza Masvidal, who had supported the Revolution, and other leading figures of the Cuban church.[39]

In the meantime, Rasco and Villarreal organized MDC in exile and issued a declaration saying that Cuba's problem had become a hemispheric concern and called on other American nations to come to the support of Cubans. "Today," noted the declaration, "Cuba is unfortunately the first battleground of the forces that are fighting for possession of the American continent. What is happening in Cuba is only the beginning. Its tragedy can and will involve the whole continent."[40] The declaration went on to say that Christian Democrats had initially supported the revolutionary government but its total disregard for elections, civil liberties, and rational economic policy forced them into opposition. "It is a regime," it noted, "that worries more about training leaders to expand communistic infiltration than with promoting the welfare of the people; a regime that talks only about Cuban sovereignty in relation to the U.S. but yields to the U.S.S.R in every detail."[41]

In addition to establishing the main office in Miami, MDC offices opened in Caracas, Mexico City, Madrid, Bogotá, and Puerto Rico as well as in the United States, including New York, Washington, DC, Chicago, Tampa, and California. Convinced that Castro would not last, the MDC prepared itself to take its place among the island's political parties in a restructured Cuba.[42] The organization also established a military wing under the direction of Laureano Batista (no relation to Fulgencio Batista), a thirty-year-old graduate in law from the Villanueva University. Batista had been national president of the JEC in 1952–1953 and in 1959 worked for the Trust Company of Cuba; he was a founding member of the MDC. On leaving Cuba in 1960, he dedicated himself to building the movement's clandestine organization to support the insurgents in Cuba.[43]

Another group of Catholics focused on defending traditional university autonomy from the increasingly aggressive government that seemed intent on controlling all aspects of Cuban civic and political life. The problem became acute after October 1959, when the Castro brothers interfered directly with student elections at the University of Havana, an action that historically would have been sufficient to provoke mass opposition by students. Indeed, students had fought the Batista dictatorship, resulting in the closure of the university for two years. With the reopening of the university, student politics reappeared to great controversy when Castro publicly supported Rolando Cubelas, a government official who resigned his job to run for head of the student confederation. He was opposed by Pedro Luís Boitel, a Catholic and popular leader of the 26th of July Movement. "Instead of fighting," Castro declared, "what all students should do is to embrace each other with revolutionary spirit, and unanimously elect a President and unite, so that a reform plan can be carried out without delay. This would be a victory for everybody, and not the triumph for any single group."[44] On the day of the election, Raul Castro accompanied Cubelas to the university, and the government candidate won a narrow victory, representing a first step in direct government control of the university system.

Among those supporting Boitel and opposing the government's involvement in the elections was a group of Catholic students led by Alberto Muller, nephew of the Catholic bishop of Camaguey, Alfredo Muller. A member of ACU, Muller founded a newspaper, *Trinchera,* in defense of traditional university autonomy. *Trinchera* emphasized the need to defend an independent university and asked all to remember the student martyrs of the past who had died to defend the university from government interference. "Let us raise our voices to our martyrs once and for all," the newspaper declared, "so they will know that here still exist youth with hope, with a spirit of sacrifice, and with sincerity in their hearts, sufficient to defend AUTONOMY, SYMBOL OF OUR LIBERTY, for which they died" (emphasis in original).[45]

Shortly after taking over as president, Cubelas announced the formation of student brigades of the newly formed national militias to "defend Cuba and the revolution" and at the end of November affiliated the student federation with the communist-controlled International Union of Students. *Trinchera* criticized the new student leaders for their pro-communist stance and tensions among pro- and anti-communist students increased.[46]

In January, the students again responded angrily when the government announced Soviet Vice President Anastas Mikoyan's visit to Cuba to open a cultural exposition and to negotiate commercial agreements. A group led by Muller and Manuel Salvat, both leaders of the ACU at the University of Havana, along with students from Villanueva University, organized a demonstration. At midday on February 5, at a wreath laying ceremony, Mikoyan placed flowers arranged in the shape of the hammer and sickle at the statue of José Martí in Central Park in Havana. In protest, the Catholic students marched to the park that afternoon with their own wreath shaped like Cuba and in the colors of the Cuban flag. As they approached the statue, supporters of the Revolution assaulted the students, who were then arrested by the police.

During the next days and weeks students continued their protests, expressing their discontent with the government and the student federation led by Cubelas. They even demonstrated against Carlos Rafael Rodríguez, perhaps the best known of old-line communists, when he received a position as professor of economics in the Faculty of Social Sciences and Public Law. Several additional confrontations and the closing of independent student newspapers finally convinced dissident students that university autonomy and freedom of expression had been destroyed. By summer 1960, the students had gone underground and established the Directorio Revolucionario Estudiantil del MRR (DRE), associating with Artime's group, but the pursued leaders soon sought refuge and left Cuba through the auspices of the Brazilian embassy.

Once in exile Muller, Salvat, and others separated themselves from MRR and continued on their own.[47] At the first plenary meeting in exile the DRE declared itself the inheritor of the traditions of the Catholic student leader José Antonio Echeverría, killed in the struggle against Batista. They declared their intention to defeat communism in Cuba and reiterated their denunciation regarding the crushing of university autonomy on the island.[48] DRE also articulated a strong commitment to faith, declaring their organization "one of the vehicles for planting Christian doctrine in Cuba." "We aspire first to change mankind, educating and forging a moral foundation based on Christian principles." Their first task was to overthrow Fidel Castro, and their second would be to advance their ideas, based on the Gospels and Catholic social thought.[49] At the end of November, determined to support the insurrectionary activities of insurgents in the Escambray Mountains, Muller, Salvat, and others returned to the island with supplies and munitions and continued their clandestine organizing work, anticipating an exile invasion of the island early the next year.

Many social democratic leaders formerly associated with the first revolutionary government also went into active opposition, organizing the Movimiento Revolucionario del Pueblo (MRP) in July and August 1960. MRP represented a fusion of three different groups, including members of JOC and important Catholic intellectuals strongly associated with the Revolution.[50] Among them, JOC leaders Reinol González and José Plana became members of the executive committee of the Cuban labor federation (CTC) early in 1959, but their association was terminated at the end of 1959, when Castro successfully influenced elections to ensure his control. At the Tenth CTC Congress held November 18–22, 1959, as with the university elections, Castro delivered a dramatic speech when it became apparent that the assembly was unwilling to accept a "unity" or pro-government slate for the new executive council. Though Castro did not obtain the slate he wanted, even with his charismatic appeal, he certainly gained a generally cooperative group, and González and Plana were among those unseated. Castro established definitive influence over the labor confederation in subsequent months, and throughout 1960 government loyalists and communists purged the CTC unions of their independent leaders. At the next congress, in November 1960, a unity slate emerged victorious, and communist leader Lázaro Peña became the new secretary general, leading eventually to loss of labor union autonomy.[51]

After the Tenth Congress, González moved into open opposition, helping organize the MRP. He rose to head the organization in Cuba after its leader, Manuel Ray, former Secretary of Public Works in the revolutionary government, went into exile in late 1960. González maintained the MRP actively until his arrest during summer 1961, when he publicly confessed to his clandestine activities on national television in exchange for a twenty-year sentence and the lives of his comrades.[52] Other Catholic members of MRP included Valdespino, Fiallo, Rumbaut, and Cerro, who also denounced the Revolution during spring 1960 and spoke up against communism, political repression, and the government's pro-Soviet foreign policy. Though highly critical of Artime, Rasco, and Muller earlier in the year, they too became disillusioned and worked actively against the government as members of MRP.

The church hierarchy followed the lead of the Catholic laity. Until late spring 1960, the bishops had only spoken up in early January 1959, when they confronted the government over its efforts to decertify diplomas issued by Villanueva University during the last years of the Batista regime.[53] This was the Ministry of Education's effort to punish the Catholic university for remaining open during the two years the University of Havana had closed its doors to protest Batista. Though a compromise resolved the potential for an immediate confrontation between church and state, events throughout 1959 and early 1960 increasingly caused the hierarchy concern. Initially they avoided a strong public stand against the Revolution, fearing they would not prevail in the event of a showdown with Castro.[54] Now the bishops felt they had little choice but to challenge the regime.

In May, Archbishop of Santiago Pérez Serantes issued a pastoral letter titled "For God and for Cuba," declaring that communist influence in the government was no longer a matter of rumors. "We cannot say," he declared, "that the enemy is at the gates, because in reality he is inside." The archbishop told Catholics they should not forget that throughout the ages "los nuestros" had believed it better to lose everything, and even spill blood, rather than to renounce the liberties granted by God. After denouncing the philosophical tenets of communism, his pastoral called on the faithful to refuse to cooperate with communism, to study the social doctrines, and to endorse the better distribution of material wealth in a way consistent with

Catholic teaching. He also called for evangelization to combat ignorance about God.[55]

Besides Pérez Serantes, perhaps the strongest voice in opposition to the government was Auxiliary Bishop Boza Masvidal of Havana. He became bishop in February 1960, but for sometime before this he had already spoken up to criticize certain government actions. In July 1959, he, like Rasco, had questioned why the Fundamental Law of the Republic (which replaced the Constitution of 1940) omitted the reference to God found in the previous governing documents. He thought this omission important, since "with God the agrarian reform will reflect the Christian justice of the papal encyclicals, of brotherly love, of making everyone a small landowner, of removing inequality and injustice, of recognizing dignity and the rights of the human person made in the image of God." Without God, agrarian reform "would be the communist yoke of hate and class struggle which as a tactical measure would give the campesino a fictitious right to property but only as a first step toward man's absorption by the State."[56]

The entire Cuban episcopate issued a pastoral on August 7. They applauded the government's social programs, including agrarian and urban reform, fighting racism, building housing stock, eliminating gambling, and other measures, but also expressed concern that many government officials, journalists, labor leaders, and others were publicly pronouncing their admiration for communism and supporting policies clearly inspired by that system. "It should not occur to them, then," they declared, "to come and ask Catholics, in the name of some poorly understood unity, to cease our opposition to these doctrines because we could never accept them without betraying our most fundamental principles."[57]

During the next months Pérez Serantes issued three additional pastoral letters, reiterating an unconditional rejection of communism while emphasizing the church's commitment to social change. The archbishop challenged the government's accusations that the church was a traitor to the nation and was pro-United States. In his pastoral "Neither Traitors Nor Pariahs" he wondered who could reasonably equate opposition to communism and atheism with a lack of patriotism. He declared the choice was not between Moscow and Washington, but rather between Moscow and Rome.[58] In late 1960, when the opposition and Catholic press no longer published, Boza Masvidal spoke frankly from his parish pulpit at Caridad Church in Havana and circulated his anti-communist views in his clandestinely distributed parish newsletter.[59]

Confrontation and Repression

Catholic civic and underground responses to the Revolution's path led to open confrontations in late spring 1960 that during the next year grew into a government policy of wholesale repression of Catholics opposed to the regime. Orchestrated assaults on the church began with demonstrations by supporters of the Revolution, often led by *milicianos* (members of armed militias), calculated to generate popular reaction to the hierarchy's criticisms of the government. In a provocative gesture, on July 17, 1960, Boza Masvidal said a mass at the Havana cathedral in memory of the victims of communism the world over and denounced communist persecution of the church. Pro-government demonstrators gathered at the cathedral and clashed with worshippers who emerged from the temple shouting "Cuba, Sí!; Russia, No!," resulting in the arrest of thirty Catholics. The next day, *milicianos* assembled outside the Jesús de Miramar Church, provoking further confrontations during which a priest and several others sustained injuries. Later that same day, government-controlled Radio Mambí launched a strong denunciation of Boza Masvidal's sermon the previous day, and Castro himself on television characterized the clergy as "falangist" and essentially "foreign" and unpatriotic.[60] Castro taunted Catholic women, saying, "they should leave their temples and go to the countryside and help the agrarian reform, and sew and border clothes for children who have none."[61]

At about the same time, in Camaguey, government supporters incited campesinos against the church. At a meeting held in Batey del Central Santa Marta in the municipality of Santa Cruz del Sur, anti-Catholic speakers told the workers that "the counterrevolution now utilizes the motive of religion to attack and divide us." One speaker, identifying himself as a practicing Catholic, complained that priests divided Cubans. "There is a reason they don't want us to read the Bible," he noted, "because they don't want us to establish an understanding directly with God." Another speaker, a member of the municipal government of Ciego de Avila, called the priests "impudent and shameless, who pretend to be the exclusive interpreters of our people's Christian sentiments." He warned that they "will be the first to be executed when the first shot from a counterrevolutionary is heard. The people will take justice into their own hands and hang them."[62]

The government continued fanning anti-clerical sentiments and encouraging resentments toward the church, leading to more confrontations and violence. One observer reported that "a campaign already was well under way to discredit the clergy in every ruthless manner, including the appearance of hoodlums dressed in priests' robes in night clubs and places of disrepute."[63] The bishops' critical August 7 joint pastoral also provoked demonstrations and violence. As pastors read the letter in the churches, pro-government demonstrators appeared, heckling and clashing with worshippers inside and outside the buildings. At Havana's Jesús del Monte Church, militia forced the congregation from the church and closed the doors, while in the Luyanó neighborhood police intervened to stop demonstrators from interfering with worship services.[64] In Bauta, outside Havana, a priest was shot in the leg. Six Catholics were beaten and then arrested during clashes with demonstrators at Sagua La Grande. *Milicianos* in Havana surrounded a gathering in Caridad Church and shouted profanities and abuse at the worshippers.[65]

Protesting this violence, Archbishop Díaz made a personal visit to the office of President Osvaldo Dorticós, who refused to receive him. The archbishop told Dorticós's secretary that if the violence continued he would close the churches and call the attention of the world to the repression of the Cuban church, which was becoming a "Church of Silence."[66] Several days later, Dorticós told a labor rally that, despite the many provocations, the government would respect all religious denominations, though he made no specific reference to the bishops' pastoral or Díaz's ultimatum. Castro, however, was less circumspect. On August 11, during a three-and-a-half-hour speech, he denounced Catholic charges of communist infiltration, saying that his critics "would be capable of crucifying Christ Himself again." He linked the "fascist" priests to conspiracies in the U.S. embassy, which he charged had an interest in disrupting church-state relations. Subsequently, in the Communist Party newspaper, *Hoy,* Secretary General of the Communist Party Blas Roca linked the church directly to the growing counter-revolutionary activities organized in the United States. He declared that "the reactionaries, agents of imperialism and the big Cuban landholders . . . cannot be permitted to use the churches . . . to make counterrevolutionary propaganda."[67]

Interested in encouraging divisions among the many Catholics who felt deeply torn in their loyalties to their faith and to the Revolution, the government facilitated the activities of a pro-government Catholic organization, With the Cross and With the Fatherland, headed by Father German Lence.

In late 1959, some in the government had briefly considered attempting to create a national church using the Chinese model, but when this proved unworkable, authorities instead supported Lence. In August, Lence held a pro-government rally attended by thirty thousand people and said a Mass for Castro who was ill. He concluded his sermon shouting, "Long Live Fidel Castro." On September 1, obviously reacting to Lence and his organization, Pérez Serantes issued a letter calling on Catholics to maintain unity and denounced efforts of those organizing unauthorized "actas" in the name of the church.[68]

In the fall the government, which during spring 1960 had already intervened in most of Cuba's independent newspapers, also closed the Catholic media and prepared the way for nationalizing the private schools. It first targeted ACU's several television and radio shows sponsored by the Telemundo television network and *El Mundo* newspaper. Authorities either ended or censored the programs. Government officials also closed the JOC radio hour dedicated to disseminating information on Catholic social teachings and intervened in Televisión CMQ, ending *Un mensaje para todos,* José Ignacio Lasaga's Saturday morning broadcast sponsored by the National Catholic Organizations Association. When Lasaga pointed out that his program simply spoke of Catholic theology and contrasted it with communist theory, he was told that this was obviously an implied criticism of the government. The station's new administrators replaced it with a Russian news program.[69] Throughout Cuba Catholic media closed in the face of direct interventions and intimidations.

In October, rumors circulated of an impending new law to regulate Catholic education that would make all private school teachers, including priests and nuns, government employees under the supervision of the Ministry of Education, whose authority would supersede that of the religious orders themselves. The government press declared that this would make for "truly democratic education without privilege and discrimination," while members of Confederation of Catholic Schools of Cuba interpreted the move as another step toward the eventual nationalization of the schools.[70]

Catholic organizations across the country responded to the increasing repression and violence. At a week-long national congress of Catholic youth attended by two thousand delegates at Colegio La Salle, Archbishop Díaz asked that young Catholics remain united, reject violence, and be always ready to forgive and do good. Despite his call for moderation, delegates vented their anger, shouting "Cuba, sí! Communismo, no!," expressed full support for the bishops' pastoral letters, and denounced "communist infiltration" in the government. The assembly's resolutions denounced the break-away Catholic organization headed by Lence and insisted that the government respect the clergy and guarantee priests the right to conduct their ministries. They also reaffirmed their intention to defend Cuba's national sovereignty from any outside power, referring to the Soviet Union.[71] JOC called the *miliciano* activists "cowardly and despicable" communists dedicated to destroying all anti-communist organizations. "We fight to preserve respect for the dignity of man, while they fight for the total slavery of the human person," declared a JOC statement.[72]

The capture of Catholic student leader Porfirio Ramírez, president of the student federation at University of Las Villas and former Villanueva University student, ignited even more demonstrations. In August 1960, Ramírez had led an assault on the provincial government palace in Santa Clara and retreated into the Escambray mountains, where he intended to operate guerrilla operations.[73] After he was captured on October 8, the authorities quickly tried and executed him. Before his much publicized and reportedly gruesome execution, Ramírez assured his comrades, "I am not afraid; on the contrary, I have never felt more sure of myself; I know my death will not be in vain and the students will struggle to free my brothers, my country, from the treason of the monster communist of the Caribbean."[74] In defiance, many Catholic high school students went on strike the next day and attended masses in his honor.[75]

The following month, Bishop Boza Masvidal became embroiled in a controversy when pro-government students at Villanueva University denounced the school's administration for conspiring against the Revolution. The bishop expelled the students when they refused to retract their accusations, initiating a cycle of sharp denunciations from the press.[76] An article in *Bohemia,* which by then was in the hands of the government, published further denunciations by the expelled students. Accusing the University of being a "fifth column," working against the Revolution, the students offered as evidence that Augustinians from the United States owned Villanueva University and catered to the country's wealthy. The students charged Bishop Boza with being the "ideological and political guide of the counterrevolution in the church and Catholic associations and schools."

His goal, the article declared, was to encourage a confrontation between the church and the revolutionary government. The article further characterized the faculty as essentially "franquista" and pointed out the close relationship between the university and the ACU. "It must be taken into account," the article declared, "that the leadership at Villanueva and the rest of the Catholic education centers is the Agrupación Católica Univesitaria," pointing out that the "traitor" Artime came from its ranks.[77] Castro also weighed in on November 27, again denouncing the "anti-revolutionary activities" of Catholics. He called priests counterrevolutionary "henchmen in cassocks," accusing them of taking money from sugar companies in return for preaching against the Revolution, and denounced Villanueva University as "yankilandia." During the first week in December, bombs exploded in three Havana churches, including Boza Masvidal's Caridad Church.[78]

This prompted another collective letter from the bishops addressed to Castro, read in churches on December 4. Cuba's bishops charged that "an anti-religious campaign of national dimensions has begun and each day has been growing more and more virulent." The letter accused the government of orchestrating a campaign to destroy the church, including insulting Catholic priests and institutions, closing newspapers and radio and television shows, inciting violence against Catholics, leading to the bombing of churches, and encouraging a schism by supporting Father Lence's activities.[79] On December 23, 1960, after an active two years of raising his voice in defense of Catholic thought, Pérez Serantes issued his final major pastoral letter, "With Christ or Against Christ," in which he declared the church's intention to combat the communization of Cuba openly and uncompromisingly. The struggle was between "Christ and the Anti-Christ," and he told Cubans they each had to choose their preferred leader. As for Catholics, "know that the time has arrived to demonstrate our capacity to resist and our disposition to struggle." The pastoral then went on to reiterate the church's opposition to communism and why Cuba's deep social problems, which urgently needed to be remedied, could only be successfully resolved by following Catholic social thought.[80]

At an assembly of Cuba's labor federation later in the month, Castro again responded with anger, accusing the hierarchy of being hypocrites and denouncing Cardinal Arteaga, and by implication the church, as collaborators of the Batista government. "When the bloody tyrant," Castro charged, "needed His Excellency or His Highness, as they called him at the presidential palace, he appeared at that palace, so stained with blood and corrupted by the tyrant . . . to give the kiss of Judas." On the other hand, he defended Father Lence, declared that the principal objective of the working class was to gain political power, and announced that to be anti-communist was to be counterrevolutionary.[81]

Tensions and confrontations became even more aggravated after January 3, with the rupture of United States-Cuban relations. During the final third of the year, Cuba's trade relations with the United States had deteriorated rapidly, and on October 13, the Eisenhower administration, already deeply involved in plotting Castro's overthrow, declared a total ban on all exports to Cuba. Immediately, the Cuban government took over 382 large private enterprises, including all the banks, the remaining sugar mills, eighteen distilleries, sixty-one textile mills, sixteen rice mills, eleven cinemas, and thirteen large stores. An urban reform law declared that no one could own more than one residence. A couple of weeks later, the government nationalized 166 U.S. businesses. The United States recalled its ambassador, and on January 3, 1961, relations between the two countries were officially severed.[82] Also, by this time, the Cuban government was well aware of U.S. support for counterrevolutionary activities and exile plans to invade the island.

As Catholic resistance continued to grow, *milicianos* intensified their activities against the church. Just three days after the rupture of relations, citing the dangers of an impending invasion from the United States, pro-government militants occupied various churches, seminaries, educational centers, and Catholic associations like ACU and JOC. Castro accused the "lackies in cassocks" (*esbirros con sotana*) with providing an ideological weapon to justify counterrevolutionary activities. *Milicianos* also closed *La Quincena* temporarily, which had criticized the government for its "anti-Catholic campaign," which, the newspaper noted, "in the last few days has acquired an increasingly sectarian demeanor and aimed its batteries our way. We are not surprised or fearful."[83]

On February 14, the Juventud Católica Cubana celebrated its thirty-second anniversary at Colegio La Salle in Havana, attended by three bishops, including Archbishop Díaz. A large crowd surrounded the school, trapping everyone inside. When the archbishop called the police, he was told that Catholics provoked the siege, and only after six hours did a submachine-gun-toting militia official inform Catholics they could leave. In response,

Catholic students initiated strikes, and Catholic schools reported absenteeism of from 50 to 100 percent. The state schools, however, remained unaffected, revealing the Catholic minority's limited leverage against the government.[84] In March, a bomb exploded in a private academy, injuring nine professors and students. Although no one claimed responsibility, the government press accused the church and the clergy of inciting the violence against the director of the school, who had publicly supported the government's educational policies. Minister of Education Armando Hart said it was the work of "falangist priests," and the following day Castro again accused the church of being "the fifth column of the counterrevolution" and alluded to the possibility of expelling all Spanish priests from the island. On March 7, Catholic students and pro-revolutionary crowds again confronted each other in Santiago on the Day of the Catholic Student after Mass at the Cathedral.

Interventions directly in Catholic schools also began. On February 19 communist labor leader Lázaro Peña charged Catholic educators with poisoning the minds of Cuba's children and demanded that something be done. In fact, the government response had already begun. On the thirteenth, for example, pro-revolutionary students took over the Escuela Electromecánica de Belén, a technical school for working-class children owned by the Jesuits, complaining that the teachers spread anti-revolutionary ideas. During the next two months, the government intervened in schools across the island using similar tactics in which students and teachers sympathetic to the Revolution organized protests accusing school administrators of spreading counterrevolutionary sentiments and demanding some action.[85]

Certainly, as the tensions between Cuba and the United States continued to grow during early 1961, and popular enthusiasm and sympathy for the Revolution increased, the government gained a freer hand to attack the church, especially by linking the Cuban church to U.S. interests. As news reports continued to suggest that an exile invasion of the island was imminent, Castro kept his inflammatory anti-church and anti-clerical rhetoric at fever pitch. Armed pro-government supporters disrupted Mass at the Cathedral in Santiago de Cuba and clashed with worshippers. In Camaguey, *milicianos* entered a parish church and sang the national anthem, leading to further clashes. When a priest in the town of Palos (Havana Province) insisted on saying Mass, a mob attacked him, forcing him to leave for Havana.[86] Also, the government reported the capture of Father Francisco López

Blazquez in the Escambray Mountains with an insurrectionary band—for many revolutionaries a clear signal of the church's posture.

In April, Holy Week activities also resulted in confrontations between Catholics and backers of the government. On the eve of traditional Good Friday processions, Castro characterized the clergy as a "plague of cassocked thugs and mercenary professors." He warned that rather than "letting the minds of our young people go on being poisoned, the revolution will not hesitate to take whatever measures it deems proper." He equated the interests of the Catholic hierarchy with capitalism and charged the church with using its freedom to promote counterrevolutionary activities in educational centers and in the churches themselves. At the Good Friday *via crucis* procession sponsored by Bishop Boza Masvidal's Caridad Church, some seventy thousand people attended. The procession itself was only marred by groups of people shouting "Fidel! Fidel!" but soon after it broke up, just after midnight, police cars arrived at the church and arrested about fifty people. As they were pushed onto buses and taken away, they shouted "Long Live Christ the King," and "Cuba: Sí; Russia: No." Earlier in the day, in Guines, southeast of Havana, militiamen broke up a similar procession attended by five thousand and detained the entire cast of enactors. Though shots were fired, no one was injured. At yet another Good Friday procession in Havana, *milicianos* shouted "Fidel!" The worshippers responded with acclamations of support for the pope and Boza Masvidal.[87]

Deportations and Silence

Shortly after Easter, on April 17, 1961, Cuban exiles funded by the United States launched the Bay of Pigs invasion, which provoked the final assault on Catholics by the Castro government. Well aware of the impending invasion, the Cuban government declared a national emergency, mobilized defenses, and in a matter of days defeated the exile brigade. The government captured 1,180 of the 1,297 invaders, held them in prison, and eventually negotiated a release. Not taking any chances, even before and especially after the invasion, authorities rounded up possible sympathizers, perhaps as many as 100,000, including many Catholics, who were seen as particularly complicit. The invasion gave Castro political cover, and the strong Catholic character of the invaders provided a good pretext for targeting the church.[88] The work of intimidation begun the previous summer now moved into still higher gear, and authorities crafted a careful campaign to discredit the church and destroy its ability to challenge the Revolution.

The government held and screened detainees in public buildings, theatres, and other places, but released most within a couple of weeks. Those identified as actively resisting the Revolution remained imprisoned. Cuban authorities closed churches and parochial schools and stationed *milicianos* at the doors. The churches opened later, but the schools never reopened. Authorities also occupied Villanueva University and placed the Augustinians, mostly U.S. citizens, under armed guard on the grounds. Overly zealous *milicianos* desecrated some of the churches, and the government closed all Catholic lay associations, including Catholic Action, ACU, JOC, and CYO; they, like the schools, never reopened. Authorities detained hundreds of lay leaders and activists, some before and others after the invasion, including José Ignacio Lasaga; Elordio Solzano de Villalón, president of the Catholic women's organization; Mateo Jover, president of the CYO for boys; Marta Díaz, president of the CYO for girls; Ramón Casas, national president of Catholic Action; and Alberto Cao, national president of JOC. Ailing Cardinal Arteaga and Bishop Rodríguez Rosas of Pinar del Rio sought refuge in the Argentine embassy, while the government placed bishops Díaz, Pérez Serantes, Boza Masvidal, and Ríu Anglés under house arrest. *Milicianos* arrested priests all over the island and even entered the convents and evicted the nuns.[89]

On April 18 and 19, to demonstrate what opponents of the Revolution could expect, the government executed several of the underground Catholic leaders who had been caught and arrested during the previous months, including González Corzo, Sorí Marín, and others.[90] Two members of the DRE, Alberto Tapia Ruano, age twenty-one, and Virgilio Campanería Angel, age twenty-two, were also executed. In his final letter to his parents, Tapia wrote, "Today at my trial I saw my brothers and godparents crying, but why? No, a thousand times no; I know it is painful for you but I want you to overcome this and think that God in his infinite generosity has given me this grace to be well with him and we should all thank him. Good-bye. . . . Have faith in the Eternal Life and I will intercede for all of you. Long live Christ, the King!"[91]

Castro formally declared the Cuban Revolution to be socialist on May 1, International Workers' Day. In a triumphant mood after the failed invasion, and with the backdrop of overwhelming support of the Cuban people, Castro reaffirmed that elections would not be held anytime soon, that the Constitution of 1940 was antiquated and obsolete, and that all private and church schools would be nationalized. He also announced that foreign priests opposing the Revolution should leave the country.[92] Initially, many priests returned to their parishes, and the bishops returned to their work, though Cardinal Arteaga remained in the Argentine embassy, by now gravely ill. He never recovered and died in March 1963. Despite their efforts, the clergy could not return to their normal routines. *Milicianos* maintained their campaign of intimidation, frightening clergy, religious, and laity and causing many to leave Cuba.

With church blessings, hundreds of Cuban and non-Cuban nuns—without any means of livelihood and who had staffed schools, orphanages, and homes for the elderly taken over by the government—left first, taking new assignments in the United States, Canada, Spain, Latin America, and elsewhere.[93] On May 19, 1961, a Pan American Airlines flight arrived in Miami from Havana carrying fifty-one North American and forty-six Cuban evacuees. United States citizens included several newspaper correspondents and six Augustinian professors of the now closed Villanueva University, including Father Lorenzo Spirali, its founder.[94] This continued during June and July, as numerous flights brought out the Catholic religious. One charter flight in July carried 108 religious, including fifty priests of the Franciscan, Vincentian, Redemptorist, Jesuit, Dominican, and Carmelite Orders. An earlier flight had brought the final twenty-four of the 150 Apostolate of the Sacred Heart nuns who had been in Cuba.

To be sure, the departure of the Catholic religious from Cuba was a sensitive problem for the government, since it would certainly not play well internationally. To avoid criticism from abroad, the government tried to give the appearance that the church was abandoning the island voluntarily. A Dominican lay brother told reporters on arriving in Miami that the regime continued to imprison priests, creating tremendous tensions among the clergy in Havana. "The streets of the city look like an armed camp," noted a priest, and the intimidation and harassment made it impossible for the religious to carry out their work. The religious complained that they received unsigned expulsion documents from the government, though their exit visas indicated they were leaving voluntarily. One priest reported that government officials told him that only those who "behaved themselves" would be allowed to stay in Cuba.[95] Those opposed to the regime had to leave or remain in silence with the constant fear that they could be assaulted or detained at the whim of national or local authorities. Certainly, for those old enough to remember, these events seemed reminiscent of the Spanish Civil War or perhaps the assault on Catholicism during the Mexican Revolution. While the government did not technically expel many of the religious who left during the summer, it certainly did what it could to convince them that they were not wanted or even safe in Cuba. The church also encouraged many to leave, hoping the exodus would create international pressure on the Cuban government.

Those clergy the government failed to intimidate, however, did suffer formal deportation in mid-September. By the end of the summer, the Catholic Church, as an institution, had been crippled. Without access to the media, the bishops could not speak to the faithful, and the militia watched priests during masses to ensure they did not criticize the regime in their sermons. Boza Masvidal, for one, continued his activities anyway, quite publicly meeting with Catholic lay leaders, criticizing the government in sermons, distributing newsletters, and sponsoring informal gatherings where he taught and spoke about Catholicism and its social thought.[96]

As the September 8 feast day of Nuestra Señora de la Caridad approached, Boza made arrangements to celebrate the occasion at his Caridad parish church. He initially obtained permission for a procession at 5:30 p.m. on Sunday, September 10, but then received instructions to begin the event before 9 a.m. and traverse only designated streets. Rather than comply, the bishop cancelled the procession, but some four thousand worshippers appeared at the church anyway at the originally announced time to protest. *Milicianos* and supporters of the government also gathered, leading to confrontations and a shooting that left a seventeen-year-old JOC activist, Arnoldo Socorro Sánchez, dead, and over one hundred demonstrators under arrest. The bishop and the government accused each other of instigating the confrontation, but the government had the upper hand and sponsored a public funeral for the youth, declaring he had been a supporter of the Revolution killed by Catholics. On September 12, the government published its accounts of what had transpired, interpreting the incident as a Catholic counterrevolutionary effort to undercut the Cuban Revolution. Authorities arrested Boza Masvidal and during the next days rounded up religious from across the island, forcibly placing about 135 on a Spanish steamer, *Covadonga*.[97] After five days of detention, on the seventeenth, escorted by seven men with machine guns, the bishop joined his colleagues on board. Among those expelled were forty-six Cuban clergy, making it clear that any religious publicly opposing the Revolution would be expelled from the island, whatever their nationality. Only about two hundred priests remained in Cuba by the end of September.[98]

In a speech after the *Covadonga* had departed, Castro accused the church of training and encouraging "saboteurs, fifth columnists and terrorist bands," and announced new restrictions on the church. He prohibited religious processions outside the churches and warned that Cuban priests "conspiring against the *patria*" would lose their citizenship. Boza Masvidal also spoke. "I have sailed from Cuba against my will," he declared. "In spite of my Cuban birth, I was physically forced on board." "My desire," he said, "was to tend and serve the needs of my people, share with them all the risks and adversities, whatever they might be."[99]

After the deportations, the church fell silent. It could no longer confront the government without incurring costs that threatened its very existence on the island. At the end of 1961, Castro declared himself and his revolution Marxist-Leninist. Fidel Castro's rapid consolidation of the Revolution through his charismatic relationship to the mass of the Cuban people, control of the rebel army, astute political maneuvering, and embrace of communism left Cuban Catholics stunned, to say the least. In a matter of two short years, Castro had suppressed and demolished what Catholics had constructed over half a century.

Chapter Three

FAITH COMMUNITY

At this moment of such uncertainty in exile, of privation, of confu-
sion, of doubt, the only thing that can put an end to our tribulations
is to turn to Christ.

—Carlos Obregón (1962)

Cubans who fled their homeland in the 1960s left for many reasons, but fundamentally because the Revolution systematically and radically transformed
what they knew and valued. Their departure left them dispersed and disoriented, but they immediately sought protection and comfort by attempting
to recreate abroad what they had abandoned. Catholics turned to their faith
for solace, one of the few things they carried with them to anchor their new
lives. In south Florida they used their militant faith experiences to establish
Catholic communities that provided safe settings for assessing their new
situation, including reengaging their spiritual and faith traditions. Catholic
settings, whether in parish churches, schools, or lay communities, provided
not only spiritual nourishment but also economic, political, and social
contact and networking possibilities that enhanced their ability to survive
in their new environment while maintaining a commitment to their faith.

Resettlement

Almost 700,000 overwhelmingly white refugees of all Cuban social classes, regions, and religions arrived in the United States during the first twenty years of the tumultuous Revolution. Though heterogeneous as a whole, the various waves of refugees consisted of people with very specific characteristics, from the departure of the white upper and middle classes in the early 1960s to the arrival in 1980 of significant numbers of blacks and mulattos of the working classes. Cuba's privileged classes began leaving in early 1959 in response to the executions of many *batistianos* and the transformation of the country's economic system signaled by the radical agrarian program. The next year, the government expropriated U.S.-owned property, and urban reform laws confiscated rental properties in the cities, affecting the middle classes and business sectors. Deepening tensions after the failed Bay of Pigs invasion in April 1961 intensified the exodus, and people escaped in a number of ways. Some Cubans received U.S. visa waivers handled through the Swiss Embassy in Havana, while others left to "third countries" (countries other than the United States and Cuba), especially Spain, Venezuela, and Mexico. Those prohibited from leaving by Cuban authorities found clandestine solutions, including seeking political asylum in foreign embassies and leaving on private boats, planes, and even rafts. During this time perhaps 150,000 Cubans arrived in the United States, for the most part believing that the regime would not survive, either because it would become a victim of its own ineptness or as a result of U.S. military action.[1]

The Cuban missile crisis in October 1962 closed all direct migration from Cuba to the United States, and during the next three years only about 56,000 Cubans emigrated there, mostly via third countries, though many continued to depart Cuba clandestinely. During the summer of 1964, for example, 554 Cubans arrived in south Florida in 66 boats, including 381 men, 87 women, and 86 children. As one report noted, "In their desperation to escape . . . the Cuban people have escaped in the most unbelievable ways: a trailer's roof converted to a boat, a rustic raft made out of bamboo with ropes and five inflated innertubes, even a weak kayak."[2]

The numbers fleeing Cuba again increased, beginning in September 1965, when Castro, responding to the U.S. government's use of the exodus for propaganda advantage, declared that Cubans in the United States could pick up their relatives at the port of Camarioca, a fishing village on the coast of Matanzas province. During the next three months exiles rented boats of all kinds and picked up their loved ones in Cuba. About three thousand arrived in this way, but many more entered after the United States and Cuba signed an agreement establishing what became known as the "Freedom Flights." Beginning that December, two flights a day between Miami and the port of Varadero transported some three thousand Cubans a month to the United States. By the time the flights ceased in 1973, almost 300,000 Cubans had reached the United States.

Those arriving on the regular flights reflected a broadening demographic cross-section of Cuban society. During the final years of the 1960s, the government moved to nationalize Cuba's entire urban economy, displacing thousands who either had to integrate into the new socialist economy and work for the government or had to leave the island. The establishment of a hemispheric trade embargo in 1964 against Cuba also aggravated the economic situation on the island, increasing shortages and causing further distress. Those leaving in the decade after Camarioca were largely people of the working classes and the petit bourgeois, including employees, independent craftsmen, small merchants, and skilled and semi-skilled workers.[3] With the end of the organized flights from Cuba in 1973, immigration ceased except for those who had managed to leave for third countries, especially Spain, and then managed to receive visas to travel to the United States. Some continued to arrive on boats and rafts, but not until 1980 did another flood of refugees arrive.

At the end of March 1980, six Cubans in a bus crashed through the gates of the Peruvian embassy in Havana and asked for political asylum. Furious with the Peruvians for allowing the asylum seekers to stay despite the death of one of the embassy guards, Castro removed his sentinels from the embassy, and within a short time ten thousand Cubans entered the grounds hoping to get out of Cuba. In the midst of great tensions in Cuba, including large and aggressive pro-government demonstrations, the United States, Peru, and other countries agreed to accept the Cubans in the embassy. During the next month, Castro castigated the United States and the Cuban exile community for aggravating the situation and, again reacting to U.S. criticisms, announced on April 20 that all Cubans with relatives in the United States could leave. In a replay of Camarioca, Castro invited exiles to pick up their relatives but this time at the port of Mariel. Thousands in south Florida rented boats and ferried their Cuban relatives and thousands of others across the Strait of Florida, an exodus that continued until September, when about 125,000 Cubans had arrived in the United States.[4] These arrivals contrasted sharply from previous refugees. Mostly young, mulatto and black, and overwhelmingly working-class semi-skilled and unskilled laborers, this migration included people who would have been expected to be among the Revolution's strongest supporters.[5]

As Cubans arrived over a twenty-year period, they created numerous and diverse communities, with south Florida the largest by far. By 1980, Cubans in the Dade County metropolitan area, which includes cities such as Miami, Hialeah, Sweetwater, and Miami Beach, numbered almost 600,000, producing an entrepreneurial and dynamic economy that literally transformed the region. Large numbers of Cubans also settled in the northeast, mostly in New Jersey and New York, establishing communities in Union City and the city of West New York, two New Jersey towns on the Hudson River across from New York City. By 1970, a little more than one-third of West New York's total population of 40,666 was Cuban, and by 1980 the Union City–West New York area had incorporated about 100,000 Cubans. Smaller but distinct Cuban populations also appeared across the country, including, by 1980, some 30,000 Cubans in Los Angeles; 24,000 in Chicago; 13,000 in Boston; 10,000 in Atlanta; 8,000 in Washington, DC; 5,000 in Dallas–Fort Worth, and 2,000 in New Orleans.[6]

As Cubans flooded into Miami in 1960 and 1961, with only the clothes on their backs, they received almost immediate support from the local community. Faith communities, including Catholics, Jews, and Protestants, and volunteer relief agencies, including Catholic Relief Services, the Protestant Latin American Emergency Committee, the International Rescue Committee, and the United HIAS, worked to provide the arriving refugees with economic assistance and shelter.[7] Since Catholics represented a large proportion of refugees in the early years, the church played a critical role in helping Cuban refugees financially as well as in pastoral matters, which no doubt gave the newcomers comfort and may have reinforced the religious commitments of many.

The diocese of Miami played a particularly active role in refugee relief organized through its Centro Hispano Católico (CHC). The CHC opened during fall 1959, at the initiative of Father Bryan O. Walsh, director of Catholic Charities, to serve the growing number of Hispanic Catholics in south Florida, mostly Puerto Ricans, Colombians, and other South Americans. The staff included four sisters of the Dominican Order and several Spanish Dominican priests, including Angel Vizcarra who became very active with the Miami Cuban community. The CHC was the only community social service agency with a bilingual capability, and its initial services included religion and English classes, a medical out-patient clinic, a dental clinic, a day nursery, a high school for Spanish-speaking teenagers, and a radio station. As the number of Cubans refugees increased, so did its work, including administering food and clothes distribution and offering a variety of other direct aid programs.

The Catholic Church in Miami offered Cubans strong and consistent support. In addition to financial help, church officials defended Cuban refugees from the reactions of Anglo-Americans and others bewildered by this sudden and unprecedented influx of foreigners. In 1963, Father John J. Fitzpatrick, in charge of matters having to do with the Spanish-speaking for the diocese, sought to calm fears in an address to the Miami Sierra Club. "The Latins in our midst are not our problems; they are our opportunities," he declared. "They are our brothers in Christ and we must be the first to know them and to love them." Fitzpatrick emphasized that though overall Cuban refugees are not well "churched," they possessed strong religious values and sense of community. He said that North Americans practiced an "individual worship, with a sort of cold, provincial 'mind your own business' type of religion," while Latin religiosity "is based upon Christian principles of love and sacrifice, as preached and practiced by Christ himself." For them, he declared, community and public worship were more important than individual worship. He asked his audience to be tolerant of their differences and not to insist on too rapid assimilation that would destroy their "most cherished values." He reminded his audience that "the peoples of many nations—the Irish, the Italians, the Poles, and others—have brought many fine things to the United States which have contributed greatly to our cultural and economic development."[8]

Father Bryan Walsh also came to the defense of Cuban refugees and, in fact, became their strongest advocate in those early years. He arranged for them to receive living expense stipends and opposed efforts to intern the refugees at the Opalocka Naval Air Station as advocated by some local politicians. Cubans needed to be out in the community, Walsh argued, where they could find jobs and take care of themselves. "They were entrepreneurs, they would manage," he remembered advising everyone. He especially wanted to avoid making dependents out of them and creating "another West Bank," referring to the Palestinian refugee experience. "This is where the church emerged as defenders of the refugees," Walsh noted. "I remember preaching at churches where people walked out in the middle of the sermon [for advocating for the refugees], and the mail was horrible."[9]

Walsh also helped large numbers of unaccompanied children arriving in Miami. Frightened by the Revolution's increasingly aggressive tone, people of the middle and upper classes particularly feared that the government would take charge of their children. The Revolution's literacy campaign in 1961 sent thousands of teenagers to the countryside to teach campesinos to read and learn revolutionary ideology. The nationalization of the schools disturbed parents, but of even greater concern was the rumor that Cuban children would be sent to the Soviet Union for school. Thousands of families sent their children unaccompanied to the United States. Parents hoped to follow as soon as possible, but, for many, events turned an expected short separation into something much longer, as travel ceased in October 1962 with the outbreak of the missile crisis.[10]

In November 1960, Walsh learned of a young Cuban boy being passed around among several Cuban families and offered to help. As director of the Catholic Welfare Bureau, mostly a child-care and adoption agency, Walsh placed the boy with a local family. He later discovered many others in similar circumstances and placed them as well. The break in United States–Cuban relations and the failed Bay of Pigs invasion created greater desperation, and even more families sent their children abroad. Since they were unable to obtain visas at the U.S. embassy, a clandestine network developed in Cuba to get children off the island with visa waivers made available by Father Walsh. When waivers could no longer be obtained, the network in Cuba forged documents and, with the cooperation of the airlines, secured seats on outgoing flights to Miami. Through Operation Pedro [Peter] Pan, some fourteen thousand Cuban children during 1962 and 1963 arrived in Miami, where Walsh took charge of them. Initially Walsh succeeded in placing the children in private homes, but as the numbers grew, this became more difficult. The diocese established five camps in Dade County to house the children. The church raised funds locally for the care of the children, but the Kennedy administration soon provided additional necessary resources. In time, most of the children found homes, though many ended up across the country, away from their community.[11]

As the number of refugees arriving in south Florida increased, the local church intensified its activities. By the end of 1961, the diocese of Miami had provided nearly $1 million worth of welfare and health services, including food, housing, hospital care, schooling, and other services, but the resources remained inadequate.[12] The diocese spent about $2.5 million by 1965, and in 1975 the annual budget of the CHC reached $250,000 a year.[13] Besides diocesan resources, Catholic Relief Services in Miami obtained private contributions, including from large North American businesses that had been in Cuba. In late 1960, Texaco Oil, Inc., for example, gave $100,000 to Cuban refugee relief, $50,000 of which went directly to the CHC.[14]

The emerging Cuban community itself also provided funds for the CHC's mission. In November 1960, more than two hundred Cuban women, organized as the Sección Cubana Centro Hispano Católico, contributed $10,000 for CHC relief work. Presenting the gift to Bishop Coleman Carroll at a luncheon, Mrs. Alfonso Fanjul, president of the Sección Cubana, noted that this marked the start of an ongoing effort to provide resources for food, clothing, housing, education, and employment for Cuban refugees and called for volunteers to help the CHC staff. Fanjul also announced Sección Cubana's plans for a benefit dinner-dance that would include an "Extravaganza Latina" show of "top talent from Cuba."[15] By June 1968, the CHC had handled some 450,000 cases, mostly Cuban.[16]

Despite these efforts, by the end of 1960 about forty thousand refugees had arrived, and their numbers increased by at least one thousand to 1,500 per week. Still facing shortages of funds, Sister Miriam Strong, administrator of CHC, told reporters that "People who formerly were seeking jobs are now begging for food and in many cases going hungry." She emphasized that the community needed to do more. "Although many donations have enabled us to give immediate aid, there is still a tremendous need, and all Americans should feel a personal responsibility to help these people who are refugees from communism."[17]

Finding his diocese financially stretched, Bishop Carroll convened a meeting of influential business and political leaders and through them appealed for help in Washington. President Eisenhower responded by officially designating Cubans as political refugees fleeing a communist state and released $1 million in contingency funds to support the ongoing relief. Eisenhower also appointed Tracy Vorhees, who had headed the 1956 Committee for Hungarian Refugee Relief, to investigate the Cuban refugee situation. In response to Vorhees's report, submitted on December 7, 1960, the administration established a Cuban Refugee Emergency Center in Miami to coordinate relief activities and initiated a resettlement program, giving Cubans a "parole" status that allowed them to seek employment in the United States. This reflected the government's hope that their stay in the United States would be temporary. Not until 1966, with the passage of the Cuban Adjustment Act, did Cubans receive the right to apply for permanent residency after one year in the United States. Since federal funds were used exclusively for resettlement activities, private relief agencies remained deeply involved in raising funds for direct assistance, including food, clothing, medical care, and other needs.

The limited support for refugees by the Eisenhower administration changed with the new Kennedy government, which in March 1961 announced the creation of a full-fledged Cuban Refugee Program (CRP) in the Department of Health, Education and Welfare and in coordination with the departments of State, Labor, Defense, and Agriculture. Under the CRP program, funds were used for more than resettlement, including direct relief like stipends, food, health services, schooling, and training. In 1962, Congress passed the Migration and Refugee Assistance Act, which established permanent authority for CRP.[18] The refugee center provided Cubans access to financial resources never accorded any other immigrant group to the United States, but it also established a program of geographic relocation when south Florida could no longer manage the influx. By 1978, almost 470,000 Cubans had been relocated away from Miami, though in subsequent years many returned to the region on their own.[19]

Among those departing Cuba in the early 1960s were the Catholic leaders and intellectuals who had criticized and resisted Castro. Most went to Miami but dispersed as they found educational and professional opportunities across the United States and other places. Rubén Rumbaut, for example, arrived in Miami in mid-July 1960, just as the government initiated its overt anti-Catholic campaign. "We flew away from Cuba without knowing when we would return to her," wrote Rumbaut's wife, Carmen. She and her husband did not know "what would happen . . . if our exile would be long or short." While Carmen set up a household and settled their five children in new schools, Rubén became involved in exile political activities and explored employment possibilities. He enrolled in an intensive English course at the University of Miami and took a course in medicine at Miami's Jackson Memorial Hospital for Cuban doctors wanting to take the Foreign

Medical Exam for licensing in the United States. On passing the exam he accepted a job with the Veterans Administration as Chief of Mental Hygiene Clinic Outpatient Service in Albuquerque, New Mexico. They left Miami at the end of 1961.

"We said goodbye to our many friends in Miami," Carmen remembered, "and with a debt of over $1000, without furniture or appliances for the home, with only $50 in our pocket, and without knowing what this new exile stage had in store for us, we boarded the plane with our five children and started our new life of work in this great nation."[20] Others did the same. Lasaga accepted work in Maryland, Valdespino started doctoral studies in literature in New York, Rasco joined the Inter-American Development Bank in Washington, DC, and Cerro relocated to Venezuela, where Boza Masvidal already lived. For the most part, Cuban professionals fared well, translating their education and skills into successful careers in the United States. In some ways their success should have made it easy for them to simply forget Cuba and leave it behind, but this did not happen. As exiles, more than anything else, they wanted to return home.

Those who remained in south Florida created a dynamic community that transformed the region economically and culturally. In the 1980s, Cuban exile scholar Alejandro Portes described the south Florida Cuban community as an economic enclave with an independent entrepreneurial base that served its own ethnic market as well as the general population. The community included a population with considerable education, experience with capitalism, and possessing some capital either brought from Cuba or accumulated in the United States that allowed for relative autonomous economic growth. The Cuban enclave included entrepreneurs transplanted from Cuba who laid the foundations of a local economy with an extensive division of labor and employment possibilities at all levels for subsequent Cuban immigrants. The community relied on personal relationships and business networks often reproduced from the island that contributed to a sense of ethnic solidarity. These networks influenced decisions about loans, hiring, and many other economic matters, giving Cubans access to private capital, federal loans, and job opportunities that they might otherwise not have had.

The ever increasing number of Cuban arrivals, as well as the North American market, provided a customer base for a diverse set of economic enterprises established by Cubans that expanded rapidly. Many eventually established small businesses that required little initial capital, while others took nonunionized garment and construction jobs. Business ownership increased rapidly. In Miami, Cubans owned 919 enterprises in 1967, but within ten years this had increased to eight thousand, mostly small firms with an average of about eight employees. Cubans established restaurants and cafeterias, gas stations, grocery stores and eventually supermarkets, book and record stores, hardware, appliance and furniture stores, funeral homes, radio stations and newspapers, theaters, pharmacies and clinics, and the whole range of businesses that a community required. In time, these enterprises also sought markets outside of Miami, in other parts of the United States, and in Latin America, providing tremendous economic possibilities for the Cuban business community. As Cubans continued to arrive during the next decades, they also found jobs in this community, further expanding the economic enclave.

Cubans reproduced their professional classes. At first many professionals could not practice their vocations and therefore abandoned them, but with the support of the Cuban Refugee Program others learned English and underwent professional relicensing to work in the United States. These professionals and others in the community emphasized education and invested a great deal in sending their children to colleges and universities, another factor that in time strengthened the enclave and allowed it to grow. As a whole, the Cuban communities that formed as a result of the post-1959 migrations fared relatively well economically. Median family incomes surpassed other Hispanic groups, although they did not reach the income levels of Anglo-American society. This higher income resulted from several factors, including their peculiar demographic characteristics, United States government support of the refugees, the benefits of Miami's enclave economy, and the successes of Cuban women entering the labor market who contributed substantially to family incomes. This naturally gave new arrivals considerable opportunity that would not have existed in a normal, undifferentiated working-class immigrant community without a dynamic entrepreneurial element.[21]

Faith

Cubans who arrived in south Florida in the 1960s included devout and nominal Catholics, as well as non-Catholics, though various observers thought the vast majority did not practice their faith very fervently, certainly not going to church on a regular basis. Msgr. John Fitzpatrick, for example, noted that Cuban students who did not receive their religious training in parochial schools generally remained unchurched. In many Cuban homes parents "teach very little," and they did not take their children to Sunday Mass. This lack of engagement with the faith also translated into little material support for the church. "For many Cubans," Fitzpatrick continued, "contributions to the support of the Church are the last line on their budget, if it even has a line." Other American priests also noticed a informality among Cubans about their faith and a tendency to engage the sacraments for social rather than spiritual reasons. At weddings, one priest commented, Cubans often arrived late. "This is not only a discourtesy to the priest," he noted, "but very disconcerting to a priest who has other important duties to perform." Other Cubans were more interested in "the extravagance of their showings at weddings and first communions" than with the spiritual significance of the event. On the other hand, Father Emilio Vallina of San Juan Bosco Church took a more optimistic attitude. Though he did not deny the traditional lack of devotion among Cubans and recognized the superficiality of many, he did notice a considerable change over the years. "The indifference of many toward their faith in the years before Castro's take-over," he explained, "has been replaced by a new dimension in religious fervor." This resulted from the fleeting nature of material things and "the fact that the exiles were forced to seek consolation in spiritual things."[22]

Whatever the percentage of practicing Catholics in south Florida, however, sufficiently dedicated and devout Catholics did exist among the refugees to forge a visible and devout Cuban Catholic presence. Those who arrived devout generally remained so in exile and initially focused their energies on reorganizing their faith communities. They eventually engaged in evangelization, reaching out to those Catholics who exhibited only lukewarm attitudes about their church and religion but who often resorted to faith to make sense of their refugee experience. Cubans interested in Catholicism founded a rich array of culturally familiar institutions through which to engage their religion. Networks dedicated to living and deepening faith during this time of insecurity and vulnerability represented one of many important sources of guidance for Catholic exiles struggling to reorganize their lives. Institutions grew out of the community itself over a period of some fifteen years, including majority Cuban parishes, lay movements, shrines, schools, and media. The number of practicing Hispanic Catholics in south Florida grew, and the church took an important place within the Cuban community in the region.

Despite residing in Venezuela, Bishop Boza Masvidal played a particularly significant role in encouraging and organizing south Florida Catholic exiles, establishing a long and enduring relationship with the community. On the evening of January 27, 1962, the bishop celebrated Mass on an altar erected in the center of the baseball diamond in Miami stadium, attended by some thirty thousand people. Already the moral symbol of the exile struggle against communism, he was received by Miami Catholics just four months after his expulsion from the island. With the full support of Bishop Carroll, Cuban priests Francisco Villaverde and Angel Villaronga organized the event with the help of prominent former lay leaders from Cuba. Preliminary activities included a triduum of prayers in six Miami parishes, beginning on January 24, conducted by exiled Cuban priests. These days of prayer prepared Cuban Catholic exiles for a public profession to the Virgen de la Caridad at the culminating Mass sung by Bishop Carroll in which the Cuban bishop delivered a sermon.[23]

The solemn Mass began with a procession of men carrying lighted torches, forming a cross on the field, as more than twenty Spanish-speaking priests heard confessions. A choral group from St. John Vianney Seminary, attired in cassocks and surplices, provided music. In his sermon Boza Masvidal called on Cubans to embrace their faith, which would get them through these difficult times. "The ideal of faith," he noted, "will give our lives a new view of things, a new sense of our work, to understand suffering and to illuminate the realities of our lives in a new light."[24] Beginning with this trip to Miami, Boza Masvidal earned his place as the pastor of exile who spoke to and encouraged Catholics wherever they lived in the diaspora.

After his deportation, Boza Masvidal spent some time in Spain and then traveled to Rome and briefed the pope on conditions in Cuba. By early March he had been assigned to a parish just outside Caracas, in Los Teques, from where he initiated an international effort to organize exile Catholics. Boza Masvidal's activities, with the support of prominent members of Cuba's exiled laity, resulted in the foundation of the Union of Cuban Exiles (Unión de Cubanos en el Exilio; UCE) in Caracas, Miami, and New York.[25] Headquartered in Caracas, the UCE proposed to "reaffirm our Christian faith by making it alive, dynamic and commanding" and "to cooperate with the religious authorities in each place [where Cubans lived] to provide attention and spiritual assistance." "Live our faith," he told Cubans. "In the face of the materialism that surrounds us, become aware that faith is life, be formed by faith and live it with intensity."[26]

While Boza Masvidal's presence provided a sense of comfort and encouragement, serious Catholics arriving in Miami in the early 1960s did not really need to be urged to look to their faith during this time of distress. They did so instinctively and quickly reorganized their faith communities. Cubans initially settled on Eighth Street near downtown, which became known as Little Havana or Calle Ocho ("Eighth Street"). Catholics attended church in the nearby parishes and sought out friends and acquaintances from the apostolic networks they had worked with on the island. These simple acts were the first steps in reorganizing their faith communities in a new environment, a process that included a determination to maintain identity and culture while at the same time recognizing the very significant structural and cultural differences of church life in the United States.

Cubans immediately noticed the extent to which North American church life revolved around the parish. Deeply influenced by a highly activist laity, Catholic life in Cuba revolved less around the parishes than the lay organizations that had regenerated Catholicism on the island. At home, Catholics did not necessarily attend Mass in their parish churches, often preferring to attend services with the membership of their lay organizations. Similarly, apostolic and evangelization work was not organized in the parishes but by national lay organizations that often worked independently of the parishes and pastors and in greater coordination with the lay organizations' spiritual counselors. For Cuban Catholics, then, accepting the centrality and power of the parishes and their priests did not come easily, and the diocese found itself constantly reminding parishioners of their obligation to attend Mass and establish community with their local parishes and parishioners.[27]

As the Cuban presence expanded dramatically in the early 1960s, Cuban congregations also grew. By early 1962, Cubans belonged to at least thirteen parishes, extending from St. Patrick's Parish in Miami Beach, west to St. Brenden's Parish just beyond Southwest Sixtieth Avenue, and on the north, from St. John's Parish at about Northwest Thirty-third Street to Epiphany Parish, south of U.S. Highway 1, also known as Dixie Highway.

Three years later, a census revealed that several parishes had a Cuban presence numbering in the thousands, including San Juan Bosco (14,284), St. Michaels (11,679), SS. Peter and Paul (9,392), Gesu (7,322), Corpus Cristi (7,303), and St. Mary's Cathedral (3,110).[28] Subsequently, new parishes with large Cuban congregations emerged throughout Dade County. In December 1963, with one thousand parishioners looking on, Bishop Carroll blessed the temporary church of St. Dominic Parish, an area northwest of downtown Miami that had become heavily Cuban. The church stood at the corners of LeJune Road and Flagler Street and was led by Father Angel Vizcarra. In his talk to the assembled, Carroll lauded Vizcarra for his hard work in developing the parish and noted with satisfaction how Cubans and other Spanish-speaking parishioners had become active in parish work.[29] St. Kevin in 1963 and St. Kieran in 1967 followed. In October 1968, the diocese established St. Robert Bellarmine parish, in an area with one thousand mostly Cuban families, and others included St. Raymond (1969), St. Agatha (1971), St. Cecilia (1971), St. Joachim (1972), Our Lady of Divine Providence (1973), and St. Benedict (1973).[30]

Within the parishes numerous churches included Spanish-speaking priests, many who first arrived from Spain in the 1950s to work mostly among Mexican American and Puerto Rican farm workers spread across the rural areas of south Florida. The church recruited these priests through the Obra de Cooperación Sacerdotal Hispanoamericana (OCSHA), a Spanish church organization established to provide clergy for Latin America but also for areas of the United States with significant Spanish-speaking populations. After the Revolution in Cuba, many OCSHA priests initially assigned to the island relocated to south Florida and remained close to the Cuban exile community.[31] Also, many of the hundreds of Cuban priests who left the island during 1961 ended up in Miami, where they ministered to the exploding Cuban and Hispanic population. By May 1962, the staffs of sixteen churches in the Miami area included nineteen Hispanic priests, and at least ten churches offered confessions in Spanish and Spanish-language sermons at Sunday Mass, though these masses were often not authorized in the main church and were instead conducted in the parish halls.[32] The parishes offering Spanish-language services included five in Miami, in the area of greatest Cuban concentration, but also at Little Flower in Coral Gables, Santísima Trinidad in Miami Springs, Santa Inés in Key Biscayne, and Inmaculada Concepción and San Juan Apóstol in Hialeah.[33]

Within five years, after the liturgical reforms of Vatican II, thirty Spanish-language masses were being said weekly in fourteen Dade County parishes. A directory of Cuban religious and priests in the archdiocese of Miami published in 1975 included ninety-two priests, most of whom worked in parishes, schools, and seminaries.[34]

Though Cuban and Spanish priests in the archdiocese were quite numerous in the 1960s, the numbers could still not keep up with the expanding Latino population during the next decade. In the short-term the church requested more priests from Spain, but over the longer run only vocations among Cuban and Hispanic youth could provide the necessary clergy for their community. In a highly symbolic ceremony in August 1962, the Cuban Catholic community celebrated the first ordination of a Cuban in south Florida, with a ceremony at the Miami Beach convention hall. An editorial in the Catholic newspaper *The Voice* declared Daniel Sánchez "a symbol of hope for the future" not only for Cuba but for Latin America in general, where priestly vocations lagged. The event even attracted Cardinal Francis Spellman, archbishop of New York, who conducted the ordination, drawing a congregation of more than twelve thousand people.[35] A group of nine Cuban seminarians, most of them sponsored by the Peter Pan program, entered the St. John Vianney Minor Seminary in Miami in fall 1962, and by 1967 fourteen Cubans studied for the priesthood.[36]

Cuban and Spanish priests played critical roles in helping Cubans adapt to the parish-centered church in the United States. They helped Hispanic parishioners to develop their places of worship not only as centers of religious life but also as general support for a disoriented and demoralized population. St. John Bosco was perhaps the most important of Cuban parishes in the early years. Founded initially as a mission of St. Peter and St. Paul Parish in February 1963, St. John Bosco began on Flagler Street in the heart of Little Havana. In June, Father Emilio Vallina, a Cuban, became the administrator of the mission and offered the first masses with sermons in Spanish at the Trivoli movie theatre on Flagler.[37] In late 1963, Archbishop Carroll asked Vallina to meet him at the corner of Flagler and Northwest Thirteenth Avenue, in the heart of little Havana. "When he saw me," Vallina explained, "he gave me some keys, pointed to an old garage and told me it was mine. . . . It was a great responsibility, but at the same time he gave me his vote of confidence." By January, now in the new facility, Father Vallina, with the aid of a pastoral assistant and three Cuban Christian Brothers, provided six masses on Sunday, five with Spanish sermons. With renovations completed in 1965, Bishops Carroll and Boza Masvidal dedicated the new St. John Bosco Church, and it became a parish in 1968.[38]

San Juan Bosco, as the Cubans called it, became a symbol of Cuban Catholic community life. A youth center offered adolescents a place to participate in sports, social activities, and a film club, where they watched, discussed, and critiqued films. A social assistance department visited needy parishioners, especially the newly arrived refugees from Cuba who always especially lacked food and clothes. An annual festival raised funds for the church. At the 1969 festival, Father Vallina announced plans for the coming years that included expanding the school and the kindergarten, constructing a stage in the parish hall, building a cafeteria, installing sports facilities in adjacent lots, and targeting outreach activities to the community's youth.[39] In time, the parishioners of San Juan Bosco involved themselves in the various groups and apostolic movements organized by the exile community, including Women of Catholic Action, Catholic Student Youth, the Christian Family Movement, Knights of Columbus, the National Council of Our Lady of Charity, and many others. The church also celebrated the Patron Saint feast days of all of the nations of Spanish America, though, of course, the feast day celebration of the Cuban patroness, Nuestra Señora de la Caridad del Cobre, remained the most important and most attended. This practice also attracted Latino parishioners of other Latin American nationalities.[40]

For the diocese of Miami and the religious leaders arriving from Cuba, deepening the faith of the dispirited refugees through evangelization and pastoral care ranked among their most important goals. The Cuban parishes worked to reconstitute a Catholic community but also engaged in systematic outreach to arriving refugees who they felt would be especially receptive to a new and deeper encounter with their faith. In September 1964, for example, Father Javier Arzuaga, assistant pastor at Corpus Christi, visited some 250 Cuban homes, urging them to attend a religious gathering in a neighborhood vacant lot close to the church where he would preach Christ's message. The first evening some one hundred people attended, and the activity continued throughout the week with talks by the priest on the relationship between God and humankind, Christianity, the church, rituals, and liturgy. The following week, the priest did the same in another parish neighborhood and reported an overall increase in mass attendance, especially among children.[41]

Despite the initial skepticism of many unchurched new arrivals, the large number of parishes in the diocese provided newcomers with comfortable settings in which to learn about Catholicism and maintain and cultivate their cultural identity. At St. Bellarmine parish, Father Eugenio del Busto, who also served as auxiliary chancellor of the diocese, offered masses in Spanish and regularly visited the homes of the parish families. He offered religion classes for children on Saturdays and Sundays, and encouraged the laity to establish parish chapters of the numerous Cuban apostolic movements flourishing in the diocese. "The result we have achieved is fantastic," del Busto noted. "We always have a new experience, a positive experience, an extraordinary enthusiasm."[42]

The reenactment of Christ's passion became a common Holy Week ritual in Miami. The ritual appeared at San Juan Bosco around 1970, where the director of the production characterized it as a "labor of evangelization." At St. Stephan parish, the event began when the community felt the need "to live Holy Week according to our custom," and although the parish did not have a Spanish-speaking priest, they performed the play anyway, attracting more than two thousand participants. After this the diocese sent them a priest who could "coordinate the activities and speak our language." Cubans also participated in "El Encuentro de la Virgen Dolorosa con El Nazareno," in which members of various churches carried images of Jesus and the Virgin in procession to Martí Park. Parishioners from San Juan Bosco carried the image of the Nazarene while members of St. Peter and St. Paul Church carried the Virgin. At the park, parishioners reenacted Christ's passion.[43] Masses and confessions in Spanish, Cuban faith practiced at home and in the parishes themselves, and evangelization among Cuban families, including new arrivals from the island, reinvigorated the faith of many.

Cuban lay apostolic movements also played a critical role in deepening faith and encouraging evangelization among exiles. They emphasized personal conversion, promoting the Christian family and Catholic formation of their children. The only Cuban apostolic organization that managed to make the transition to Miami relatively unchanged was ACU, which moved there subsequent to the intervention by the Cuban government after the Bay of Pigs invasion. Still led by Jesuit Father Armando Llorente, the organization's spiritual leader in Cuba, ACU acquired a permanent location in Miami in 1965.[44] ACU reinitiated its publications, the journal *Mundo Nuevo* and internal bulletin (*hoja intima*) *Esto Vir.* While the bulletin served to maintain communication among the various chapters of the ACU in the

United States, Venezuela, Spain, and other places, the journal focused on theological and political questions. After reorganizing in Miami, Llorente traveled to other cities helping exiled ACU members rebuild a cohesive organization dedicated to spiritual growth and their homeland.[45]

Maintaining a sound family life emerged as perhaps the most pressing issue for refugees during the first decade in south Florida. While the local church did what it could to help their transition, Cuban Catholics acted on their own, drawing from their own traditions to create lay organizations that could immediately meet their needs and asking Cuban priests to act as their spiritual counselors. In January 1963, Cubans founded the Movimiento Familiar Cristiano (MFC) to address the critical issues faced by Cuban Catholic families during this time of displacement and resettlement, including questions of faith, psychological distress, and assimilation pressures. Cubans in Miami based the MFC on Equipos de Nuestra Señora (Our Lady's Teams), a family movement in Cuba founded by Christian Brother Augustín Victorino at La Salle School in Havana. Former movement activists in Cuba, Humberto López Alió and his wife, María Antonia Clark, founded the first MFC team at St. Agnes parish on Key Biscayne, which was dedicated to strengthening Latino families in south Florida. Advocating a theology of marriage to help couples find happier relationships, the ministry, noted López, "is the family saving families for Christ, taking Christ to families, with our testimony, with the example of lives that radiate Christ in their joy, in their happiness, in their love and in their harmony, and also in their pain and in life's tests."[46]

By June 1963, besides the St. Agnes group, MFC teams included some fifty-four couples at St. John the Apostle (Hialeah), Little Flower (Coral Gables), and three heavily Cuban parishes in Miami.[47] Father Angel Villaronga, who served as MFC's spiritual counselor, became very active not only working regularly with the organization but also writing columns about pastoral issues and family life in the Spanish-language section of the diocesan newspaper. His reflections usually focused on Christian marriage, often connecting doctrinal issues with the daily problems faced by the exile community in Miami. As the movement continued to grow into the early 1970s, Father Villaronga also edited two magazines, *Movimiento Familiar* and *Caná*.[48]

MFC addressed its concerns about protecting and cultivating the Cuban family in exile at meetings in 1964 and 1966 attended by one hundred and five hundred couples, respectively. Almost two thousand participants, representing forty MFC groups and sixteen parishes, heard talks on a variety of themes, including "The Family under Communism" and "The Family in the Miami Environment." Speakers offered optimistic thoughts about the situation in Miami but also warned that the move from a traditional, family-oriented society to a highly materialistic country where the family seemed less central presented a potential threat to the integrity of their faith and community. They grappled with the problems of adaptation to a foreign culture but also noted with optimism that the Cuban Christian family was certainly strong enough to withstand the stresses of exile: "Our posture is to confront the issues, and triumph."

As a practical consequence of these meetings, MFC established a special bureau with doctors, priests, teachers, social workers, and psychiatrists available to support all families.[49] Several other lay organizations also dedicated to preserving families formed in the early 1970s. Encuentros Familiares (1971) encouraged retreats for entire families; Impactos (1973) worked with families with children between ages three and ten; and Caminos al Matrimonio (1973) offered premarital counseling. Also in 1973, Cubans established Encuentros Juveniles for adolescents between sixteen and twenty years of age.[50] Initially seven parishes participated with this youth organization, sponsoring weekend retreats every forty-five days, in which young people talked and reflected on their faith. In 1976, Cubans interested in missionary work established Amor en Acción, based on the principle that "faith without action is dead." They worked first in the Dominican Republic and Mexico, and then in Haiti.[51] Certainly, the trauma of displacement caused many exiles to turn to religion for solace, and they created these grassroots movements in response to the spiritual needs of the Cuban Catholic laity, supported by Cuban and other Hispanic priests and religious. For many years these organizations operated relatively autonomously, independent of the diocese, which did not recognize them officially, but in time they became officially connected to the archdiocese.

Diocesan supported-activities dedicated to cultivating personal spiritual growth and formation in the church also attracted Cubans. Organizations that worked in the parishes and across the diocese included the Legion of Mary, St. Vincent de Paul, Knights of Columbus, and, perhaps the most appealing to Cubans, the Cursillos de Cristiandad.[52] Though Latinos from all over Dade and surrounding counties participated, the *cursillos* (mini courses) in Miami took on a strong Cuban identity.

Founded in 1949 in Mallorca, Spain, the *cursillos* ignited Christian militancy among Catholics at the grass roots by encouraging spiritual self-reflection and conversion through religious retreats. The *cursillos* promoted a personal and relational faith experience that attempted to break through "the culturally conditioned, ritualistic, habitual faith into which most Hispanics are born," by encouraging testimony and community.[53] Characterized by displays of emotion, songs, and sharing of experiences, the *cursillos* spread throughout the Hispanic Catholic world, arriving in the United States (in Texas) in 1957, first among Mexican American Catholics. The *cursillos* started in Miami in March 1962, when some forty men, all Cuban exiles except one, participated in a retreat led by Father Gus Petru, who was visiting from Guadalupe Church in Laredo, Texas.[54] Father Primitivo Santamaría, chaplain of the CHC, took charge of organizing the second *cursillo* in June with thirty participants.[55] A third, organized in September, received public support from Msgr. Fitzpatrick, who exhorted Spanish-speaking Catholics to attend: "it is not necessary that they be practicing Catholics, just that they are Catholics with good qualities and personality."[56]

After the third successful *cursillo* the bishop announced the creation of a Diocesan Secretariat headed by Father Santamaría and aided by several other priests and lay officials, including Father Miguel de Arrillaga, who later followed Santamaría as the movement's counselor in Miami.[57] The following June, forty-nine women, mostly Cubans, attended the first session for women directed by a team from Caracas.[58] By 1966, some seventy *cursillos* had been held in the Miami area, and the organization began publishing a newsletter, *Militante,* reflecting the enthusiastic Catholicism that *cursillos* engendered among Cubans and other Latinos.

In 1977, Father José L. Hernando, named diocesan spiritual counselor for the *cursillos* in 1969, explained that the retreats helped "to construct man from the inside," which first meant "fixing his heart." "When the heart becomes transparent, what is revealed are complexes, repressions, prejudices and pressures, insecurities and fears, guilt and sin, apathy and ignorance, pride and conceit, rebelliousness and injustice, vice and weaknesses, broken dreams and hidden failures." Hernando explained that to heal these kinds of wounds, the *cursillos* encouraged people to love and seek reconciliation—with themselves as well as the world around them.[59] Particularly in the 1960s and the early 1970s, the *cursillos* attracted the attention of many exiles seeking spiritual comfort in an effort to overcome their haunting experiences of flight and displacement. The *cursillos* brought many nominal Catholics more fully into the church. Exile Carlos H. Obregón, for example, admitted that in Cuba his Catholicism had not been very active. "From my infancy," he wrote, "my mother tried to guide me toward Catholicism. But how far I was from it." He acknowledged that prior to attending the *cursillo* he and most of his friends and acquaintances had the idea that being Christian was a personal thing, very subjective, and each to his own. After the *cursillo* he felt that to be Christian was to be an apostle, to speak to others about Christ and the church. "At this moment of such uncertainty in exile," he observed, "of privation, of confusion, of doubt, the only thing that can put an end to our tribulations is to turn to Christ."[60] Referring to the work done by the *cursillos* among Cuban exiles, one observer in 1966 noted: "it is easy to recognize that it is there that the great battle of exile has been waged; there, men and families have been perfectly prepared for the reconstruction of Cuba and for the benefit of all America."[61]

Miami Cubans also participated with the diocesan-run Confraternity of Christian Doctrine programs (CCD), dedicated to formal religious instruction among the faithful of all ages. In June 1962, Father R. E. Philbin, diocesan director of CCD, announced an initiative to recruit Spanish-speaking Catholics and brought Father Raymond García, from San Antonio, Texas, who had considerable experience establishing CCD programs among Spanish-speaking communities in the U.S. southwest and Latin America. After García's visit, Father Vallina assisted Philbin in organizing the program for Spanish speakers. On October 2, Vallina launched the program with representatives from Miami's largest Cuban parishes and in the first years trained 150 teachers and attracted over 3,500 children to the catechism classes. Vallina also became well-known as the spiritual counselor for the movement with his Spanish-language columns about CCD that appeared regularly in the diocesan newspaper during the 1960s.[62]

Catholic education, which perhaps more than anything else had been responsible for the revival of Catholicism in Cuba during the first half of the twentieth century, became an important priority for those able economically. Many Cubans placed their children in parochial or private schools, but since most children attended public schools, the parish also played an important role in religious formation. The diocese at first offered free schooling for arriving refugee children. A Spanish-language high school, known as Bachillerato del Centro Hispano Católico, opened in January 1961 and was designed to "maintain [student] . . . scholastic standing until they return to Cuba." In June, twenty-three students graduated from the school, having been instructed in religion, Spanish, English, mathematics, science, social studies, and U.S. history.[63] In testimony to Congress in late 1961, Bishop Carroll reported that four thousand of the fourteen thousand refugee children enrolled in Dade County schools attended private, mostly Catholic schools. In that year, the diocese supported children attending the parochial schools to the tune of $275,000. Later, as more Cubans became economically able to pay tuition costs, they remained committed to Catholic education.[64] By 1982, Latino (mostly Cuban) enrollment accounted for more than 65 percent of the more than nineteen thousand students enrolled in thirty primary and eight secondary Catholic schools in Dade County.[65]

For the wealthiest, elite private Catholic schools transferred from Cuba played an important role in the community. In Cuba these schools provided an important combination of religious formation and socioeconomic networks, which Cubans tried to recreate in south Florida. The nationalization and confiscation of Catholic and other private schools during the first half of 1961 led to the reestablishment of several in Miami, including *colegios* La Salle and Belén, which opened in September 1961. La Salle operated in a building with eight classrooms constructed next to Mercy Hospital, facing Biscayne Bay. On opening day the faculty included twelve Christian Brothers with advanced degrees in their fields of expertise. Among the seven Cubans, several had studied in the United States, including at University of Notre Dame and Georgetown University. Brother Alfredo Joaquín, the superior of the Cuban community, had taught in Cuba for eleven years, and most of the others had served as principals in various Cuban schools.[66]

Jesuits at Havana's Belén explored with Bishop Carroll the possibility of transferring the school to Miami in early 1961, when government intervention seemed all but inevitable. They obtained funds from Jesuit provinces in the United States and, shortly after the school's expropriation, reorganized in Miami.[67] The bishop gave the school permission to open but only if it incorporated a U.S. curriculum, in English, with diocesan, county, and state standards and requirements.[68] Headed by the Rector Father Luís Ripoll, the faculty included mostly English-speaking Spanish and Cuban Jesuits, but also some Jesuit personnel from the United States. During the first year Belén operated in classrooms at the Gesu parish school in downtown Miami, but in September 1962 the school occupied its new quarters in Little Havana.[69] Some years later, the school moved to a permanent site in west Dade County. The children and grandchildren of alumni attended the new school, and a new generation initiated their studies. Alumni association meetings raised money for the school, encouraged networking among former students, and gained support by promoting nostalgia for the Cuban past.[70]

In June 1962, Belén held its first graduation ceremonies, and twenty-six students received their diplomas from the hands of Bishop Carroll. The bishop's comments, in Spanish, emphasized the importance of Catholic education and the commitment of the diocese to the education of the refugee children arriving in Miami. He congratulated the students saying that their graduation "revealed that you are anxious and disposed to undergo great sacrifices for a good Catholic education and you understand perfectly well the importance and necessity of knowing about faith."[71] Other schools also opened during 1961 and 1962 in and around Miami and Ft. Lauderdale, including a primary and secondary school in Opa Locka headed by the former director of a Marist school in Cuba, Colegio de Cienfuegos.[72] Less affluent Cubans, initially avoiding the public school system, which they did not trust to instill proper values, often preferred a network of private neighborhood schools known as the escuelitas cubanas (Little Cuban Schools). Though secular, many of these bilingual schools sought support from the church for religion teachers.[73]

The media, including newspapers, radio, television, and magazines, helped evangelize and consolidate the sense of faith community among Cuban Catholics. The diocesan newspaper *The Voice,* from its very inception in 1959, published several pages in Spanish. The Spanish-language insert covered affairs of interest to the Hispanic population in south Florida, including editorials; local and international news; reviews of Christian-inspired books, movies, and theatre; and many other topics.[74] From the beginning of the Revolution in Cuba, *The Voice* covered events quite closely. Both the English and the Spanish sections tracked political developments on the island and reported on the diocese's response to the flood of arriving refugees. The newspaper offered information on Catholic services available to refugees and commented on many aspects of the Cuban question, internationally and domestically. Within a couple of years of their arrival, the Cuban editors of the Spanish-language insert published regular columns and commentaries on spiritual and inspirational matters by Cuban clergy and lay leaders that had great public appeal.

Other media outlets controlled by Cubans and concerned principally with Cuban Catholic matters also appeared. The UCE bulletin, *Unión,* published by Bishop Boza Masvidal in Caracas but distributed to Cuban Catholics throughout the United States, Europe, and Latin America complemented the official diocesan newspaper in south Florida with a strong focus on their faith and community. In Miami a Cuban Catholic magazine called *Ideal* began publishing in 1972. While *The Voice* covered the broader Hispanic community in south Florida, not focused exclusively on the Cuban community, *Ideal* offered an overt political agenda. Founder Lorenzo de Toro, an activist in the *cursillo* movement, explained: "The work of the journalists in charge of the Hispanic section [of *The Voice*] has been laudatory and continues to be of great use in orienting Catholics, but with the unanticipated growth of the Latin population of south Florida as a result of the massive Cuban exodus, the hunger for [Catholic] orientation and formation grew and it was necessary to increase the sources of informative Christian writings." De Toro visualized a publication that would take to Spanish-speaking Cuban Catholics "the Christian message applied to the present moment, without putting aside political and social orientations, realities to which today's Christians cannot be indifferent."[75]

In addition to print media, Cubans took to the airwaves to evangelize and promote a tight-knit community. Cuban-owned or managed radio and television stations offered free airtime to priests interested in reaching the broader community. In August 1966, Spanish-language station La Fabulosa (WFAB) began airing a forty-five minute program, "A Happy Sunday." Hosted by Fathers Agustín Román and Angel Villaronga, the program began with practical problem-solving advice from a theological perspective and concluded with a Sunday homily focusing on "current, everyday problems in our community." In March 1970, the Spanish-language television station (Canal 23) began offering a Spanish-language Mass. Originally coordinated by Father José L. Hernando with the help of María del Pilar Osa and Araceli Cantero, the Mass reached a large number of Cubans who attended church only irregularly. In 1971, a program called "The Paths of God," hosted by Hernando, appeared on radio station La Cubanísima (WQBA), and in 1973 Radio Alegre (WCMQ) began airing "Focus on Miami," directed by Father José P. Nickse. The former was a fifteen-minute religious message, while the latter offered a varied format, including news, interviews, religious orientations, music, and community issues. Together these shows, known as "A Parish on the Air," reached out to evangelize the Cuban exile community and to reinforce their Catholic traditions.[76]

The most important and revered devotional space for south Florida Cuban Catholics was the Ermita de Nuestra Señora de la Caridad del Cobre, dedicated to Cuba's patroness. Events leading to the creation of the special shrine for the Virgin of Charity began on the evening of September 8, 1961, when thousands of exiles gathered to celebrate her feast day, the first since the exile defeat at the Bay of Pigs. "Tens of thousands of Cuban refugees filled the Stadium . . . surrounding the improvised altar that held the image of the Virgin of Cobre," a statue that arrived that very day, smuggled from a parish church in Guanabo Beach, east of Havana. "Waving white handkerchiefs they welcomed the beloved Patroness," observed a reporter, "reminding one of the grand Catholic Congress held in Havana two years ago, in which a million Cubans gathered in the Civic Plaza, announcing their Christian spirit, rejecting materialistic and atheistic doctrines, dispossession and oppression, which were already becoming clear." At eight o'clock the Mass began, conducted by Bishop Carroll, and Father Francisco Villaverde delivered the homily. A rosary for the salvation of Cuba followed the Mass, accompanied by a ceremony in which Cuban exile youth with torches formed the likeness of a large rosary. The children shouted "'vivas' for Christ the King (Cristo Rey) and for a Free Cuba and sang songs for the Virgin, closing with the [Cuban] National Anthem."[77] Every year afterward Cubans met to commemorate this day of devotion.

At the September 1966 celebration, commemorating the fifty-year anniversary of the pope's naming Our Lady of Charity the patroness of Cuba, Bishop Carroll announced to a gathering of twenty-five thousand people that a permanent shrine would be built to the Virgin. "We sincerely hope the aspirations and the prayers of the Cuban people will obtain from God," he declared, "through the intercession of Mary, the religious liberty that was defended so clearly by the Ecumenical Council [Vatican II]." Reminding exiles that their own country possessed many monuments and sanctuaries, he said: "it is only appropriate that the same God-loving people who now find themselves torn away from their beloved country, exiled in a strange but hospitable land, erect a shrine attesting their deep love for their very dear patroness, Our Lady of El Cobre." He then called on all Cubans to provide their talents and material resources to make it possible. In the homily Villaronga exhorted Cubans to become united. "Cubans," he said,

"It is true that we need something to unite us. Here we have it. Just as the Eucharist is the symbol of unity with charity, let Our Lady of Charity be the symbol of unity for the Cubans."[78]

Days before, as preparations for the commemoration proceeded, Father Eugenio del Busto also emphasized to the press and radio the theme of Cuban unity: "We want the Virgin of Charity, that was in the past a symbol of unity for the Cuban people, to become, now in exile, the fundamental stone of patriotic and spiritual unity for exiled Cubans."[79] Within two weeks, Bishop Carroll announced specific plans for the shrine, which was to be completely financed, designed, and managed by the Cuban exile community. The diocese also announced the donation of land on Biscayne Bay, next to Mercy Hospital and La Salle School. A committee of Cuban laity, headed by Manolo Reyes, a journalist and television personality and associate editor of *The Voice*'s Spanish-language section, set up an office and took the idea to the Cuban community.[80]

By September, a temporary chapel had been built, and Bishop Carroll, with two of Cuba's most conservative former bishops of the 1950s, Msgrs. Carlos Ríu Anglés and Eduardo Martínez Dalmau, concelebrated the annual feast day commemoration. During three days of preparation for the celebration, parishes in the Miami area participated in a triduum of prayer, and two Spanish-language radio stations—WMIE ("Radio Continental") and WFAB ("La Fabulosa")—provided free time in the mornings to transmit religious programming about the Virgin of Charity.[81] After the Mass, Bishop Carroll blessed the chapel and announced the appointment of Father Agustín Román to be the shrine's chaplain. Originally from San Antonio de los Baños, a town near Havana, Román studied at a seminary in Matanzas and then in Montreal, Canada. He returned to Cuba in 1959 for his ordination by the bishop of Matanzas, Alberto Villaverde. Among those deported in September 1961, Román, like most of the others, had had no intention of leaving Cuba. In exile, he initially accepted an assignment among Chile's Araucanian Indians but in 1966 transferred to Miami.[82]

In an interview shortly after his appointment, Román declared: "the principal objective of the Chapel of Charity is to maintain alive and deepen the devotion to the Virgin of Charity in the Cuban exile community." "It will be a place," he went on, "where after spending time with our patroness we can live more Christian and Cuban." Besides already planning the shrine's future religious activities, Román hoped to make it the first place newly arrived refugees would visit.[83] He also established the Confraternity of Our Lady of Charity of Cobre to institutionalize support and raise funds. Cubans contributed hundreds of thousands of dollars for the construction of the shrine, which was consecrated by Cardinal John Krol of Philadelphia on December 2, 1973.[84] The shrine to the Virgin became a place of particular religious and spiritual importance for south Florida Cuban Catholics and, indeed, for many others across the country.

The Cuban Catholics who fled their homeland in the 1960s reorganized their life around their faith and family. The experience of displacement strengthened the commitment of many to personal piety, but it also re-invigorated their activism displayed so clearly in Cuba in the 1940s and 1950s. They used their Catholic Action experience to create their own, often autonomous institutions capable of immediately meeting their particular spiritual and family needs. Inevitably, they also articulated their faith within the reality of their exile experience and frame of reference, linking their Catholicism to their understanding of Cuba's past, troubled present, and desired future.

Chapter Four

IDENTITY AND IDEOLOGY

We are a people with particular values, history, traditions, language.
Why lose that? Why stop being who we are?
                    —Bishop Eduardo Boza Masvidal

Cubans living in exile after the 1959 Revolution developed an intense and single-minded nationalism and a clear and unflagging militant, anti-communist, anti-Castro discourse that became a part of the community's very identity. In creating new communities abroad, Cubans did not relinquish their claims to the land they had left. They celebrated their past, denounced the "new Cuba," and articulated their intention to reconstruct Cuba once freed from the Marxist nightmare. In time, nostalgia for the homeland colored memories, intensifying the exile drama and deepening the determination with which they acted.

For years after the events leading to their departure, exiles filtered life through a lens colored by their sense of betrayal, not just intellectually and ideologically, but emotionally, born of displacement and experience. Most exiles could not come to terms with the enormity of the catastrophe, and they began new lives driven by the pain and anger of their trauma as well as their determination to return. They found jobs and adjusted to the new environment but held on to their identity with an intensity that seemed to increase with time. This trauma molded their political style, behavior, and discourses, characterized by militant politics, violent language and action, and little tolerance for compromise. Their deeply felt sense of loss did not reside in quiet anguish; it waited in ambush to explode in fierce rhetorical episodes whenever the question of Cuba emerged in structured debate or polite conversation. Their rhetoric and tone often shocked North Americans used to comparatively moderate discourses in their own politics. Cubans displayed a zeal fueled variously by a crusading spirit, anger and outrage, a sense of patriotic obligation, and perhaps more. They gained a well-deserved reputation for their emotionally charged discourses expressing absolute contempt for the Cuban Revolution and seeking its destruction.

If faith traditions provided Cuban Catholic refugees with the basic principles and institutions around which to form new communities, faith in the same way influenced how they thought about themselves as exiles. Consciousness of exile involved their sense of nationality as well as their opposition to the new political and socioeconomic forms emerging in their homeland. They did not think of their nationality independently of their faith; indeed the two remained inseparable. At the same time, faith and communism remained always irreconcilable, prompting them to maintain a commitment to the church's social doctrines as a concrete alternative to totalitarian forms. Recovery of their nation required retaining a commitment to nationality and articulating constantly their intransigent rejection of communism. These two ideas permeated their thought and remained constant companions in Catholic exile identity and ideology.

Nationalism

During the nineteenth century many Cubans had perceived the Catholic Church to be linked with Spanish colonial interests and not much related to the aspirations of the Cuban people themselves. As the church became increasingly Cuban during the twentieth century, Catholicism on the island incorporated nationalism and patriotism into its expressions and aesthetics. By the 1940s and 1950s, Catholics sought what they considered to be a healthy balance between the universal precepts central to their faith and allegiance to their particular history and culture, and they defended Cuba's national integrity and independence at a time when their country remained dominated by the United States. At the same time, most Catholics rejected what they considered extreme or xenophobic nationalism often accompanied by anti-clericalism and associated with socialism, which they viewed as promoting secularism and state control of the educational system.

At the National Congress at the end of 1959, Catholic Action leader Mateo Jover explored the relationship between nationalism and faith, outlining the patriotic obligations of Catholics. In his address "Charity and Love of Country," Jover noted that because humankind lives in concrete and imperfect social and political settings, patriotism has to be more than an abstract and sentimental idea. True nationalism and patriotism for Cubans, therefore, meant developing a daily and habitual commitment to improving Cuba, which included thinking about the common good, participating in the country's public life by voting, remaining vigilant and criticizing developments when necessary, maintaining a sense of social obligation, observing the law, and opposing colonial and imperial impositions that undermined the nation's integrity. At the same time, Christians needed to avoid "exalted, blind, fanatical, and indiscriminate" nationalism and disrespect for other nations as well as totalitarian systems of the right or left that disregarded individual freedom. Jover called for an "honest nationalism" that sought a balance between Christians' particular allegiance to their nation and their obligation to universal Christian values. Christians should be ready to die for this kind of nationalism, but above all "for the patria we should be ready to *live* every day offering the fruits of our efforts, our work, our sacrifice, our quiet heroism, to make her prosperous, happy, virtuous, united, Christian."[1] Not surprisingly, nationalist feelings among Catholics as well as most exiles grew stronger and even strident in exile. While Catholics in Cuba had embraced a moderate nationalism, once outside their homeland an intense nationalism became a critical aspect of their exile identity; their sense of exile could not have survived without a consciousness informed by national values, historical memory, and sense of *cubanía*.

On his first trip to Miami, Bishop Eduardo Boza Masvidal counseled exiles to remain engaged with their history and sense of nationality. He understood the disruptive and demoralizing effects of dispersion and exile, as well as the potential threat to faith and national identity, and used the UCE to maintain links and communication among Cuban Catholics. Besides Miami, UCE chapters emerged in New York, Atlanta, Orlando, Dallas, and other places, serving as gathering places for Cubans in cities where they enjoyed little residential cohesion and cultural visibility. The various chapters published newsletters, keeping their readers updated on UCE's activities and offering perspectives on religious and political questions. Boza Masvidal counseled Cubans to maintain a "national soul," fan "the flame of faith in the destinies of our *patria*," and "conserve our values, our own being." "We are a people with particular values, history, traditions, language. Why lose that? Why stop being who we are?" "Only if we continue being ourselves will we continue loving our nation and being, able to assume our proper responsibilities," the Bishop emphasized.[2]

UCE encouraged Cubans to integrate into their countries of refuge but without losing their Cuban national identity.[3] Boza Masvidal's inexhaustible flow of articles, newspaper columns, and other writings in literally dozens of exile newspapers and magazines kept his call for defending Cuban national identity in the forefront of public consciousness.[4] In 1978, the Miami UCE chapter disseminated "the prophetic thought of our Bishop Boza Masvidal," in a collection of his writings titled *Voz en el Destierro* (Voice in Exile), much of which touched on the intersections of faith and national identity.[5] In addition to becoming the most important exile pastor and moral teacher, Boza Masvidal also distinguished himself as among the strongest advocates for encouraging Cubans to maintain their sense of nationality and hope of someday returning home.

During the first twenty years of exile, Catholics countered communist interpretations of Cuban nationality and history with their own, emphasizing the country's intimate links with Catholicism. They saw themselves as inheritors of the traditions of Cuba's independence fighters of the nineteenth century whom they also viewed as struggling for nationality and faith. Exile religious leaders sought to expose their communities to a positive assessment of Catholicism's role in Cuban history, often taking a triumphalist view that contradicted Marxist critiques of the church's role in Cuban history as simply a tool of Spanish colonialism. The exile bishops portrayed a compassionate church historically in communion with the country through all its eras.[6] They took a special interest in Félix Varela, the Cuban exile nationalist of the early nineteenth century whom they characterized as a critical influence on José Martí, Cuba's national hero.

A priest who ministered among poor Irish immigrants in New York, Varela especially appealed to exiles in the 1970s.[7] He prepared the way for Martí, they argued, who was born less than a month before the priest died

and inherited his intellectual mantle as the leading exile activist and nationalist visionary. Though Martí had not been a practicing Christian,
Catholics nevertheless argued that his writings revealed a clear spiritual
dimension that informed his concerns about justice and dignity, a legacy,
they imagined, of Varela himself.[8] In 1972, *Ideal* published a facsimile of
Varela's newspaper *El Habanero,* with a preface by Father Román, linking
Catholic exiles with the earlier Cuban exile era, and in 1979 Miami Catholics
initiated what became a traditional annual pilgrimage to Varela's original
tomb in St. Augustine, where he had died in 1853.

Cubans also created symbols and narratives of their own historical experience in exile, including honoring their martyrs in the struggle against
Castro. In 1968, for example, Christian Democrat Antonio Calatayud argued
that the U.S.-sponsored and funded Bay of Pigs invasion in April 1961,
though unsuccessful, was a symbol of the exile struggle and needed to be
honored with a memorial. The Bay of Pigs, he declared, "is a shout for liberty, it's the bugle that calls us to battle, it is the raised arm that points south,
toward the inevitable encounter without our homeland, feet on the ground
and rifle in hand, to redeem our country from the chains of slavery, to
build with the help of all a new democratic Cuba."[9]

In 1971, responding to this kind of rhetoric, the community inaugurated a memorial to honor the invasion brigade and exiles gathered at San
Juan Bosco for a Mass dedicated to those who died.[10] The next year on the
occasion of the unveiling of the monument, *Ideal* dedicated its cover to
those who lost their lives with an image of their names encircling the in-
signia of the brigade, a cross and a Cuban flag emblazoned on an outline
of Cuba. The headline read: "Bay of Pigs: Christ Also Died There . . . But
He Will Resurrect!" Carlos Allen, a badly injured Brigade member, devout Catholic, and lay activist at St. Brenden parish offered a personal testimonial titled "I Saw God at the Bay of Pigs," in which he concluded that
"our Christian faith will help us continue struggling for our motherland."[11] The monument became a place for patriotic events usually accompanied by a religious service dedicated to those who fell in the fight against
communism.

Ideal dedicated abundant space to issues of Cuban history and nationality
generally, especially promoting Catholic themes in a regular column titled
"De La Historia de Cuba" ("From Cuban History"). One issue, for example,
reproduced a historical narrative of the taking of the town of Cobre by

Cuban insurgents during the Ten Years War in the 1870s. It related the arrival of independence fighters Carlos Manuel de Céspedes, Maximo Gómez, Francisco Aguilera, and numerous other Cuban leaders to the town and their encounter with Our Lady of Charity. "All were visibly moved when the Captain General [Céspedes] surrendered his sword before the Virgin of Cobre, offering homage and devotion to the Queen and Lady of all Cubans."[12] The message was clear; the independence activists were motivated not only by patriotism but also by their Catholic faith.

The intimate linking of Catholicism with Cuban history also appeared quite explicitly at the shrine to Our Lady of Charity. Catholics identified their own experience of dislocation with symbols and images of faith and nationality, themes central to a large mural painted behind the shrine's altar by Cuban artist, Teok Carrasco. Thirty-six feet tall and just over twenty-three feet wide at the base (a width maintained to a height of ten feet, then progressively closing to a width of ten feet at the top) the mural depicted geographic, religious, and patriotic symbols of Cuba. At the very center of the work stands the Virgin holding the Christ child, while at the top a Cuban flag, representing a suffering nation, is draped over a cross and carried by two angels. Just below the flag is Father Varela, who symbolically unites the themes of faith and nationality. Around the Virgin are important religious and secular historical figures who for many Cubans had traditionally defined Cuban origins and nationality, including Christopher Columbus, Father Miguel Velázquez (the first Cuban priest, son of a Spaniard and an Indian woman), Bishop Juan José Espada y Landa (eighteenth-century prelate known for his good works), Father José Agustín Caballero (important Cuban intellectual and teacher of the early nineteenth century), Carlos Manuel de Céspedes (initiator of the Cuban struggle for independence in 1868), Perucho Figueredo (author of the national anthem), José Martí (Cuba's national hero), Havana Archbishop Manuel Arteaga Betancourt (Cuba's only Cardinal up to that moment), Bishop Boza Masvidal, and many others. In addition, the mural includes symbols of Cuba's relationship to the United States, including the Plaza of San Agustín, Florida, in the eighteenth century, various Franciscan martyrs of the Florida missions, and bishops and teachers in Florida during the same period. Non-Cuban figures of importance appearing in the mural include Popes Benedict XV (who named Our Lady of Charity patroness of Cuba) and Paul VI and Bishop Coleman Carroll, for his generosity to the exile community. Finally, the mural includes familiar geographic and architectural scenes, including the Pico Turquino (the highest peak), the sanctuary to the Virgin at Cobre, the towers of the cathedrals in Havana and Santiago, Havana's historic Morro Castle, and a monument to Cuba's unknown soldiers in Matanzas. At the bottom right a scene of refugees in a boat rendered next to the Statue of Liberty offers a sharp statement about the exiles' "flight to freedom." The overall interpretive impact suggests a historical trajectory deeply influenced by and connected to the Catholic faith, reminding exiles of their past struggles for independence, nationality, and liberty, their historical connections to Florida, as well as their current gratitude to the United States for receiving them in their moment of crisis.

As exiles visited the shrine and prayed to the image of Our Lady of Charity placed on a pedestal attached to the mural, they could not avoid the clear message that their Catholic faith was woven into the history and identity of the Cuban nation, a fundamental truth that the communist regime in Cuba had worked to undermine. In effect, the mural offered a visual historical interpretation for visitors that daily countered the new Marxist historiography developed on the island after 1959. More fundamentally, however, the artist, reminded exiles that "The Cuban people will find their salvation in the arms of the Virgin of Charity."[13]

In reality the entire tradition of celebrating the Virgin's feast day on September 8 and building the shrine was inextricably linked to the powerful blending of faith, history, and nationality expressed almost from the beginning in exile. The first public devotion in 1961 captured the imagination of Cuban Catholics, and each year the celebration grew and became an important public demonstration of faith, identity, and political opposition to the communist regime in Cuba. Church leaders made explicit links between their faith expression and their patriotic sentiments. In September 1962, some twenty-eight thousand Cubans jammed Miami Stadium, filling it to capacity and forcing officials to turn thousands away. Though Bishop Carroll officiated, Father Villaverde delivered the sermon, emphasizing the two things that drew Cubans together that night: "The love of Mary, Mother of God and our Mother, and love of the Motherland, destroyed and bloodied."[14] The next year, more than twenty thousand exiles congregated at Tropical Park in Miami to honor the Virgin at the end of a novena of prayers that had been heard in various parishes for the "Silenced Church," the theme of Father Bez Chabebe's sermon. He reflected on the differences in the way this feast day had been celebrated in the past and in the present. In the past, he said, the event was joyous, full of demonstrations of love for the Virgin, but now, "although the love of the Mother remains the same, the commemoration has a more serious meaning, deeper, because we join in the pain of the Silenced Church." Meditating on the Silenced Church, he pointed out, was to find lessons about the victory of Christ over his enemies. In finishing he asked Cubans to pray for grace, for the liberation of Cuba, and for the breaking of the silence of the church.[15]

Every step of the way, supporters of the shrine appealed to the nationalist sentiment of exiles as a fund-raising strategy for its construction. In 1967, the shrine's finance committee chose the occasion of May 20, Cuban Independence Day (celebrating independence from Spain), to hold a fund-raising event. After a procession, at three in the afternoon, several well-known Cuban priests representing Cuba's six provinces concelebrated a Mass. In the days leading up to the gathering, a much listened to Miami talk radio host, Tomás García Fusté, exhorted exiles to participate in the event and to support the shrine.[16] Father Ismael Testé, a popular priest and radio commentator in Cuba who had founded and directed Cuba's Boy's Town, traveled from his parish in Houston, Texas, to give the sermon. He asked for the support of all exiles, saying, "We want to build a shrine that will tell all coming generations that here came a people, carrying the chains of exile, and not only rebuilding their lives, but making outstanding contributions to the cultural life and industry of the United States." He thanked the bishop, represented by Mons. Bryan Walsh, and the United States in general for their generosity with the Cuban people.[17] Ritual at the shrine linked place to memory and personal experience.

As chaplain, Father Román consciously cultivated among visitors the ideas of exile, faith, and nostalgia. Starting in 1967, Román invited the faithful from each of the Cuban municipalities represented in exile to become pilgrims, gather at the shrine, and participate in a Mass for their faith and country. Within two years, exiles participated in 127 of these *perenigraciones* (pilgrimages) so that "Catholic devotees to the Virgin of Charity continue forgetting about their necessities in order to think about our brothers in the beloved homeland." "Thousands of Cubans," Román explained, "of the different provinces and municipalities [of Cuba] have come to the feet of the Virgin praying for the suffering motherland, for the prisoners and for the dead." "There is not one corner of Cuba," he emphasized, "that can say, 'they did not remember me.'"[18] The Ermita also sponsored gatherings of the faithful every two months known as *romerías,* which brought together larger groups of exiles representing Cuba's pre-revolutionary provinces. They held picnics with music, entertainment, prayers, processions, and a variety of other activities to reassert their faith, establish stronger exile ties, and remember their homeland.[19] At the Romería Pinareña, in early May 1969, for example, families (parents, children, and grandparents) from Cuba's westernmost province Pinar del Rio gathered, many with flowers, at the shrine on Sunday afternoon. Activities began with a rosary and song in front of the Ermita. As Father Román noted, "The pilgrims prayed, remembering the past and making offerings for the present and for the future that is in the hands of the Son of the Mother." After prayers they turned to the *merienda* (afternoon snack) and people approached a long table full of *pastelitos y frituras dulces* (cakes and fried sweets). They ate, talked, exchanged stories, and remembered their towns, villages, and farms in Pinar del Río. As the sun began its descent, people cleaned up the grounds and prepared to leave, amazed that "having been born so close to each other we would have met in Miami." "The Mother," observed Father Román, "gathered together her sons in this small house in exile so that they would not forget the many who suffer in that valley of suffering.[20] The shrine also received daily visitors from the exile community who offered solitary prayers and left flowers, candles, money, and other signs of devotion.[21] All of these activities served to maintain unity and a heightened sense of Cuban national identity mediated through faith and the Catholic tradition.

This commitment to homeland was not only evident at the shrine. Virtually all exile Catholic organizations linked faith and nationalism. Lay apostolic movements, especially MFC in the early 1960s, promoted a strong sense of national and cultural identity among their members, including their children. "We must always be cognizant," an MFC document counseled, "that as parents we should be driven by the idea of returning to the liberated motherland." Nevertheless, they recognized that many of their children "do not know, or remember little, of Cuba, which makes even more urgent our obligation to keep alive the fires of tradition." They instilled in their children a love of patria, hopefully even to the extent of responding "to the call for arms to defend liberty anywhere in the world." Furthermore, to avoid a loss of identity, MFC urged Cubans to take advantage of the opportunities provided by the church, especially the parochial structure that offered space to promote a rich integrated community life where they could worship within a familiar cultural environment. Hoping to foster greater community cohesion, they also urged families to maintain close communications and even move geographically closer to each other whenever possible, in addition to holding frequent family gatherings and celebrations, preferably centered in church and the liturgy.[22]

As an additional way of preserving their heritage, MFC members in Miami established ties with the Latin American MFC. This reinforced their cultural ways, including working within a Spanish-language environment, reflecting their confidence that they would eventually return to Cuba. As part of a tour of Latin American countries in 1963, leaders of the Latin American MFC met with some seventy Hispanic, mostly Cuban, couples in Florida to offer stimulus and ideas about how to expand their activities. This relationship with the Latin American MFC reinforced the Miami group's sense of exile, fostered allegiance to Hispanicism, and contributed to their feelings of nostalgia for their homeland.[23]

One parish, La Inmaculada in Hialeah, promoted cultural awareness and pride in Cuba through its youth folkloric musical program, directed by Father Bez Chabebe and called "Añorada Cuba" (Yearning for Cuba). It gained a wide following in the community and with the help of several lay organizations presented a show that in May 1964, for example, attracted some five thousand people. According to the program notes, "Cuba has produced many musical genres with a melodic and rhythmic richness that has traveled the world; and these Cuban sketches along with the typical dances and costumes project a vision of the musical soul of the Cuba of Christ and Martí."[24] Bez Chabebe described the musical review as "a message to Cuban children and youth; an invitation to enter the emotional history of their grandparents and the customs of their parents." "It intends," he went on, "to recall, to feel, and to bring to life the memory of the far away motherland." Through song and dance, and with "tropical flavor," the review also, according to Bez Chabebe, sent a message to the free world, that a suffering nation waited. The show highlighted the exile community's continuing struggle to "rescue Cuba's sovereignty."[25]

Schools did their part as well. At Belén, for example, though fully "Americanized," the school's curriculum required Spanish-language education and Cuban history, while the social environment reinforced Cuban customs and ideas. In January 1963, the school celebrated its patroness,

Nuestra Señora de Belén, and, in anticipation, eighty students spent three days in spiritual exercises that closed with a Mass on January 30 attended by a number of alumni. The next day, at a literary evening sponsored by alumni, students demonstrated their debating skills in engaging the theme of "Evolution and Revolution in Cuba." Javier Figueroa, Alberto Morales, and Jorge Ruíz defended the need for a revolutionary process in Cuba in 1959, while Orlando Espín, Emilio Bejel, and Humberto Ravelo argued the merits of an evolutionary process. The event concluded with a speech by a prominent alumnus of Belén, Dr. Francisco Pérez Vich, who thanked the school and offered remembrances "de los tiempos ya idos" (of times past).[26]

For those unable to attend Catholic schools, the parishes often provided the nationalist and cultural context for many Cuban children. In February 1968, for example, San Juan Bosco established the Escuela Cívico Religioso (Civic Religious School), which taught Cuban geography and history; Spanish; Cuban, Spanish, and Hispanic American literature; and Cuban and Latin American culture. The purpose was "so that these children and youngsters maintain their love and appreciation for those things from their land of origin and so that they might one day return and be useful in the creation of a new society."[27] In this way, national identity remained a central feature of daily life for Cuban refugee children.

Spanish-language media networks regularly combined pride in culture and language with a strong nationalist and political message. During its first year, for example, *Ideal* featured articles on a variety of traditional Catholic issues and values but also focused on events in Cuba, international relations, communism, and Cuban history. In 1972, articles by Bishop Boza Masvidal outlined the church's traditional position with regard to communism, and an interview with a young Cuban, Santiago Díaz Arvesú, related his experiences fighting communism as a helicopter flight engineer in Vietnam during 1968–1970.[28] *Ideal* embraced faith and identity issues in ways that this highly politicized anti-communist exile community could relate. In the late 1970s, UCE also published *Cuba Diáspora,* a journal that dedicated a great deal of space to the church in Cuba, before and after the Revolution, encouraging Cuban Catholics to recall with pride their traditions and the work they had accomplished in their homeland before the coming of communism.

This desire to maintain awareness of Cuba's pre-revolutionary traditions among exiles in the face of the significant historiographic and literary revisionism in Cuba engaged numerous talented intellectuals and academics,

Catholics and non-Catholics alike. They produced a flood of literary and historical work, and a new generation of scholars trained in universities in the United States became academic leaders in the study of Cuba and their diasporic experience. Among the most influential promoters of this literary production in Miami was Manuel Salvat, the anti-communist Catholic student activist of the early 1960s turned businessman, who established a small family-run bookstore and publishing company called Universal. Salvat specialized in Spanish-language Cuban texts, ranging from reedited works of pre-revolutionary historiography to the writings of exiles. The availability of these works reinforced exile interpretations of their history, but Salvat's publishing house also provided an outlet for exile texts and debate.[29] The predominantly Spanish-speaking Cuban exile population in Miami created their own literary world tied more to the Hispanic world, especially Spain, than to the United States.

Throughout the 1960s and 1970s, Cuban Catholics in south Florida built a community, relying on the faith, values, and traditions from their homeland. They obviously did not re-create their new world in the exact image of their homeland, but they did continue networks and relationships that kept their focus on the past as they created themselves anew. Catholic Action activists remained committed to their faith traditions, working with many different organizations in parishes and other settings. Members of the FJC (men's section of Cuban Catholic Action) in the United States, Puerto Rico, Venezuela, Spain, and other places reorganized themselves in 1973 as the Antiguos Miembros de las Juventudes de Acción Católica Cubana.[30] Though mostly an organization dedicated to reestablishing old friendships and relationships and renewing communication among people with similar experiences in Cuba, it maintained a spirit of religious and patriotic activism, as well as nostalgia, among many of its members. In 1976, soon after the premature death of Andrés Valdespino, several Catholic Action members established the Fundación Dr. Andrés Valdespino to honor the Catholic nationalist activist, and offered an annual scholarship in his name to the best study promoting Christian ideals and the love of Cuba.[31] At a fiftieth anniversary of Catholic Action meeting in Miami in 1978, members reflected on their situation, celebrating the legacy of their work in Cuba, but also mourned the loss of their *patria*. As former Catholic Action activist Florinda Alzaga expressed with the great nostalgia so characteristic of the exiles, "It is a day of pain because we probably could have gathered at one of those assemblies, at one of those fantastic and florid assemblies in our homeland, and instead we are all in exile, we are scattered across the world, we are men without a land but we are united by the love of God."[32]

Anti-Communism

In addition to reaffirming nationality, history, and connections to their home-land and insisting on maintaining their heritage, creating an exile identity necessarily required delegitimizing developments in Cuba, including con-demning the ruling authorities and rejecting the communist system. For Catholics, communism represented the very antithesis of their ideas about civic society, as well as their faith. Atheism, collectivism, the negation of the individual, and totalitarianism, among other things, spelled the annihi-lation of their worldview. Cuban Catholics, like most exiles of all political and faith persuasions, became determined Cold Warriors, convinced that communism not only was destroying Cuban society and traditions and re-ducing its population to virtual slavery but also constituted a threat to Latin America generally.

To be sure, the U.S. government encouraged their discourse and pro-vided resources for its dissemination, but the content reflected the experi-ence of the exiles themselves. Exiles took seriously Castro's promise to create many Vietnams in Latin America. If Castro was capable of revolutionizing their own country and transforming what they considered to be a human-istic and democratic program into a Marxist-Leninist project, they consid-ered him perfectly capable of doing the same in Latin America, especially with the support of the Soviet Union. For all their hatred of Castro, exiles recognized his extraordinary ability to strategize and execute revolutionary agendas, and they took seriously his charismatic potential to mobilize hun-dreds of thousands, if not millions, behind a vision that exiles character-ized as repressive but that many others perceived as liberating. Catholic and non-Catholic exiles alike viewed communist ideology as repulsive, but in the hands of Fidel Castro it became more, a clear and present danger that had to be stopped. In this, an exile core remained intransigent, the carriers of an anti-communist rhetoric that marked all communities to one extent or another but particularly Miami.

The Cold War rhetoric and intransigence of exiles rivaled the most zeal-ous anti-communists of the United States. The Cuban "problem" became a central concern even in organizations not formally focused on political matters. In 1963, for example, Miami's MFC sent a letter to the MFC International Congress in Rio de Janeiro asking for their support and for personal gestures of solidarity with their exile cause.[33] At their annual reunion during 1965, MFC launched a campaign asking families to pray the rosary together for the liberation of Cuba and the salvation of all America.[34] The following year, MFC leaders Humberto López and his wife María Antonia Clark participated in the IV Encuentro Latinoamericano del MFC in Caracas along with Bishop Boza Masvidal. In addition to their contributions on religious matters, they reminded their Latin American colleagues about the situation in Cuba. "It was also our obligation," they said, "to ensure Cuba's presence [at the meetings]," since Cuba was "deeply marginalized in the Americas by a 'conspiracy of silence' and the lack of solidarity in the face of great pain." On many occasions during the meetings the López couple reminded the delegates of their plight as exiles. At one round table where the discussion focused on the problems of the disadvantaged and marginal families in Latin America lacking even minimal necessities, the Lópezes pointed out that there were other kinds of marginal families as well: "those who, though not emigrants, were forced to leave their country but who dream and are confident of a return and prepare for this day by protecting the treasure that is their moral values and traditions."[35]

Intensely angry exiles took every opportunity, however inappropriate it may have seemed to others, to raise issues about Cuba at public forums of any kind. Intensity became almost characteristic of exiles, especially of those who left during or in the immediate aftermath of the first three years of revolution. The continuous arrival in south Florida of refugees on rafts, inner tubes, rowboats, and other crafts provided ample evidence to exiles that Cubans actively rejected the communist system. Besides lamenting their personal losses, exiles believed that they, not the communist authorities in Cuba, expressed the authentic values and aspirations of the Cuban people who suffered such severe repression they had little hope of claiming their own destiny. Given the chance to vote, Cubans would rid themselves of communism in favor of a pluralistic democratic society. Though outmaneuvered and defeated by their foes in Cuba, exile leaders rejected the notion of simply accepting their fate and a new life in their adopted land. They remained fully engaged with Cuba.

Exile wrath focused especially on Fidel Castro, whom they held personally responsible for the imposition of communism in Cuba. Some believed the system in Cuba simply reflected Castro's obsessive need for power.

Psychiatrist Rubén Rumbaut even offered a psychological evaluation of Castro, characterizing him as an anti-social psychopath, with a deep and genuine and permanently deformed personality, unable to perceive anguish, guilt, or remorse. In addition, Rumbaut's analysis characterized Castro as lacking the ability to create personal, group, or societal loyalties or to develop a sense of morality and learn and change as a result of experience. These kinds of individuals, he noted, are hard and hedonistic, emotionally immature, have no sense of responsibility or judgment, and demand immediate gratification without reference to the rights and sentiments of others. They are narcissistic and suffer from delusions of grandeur and are always capable of rationalizing their conduct regardless of its impact, making it seem reasonable and justified. Rumbaut characterized Castro as an efficient manipulator and talented actor capable of feigning sincerity and persuading those around him to suspend their sense of objectivity and spirit of discernment.[36] The phrase "Castro-communism" used often by exiles to describe the system in Cuba reflected the belief that while Castro adapted the communist system as the model for his revolution, it was simply the most efficient and useful system to accommodate the absolute craving for power his personality required. Also, they viewed his social discourse as simply a justification for establishing a totalitarian regime—a system he would not hesitate to modify if a shift in model served his hunger for power.

Catholic rejection of communism of course had a strong theological basis, rooted in a tradition that provided exiles with their justification for trying to overthrow Castro. Indeed, the church's social teachings responded to the emergence of socialism during the era of capitalist excesses and exploitation in the nineteenth century. As communism made its appearance with the Bolshevik Revolution, the church's anti-communism became more strident. In March 1937, reacting to socialistic and anti-clerical advances across the world, including Mexico and Spain, Pope Pius XI reaffirmed this message in his encyclical *Divini Redemptoris,* which made the case against "atheistic communism." Just two weeks before, the pope had also issued *Mit brennender Sorge,* condemning German fascism, extreme nationalism, and "the whole Nazi conception of life as utterly, and necessarily, anti-Christian." Likewise, *Divini Redemptoris* declared that "Communism is intrinsically wrong, and no one who would save Christian civilization may collaborate with it in any undertaking whatsoever." With these two encyclicals the pope reaffirmed the church's opposition to totalitarian regimes of the right and the left and called on Catholics to support change within the guidelines of the social thought expressed in *Rerum Novarum* and *Quadragesimo Anno*.[37]

Cuban Catholics had learned to despise communism even before *Divini Redemptoris*. In 1932, for example, a twenty-year-old Lasaga revealed his anti-communist intensity in a text titled "Meditación Roja." In it he spoke of the many shared goals of communists and Catholics, including denouncing imperialism, land concentration (*latifundios*), racism, and social inequality. If communism were only that, Lasaga wrote, he could be communist. But communism was much more; it was also an unacceptable economic system, ideological creed, moral code, and pedagogical tradition. Lasaga believed in *patria*, human fraternity, family, love, liberty, private property, morality and justice, ideas he argued upheld by Christianity and undermined by communism. If only communism could deliver the poor and repressed, perhaps he would be a communist, but that was not the case, he noted. Christianity offered spiritual and temporal redemption to the workers without violating the essential values necessary for human dignity.[38]

Catholic education in Cuba certainly inculcated anti-communist values, which became even more deeply entrenched with the outbreak of the Spanish Civil War in the later half of the 1930s, when Catholics and communists brutalized each other in word and action. A large Spanish immigrant population, including many priests, brought the reality of the war to Cuba to an extent perhaps not seen anywhere else in the Americas. The strong influence of Spanish clergy in Cuba, many who had lived or heard first hand of the brutal and bloody confrontations during the civil war and perhaps seen priests executed or otherwise killed by the Republican forces, produced a deep and personal animosity toward communists.[39]

At the same time, this ideological anti-communism had not always translated into an absolute intolerance for communists in day-to-day politics. Communists had played an active and legal role in Cuban politics during the 1930s and 1940s, and though Catholics viewed them as astute opportunists, many recognized their right to participate in the political system. Some social Catholics believed that rather than spending time worrying about communist politicians, efforts should be taken to remove the social grievances on which they thrived. When Fulgencio Batista, in November 1953, outlawed the Partido Socialista Popular, the Cuban Communist Party, Valdespino objected. He thought this unnecessary, since the communist threat did not stem from the existence of a legal organization but rather from the inability of the government to resolve the nation's social problems. He reminded readers that the Constitution of 1940 allowed for legislation to confront social ills but that no effective implementation had occurred. Rather than conforming to the exaggerated and "hysterical" anti-communism emanating from North Americans, Cubans should turn their attention to the nation's social realities, implementing Catholic social doctrines and making communism irrelevant.[40]

Nevertheless, in 1960 most Catholics did perceive a communist danger, and some warned of this almost from the outset of the revolutionary victory. Villanueva University student and Catholic Action activist Lourdes Casal, for example, denounced communism in several articles in *La Quincena* from February through April 1959. She explained Catholic social thought to her readers, condemning both liberalism and communism. Communism, she declared, had to be condemned for being "totalitarian, materialistic, determinist, and atheist."[41]

As one might expect, by the time Catholics went into exile, they had become militantly anti-communist and increasingly doctrinaire. Exiles believed that reformists in Latin America and the United States, Catholic and otherwise, did not recognize this reality, mistaking state paternalism, repression, and absolute control for social justice. They recognized that the Revolution had managed to present an image of liberation and social justice, but their own experience from 1959 through 1961 convinced them otherwise. Their own experience suggested a totalitarian and inhumane system totally controlled personally by Fidel Castro, a viewpoint they publicized at every opportunity.

Catholics expressed their ideas in an array of newspapers, magazines, and pamphlets, often funded by the U.S. State Department, the CIA, or other governmental or private sources. In late 1960, for example, Angel del Cerro edited the U.S. government–funded *Boletín Semanal Informativo,* distributing over 65,000 copies throughout the Americas in an effort to sway opinion against the Cuban Revolution.[42] Late the next year, Cerro, along with Catholics Rumbaut, Fermín Peinado, and another collaborator, Andrés Suárez, sought funds from the U.S. State Department for a new expanded journal to replace the *Boletín.*[43] In addition to the news and information contained in the *Boletín,* this new outlet for a Latin American audience intended to provide a deeper analysis of the Cuban situation and its implications for the hemisphere. The proposal for a distribution of thirty thousand included a monthly budget of a little more than $12,000.[44] Presumably funded by the U.S. government, the *Cuba Nueva* appeared on March 15, 1962, under the guidance of José Ignacio Lasaga, chief of propaganda for the CIA-sponsored exile organization Consejo Revolucionario Cubano.

Though initially directed by Fermín Peinado, an attorney from Guantánamo and professor of political theory at University of Oriente, who worked with Catholic Action in Santiago de Cuba, Cerro became editor in August 1962. Not technically a Catholic journal, *Cuba Nueva* nevertheless provided a mouthpiece for exile Catholic intellectuals who viewed Cuba's future tied explicitly to Christian traditions in clear contradistinction to the communist revolution on the island. While Castro defined the Cuban process as a popular revolution aimed at liberating the people from injustice and US imperialism, the journal offered a portrait of a revolution that took away people's rights and turned the country over to Soviet imperialism.

Recognizing the popularity of the Cuban agrarian reform process among progressive forces in Latin America, *Cuba Nueva*'s contributors reiterated their own view that the agrarian reform law of May 1959 was not necessarily inconsistent with the nation's needs or economic rationality, though Castro's implementation violated both the letter and the spirit of the law itself. Instead of a land reform based on the basic principles of private property and judicial procedure, the practical application of the law became a massive project of expropriation, without due process or compensation, dedicated to creating a system of state farms along Soviet lines. In reality, the exiles declared, the agrarian reform program's main goal was fundamentally political, not economic—to liquidate the opposition. Lacking economic rationality and characterized by coercion, administrative chaos, and low worker productivity, the agrarian system not only failed to increase production but also denied Cuban citizens the basic right of determining their own destiny.[45]

Other articles looked at the situation of Cuban workers, emphasizing how the traditional Cuban labor movement had been taken over by the state, leaving workers without autonomous power of their own. Worker resistance, they noted, led to the imprisonment and exile of many and even to a constant denunciation by the revolutionary leadership of Cuba's "inefficient" workers. The journal reported, for example, a meeting of the council of the government's labor federation during which the national leadership including Che Guevara reminded workers that under socialism their values had to change. He reprimanded their low productivity and absenteeism and announced a national compensation plan that equalized salaries for workers in similar classifications, admitting this required a reduction of compensation for many. In order to combat absenteeism, Guevara declared that the moment had arrived to "use compulsory methods" to ensure production and certainly workers no longer had a right to strike. One contributor, Carmelo Mesa Lago, viewed these developments as contrary to the interests of workers who decidedly lost—not gained—rights and security under this new system. The editors of *Cuba Nueva* concluded that "the enslavement of the Cuban worker was now clearly delineated."[46] The magazine also tackled numerous other issues relating to Cuban communism, including education. Andrés Valdespino and others, for example, characterized the government's complete takeover of Cuban education, from primary school through the university, as simply motivated by political goals, without reference to the intellectual freedoms necessary for a genuine educational experience.[47]

For these critics perhaps the greatest symbol of the system's inherently repressive nature was the government's heavy reliance on imprisonment and executions to maintain conformity and order. Exiles described a totalitarian reality in Cuba that demanded "revolutionary unity" and total submission to government political and socioeconomic policies. The regime created a security and judicial network composed of *milicianos* and military personnel, interior ministry officials, police, secret police, and neighborhood watch groups. During the 1960s, the government systematically arrested political and literary dissidents, urban resistance fighters, insurrectionists in the mountains, exile infiltrators, gay people and prostitutes, Catholic lay activists, evangelical preachers, black marketers and contrabandists, and generally made life difficult for most nonconformists. During these years, thousands of Cubans languished in prisons, and many faced execution—for exiles a concrete sign that the Revolution could only survive through intimidation and repression.[48] Even for progressive Cuban Catholics, no amount of social reform on the island could justify these basic violations of human rights.

Fundamentally, Catholic exiles, and indeed most exiles, characterized the Revolution as an immoral political and socioeconomic process designed to establish totalitarian control by violating the basic rights of the Cuban people for the purpose of advancing the personal and grandiose agenda of Fidel Castro and a small cadre of communist elites not only in Cuba but also across the hemisphere. It was this zeal, born of their own experience with Castro and the Revolution in the early 1960s, that maintained exiles on this constant anti-communist crusade. As one Catholic, Manuel Maza, writing in ACU's journal *Mundo Nuevo*, wondered: When was the Western, free, Christian world going to stand up to communist expansion? "Anyone who is somewhat informed knows that the basic program of Soviet Russia, the maximum standard bearer of international communism, is, in synthesis, the conquest of the world." After listing the areas of the world taken by the "red advance," the editorialist faulted Western Christianity for its failure to confront communism in a firm way, with conventional—not atomic—weapons. "Because," the article ended, "if we only die one time, its better to do it on our feet, in defense of eternal ideals, than to live devastated by the worst form of slavery the world has ever seen."[49]

The development of exile identity and ideology among Catholics included a consciousness of Cuba's past and present. In 1982, on the occasion of the commemoration of the eightieth anniversary of Cuban independence from Spain, Bishops Boza Masvidal and Agustín Román issued a pastoral document that outlined the broad themes they believed fundamental to their exile experience. The message of "Cuba Ayer, Hoy y Siempre" ("Cuba Yesterday, Today, and Always") reflected the numerous strands of exile thinking evident during the previous twenty years.[50] Restating the exile belief in the essentially Catholic character of Cuba's history, the bishops reasserted the historical contributions of Catholicism in Cuba and argued that the communist imposition represented a deviation from genuine Cuban traditions. The pastoral firmly denounced communism as fundamentally incompatible with Catholic faith and doctrines as well as with notions of Cuban nationality. The Revolution, they insisted, had derailed Cuba's "authentic" destiny as a Christian nation. "In 1959, with the Marxist-Leninist nature of the revolution, the process of liberation was harshly halted," declared the 1982 document. "Instead of faith and spirituality, militant atheism; instead of respect for human dignity, oppression and violation of all rights; instead of sovereignty, submission to the Soviet Union and total dependence in politics, economics, ideology, and military affairs."[51] They looked to Cuba's Catholic past to help them retain their sense of connection and relationship to history, culture, and values, as well as to legitimize their efforts to restore a Christian heritage. The Cuban present under communism represented an absolute negation of Cuba's genuine traditions and necessarily had to be combated in the most uncompromising terms. Nationalism and anti-communism, then, went hand-in-hand in the Catholic articulation of exile identity.

To struggle against communism was not sufficient, however. The discourse of exile also included a vision of returning to their devastated country and re-creating from historical tradition and a reinvigorated social Christian heritage a new nation capable of providing for all its citizens. Exile was not only about the past and the present but about the future nation. The 1982 document pointed out that despite historical developments since 1959, exiles remained Cuban with a continuing claim to their land of origin. Exiles remained an integral part of the Cuban nation: "Geographically we see a Cuba divided in two; the Cuba inside and the Cuba outside; the island and exile." At the same time, "we cannot allow this simple geographic accident to divide us because we are one people and we have to embrace our fundamental unity, share sorrows and joy, suffering, yearnings, struggles, and hopes, those on the inside and those on the outside."[52] As such, they considered their voices to be legitimate Cuban voices with a right to be heard. They had to prepare for the future, and they looked to their faith for guidance.

Chapter Five

THE SOCIAL QUESTION

> *From the ideological point of view we will follow the pontifical orientations that are the basis of social Christian doctrine; we will combat modern errors, from 'laissez faire' capitalism to fascism and communism.*
>
> —Carmelo Mesa Lago (1964)

Though Cuban exiles of whatever political persuasion embraced nationalism and opposition to communism as fundamental aspects of their exile identity, Catholics in particular remained true to their long-standing concern for social justice. Even as they departed a Cuba in the throws of social revolution, they continued to support the church's social teachings and during the next decade observed a Latin America painfully burdened with economic stagnation, increasing poverty, social stratification and unrest, guerrilla movements, military coups, and repression. Many Catholics maintained an interest in their country's potential future as a socially just democratic and Christian nation and fully engaged the emerging theology of the Second Vatican Council and discussions about the church in the modern world. The social question went to the very heart of their theology.

Theirs was not a spiritual journey unrelated to temporal realities but one dedicated to connecting spiritual and worldly matters as a method for improving the condition of all Cubans. In this spirit, many Catholic exiles continued to struggle with social concerns, remained committed to the Vatican teachings, and sought to convince others of their conviction that social justice and communism were fundamentally incompatible.

The Social Imperative

The Cuban Revolution caused a deep personal crisis for many involved in issues of social justice. Though enthusiastic or at least open to the social discourses in their homeland in the 1950s, many exiles lost all interest in such issues as their anti-communism deepened and defined their political perspectives. Even exile Catholics still engaged with social thought could not ignore all that had occurred. At first, their experiences of displacement and flight threatened to push aside their social Christian traditions. Not only did they face numerous pressing matters, including finding their place in a new society, but they also committed to struggling against the Castro regime.

Especially troublesome after the Cuban Revolution was how to understand the relationship between the practical aspects of resolving poverty and other social problems with the dangers of communist revolutions. Long-held values had to be rethought in light of new conditions; those deeply influenced by the teachings of the church struggled to make sense of their social obligations in light of their experience with communism as well as the realities of their new places of residence. This constant memory of the homeland made reform-minded social thinking increasingly difficult as Cubans reacted to socioeconomic issues and movements from the perspective of their increasingly doctrinaire anti-communism. Many came to believe that a non-communist social movement was a contradiction, viewing social activism as merely a tool for communist opportunists and their sympathizers to advance hidden agendas.

Nevertheless, Catholic leaders and intellectuals insisted on the relevance of social thought even for their situation. Even in the face of mass disillusionment and considerable ambivalence among most exile Cubans, some Catholics, and non-Catholics to be sure, continued to advocate for a humane social order. Forward looking Catholic leaders thought of their predicament as an opportunity to reflect, rethink, and prepare for the reintroduction of a socially conscious Christianity to Cuba when Castro fell, which they imagined would be shortly. Intent on maintaining a measure of balance, numerous leaders spoke of their social obligations even as they denounced and acted against the communist revolution. They encouraged their compatriots to remain engaged with social concerns and argued against a reactionary response to events at home. Rejecting the obvious imperative for social change, they reasoned, would not only frustrate future efforts to reconstruct Cuba along socially conscious Christian lines but also allow Castro to depict the exile communities as retrograde. Catholics of differing persuasions counseled their compatriots to keep matters of social concern at the center of their discourses.

In 1960, for example, after leaving Cuba, Manuel Artime reaffirmed his social Christian philosophy that evidently drew heavily from the Jesuit activist Manuel Foyaca. Emphasizing the deficiencies of materialist-centered communism and liberal capitalism and drawing on Spanish *Hispanismo,* Artime advocated a new civilization based on Hispanic, Humanist, and Christian traditions, one based on private property and freedom where even the weakest would be provided the resources to live a dignified life.[1] Artime's vision of a genuine Christian society required creating an environment of harmony and mutual respect between capital and labor.

He called for cultivating employers who cared about their employees like younger brothers, who ensured that they had what they needed to live honorably and with dignity. "In the end," he wrote, "the employer should in his conscience feel the problems of the workers as if they were his own, just as Jesus suffered on the cross for our sins." At the same time, the employees needed to keep in mind the requirements of the employer, as if he were an older brother, to ensure the health of the business enterprise and to promote his welfare. All of this would be ensured by a Christian state with the authority to intervene when necessary to ensure the welfare of all the citizens. The state would protect the freedom of citizens as long as they did not disturb the common good and transform liberty into libertine ways. The state would also guarantee the requirements of those most in need by establishing economic enterprises not viable for private capital, including public service enterprises. Finally, a Christian state would establish an educational system for all the nation's inhabitants that not only instructed students but formed them morally and with civic responsibility to achieve the necessary consciousness.[2]

Though an ardent Catholic reformer, many considered Artime a right-wing ideologue. One colleague who left MRR in 1961 characterized him as having "fascist tendencies."[3] Artime, however, always rejected such accusations, saying his views did not represent support for Franco Spain, falangist ideology, or religious intolerance that would lead to a totalitarianism of the Catholic Church. He opposed the fascist right, he said, as much as the totalitarian left.[4] Nevertheless, his ideology, like that of his Jesuit mentors, certainly reflected the influences of Spain's Catholic-corporatist tradition, which did not generally prosper among Cuban Catholics. It was the Christian Democratic Movement (MDC) that more closely represented mainstream Catholic social thought among Cubans.[5]

Andrés Valdespino and others influenced by Jacques Maritain and the emerging Latin American Christian Democratic tradition also remained cognizant of the importance of Catholic social doctrines for Cuba and the world around them. In 1960, even after leaving Cuba and despite what he considered to be Castro's betrayal, Valdespino believed that the Revolution still carried "the seed of social justice, [and] that if projected with a Christian sense, will bear fruit in the future *patria*. That is the Revolution we must rescue from the traitors. . . . That is the Revolution we must save."[6] At the same time, Christians found promoting social advocacy among an exile population that had just escaped a communist revolution to a secularized and Protestant nation to be a daunting challenge indeed.

Some asked exiles to reflect on how and why leaders with radical and totalitarian methods had managed to gain the enthusiastic support of the mass of Cuba's population in the first place. In September 1961, for example, Jesuit Francisco Dorta Duque warned his compatriots and Latin Americans generally at a Catholic conference on Latin American social problems that the "tragic process of the Cuban revolution" resulted from the lack of attention to the difficult social realities on the island, especially in the rural areas. "Perhaps Cuba's destiny during this century," he noted, "will be to serve as a great lesson to the political, economic and religious leaders of our hemisphere." He reminded his audience of Cuba's historically inequitable agrarian sector in which some ninety-six owners possessed a fifth of the national territory and four companies controlled a quarter of the sugar cane harvest. Low wages and unacceptable levels of poverty characterized the Cuban countryside. All of this, he noted, led to an unfortunate communist program of radical change that had severe repercussions for the nation's economic, social, and judicial order and sinned against basic human values.[7]

One of the repercussions was a generalized reaction in the exile communities against discourses of social change. One observer writing in UCE's bulletin *Unión* noted that many Cubans had recognized the social injustices in Cuban society and supported movements for change, but their sense of loss and betrayal now overshadowed their sense of social responsibility. Instead of seeing a revolutionary dream that promised "bread, work and justice for all," a "cold tyranny, like never before seen" enveloped the island nation, leading exiles to conservative political postures. Unfortunately, he noted, by 1965 the experience of revolution and flight had left a deep imprint on the spirits of many Cuban exiles, one that "still continues to bleed and which will be difficult to dispel for a long time to come." The grave results of this bitter experience, according to the columnist, caused many exiles to assume an attitude of suspicion and, often, outright opposition to socioeconomic reform. For some exiles, "the very word reform brings with it connotations of communism." Many who suffered the consequences of the radical revolution responded to talk of reform and change with bitterness and anger. While understandable, reasoned the columnist, this growing retrenchment only played into the hands of communists who always took advantage of social injustice to promote their ideology. As witnesses of what occurred in their homeland, exiles should speak with authority about the dangers of communism but without neglecting the necessary task of advocating for social change and greater justice throughout the hemisphere.[8]

Valdespino too believed that change, and not retrenchment to the status quo ante, continued to be the appropriate response to injustice. He lamented the communist betrayal but argued that when the Castro regime fell—an inevitable event, he thought—Cubans would reconstruct a democratic and just society. He warned of the "danger of reaction," of the possibility that a post-Castro Cuba would be governed by an extreme right-wing government opposed to even the modest social advances made under the Constitution of 1940. He feared that under the influence of right-wing leaders the Cuban people would equate social justice with communism and totally abandon the social Christian agenda.[9] The logical response should not be retrenchment and a lack of action, but just the reverse.

Leading Catholic lay intellectuals communicated a similar message to an international audience, mainly Latin American, in the exile journal *Cuba Nueva*. José Ignacio Lasaga asserted that exiles aspired to create "a Cuba proud of its traditions, but anxious for definitive reforms where the imperative of social justice for contemporary man join with the norms of liberty and democracy . . . and the secular principles of our Christian heritage."[10] In part a warning to their Latin American friends, Catholic intellectuals did not hesitate to point out the failures of Cuba's leaders, who had created a void that was ultimately filled by communism. A spiritual crisis had paralyzed Cuba's leaders in the past, and the future, with communism defeated, required the building of a new Cuba utilizing a profound social ethic that could only emerge from the principles of "our Christian heritage." All the reforms necessary for solving Cuba's and Latin America's political, social, and economic problems would be of little consequence if not accompanied by "religious energies." As for Cuba, it was not a matter of reconstituting things as they were but rather of founding the nation anew.[11]

The editors of the *Cuba Nueva* elaborated their social Christian agenda in a series of articles they called "A Vision of the New Cuba" ("Imagen de la Cuba Nueva"). The first, by noted essayist Luís Aguilar León, former professor of history and philosophy at University of Oriente and at that time professor of Latin American history at Columbia University, warned Cubans that when Castro fell, the country would be in ruins. Now was the time to think about reconstruction and the pressing questions included how to re-create democratic institutions, what to do with a generation indoctrinated with Marxist-Leninist thinking, how to refashion a workable political economy, and how to recover the spiritual currents so devastated by the Revolution.[12]

Valdespino's essay argued for the construction of a nation with a new moral code and commitment to social responsibility, a noncommunist nation different even from what had existed before the Revolution. The scandalous corruption in Cuban public life before the Revolution, Valdespino pointed out, had produced a desire among the Cuban people for honesty that fueled the revolutionary process, and while on the surface Castro's system seemed to provide this honesty, in reality corruption simply took different forms as a "new class" took control of everything. Administrative honesty and a "morality in our public life" would be crucial for a post-Castro Cuba.

At the same time, the moral laxity that had existed in pre-revolutionary public life simply reflected a deeper malaise, the lack of a true sense of social consciousness in broad sectors of national life. Valdespino charged that Cubans had been frivolous, lacked social responsibility, were excessively individualistic, lacked a communal spirit, and thought and functioned more in their own interests than for the common good. Everyone had invoked their rights and few their obligations. These characteristics had been reflected in the parliament, in the political parties, in the judicial system, in the press, in the unions, and among the industrialists, owners of property, and all the professional classes. In the end, concern about these deficiencies had produced a revolutionary movement hijacked by communism, leaving Cuba in an even worse moral situation than before. In order to build, after Castro's fall, a genuinely democratic system in which principles of freedom and dignity would be affirmed, Cubans needed to establish a moral foundation based on a true Christian sense of "social obligation."[13]

Fermín Peinado elaborated further, suggesting that the creation of a moral Cuban society was a matter of honesty not simply in public office but in all aspects of society, which required placing emphasis on broadening the spiritual dimensions in Cuban life. Nineteenth-century positivism and twentieth-century Marxism had advanced materialist visions and stunted spiritual growth. A much-needed religious and spiritual renaissance, social responsibility, and a communal national spirit needed to be cultivated through an educational system that taught Christian values, best accomplished through a decentralized political and economic system that protected human liberties.[14]

Cerro also highlighted the need for social reform, urging exiles to honor the revolutionary spirit unfortunately taken hostage by Castro and to remain committed to a genuine agrarian reform. Castro's forced collectivization had to be dismantled and replaced with a distribution of lands to the campesinos. "The dignity of the campesino," he noted, "requires that he own his own land, that he be allowed to exploit it freely, that he be aided by the State to leave ignorance and backwardness behind and to become a progressive member of a society of free men." Certainly, the post-Castro period would be characterized by ideological battles and policy debates, but everything should not be left for future decision-making. He warned that "if we are not from this moment capable of offering a convincing alternative vision, we should prepare for the next chorus of lamentations."[15]

Clerical leaders, too, spoke of the social concerns. During his visit to Miami in January 1962, Bishop Boza Masvidal reminded Cubans to remain committed to social justice but also spoke about Latin America generally. "The selfish class differences," he declared, "must disappear whereby some have too much and others die in poverty."[16] Fearful that the increasingly popular Cuban Revolution would succeed in exporting its ideological and political system to Latin America, Boza Masvidal wrote forthrightly about the need for a Christian revolution in the region, citing concrete statistical evidence of the rampant poverty and socioeconomic misery. Declaring "the situation in our countries not Christian," the bishop rejected the arguments of "some anti-communists" who denied the existence of deep social problems and criticized Cubans who insisted all was well on the island before the Revolution. "Either we create the Christian revolution or God will punish us, letting us fall into the hands of communist revolutions, which are nothing more than desperate expressions, jealousy, and hatred unleashed by the oppressed." A Christian revolution required, as a point of departure, "that great revolution of evangelization" and the development of a Christian consciousness that would allow for the blossoming of love among humankind. The Christian revolution would have to ensure human dignity, which could not be accomplished through the materialistic assumptions of communism or individualistic capitalism. Any new society had to be based on the precept that labor was not merchandize and could not be ruled by the laws of supply and demand. Workers are not machines. If respected, these truths would bring social justice.[17]

New Theological Trends

As exile Catholics reaffirmed their commitment to matters of social justice during the early 1960s, the Second Vatican Council along with new papal encyclicals and stunning pronouncements by Latin America's bishops brought new focus on the issue in the second half of the 1960s and throughout the 1970s. Innovative church documents called on Catholics to be more understanding and compassionate, less dogmatic and intransigent, and more open and involved in the world. Besides reaffirming and updating the church's social commitment, the documents also counseled greater tolerance for cultural diversity within the church, emphasized the need for greater participation by the laity, offered new ideas about dealing with communism, outlined liturgical reforms, and inspired theological innovations.

Beginning with Pope John XXIII, concern about poverty and marginalization in human societies took on a heightened importance in Catholic theology, which increasingly concerned itself with the place of the church in the modern world. Besides their traditional spiritual and evangelizing commitments, Catholics heightened their concern for temporal matters in an increasingly polarized world in which social inequalities divided the technologically and industrially advanced West from less developed and poverty stricken regions. Catholics advocating social justice received powerful moral support from the Vatican, not only in the texts of the Vatican Council (1962–1965) itself but also in the papal social encyclicals of the era. Pope John XXIII's *Mater et Magistra* (1961) and *Pacem in Terris* (1963), the Council's document *Gaudium et Spes* (1965), and Pope Paul VI's *Populorum Progressio* (1966) all pointed to the centrality of the social questions for humankind and demonstrated the intricate relationships among social problems, pressing international economic realities, political trends, and religious matters.

Together these documents, while ratifying the church's qualified support for capitalist-based economic development, critiqued dominant trends and sought new, more humane approaches to economic growth. In general, the writings expressed confidence in Western economic development but recognized its limitations, especially in the face of growing poverty. The sanctity of private property became less important to a church that now focused on the needs of the majority poor in the world. Measures had to be taken to make Western capitalism less exploitative, including the promotion of fair land expropriation and distribution, greater economic autonomy, and a more democratic control of production and investment. The writings also noted that people had the right to defend themselves when state authorities insisted on oppressing them rather than working in their interests, and that the church had the right to point out moral concerns, even to criticize the political order.[18]

During his reign Pope Paul VI brought a critical eye to problems associated with capitalist development, which offered power and wealth to the few "while whole populations destitute of necessities live in a state of dependence." The pope questioned the justice of the existing international economic system and condemned the misery it created through the perpetuation of unequal socioeconomic systems ruled by small groups of oligarchies. Dominated by international corporations, modern capitalist economies created deeper divisions and greater poverty. Paul VI suggested that political measures had to be taken to create a more just socioeconomic order. Modern forms of democracy should find imaginative approaches in tune with local realities. This represented a commitment to grassroots approaches to change rather than the state-sponsored corporatist recipes included in the traditional encyclicals. Extensive and complicated, these documents often mixed contradictory traditional and radical ideas and as a whole produced a critique of modern capitalism that caused considerable intellectual and theological discussion and controversy.[19]

This increased interest in Catholic teaching on matters of socioeconomic concern exerted a dramatic influence in Latin America, where the church began to acknowledge and criticize the region's long-standing social inequities and injustices. The Latin American bishops called for change in the region to reduce the suffering of the poor and eliminate the military dictatorships that responded to social unrest with brutal retribution. In 1960, for example, the Colombian bishops published a pastoral letter on agrarian reform that caused immediate alarm among conservative sectors not only in Colombia but Latin America generally.[20] Two additional letters by bishops in Chile and Brazil, in 1962 and 1963 respectively, delivered an even stronger message. In the Chilean pastoral, the bishops offered statistics on housing, unemployment, salary, and education to demonstrate the existing social inequalities and called for structural reforms to relieve poverty. "The Christian must favor those institutions that demand social action," declared the bishops, "and if the problem directly concerns him, he should participate in social action." Beyond that, the Christian also had the obligation to support institutional changes, including agrarian, fiscal, and administrative reforms. The Brazilian bishops urged similar measures in their country to dismantle a system "in which money and economic power are the underlying determinants in all economic, political and social decisions. It is an order in which a minority has access to culture, a high standard of living, health, comfort and luxury, and in which the majority, having no way of obtaining these goods, are by that very fact deprived from exercising many of man's basic and natural rights."[21]

The impact of these new perspectives in Latin America contributed to a rather significant reconsideration of the church's role in the hemisphere, especially with regard to the poor. Institutional changes within the Latin American church during the 1950s created a national council of bishops, which in 1955 linked into a regional body (CELAM). This provided the Latin American church with a vehicle to address hemispheric concerns, which it did during the 1960s in the wake of the Cuban Revolution, Vatican II, and the new papal encyclicals on the social question. Inspired by Pope Paul VI's 1966 encyclical *Populorum Progressio,* known as Latin America's encyclical, and deteriorating conditions in the region, a new generation of Catholic religious, laity, and bishops came together in 1968 at a landmark council in Medellín, Colombia, and articulated a powerful message about the need for social change in the region. Opened by Pope Paul VI, in what was the first visit by a pope to the region, CELAM squarely confronted the pressing issues of social inequality and injustice. The final Medellín document described Latin America as marked by deep social stratification and by external dominance, and the bishops agreed that in such circumstances the church had to stand with the poor, to help them and the whole region.[22]

Cuban exile Catholics reacted to these documents in a variety of ways. Many viewed them with suspicion, especially the pronouncements on relations with communism, but social Catholics applauded this renewed interest in social matters. They rejected the charges of some exiles that the new Catholic teachings simply accepted communism. Bishop Boza Masvidal, for example, insisted that the Vatican teachings did not in any sense backtrack on the traditional and vigorous defense of the dignity of the human person and his/her rights. In 1965, in a brief stopover in Miami while returning from the final session of the Vatican council, he again argued that the church's position with regard to communism had not changed but the council "only wanted to emphasize the sense of charity and love toward our enemies."[23]

Valdespino endorsed Boza's interpretation, saying that while the church did urge less intransigence, documents did not waver on the church's opposition to communism.[24] Earlier, in July 1961, for example, on the occasion of the publication of Pope John XXIII's encyclical *Mater et Magistra,* Valdespino had argued that though the particulars were different, this new document resembled the earlier teachings urging Catholics to work for social justice without appealing to totalitarian systems or liberal capitalism. The main historical difference, Valdespino thought, was simply that at the time of *Rerum Novarum* unbridled capitalism ravaged Europe, but now totalitarian communism also constituted an obstacle to social justice. The pope's message, Valdespino argued, is "profound and vigorous in that it not only condemns solutions to social ills that do not take into account the values of the spirit, but advocates for a social order—domestically as well as internationally—that respects the dignity of the human person, condemning the exploitation of man by man and the enslavement of man by the State."[25]

MDC also played an important role in maintaining the social discourse before the exile community. Institutionalized in the 1960s, MDC held congresses twice a year, strengthening relations with the international movement, particularly in Latin America, and disseminating its thought among exiles in preparation for a return to Cuba, where MDC intended to become an active political party in a restored democratic system. MDC relied on Maritain's thought but also embraced the ideals of the Latin American Christian Democratic movement during the 1960s, including the primacy of the individual, democracy, the social function of property, limited but effective state intervention in the economy, political decentralization, support for unions and other civic organizations, cooperatives, and worker involvement in the running of capitalist firms.[26]

In 1964, Miami MDC leader Enrique Ros pointed to the centrality of the encyclicals to his faith on the occasion of the upcoming Sixth Latin American Congress of the Christian Democratic Parties in Venezuela. The meeting itself, he noted, constituted a tribute to *Rerum Novarum* and *Mater et Magistra,* since these documents provided the ideological continuity and inspiration for the Christian Democratic organizations. "When John XXIII, the exceptional pope" outlined in *Mater et Magistra* Christian social concerns, "he seemed to offer solutions to the critical problems of our continent whose economy—fundamentally agrarian—still maintains a feudal structure." Ros declared that the encyclicals inspired Catholics to promote political positions aimed at alleviating Latin America's problems, including protecting the region's primary products; regulating capital investments; promoting regional political, economic, and social integration; defending labor's right to employment; and pushing for social security, among other things.[27]

Better known and a more prolific writer, MDC leader José Ignacio Rasco also expressed support for the church's social agenda. He had initially outlined many of his ideas in Cuba during the later half of 1959; he had voiced his support for Catholic social thought, calling for an equitable re-distribution of agrarian land in the hands of individuals and the immediate implementation of democratic procedure.[28] Once in exile, Rasco remained committed to the ideas of Maritain, established the Instituto Jacques Maritain in Miami, and in 1980 published a brief essay on the French philosopher and Christian Democracy.[29]

As an employee of the Inter-American Development Bank in the 1960s, Rasco also articulated hemispheric concerns, emphasizing the need for Latin American economic integration and cooperation in the spirit of the encyclicals. The social problem, he argued, no longer reflected tensions just between capitalists and workers but also between rich and poor nations and regions. Solutions required multilateral visions and moral obligations dedicated toward attaining social justice.[30] "Genuine necessity, as well as justice," he quoted *Mater et Magistra,* "requires that whenever countries give attention to fostering of skills or commerce, they should aid the less devel-oped nations, without thought of domination, so that these latter eventu-ally will be in a position to progress economically and socially on their own initiative." Rasco saw Inter-Americanism, economic integration, and greater international cooperation among Latin Americans as an alternative to the U.S.-dominated Pan-Americanism of the previous half century. He urged Latin America to establish regional common markets, in effect, a "United States of the South," which could engage in multilateral, rather than bilateral, economic relationships with the United States. But this had to be done within the context of a commitment to international social justice and ethics.

"We do not pretend to solve complicated problems with utopian ideal-ism," Rasco noted, "but we do think that only with a lofty concept of the moral responsibility that is latent in all human affairs can we harmonize the problems that both unite and separate. . . . For the progress and inte-gration of Latin America, billions of dollars, plentiful technical assistance, and stable and reasonable prices are required; but the architectonic for the values guiding international politics must be the dignity of man." Rasco recognized the important work of the Latin American and North American Catholic Churches in "fighting very effectively in defense of social justice, against the exploitation of man by man." This should continue with "the ecumenical sense of our times, without arrogance, or false mysticism, or messianic fervor, but with the genuine and real charity of which St. Paul so genially spoke."[31]

Grassroots Activism

Cuban Catholics in Miami revealed their commitment to the social doctrines by spending considerable time disseminating the teachings within their own community in the 1960s. The diocese of Miami announced during July 1962 the creation of the Institute of Social Action (ISA), headed by Father Salvador de Cistierna, a Capuchin priest with an extensive background in the social teachings and analyzing social problems particularly in Spain and Latin America. He had founded and headed the Pius XII Social Institute at Villanueva University in Havana in1960 with a similar goal of disseminating Catholic social thought at that time of revolutionary ferment. Very much in line with Foyaca's thinking twenty years earlier, Cistierna promoted conventional social Catholic thinking about property and its role in society, relations between capital and labor, the role of the state, and the desirability of nontotalitarian corporatist structures as an alternative to capitalism and communism. Though he acknowledged that corporatist ideas had never really prospered, except in a distorted way among those with totalitarian goals, he insisted that the idea as defined in the social encyclicals had never received due attention or given a realistic chance to work. Instead, those dedicated to social change had embraced the "dangerous and slippery road of direct state control and nationalization of firms."[32]

Cistierna intended to take the social teachings to rank-and-file Catholics, saying that the church, despite some progress in recent years, still did not concern itself sufficiently with the socioeconomic arena. "It is a painful phenomenon," he noted, "that the mass of workers no longer belong to us; they may not be against us but they surely are not with us." This neglect of the workers, Cistierna believed, allowed the enemy to sow the "discord inherent in liberal capitalism and communism." To bring workers back to the church, he noted, it was necessary to select from their ranks, instruct them and make them "auxiliaries of the Church." For the social teachings to be of value, they had to be lived, communicated, and applied; they had to be acted upon. To bring reforms to Latin America, "we have to prepare the hearts and minds for the sacrifices that reforms require," Cistierna declared. This task included convincing individuals and nations not to fall to the temptation of communist doctrine.

In addition to educating Cubans in Miami about the social doctrines, ISA—through conferences, pamphlets, and radio programs—promoted the church's thought as the basis for social and economic reforms in Latin America and alerted Latin Americans about the dangers and false promises of communism. In 1963, for example, ISA published a pamphlet by Foyaca, "Crisis en Nuestra America," which blamed the communist victory in Cuba and its expanding influence in the hemisphere to the "demographic-economic-social" problem. The pamphlet offered a detailed statistical analysis of the Latin American reality and pointed to the urgent need for structural changes in the region.[33] Relying on this kind of research, ISA intended also to offer policy suggestions for concrete reforms in the areas of industrial and agricultural development in Latin America.

ISA's first course began on May 30, 1962, and attracted one hundred students. Boza Masvidal delivered the inaugural address, emphasizing the need for social reform but without authoritarian rule.[34] On September 1, Bishop Coleman Carroll officially inaugurated ISA with a Mass at Gesu Church celebrated by Boza Masvidal, who again traveled from Venezuela for the occasion. Father Mauricio de Begoña, a Spanish Capuchin priest, offered the sermon and spoke of ISA's objectives, pointing out that unlike all the other "isms," Catholicism incorporated the material and spiritual needs of humankind. "We are interested in all of mankind's dimensions," he noted.[35] The faculty consisted mostly of former teachers at Villanueva University but also included prominent leaders of Cuba's activist laity.[36]

Cistierna designed ISA to interact with many Catholic audiences, including a mid-level program housed in the Centro Hispano Católico (CHC) and intended for the general public, a program for the parishes, and a university-level program.[37] The program at the CHC, directed by Cistierna, held its classes Monday through Friday evenings, except Thursday, which was reserved for public lectures on social and economic themes.[38] The first year, courses included social doctrines of the church, psychology and communism, geography, economy, business, and the Latin American condition. The first courses drew some two thousand students, and by 1967 enrollment had increased to six thousand. In addition to its regular classes, ISA organized special workshops for particular constituencies.

In February 1963, for example, it offered a twelve-week program held on Tuesday and Thursday evenings for the Miami-based Sociedad Interamericana de Hombres de Empresa. Mostly Cuban businesspeople whose businesses had been confiscated in Cuba, the program's participants in-cluded bankers, industrialists, merchants, and publicists. One student noted that it was necessary to analyze the collapse of the economic system in Cuba in order to be able to create a vision for the future. One of the instructors, José M. Illán, thought it commendable that these businesspeople took time from their busy schedules to study "the socioeconomic problems of our times" in order to avoid again falling into the errors and omissions that led in part to the dramatic situation in Cuba. Enthused over the interest demon-strated by the business community, Cistierna emphasized that "it is our goal to work with the Cuban businessmen in the construction of that new society . . . a truly Christian society where social justice is a reality."[39] In February 1963, ISA sponsored the first in a series of debates open to the public that addressed the issue of worker participation in running business enterprises. ISA also supported the work of the church with the Latino migratory labor population in south Florida by carrying out a research project on the history and current conditions of the migrant workers, in-cluding their economic, social, cultural, and religious situation.[40]

During its second year, ISA launched its work in the parishes under the direction of Angelita Esparraguera, a former Catholic Action lay leader in Cuba. Beginning at Corpus Christi Church, ISA invited parishioners to a series of fourteen conferences, offered once a week. Many students felt the conferences, in combination with their lived experiences in Cuba, increased their understanding of events and inspired their support for Cuba's restora-tion on the basis of Catholic social teachings. The second parish program took place at Inmaculada Concepción and the third at San Juan Bosco. In all, 152 parishioners received diplomas. At San Juan Bosco the conferences examined three basic issues: the socioeconomic crisis in the world, espe-cially Latin America; Christian principles embodied in the papal encyclicals, particularly about the family, work, society, and the state; and possible so-lutions to social problems, such as cooperativism and syndicalism.[41] Per-haps it was these teachings that in 1967 inspired parishioners at San Juan Bosco to promote a cooperative experiment. In January, a group of twenty-five Cubans, led by Esparraguera, Ramón Rasco, José Campos, and others, established a nonprofit cooperative credit union for the community. Sup-ported by Father Vallina, the group set up its offices in parish facilities, but initially the idea created great suspicion. As a reporter noted, "in a majority exile Cuban area, the word cooperativism sounded tabu to many." The leaders set out to educate the community about their project, a "genuine democratic cooperativism, of profoundly Christian roots," and within a year membership increased to one hundred.[42]

The college program, headed by Carmelo Mesa Lago, appeared in January 1964, when ISA offered conferences at Barry College that were also open to Biscayne College students. Like the parish and mid-level programs, the new university program focused on an analysis of the socioeconomic problems afflicting Latin America and on finding solutions consistent with Catholic social teachings. "From the ideological point of view," said Mesa Lago, "we will follow the pontifical orientations that are the basis of Social Christian doctrine; we will combat the modern errors, from 'laissez faire' capitalism to fascism and communism."[43]

The diocesan newspaper *The Voice* covered ISA activities quite closely, regularly disseminating to Catholic readers the ideas offered in the various conferences, lectures, and workshops. During summer 1964, the newspaper reported on an ISA course on Catholic social thought in considerable detail. Father Cistierna, for example, spoke about the elements of the social question from a Catholic point of view.[44] Mesa Lago also participated with a presentation on the church's right to intervene in social questions, which, he argued, stemmed from the moral dimensions of all social problems. Other lectures focused on property rights, agrarian reform, and social security, among other things.[45] This extensive coverage obviously sought to broaden ISA's audience and encourage the Catholic social message within the Cuban Catholic community of Miami. Drawing from ISA presentations and other sources, Boza Masvidal's newsletter *Unión* also maintained a continuous flow of information and commentary on social doctrines for its readers throughout the United States and other countries, constantly reminding Cubans of the centrality of social issues to Catholic thought and the need to incorporate these teachings into day-to-day life and religious practice.

Finally, ISA activities also inspired Bishop Carroll to propose a similar program of outreach beyond the Miami Cuban community to Latin America in general. As a member of the Subcommittee for Inter-American Cooperation of the U.S. Bishops Committee for Latin America, Carroll participated in the committee's continuing concern about Latin America's social situation and the need to offer practical Catholic solutions.[46] In 1963, the subcommittee created the Catholic Inter-American Cooperation Program (CICOP) to take the lead in these matters. At its first meeting in January 1964, with the efforts of Father Bryan Walsh, CICOP supported the establishment in the diocese of Miami of the Inter-American Institute for Social Formation (IAISF).[47] In promoting IAISF, the bishop saw an opportunity for Miami, and the diocese of Miami in particular, to reach out to Latin America. Carroll recognized that the long involvement of Cuban Catholics in the social questions of Cuba and Latin America generally offered a wonderful resource for the diocese. The large and growing Cuban presence, in combination with significant communities of Latinos from Colombia, Puerto Rico, and Mexico, provided Miami an opportunity to become an important gateway to Latin America.

The Miami diocese in particular was an appropriate place for an organization that could train social reform specialists to work in Latin America's public and private institutions. IAISF also hoped to train young Cuban exile professionals, university students, and labor leaders in preparation for a return to their homeland after the fall of Castro's government.[48] Relying on the Cuban staff of IAS, IAISF operated for a number of years training students and labor leaders from the Dominican Republic, Puerto Rico, Central America, Venezuela, and Colombia.[49] At one of the graduation ceremonies, Bishop Carroll counseled the students to return home and spread the message of Catholic social thought. One student responded for the group, saying that they intended to condemn capitalist exploitation as well communism, which had taken control of Cuba through force of arms. Cuba and Latin America, he added, needed to rely on Christian social thought.[50]

At a UCE gathering in Miami in the late 1970s, Cuban Catholic activist Amalio Fiallo, a sociology professor at the Catholic University Andrés Bello in Caracas, articulated yet again that basic mantra. Fiallo offered Christianity, not capitalism or communism, as the just approach to resolving human spiritual and social problems, which were intimately linked.[51] Capitalists worship money, he noted, while communists advocated a determinist and atheist vision of the world. For exile Catholic leaders, the traditional call for rejecting communism as well as liberal capitalism remained the central message.

Challenging the Catholic Left

Catholic theological innovations during the 1960s naturally enough produced divergent interpretations among Catholics, including implications for dealing with the Cuban Revolution. In light of the Catholic Church's pronouncements in the 1960s about its obligations in the "modern world," all serious Catholics faced the challenge of having to think about political and socioeconomic realities in new ways; if reform had not historically succeeded in changing Latin America, what about revolution? If the Cuban Revolution's approach to change was unacceptable, what, in fact, were the realistic options for change in a socially polarized Latin America? Many Catholics on the political left in Latin America, Europe, and the United States sought relief from what they considered to be the tired rhetoric of traditional social doctrine and action and embraced what they interpreted as the real transformative experience of the Cuban Revolution.

Despite the Revolution's drawbacks, many social activists in Latin America viewed the Cuban experiment as perhaps the only example of a country in their region that had managed to concretely challenge, if not totally resolve, the problems of poverty, racism, illiteracy, and other pressing concerns. During this era of increasing poverty, political polarization, and right-wing military dictatorships in Latin America, many of those committed to social and economic change in the region, including Catholic reformers, seemed to accept the suppression of political and civil rights in Cuba as a necessary evil. Perhaps Castro had created a repressive state, but at least, they reasoned, he used his power to transform the country socially; the military regimes across Latin America simply supported the status quo. Cuban exiles, even many of those on the political left, considered this thinking hypocritical, to say the least.

Those sympathetic to the Cuban Revolution looked to the new Catholic theology of the Vatican Council and the papal messages of the 1960s to justify their position. These writings certainly did not advocate communist revolutions but did encourage a practical, less dogmatic response to communism, which included willingness to dialogue and an effort to understand, though certainly not embrace, the communist point of view. As part of promoting human dignity and social justice in the world, Pope John XXIII's 1963 encyclical *Pacem in Terris* urged Catholics to recognize the humanity of those that did not share Christian faith, values, or perspectives, despite their errors. Such a strategy not only promoted human relations but also provided the opportunity to evangelize and bring unbelievers to the church. This theme reappeared in *Gaudium et Spes,* the 1965 Vatican II document on the church in the modern world, which counseled Catholics to be familiar with the logic of atheism, understanding its roots while rejecting the intellectual and theological errors inherent in atheistic thinking. "Although the Church altogether rejects atheism, she nevertheless sincerely proclaims that all men, those who believe as well as those who do not, should help to establish right order in this world where all live together," the document declared, but "this certainly cannot be done without a dialogue that is sincere and prudent." The church emphasized this spirit of cooperation as a way of making a better world but at the same time demanded governments to allow "for the faithful to be allowed to build up God's temple in this world also," and invited atheists to "weigh the merits of the Gospel of Christ with an open mind."[52] While maintaining a strong intellectual and theological criticism of atheism, church documents of the early 1960s counseled dialogue and a more pragmatic attitude toward atheists, suggesting that some of their practical ideas for advancing justice had merit even if their overall philosophy remained deeply flawed.

Many Catholics took these ideas to heart and advocated active engagement with communist regimes. One well-known Belgian theologian and sociologist and member of the Latin American bishops' secretariat in Rome, Father François Houtart, observed in 1964 that the change in Vatican thinking was "not toward the ideas of communism, but toward the facts of its actual presence." He considered this change positive because it allowed for greater communication. During his own visits to Poland, for example, he found to his surprise that even among Marxists "there are quite a few people . . . who disagree with the official position of the party on several questions, who think it is very out-of-date." He noted that with the improved standard of living, many people in communist societies were more interested in social and intellectual freedom. Houtart also believed that trends suggested the possibility of eventual liberal reforms behind the Iron Curtain. He discovered, too, that many Catholics in these societies did not necessarily see their world in black-and-white terms. While not in agreement with communist ideology, they recognized certain positive aspects to the system and hoped for the day when Christian evangelization could proceed within the socialist world.

Houtart urged realism in relations with communists, including establishing active relationship and communication. At the same time, he saw little immediate prospect for fruitful dialogue between communists and Catholics in Cuba, which he visited in 1963. The Revolution was still too new and resentments high on both sides. He advised Cuban Catholics to be patient. Dialogue "at that time would be impossible, . . . the best thing to do was to be quiet and wait: later perhaps it would be possible." He reminded his readers that the problems were complex: "Often we react in such an emotional way to the problem of communism that there seems an automatic absence of rationality in our attitudes."[53] In time, however, dialogue would be appropriate and needed.

Houtart's attitudes reflected considerable openness in Latin America toward the Revolution, especially among the young who sought concrete solutions to the region's deeply entrenched social problems. During the final years of the 1950s, the Cuban and international press had closely covered this popular revolution that captured people's imaginations across the hemisphere. In the early 1960s, in the face of Latin America's economic stagnation, deepening social crisis, political polarization, and military rule, millions saw the Cuban experiment with considerable hope and optimism, which a group of Cuban JOC activists glimpsed during a trip through Latin America in 1961. Father Enrique Oslé, former spiritual counselor to the JOC; Antonio Fernández Nuevo, the last national president of JOC before its abolition; and Alfredo Cepero, a former Catholic student leader, learned firsthand of the complex sentiments of Latin American Catholics. Sponsored by the Cuban-exile affiliate of CLASC, Solidaridad de Trabajadores Cubanos (STC), the three visited Venezuela, Brazil, Argentina, Chile, Peru, Ecuador, and Colombia; they engaged in wide-ranging discussions about Cuba with diverse sectors of Latin American Catholicism. They received sympathetic receptions from the often quite conservative Catholic audiences but also learned a great deal about the deep concerns many Catholics felt about the socioeconomic reality in Latin America that informed their ideas about Castro.

In Rio de Janeiro, the Cubans spoke with an ideologically heterogeneous group of students attending a *cursillo* that included mostly Catholics but also "socialists and existentialists." During the discussion the socialists supported the Revolution quite aggressively, and though the Catholic students remained mostly quiet, they seemed in solidarity with the comments of the socialists. Somewhat perplexed, the Cubans observed that the students did not seem to care about the executions, religious persecution, brutal repressions, loss of freedoms, and emerging hunger, but only about the fact that a socialist revolution had triumphed.[54]

A later meeting with Catholic students from several universities in Quito revealed a similar perspective. Though they recognized the dangers of communism, the Catholic students also opposed the Latin American systems that perpetuated poverty and misery. They feared the consequences of an overthrow of the Cuban government that might return Cuba to its old socioeconomic structures and consolidate the capitalist system throughout Latin America. They especially resented the Cuban exiles concentrated in Miami, who spoke about the Cuban past as if it were a paradise and collaborated with the United States. The Cubans responded somewhat defensively, expressing solidarity with the generalized concerns about the social injustice all around them, but emphasized that their opposition to Castro's social revolution should not be interpreted as supporting the status quo. They opposed Castro, they told the students, because of his communism and his betrayal of the original goals of the Cuban Revolution.[55]

In São Paulo they met with passionately pro-Cuban Catholic Action students. When the exiles painted a dramatic picture of the difficult situation on the island, the Brazilians responded with equal vigor saying that the campesino and worker in Brazil supported Castro and hoped that when a Brazilian Fidel emerged, he too would execute the capitalists that oppress them.[56] Equally disheartening, in Buenos Aires they met with a group of Christian labor leaders who received them very coolly and did not seem much interested in their descriptions of Cuba under Castro. Instead, they raised questions about the material benefits the Castro government had delivered to the poor.[57]

After their trip, the three Cubans certainly had a better understanding of the complexity of the Cuban question in Latin America. What for them seemed like a clear-cut case of tyranny, for many Latin Americans had a variety of meanings and nuances that went beyond the issue of communism. Many reform-minded people in Latin America initially romanticized the Revolution and did not necessarily recognize the Castro government as a traditional communist regime. In any case, they were not unduly concerned about communist participation in the Revolution, which they viewed as a necessary aspect of the popular front tactics essential for dislodging the existing socioeconomic system. Many Latin Americans interested in reform were not in the mood to hear charges that the Revolution was communist, especially since the tactic had been used by the right-wing in Latin America and the United States throughout the 1950s to discredit progressive noncommunist political forces.[58]

Exiles also became the target of sharp criticism not only from the Cuban government but from Catholic intellectuals who shared the attitudes many had expressed to the JOC delegation. A particularly harsh assessment of Cuban Catholics by Leslie Dewart, a Christian theologian and philosopher resident in Canada, revealed his absolute lack of sympathy for the exiles. He criticized them for their anti-communist intransigence, considering it exaggerated and outdated. Originally published as a series of articles in *Commonweal* and other Catholic publications and later compiled in a book, *Christianity and Revolution,* Dewart's criticism of Cuban Catholics was based on what he thought to be their narrowly conceived and unimaginative ideological response to the Revolution during 1959 and 1960. He condemned not only the bishops for reacting to an idea and not necessarily a concrete reality but also Catholic intellectuals for their unthinking obedience to the church hierarchy. Lay leaders had the right and obligation to think creatively and offer innovative approaches to difficult situations. Cuban intellectuals like Valdespino, Lasaga, Cerro, and others, Dewart argued, had initially offered independent and progressive perspectives but ultimately failed in this respect, simply falling victim to long-standing anti-communist rhetorical formulas that led to confrontation and eventually violence.

Dewart pointed to the Catholic Church's confrontation with communism in Cuba during 1959 and 1960 as exactly the wrong approach. Clearly he thought that the church should have respected Castro's broad popular support and acted with greater reflection and restraint. In speaking aggressively against communism, an abstract idea, the Cuban bishops provoked hatred against those supporting the Revolution. "But it is those whom we hate that we should love," Dewart pointed out. "It is those who really threaten us that we are enjoined to forgive; it is those who are dangerous whom we are asked to negotiate with." He drew a parallel with Protestantism, noting that despite hundreds of years of rejecting Protestantism, the Catholic Church gained much from its inspiration. Protestantism helped Catholics "rediscover, reinvent, and refashion" their own faith, and so with communism. By engaging communism, Christians could "strive to redeem it, that is, make it truly, not spuriously, serve its own best motives and achieve its own self-realization not in error but in truth."

Dewart considered communism a challenge for the church, not a threat: a challenge to redeem communism through "the realization and actualization of communism's aspiration to truth by its transformation in the Christian intellect." But this dialogue with communism "might be redemptive of communism not simply, and, perhaps not primarily, by our adaptation and adoption of whatever good and truth communism might have to offer but, above all, by such inner purification and ever stricter sanctification of our faith and our Church as would attend upon that dialogue."[59]

By the 1970s, a deep concern about social justice emanating from Latin American Catholics, and articulated at Medellín in 1968, had coalesced into an increasingly systematic theological vision that became known as Liberation Theology. First formally articulated by a Peruvian priest, Gustavo Gutiérrez, in the late 1960s, Liberation Theology called on Latin Americans to take a forthright position against poverty. Though Liberationist thought took on various permutations, in many ways this thinking represented a logical extension in the social concerns of the church articulated since the 1940s and 1950s.[60] Nevertheless, Liberationists also represented a radical shift from the traditional social discourses of the church, drawing from very different theological roots. Unlike traditional approaches that drew inspiration from a Thomistic reliance on reason and natural law, Liberationist method also looked to scripture and concrete temporal conditions as sources of interpretation.[61] Liberationists interpreted scripture in light of the sociological and anthropological realities people faced, concluding that conditions of overwhelming poverty in Latin America required Christians to take an affirmative posture of advocacy in favor of the poor.

Influenced by Marxist class analysis and the increasingly popular ideas included in Latin American dependency theory that emphasized the imperialist nature of the economic order controlled by the United States and Europe, as well as the colonial socioeconomic structures prevailing in Latin America itself, Liberationist thinkers challenged the traditional idea that the church should remain disengaged from concrete political involvement. Traditional Catholic thought, including that of Maritain, argued that, while the church should help prepare the laity for their vocations in the world, the church itself must remain removed from the partisan politics of the temporal world. Liberationists found it impossible to separate the church from the temporal; in fact, the two could not be separated. They unapologetically and affirmatively endorsed an activist posture in support of the poor majority in Latin America, which translated into a sympathetic attitude toward the Cuban Revolution's social project. This "option for the poor" became a central inspiration for activist Christians in the 1970s, and for them Cuba represented the only concrete example of a nation in Latin America dedicated to the systematic elimination of poverty.[62]

Though Cuban exile Catholics too spent considerable energy reaffirming their commitment to notions of social justice, especially for Cuba and Latin America, they could not accept the interpretations of left-leaning Catholics. Informed by their own experiences, they did not in any way soften their attitude toward the Cuban Revolution, which they unwaveringly characterized as repressive and inherently unjust. Most exiles rejected the Catholic left's tendency to see communists as simply one more actor to be negotiated with on the political stage. While exiles supported theological discourses that called for social justice in Latin America, they also opposed blurring the line between Catholic and communist ideals. From the exile point of view, communists were not a benign minority but opportunistic and ruthless revolutionaries opposed to Christian values who if given the opportunity would impose their ideology on all. Most exiles took a firm stand against anyone who suggested the Cuban Revolution advanced the goals of social justice and human dignity.

Cubans opposed the new pragmatism of the church and especially opposed Dewart's interpretation of events. They not only resented his characterizations of their opposition to communism in 1960 and 1961 as an unnecessary overreaction but also believed his ideas lacked analytical balance. While criticizing the dogmatic attitudes and positions of Catholics, the Canadian theologian failed to apply the same scrutiny to the actions of the Cuban government itself. Exiles often pointed out that their actions in 1960 responded directly to the growing and aggressive demands by the government for "revolutionary unity," a code phrase for absolute conformity. Certainly, by early 1960, the government no longer tolerated public criticism of its policies; critics became traitors. In 1964, Lasaga complained to Vatican officials about what he perceived to be a concerted effort by left-leaning Catholics like Dewart to defame Cuban Catholics and the church. He and other exiles viewed Dewart and others like him as, at best, naïve idealists (*tontos utiles*) without any practical and concrete experience with communism and, at worst, Marxists cynically disguised as Christians.[63]

Over the years exiles consistently expressed little patience for those like Dewart whom they viewed as, on the one hand, demanding justice in Latin America and condemning repressive right-wing military dictatorships but, on the other, simply ignoring the gross human rights violations and lack of fundamental freedoms in Cuba. Cuban Catholics countered all efforts by left-leaning co-religionists to justify the Revolution. In 1963, Bishop Boza Masvidal challenged the assertions of a Maryknoll priest from the United

States who traveled to Cuba that relations between church and state were good and that reports of religious persecution in Cuba were exaggerated. He wondered how the priest could ignore the obvious repression against the church, including the expulsion of religious, repression of all independent media including banning the church from access to all radio or television, prohibition of organized lay movements, and the lack of religious education for children.[64] A decade later, the ever-vigilant Boza Masvidal responded to a book written by Ernesto Cardenal, a Nicaraguan cleric much taken with the Cuban Revolution who within a few years became Minister of Culture in the Sandinista Revolution. Boza Masvidal interpreted Cardenal as among the many leftist Catholics who saw only what they wanted. He applauded Cardenal's regular denunciations of injustices and violation of basic human rights across Latin America but could not understand how he justified them in Cuba.[65]

By the late 1970s, Cuban Catholic exiles routinely and publicly criticized tolerant attitudes toward the Cuban Revolution while simultaneously expressing support for a strong social agenda by the church. In the months leading up to a third CELAM meeting at Puebla, Mexico, in 1979, attended by the new Pope John Paul II, the Cuban exile clergy from around the world, organized as the Fraternidad del Clero y Religiosos de Cuba en la Diáspora, gathered in Miami in July 1978 to prepare a response to the preliminary consultative document. They agreed on the importance of Medellín, affirming the general outlines of the conference a decade earlier, and emphasized the social doctrines, but they also encouraged the bishops to continue to express concern about those nations suffering under oppressive regimes, including Marxist repression. The solution of Latin America's social problems, they argued, had to be more creative than a mere choice between capitalism and communism.[66]

MDC also issued a statement on the occasion of the Puebla conference echoing the sentiments of the exile clergy. MDC reiterated its own commitment to resolving social problems by embracing the ideas expressed in *Populorum Progressio* and Medellín, calling for the integration of Latin America's economies free of colonialism and outside intervention and recognizing the vocation of the Cuban people for collaborating in the struggle for liberty and justice so important for the region. Also, like the clergy, MDC emphasized that this work could only be accomplished within the context of freedom in which people could determine their own destiny.

The document concluded that though the situation in Cuba was irreconcilable with social Christian ideals, MDC's struggle should be understood as inspired not by a rejection of Marxist structures but rather by its affirmative commitment to social Christian ideals.[67]

Cuban exile Catholic advocates of change and reform who received their formation in Cuba during the 1940s and 1950s remained committed to their vision of social justice. Though they represented varying theological traditions, they agreed with the basic proposition that Cuba's eventual reconstruction required a serious focus on the social problems of the day. They expressed support for the church's emphasis on social doctrines during the 1960s and 1970s and applauded the progressive bishops in Latin America who produced the socially conscious pastoral documents at Medellín (1968) and Puebla (1979). Cuban Catholics interested in the social doctrines had much in common with progressive Catholics throughout the hemisphere. In matters of their homeland, however, they overwhelmingly parted ways with anyone who equated the Cuban Revolution with social justice. Their fundamental social message rejected Cuban communist approaches to solving poverty and human misery, relying instead on Catholic approaches that emphasized moral doctrines and practical reform.

Chapter Six

"JUST AND NECESSARY WAR"

We have not yet lost our desire for a future return.
—José Ignacio Rasco (1969)

At the end of the 1960s, José Ignacio Rasco, the prominent leader of the Cuban Christian Democratic Movement, reflected on the nature of the Cuban community in Miami. He characterized the community as distinct and deeply nationalistic. Some sectors of the community remained defiantly closed and isolated, while others absorbed some measure of North American influence, but most exhibited an exile identity that adamantly rejected any notion of assimilating into the new society. He perceived that an ethnocentric communitarian conscience thrived in Miami, "which is a bulwark against decubanization." Though outside of Cuba they did not forget; they remained focused on their homeland. "We have not yet lost our desire for a future return," he said.[1]

Exile identity existed to safeguard the possibility of an eventual return. Exile manifested itself not only in nationalism, anti-communism, and visions of a future homeland, but also in concrete and consuming activism. Literally hundreds of political organizations conspired against the Cuban

156

government, including followers of Batista, Auténtico politicians who governed in the 1940s, the Ortodoxo leaders that challenged the Auténticos during the same era, leaders of the main labor organizations, industrialists, and many others. Though unified in their opposition to Castro and communism, these various organizations represented a diversity of political persuasions, from conservatives to social democrats and of course Christian-inspired groups. All of this contributed to a highly politicized community dedicated to action that endured without weakening throughout the 1960s and 1970s.

Though Cuban exiles often disagreed about the best approaches for fighting communism, which varied over time, they did agree on the necessity of developing concrete strategies for struggle, whether through direct armed movements, diplomatic pressure, developing effective public discourses, or directly lobbying the United States government. Only negotiating with the Cuban government remained off limits, though in time this too emerged as a controversial and divisive strategy for return. Whatever their approach, as one exile declared, Cubans could never be indifferent to "the tragedy that our country is living." They did not flee to the United States to become comfortable, regain wealth, reconstitute what had been lost, or even find tranquility and peace. Instead, "We have come here prepared to fight, to organize a crusade, to struggle for God and for Cuba for as long as we have the slightest breath in our bodies." "Today our Christianity is the Christianity of the days of the catacombs, ruled by persecution and martyrdom," which requires everyone to be "on the front line, facing the enemy, willing to sacrifice all rather than abandon ground or flag."[2]

Armed Action

Despite the inability of Catholic resistance movements to slow the Revolution in Cuba during 1960 and 1961, activities continued unabated in exile with the full encouragement and significant funding by the United States. Not all exiles embraced U.S. covert support with equal enthusiasm. For some this was a bitter pill to swallow, but most believed that they had little choice and that it offered the only realistic opportunity to depose Castro, who received significant military resources from the communist bloc. Furthermore, most Catholics did not feel constrained by their faith to participate in armed actions against the government in Cuba, though the most devout did operate within what they considered the parameters outlined by Catholic tradition. Just as they thought Catholicism had permitted insurrectionary actions against Batista, most Catholics concluded that anti-Castro military operations also fell within the bounds of just war theory. Many had justified the use of violence against Batista and did so again against Castro, while others simply took it as self-evident, not needing justification and suspending religious argument altogether. As he did in 1958, church legal expert José Ignacio Lasaga expressed his opinion that exiles could act against Cuban communism as long as actions were part of an effective war effort that had a real possibility of eliminating the oppressive system on the island, though this did not include assassinations, terrorism, or other morally objectionable tactics.[3] Even the Cuban exile clergy seemed to accept this interpretation and did not speak against the constant paramilitary preparations in exile during the 1960s.

The United States quite early on decided to rely on the Cuban opposition to undermine Castro. Already in November 1959, President Eisenhower had accepted a Department of State recommendation that he discreetly organize and fund the Cuban opposition, and the following March he approved a program of covert action code-named Operation Pluto to depose Castro. Under this program the CIA was authorized to organize Cuban refugees into a public political opposition and create what was intended to be a secret military force composed of exiles trained in Florida, Nicaragua, and Guatemala for a landing in Cuba. The plan also included a propaganda offensive, including using a radio station on Swan Island, a Honduran possession off the southwest coast of Cuba, to transmit anti-Castro programming.

In the meantime, the CIA had already initiated contacts with Cuban dissidents, beginning with Manuel Artime and the MRR.[4] In November, shortly after publishing a letter of resignation from INRA denouncing Castro as a communist, Artime met with a U.S. agent at the U.S. embassy in Havana who interviewed him about communism in Cuba. The agent facilitated his escape to Tampa on a Honduran freighter, and in Miami Artime underwent detailed interrogation before being formally recruited as point man for the CIA with Cuban dissidents.[5] Artime's first CIA-sponsored assignment took him on a speaking tour throughout Latin America, during which he denounced Castro as a communist. In February 1960, CIA officials met with Catholic activists José Ignacio Rasco, Angel Fernández Varela, and Oscar Echevarría in Virginia. Another meeting with Rasco and others in Caracas in April led to the founding in June of the exile Frente Revolucionario Democrático (FRD).[6] In addition to Catholic leaders Rasco and Artime, FRD leadership included Antonio de Varona, a long-time Auténtico Party politician, and Justo Carrillo and Aureliano Sánchez Arango, two well-known political figures who had participated in a variety of governments over the years.[7] Varona coordinated the organization. The CIA-funded FRD initiated its work in Mexico City but by September had moved to Miami after they had worn out their welcome with the Mexican government.[8]

Representing five distinct political blocs, FRD condemned Castro and the Revolution's dictatorial and communist path. The organization called for the reestablishment of the Constitution of 1940 and popular elections and linked its activities with dissidents on the island through the activities of MDC leader Enrique Ros, who cooperated with MRR boss in Havana Rogelio González Corzo. Throughout 1960, clandestine groups representing many political persuasions formed in the cities, and, a little later, so did guerrilla operations in the countryside. Operating with the nom de guerre Francisco, González Corzo coordinated a sabotage campaign across the island that summer and fall.[9] Insurgents burned sugar and tobacco crops; destroyed INRA, military, and state vehicles and buses; threw grenades at the capitol building, the Palace of Justice, and the University of Havana; and spearheaded production sabotage at numerous factories and stores. By December, not a night passed without some kind of explosion in Havana.[10]

During the middle of August 1960, President Eisenhower received and approved an anti-Castro plan from the CIA that included a $13 million budget and authorized the use of Department of Defense personnel and equipment for training a paramilitary force in Guatemala. In May, the CIA arranged for Artime to meet with a group of Batista-era military officers, José and Roberto San Román, Erneido Oliva, and Alejandro del Valle. Despite their different backgrounds, the group agreed to work together to overthrow Castro and in early June, accompanied by some twenty-five recruits, departed for a CIA camp in Panama for intensive training in guerrilla warfare. After eight weeks they moved to Retalhueleu, on Guatemala's Pacific coast, to join another group already building a training camp for an exile brigade that would invade Cuba.[11]

The invasion brigade, commanded by two U.S. Marine colonels, numbered about four hundred in early November, including many Catholic activists who left Cuba specifically to join the training. Known as the Brigada 2506, after the recruitment number of ACU and MRR activist Carlos Rodríguez Santana, who fell off a cliff to his death during a training march in the Guatemalan mountains, the brigade displayed unmistakable Christian symbolism. The recruits' uniforms included shoulder patches emblazoned with a white cross, which also appeared on the unit's flag. Three Spanish Catholic priests and a Protestant minister who accompanied the invasion force to Cuba offered regular religious and prayer services for trainees and led prayers after each day's activities before retiring for the night.[12]

Once established in June 1960, FRD turned its attention to organizing the exile communities, though from the beginning they had difficulty creating unity. Initially, FRD leaders agreed to exclude supporters of the Batista regime (who predictably responded with charges that the FRD was *rosado* [pink]), but they also opposed the incorporation of many leftist members of Castro's first government now in exile, leading to even deeper factionalism. Nevertheless, FRD grew considerably, expanding its constituency and perhaps most significantly recruiting José Miró Cardona, Cuba's prime minister during the first month and a half of 1959. He had gone on to become the Cuban ambassador to Spain before finally breaking with the Revolution and going to Miami.

In January 1961, the newly elected Kennedy administration accelerated the anti-Castro conspiracy but hoped to make it more representative of the Cuban people. Despite Miró Cardona's inclusion, the new president insisted on an even more representative exile organization, specifically one that included the social democratic left represented by the MRP, headed by Manuel Ray in exile and JOC leader Reinol González in Cuba. Though many Cubans in exile characterized the MRP as "Fidelistas without Fidel," referring to their social democratic backgrounds and initial support for Castro, many in the U.S. State Department nevertheless considered MRP's inclusion imperative; it would add legitimacy to what they considered a generally conservative FRD.[13] Under pressure from the State Department and after much wrangling, FRD and MRP finally reached a tentative agreement on March 21 to unite their efforts under the umbrella of the Consejo Revolucionario Cubano (CRC) to be headed by Miró Cardona.[14] The CRC would act as Cuba's provisional government in the event of a successful invasion. MDC, for one, refused to cooperate with CRC, arguing that it was imposed by the U.S. government and did not envision an active support of the Cuban underground on the island.[15] Artime, on the other hand, became the CRC's representative to the Brigada 2506 in Guatemala and accompanied the invasion force to the island.

In the meantime, exile paramilitary groups prepared to infiltrate Cuba, hoping to offer concrete support to the Brigada 2506 when it landed. In early 1961, for example, MDC leader Laureano Batista secured two vessels and rented a farm about an hour from Miami on the road to Key West, where some twenty men trained for guerrilla duty.[16] During the middle of March, Batista's group landed supplies in Matanzas and, on the eve of the main invasion, joined with Jorge Sotus, a founder of MRR, and Pedro Luís Díaz Lanz, former head of the Cuban air force, for another expedition to Cuba.[17] This expedition included four vessels and departed Miami on April 4, also carrying MDC leaders Rasco and Luís Aguilar León, and others associated with MRR. Just before the group left, CIA agents arrived in a truck and station wagon with packs, military clothing, radios, bazookas and rockets, machine guns, mortars, automatic rifles, hand grenades, grenade launchers, and explosives, detonator caps, and fuses. Unfortunately for the exiles, a Cuban patrol boat spotted them as they approached the island; they gained speed and made their escape, but not before disposing of the weapons overboard. On their return to Miami, they learned that the invasion brigade had departed Guatemala for Cuba.[18]

In a more successful mission, DRE activists did manage to land in Cuba prior to the invasion. Alberto Muller took a group into the Sierra Maestra to organize a guerrilla force, but Manuel Salvat and many others were tracked down and arrested. For the most part, the government succeeded in disrupting the clandestine networks, and increased vigilance resulted in the capture of Muller and his comrades in Oriente during August 1961. He received a prison sentence of twenty years.[19]

In the early morning hours of April 17, 1961, the U.S.-funded and trained brigade of Cuban exiles landed on the beaches of the Bay of Pigs, on Cuba's southern coast. As news of the long-awaited and not too well disguised invasion spread through Miami, exiles filled churches to pray for those who would fall and for the liberation of Cuba from "atheistic communism." Fifteen thousand gathered at Bayfront Park for a public recital of the rosary, and exiles at Gesu church in downtown Miami initiated a novena seeking the intercession of Our Lady of Charity. A constant procession of men, women, and children kept an all-day vigil at a shrine honoring the Virgin. One evening, about five thousand refugees, many carrying signs that read "Con Cristo, Contra Castro" (With Christ, Against Castro) held a demonstration asking the Organization of American States (OAS) to help free Cuba from communism. As it became clear that the invasion had failed, Cubans in Miami pleaded with church hierarchies and laity throughout the world to pray for the fall of communism in Cuba. In a cable to the pope, a group of Cuban women asked for international intervention to help the hundreds of Catholics, including priests and lay leaders, who suffered "prison and a threat of death."[20]

If anyone had questioned the importance of Catholics in this enterprise, their role became quite clear as the events unfolded. One of the priests who accompanied the brigade, a Spaniard by the name of Ismael de Lugo, carried with him a proclamation found on his person when captured; he had planned to broadcast it to the Cuban people once a foothold had been established in Cuba. "We have come in the name of God, justice and democracy," began the document, "with the goal of reestablishing the rights which have been restricted, the freedom which has been trampled on, and the religion which has been taken over and maligned." After explaining that the invaders were all Christians and Catholics and that the fight was between believers in God and communists, the document declared, "Have faith, since the victory is ours, because God is with us and the Virgin of Charity cannot abandon her children. Catholics: Long Live a free Cuba, one that is democratic and Catholic! Long Live Christ the King! Long Live our glorious Patron Saint!"[21]

The stunning defeat at the Bay of Pigs did not dissuade exiles; they immediately regrouped, reassessed, and initiated new paramilitary operations. On November 30, 1961, President Kennedy authorized another effort, Operation Mongoose, designed to destabilize the Cuban regime by continuing training and funding exile infiltrations on the islands. Catholic paramilitary groups remained involved in these activities and contributed to increasing levels of resistance and sabotage in Cuba. Even with Artime in prison in Cuba until the end of 1962, the MRR, for example, remained active, led by José M. (Manolín) Hernández (until June 1961) and then Lasaga, who arrived from his own Cuban imprisonment. At the end of April 1961, MRR called for a continuing activism against Castro communism, which required the unity of all Cubans of all sectors, all classes, and all races, for the "just and necessary war" to defeat communism in the hemisphere. The statement reaffirmed the MRR's commitment to CRC headed by Miró Cardona.[22]

Returning to the United States in late 1962 with the release of the Bay of Pigs invaders, Artime again took charge of MRR and continued commando raids. With CIA funds, the MRR set up centers in Costa Rica and Nicaragua to infiltrate fighters and promote clandestine activity in Cuba. Among other things the MRR obtained two torpedo boats, each about one hundred feet long, with experienced crews. Each boat had a .50-caliber machine gun, four .30-caliber machine guns, and a 75mm recoilless rifle. They also had supply and refueling vessels that dropped off infiltration teams with radios. These operations continued until a change in U.S. government policy led to the withdrawal of funds for covert paramilitary operations.[23]

Additional MRR conspiratorial activities may be glimpsed through the story of Manuel Guillot. An ACU activist and deeply devout Catholic in his early twenties, he joined Artime's *commandos rurales* and later MDC's clandestine organization. In February 1960, he traveled to the United States, Mexico, and Venezuela and met with Artime, who named him MRR military coordinator. Working with members of DRE, he returned to Cuba to help coordinate MRR's activities with the FRD on the eve of the Bay of Pigs invasion. In March, anticipating the invasion, the government conducted a sweep of possible dissidents arresting many, including Guillot, who was not identified and released. He left Havana for Miami, where he continued conspiring, and traveled back and forth coordinating activities among activists in the two cities. Finally, in late May 1961, having returned to Cuba several weeks before, Guillot was caught while having breakfast shortly after attending Mass, and on August 30 was executed by a firing squad at La Cabaña fortress.[24]

Other Catholic groups also joined the renewed paramilitary activities. MDC took supplies to Cuba and also infiltrated guerrillas. In 1965, the military secretariat submitted for approval a guerrilla manual to the 8th National Congress of the Cuban Christian Democratic Movement held in Miami. A tool for training paramilitary personnel, *Guerra Revolucionaria* described the necessary conditions for launching a successful guerrilla war as well as the military phases fighters could expect. It counseled exiles not to place their confidence in simplistic solutions like assassinating Castro or naïvely placing their destiny in the hands of the United States. Only through the systematic approach outlined in the manual could Cubans hope to free their country on their own terms.[25] Despite these efforts the MDC underground eventually evacuated their people when the pressure from the government became too great. The exile students of DRE likewise launched commando attacks on the Cuban coast after the Bay of Pigs invasion. On August 24, 1962, two launches, under the command of Salvat, DRE's secretary general, departed Marathon Key at 2 p.m. On reaching the Cuban coast near Guanabo, one of the launches, manned by eight men carrying M-1 carbines, M-2 rifles, a 20 mm cannon, and a mortar, proceeded alone up the coast to Miramar, where they fired ten rounds of their cannon at the Hotel Rosita de Hornedo and the adjacent Chaplin Theatre, frequented by Soviet and Czechoslovakian technicians.[26] Though the attack apparently did not cause serious injury, the operation created an international stir, as the Cubans and Soviets protested at the United Nations and other international forums. Encouraged by the gleeful reaction of the exile community, the DRE formulated a formal military plan to guide their continuing activities against the Castro regime.[27]

Despite all these activities, for all practical purposes the armed war against Cuba by exiles was doomed, especially after the Cuban missile crisis. Subsequent to the Bay of Pigs invasion, the Soviet Union increased its military aid to Cuba, culminating in a growing tension between the two superpowers. In October 1962, U.S. intelligence confirmed the existence of Soviet missiles on the island, leading to the international crisis that produced a modus vivendi of sorts regarding Cuba. The Soviets removed their missiles, and the United States secretly promised not to invade the island, discontinuing its support for exile paramilitary activities. During spring 1963, Miró Cardona resigned as head of the CRC, protesting the lack of U.S. support, and this led to the organization's demise.[28]

Other activists followed suit. In a letter to his colleagues in New York in April 1965, DRE leader Manuel Salvat dismissed the possibility of effective armed action by the exile community. He pointed to a lack of commitment and principles by the majority in exile and their penchant for individualism that trumped the nationalist consciousness necessary for success. This, combined with the new policies of the United States "to impede independent Cuban [exile] action inside or outside the U.S.," made successful action against Castro virtually impossible.[29] Two months later, Christian Democratic military leader Laureano Batista declared that "no exile group is currently receiving *military* aid from the United States" (emphasis in original) and that paramilitary activities in general had slowed due to "the intensification of vigilance and repression by U.S. authorities."[30] As a result, the MDC decided to abandon armed actions and accelerate political strategies.[31] Artime also announced the cessation of MRR commando operations. Though in principle he still supported military raids on Cuba and encouraged those still so inclined, he shifted his energies to working with initiatives in Latin America aimed at combating communist expansion in the region.[32] Militant organizations with a clear Catholic identity like MRR and DRE disappeared as vital players in the exile communities, though many others remained active and reorganized their activities in the late 1960s.[33]

The thousands of Cubans including many devout Catholics who participated in military actions did so to stop the consolidation of the communist regime in Cuba. Certainly their opposition reflected their reaction to the Revolution's impact on their socioeconomic livelihood, but the intensity of their response also had much to do with their theological formation, their deep revulsion to an atheistic ideology that they believed sinned against humankind's basic nature and dignity. Indeed, this explains why Catholics of many political persuasions were among the first to offer resistance and form clandestine organizations to struggle against the regime.

International Diplomacy

Throughout the 1960s and 1970s, while some Cubans engaged in armed action, others simultaneously focused their energies in Latin America, where they hoped to persuade leaders to take a forthright confrontational posture with Cuba and even contribute resources for the overthrow of the government. They had every reason to expect that Latin Americans would see the dangers inherent in Castro's radical message and express solidarity with their cause.

Manuel Artime was among the first to try to persuade Latin Americans of the dangers of the Cuban regime. During his CIA-funded travel through Latin America, he met first with well-known reformer and president of Costa Rica José Figueres, who agreed with the Cuban's assessment of the situation in Cuba but cautioned him against premature action that could prove counterproductive. In time, he said, the Cuban people would perceive the truth and overthrow Castro. At the same time, Figueres told Artime that Castro's rise could be attributed to the stupid (*tonta*) politics followed by the United States in Latin America, supporting dictators instead of the democratic forces. Although Artime met with a number of well-known Latin American leaders, he and other Cuban Catholics spent most of their time briefing Catholic and Christian Democratic leaders in Panama, Dominican Republic, Venezuela, Peru, Chile, Argentina, and Brazil. Few of them expressed confidence in Artime's analysis and revealed little interest in making public declarations against the hugely popular Cuban government.[34]

Among the various organizations perhaps MDC most effectively sustained the anti-Castro diplomatic campaign in Latin America during the 1960s. It began as early as October 1959, when Rasco traveled to the Fifth International Christian Democratic Congress in Lima and in a secret session described developments in Cuba. Because his effort was obviously premature, various delegates denounced him as a reactionary supporter of the Batista regime. This experience did not distract him, however, and as a member of the diplomatic team of first the FRD and then the CRC, Rasco attended OAS meetings lobbying for action against Castro. In Costa Rica for the Seventh Meeting of Ministers of the OAS in August 1960, Rasco and his colleagues denounced the regime and watched with satisfaction as the ministers approved the "Declaration of Costa Rica," which warned against extra-hemispheric (that is, communist) interference in the affairs of the Americas. During this trip he also delivered speeches at the universities in Costa Rica warning of the dangers of communism and met with a group of Panamanian Christian Democrats.[35] The same month, Rubén Rumbaut also represented MDC at the international Christian Democratic Congress in Buenos Aires and then an international journalists' meeting in Lima, where he, too, denounced Castro.[36] In January 1962, almost a year after the Bay of Pigs invasion, Rasco accompanied a CRC delegation to a meeting of the OAS Council of Ministers at Punta del Este, Uruguay, that approved a resolution characterizing Marxist-Leninism incompatible with the inter-American system and ejecting Cuba from the organization. Though the exiles applauded Cuba's eviction from the OAS, they lamented that Cuba faced no specific sanctions.[37]

As the Revolution became more radical, exiles increased their efforts to characterize Cuba as a hemisphere-wide threat. They insisted that Castro would not be content to consolidate his revolution in Cuba; he fully intended to export his communist model across Latin America. Fermín Peinado, for example, pointed to Castro's Second Declaration of Havana, a speech to thousands of his supporters at the Plaza de La Revolution on February 4, 1962. In response to the OAS's ejection of Cuba from the organization the previous month, Castro offered his own vision of Latin America's future that included hemispheric revolutions helped along by Cuba. As in Cuba, the revolution would be fueled by discontented campesinos under the necessary direction of workers and intellectuals and supported by other progressive elements. Suspecting that no one really took this document too seriously, Peinado warned that Cuban supported guerrilla forces had already commenced operations in Venezuela and Guatemala.[38] In fact, in subsequent years, Cuban-inspired or supported guerrilla movements sprang up across Latin America, with "Che" Guevara's efforts in Bolivia in 1967 the most celebrated.

Peinado's article reflected the tone and urgency of many exiles of different political persuasions that believed Castro had the capacity to revolutionize Latin America. Numerous exile Cubans declared that Castro's presence doomed President Kennedy's Alliance for Progress announced in April 1961 to combat poverty and socioeconomic distress in Latin America generally. Valdespino, Cerro, and Valentín Arenas, for example, applauded the Alliance but argued that it would never work while Castro created revolution, undermined democratic regimes, and worked against the success of much needed economic and social reforms throughout Latin America. Only by removing the communist regime in Cuba, they declared, would the Alliance for Progress have a chance of succeeding.[39]

During these years, with the help of Venezuela, the United States took the lead in garnering hemispheric consensus against Cuba in the OAS. Provoked by Castro's direct support of communist insurgents, the Venezuelan government went to the OAS with convincing evidence of Castro's interference in its country's internal affairs. In July 1964, the American foreign ministers by a 14–4 vote broke all diplomatic and consular relations with Cuba, suspended trade, and warned Cuba of possible measures if their interventionist policies continued. Only Mexico refused to comply.[40] Cuban exiles applauded these measures that pressured Cuba economically and left the island virtually isolated in the Western Hemisphere, but they again lamented that Castro remained in power. Despite a strong effort, the United States failed to gain support for more aggressive OAS action against Cuba. Latin American governments in the 1960s had much on their plate without complicating matters with Cuba or supporting an invasion, a step that went against traditional Latin American concerns about intervention and sovereignty.

Simultaneously, throughout the 1960s, MDC built relations with the Latin American and European Christian Democratic movements and continued to lobby against the Cuban government, but remained generally disappointed by the responses. Christian Democratic governments in Chile (elected in 1964) and Venezuela (elected in 1968) did little to pressure Cuba or aid the exile activists. Though Laureano Batista, for example, supported the Chilean Christian Democratic Party's ascension to power, "this does not stop us from profoundly disagreeing with Chilean international politics, especially as it relates to the case of Cuba, its focus on the role of the United States of America, and its relations with the nations of the communist bloc." MDC politics, he explained, had to be one of maintaining cordial relations with the Chilean party, but without decreasing efforts at conferences and congresses to convince Christian Democrats of the reality of the Cuban case and the communist threat.[41]

The support they did receive from Christian Democrats came mostly in the form of rhetoric. At a hemispheric Christian Democratic meeting in 1964, for example, Cubans obtained unanimous moral support for their struggle against Castro.[42] Though this was certainly better than nothing, Cubans viewed such statements as being of little practical use and sometimes even as cynical. Perhaps typical, in May 1962, a Cuban delegation composed of Jorge Mas Canosa, César Madrid Villar, and Antonio Calatayud negotiated the passage of an anti-Castro resolution at the World Congress of Christian Democratic Youth in Caracas. Although Valdespino, Cerro, and Antonio Fernández Nuevo welcomed the statement, they decried its timidity. The resolution merely advised the nations of Latin America to do everything possible, through "peaceful means," to return the Revolution to its "authentic ideals." They also criticized the document's call for a collective mediation of the Cuban situation. The three critics wondered how the Congress could believe that the highly militarized Cuban regime with Soviet support could be removed through peaceful means or that Cuba would even submit to "collective mediation." They reminded Latin Americans that they did not expect any nation to undertake a war on their behalf. They would do this on their own, but they did need resources or at least tolerance for their efforts to organize military expeditions in various American nations.[43]

Catholic exiles also engaged the Vatican, always hoping to influence its diplomatic posture toward the Cuban Revolution. Almost from the outset, the Vatican worked primarily to ensure the continuing viability of the Cuban church and developed a cautious approach to developments on the island. In October 1961, after the deportations of clergy, the pope made his first public statement on the Cuban situation. "In the sea of the Antilles, at the door of the two Americas," he said, "lies the Republic of Cuba, a nation which is particularly dear to us, now more than ever, because for some time it has been subject to trials and suffering." "We ardently desire," he went on, "the welfare of that beloved people, their social progress, their internal harmony and the exercise of their religious liberty. And we still hope that goodwill, calmness, and a sincere search to safeguard the values of Christian civilization, which assures the true welfare of men in every field, may overcome hasty deliberations."[44] Exiles reacted to the lukewarm statement with anger and immediately challenged the Vatican to speak forthrightly about developments in Cuba. Activists in Miami cautioned the pope that in Latin America people did not perceive Castro to be a traditional communist and urged him to speak clearly about the Cuban government because "as long as they do not hear a defining word they prefer to suspend judgment and decision about Castro."[45]

Cuban exiles interpreted the Vatican's reluctance to speak forthrightly about the obvious assault on Catholicism on the island as a policy of peaceful coexistence based on an acceptance of the existing reality in their homeland. This became even more evident to them when a new papal nuncio, Msgr. Cesare Zacchi, arrived in Cuba in 1962 with a clear mandate from the Vatican to approach church concerns pragmatically. Zacchi combined new Catholic thinking regarding communism, clearly enunciated by Pope John XXIII and confirmed by Vatican II, with his own diplomatic experience in socialist Yugoslavia. He urged Catholics to remain on the island and commenced a diplomatic initiative aimed at reducing church-state tensions. Besides this, Zacchi obviously sympathized with the social goals of the Revolution and developed a cordial relationship with Castro himself. Very familiar with the highly intolerant Eastern European communists who persecuted the church unmercifully, Zacchi perceived Castro to be much more flexible and willing to accommodate the interests of the church as long as it did not openly confront the regime.[46]

Exiles did not hesitate to express their dismay. Although, for example, Lasaga in 1964 recognized the need for the Vatican to maintain diplomatic relations with the Cuban government in order to ensure the church's fundamental viability, he saw no reason for these relations to be cordial. At an opportune moment, he suggested, the church should make an official declaration regarding the lack of religious freedom on the island.[47] The exiled Cuban clergy agreed. At their first meeting in 1969, the exile clergy, organized as the Fraternidad del Clero y Religiosos de Cuba en la Diáspora, addressed a letter to the Secretary of State at the Vatican restating Lasaga's earlier request for a more restrained diplomatic attitude toward Cuba. They too recognized the necessity of formal relations between the Vatican and the Cuban government, but given the difficult situation that Cubans lived and the number of political prisoners in Cuban jails, including many Catholics, they advised the Vatican to be more discreet in its relations lest it be understood as support for the Cuban government. To emphasize the point, they attached to their correspondence a photograph of seven cardinals meeting with officials at the Cuban diplomatic delegation in Rome, which they asserted was being shown to Catholic prisoners on the island to convince them of the cordial relations between Cuba and the Vatican. Most exiles found the Vatican's silence regarding religious repression and the thousands of political prisoners in Cuba deeply disturbing.[48] In 1968, Bishop Boza Masvidal even reacted publicly to Zacchi, who commented that while Castro was obviously not a Christian, he was "ethically Christian." Boza declared that Castro's basic opposition to norms of Christian conduct and his methods for totally dominating the Cuban people made such a statement "completely absurd."[49] In 1974, some exiles even accused Cardinal Agostino Casaroli, Vatican Secretary of State, of being a "traitor to Christ" for visiting the island and meeting with Castro.[50]

Human Rights Discourse

Another aspect of exile strategies to undermine the Revolution included keeping Cuba's human rights issues as visible as possible. The Revolution's education, literacy, nutrition, and housing policies had convinced many around the world of its basic humanitarian character, but exiles regularly highlighted the compelling issue of political prisoners and human rights violations generally as evidence of the communist system's fundamental inhumanity. Their writings depicted a government that survived only through political intolerance and denial of due process, which commenced in the early months of the Revolution when the regime carried out the executions of hundreds of *batistianos*. Show trials meted out "revolutionary justice" to the worst elements of the previous regime, themselves responsible for the murder of hundreds, perhaps thousands. Though recognizing that these executions represented retribution for the bloody police and military repression of the Batista regime, exiles pointed to these actions as symptomatic of what the Revolution became.

During his visit to Miami in February 1962, Boza Masvidal spoke forthrightly to the press about human rights violations in Cuba. His resistance to communism on the island had already become legendary among exiles, and his expulsion gave him visibility that he used to mobilize Cuban exiles in a variety of ways. He especially urged exiles and the world to remember the prisoners, to do whatever they could for them, since they suffered prison for defending Christian ideals.[51] Exiles heeded Boza Masvidal's exhortations to maintain alive a public concern for those imprisoned on the island and the memory of those who had been executed for resisting.

Over the years exiles commemorated numerous martyred and imprisoned Catholic leaders who at least in their own communities became household names. Articles appeared about Porfirio Ramírez, the Catholic student leader captured in the Escambray Mountains and executed in October 1960. Written to elicit maximum emotional response, one account described his execution, including the firing squads' initial refusal to carry out the order. A second squad carried out the task, and only the next day did a revolutionary tribunal officially pass the sentence of execution. The author asserted that "a man who died like Porfirio, cannot die . . . with faith, nobody dies even if they kill him . . . so let us not look for him in the tomb. . . . Let us look for him in the luminous path that leads to a free motherland."[52]

The case of student leader Alberto Muller received attention through the distribution of pamphlets detailing his struggles against Castro and his arrest in April 1961, shortly after joining an insurrectionary group in the Cuban mountains. The document included a transcript of his trial during which he denounced the Revolution. After he was sentenced to twenty years, his colleagues in exile maintained his case before the public until the late 1970s, when he was finally released and settled in Miami.[53]

Catholic student leader Pedro Luis Boitel became a particularly well-known symbol of resistance, especially for his use of the hunger strike while in his Cuban prison. A founding member of MRR, he was arrested and sentenced to ten years but received harsh treatment for his refusal to cooperate with prison authorities. He and other prisoners engaged in hunger strikes on numerous occasions, one time refusing to eat for as many as thirty-five days, drinking only water. Finally, in April 1972, Boitel began a strike that lasted fifty-three days before he died alone in a cell of the Castillo del Principe prison in Havana.[54] Exiles ensured that his case became known internationally, and one Cuban association in Los Angeles established the Comite Munidal "Pedro Luis Boitel" to work for Cuban political prisoners. Boitel, they declared, will be the "symbol of students internationally and a challenge to the conscience of free men of the world."[55] Exiles also remembered González Corzo, the leader of the underground opposition in 1960. Captured shortly before the Bay of Pigs invasion, he was executed three days after the invasion. As one exile biographer declared, González Corzo "has not died, he lives in the soul of the Cuban people. Long Live Cuba! Long Live Christ, the King!"[56]

This was not just the work of the conservative exile sectors. A left-leaning group inspired by revolutionary Christian ideas and editing a newspaper called *Nueva Generación* also condemned the regime's repression. Editor José Prince, for example, published a letter smuggled from a Cuban prisoner that detailed the gruesome conditions and abusive treatment prisoners endured. The letter described the overcrowded cells, poor food, physical abuse (beatings, black eyes, broken arms, water deprivation, no baths) resulting in more than one hundred hospitalizations and one death. A strong supporter of social change in Latin America, Prince wondered how a revolution that began as a humanist project dedicated to the dignity of the human person could have gone so wrong. It was important, Prince pointed out, for Latin America and new generations of Cubans to learn that the real cost of the positive things provided by the Revolution had been the loss of liberty and the respect for the human person, principles that should not have to be negotiated: "If capitalism can be accused of profiting from misery and ignorance, communism should be denounced for being irrigated with the blood of totalitarian brutality." Prince also wondered how Castro could declare himself the defender of the needy, the dispossessed, when his "minions tortured workers and student revolutionary leaders, former officers of the revolutionary army in the Sierra Maestra, and former leaders of the 26 of July Movement."[57]

News of the arrival in Miami of ex-political prisoners usually included detailed descriptions of the abuse they suffered. *The Voice,* for example, published an account by José Fernández Arenal, who had served three years in prison. A former Associated Press reporter in Cuba before the Revolution, he was arrested in 1964 and accused of being a CIA operative. He revealed a bayonet scar on his back and said that many prisoners carried the scar since this was the way authorities discouraged protest and resistance. Food usually consisted of boiled macaroni without any condiment. Priests were never allowed to visit the prisons, and though Catholic inmates sometimes gathered together to pray the rosary, they paid for the action with solitary confinement if discovered. He also spoke of Catholic journalists he met in prison, including JOC activist Rodolfo Riesgo and Tomás Puig of *La Quincena.* "Riesgo was such a believer in the revolution's dedication to justice," Arenal noted, "that he naïvely thought that he could express his disagreement."[58] Riesgo remained in prison until the late 1970s.

Besides this fairly consistent media coverage of individual cases, organizations also formed to promote awareness of the political prisoners. In 1961, Elena Mederos, social welfare minister in the first revolutionary government in 1959, established an organization called Of Human Rights at Georgetown University in Washington, DC. The organization monitored human rights abuses on the island and organized marches to keep the issue in the public eye.[59] During the early 1960s, a Catholic activist, Luis V. Manrara, created the Truth About Cuba Committee (TACC), dedicated to mobilizing "public opinion worldwide and especially in the United States to gather the military support needed for Cubans to liberate our country." He opposed the isolated armed actions of paramilitary groups, encouraging the use of resources to lay the groundwork for an eventual armed struggle when more favorable conditions prevailed.[60] Though Manrara obtained funds from some wealthy exiles, such as the Bosch family of the Bacardí Rum interests, he established a grassroots network through which he disseminated information about Cuba and obtained modest contributions. He maintained correspondence with groups in several California cities, Indianapolis, Chicago, Cleveland, Houston, and many other places.[61]

Exiles also challenged the church in the United States to speak forthrightly about political prisoners. During 1972, for example, Cuban Catholic leaders in Boston, claiming to represent "no less than 50,000" Cubans in Massachusetts, expressed their displeasure with the attitude of the church hierarchy that demonstrated little sympathy for the plight of prisoners in Cuba. They charged the diocesan newspaper *The Pilot,* as well as the Latin America–based "pro-Marxist" Catholic News Agency (which the newspaper relied on for news stories on Cuba), of distorting the truth about the situation in Cuba. "To remain silent in the face of a crime is immoral," they declared in a letter to Archbishop Humberto Medeiros, "but to defend the criminal while ignoring the plight of the victim is tantamount to complicity." The letter claimed that some five hundred executions took place on the island during 1971 and estimated that between forty thousand and 150,000 suffered imprisonment. The Cubans also complained of the archbishop's refusal to offer Mass intentions for those executed, as well as prisoners and their families. "Is the salvation of their tortured souls outside the agenda of your Excellency?" The hard-hitting letter asked the "Holy Ghost" to "enlighten our Church leaders away from the possible fallacy that some form of accommodation with Marxism will result in temporary advantages."[62]

In another case, journalist Humberto Medrano, contributor to the Miami newspaper *Diario Las Americas,* in 1974 challenged the U.S. bishops to examine the question of prisoners shortly after the Vatican established formal diplomatic relations with Cuba. In one interview he said imprisonment in Cuba "is characterized by murders, torture, scarcity of food, lack of medical attention, forced labor, denial of basics," and numerous other abuses. As national coordinator of the Committee to Denounce Cruelty to Cuban Prisoners, Medrano transcribed and published letters from prisoners smuggled from Cuban prisons to document his claims that conditions in Cuba were not only not getting better in the mid-1970s, but actually getting worse. He sent the materials to the Bishops' Committee on Social Development of the U.S. Catholic Conference.[63]

Lobbying in Washington

By the end of the 1960s, Latin America's general disinterest in helping exiles and changing U.S. policy toward communism in general and Cuba in particular prompted exiles with a growing sophistication of international politics to devise new strategies. After taking office in early 1969, President Richard Nixon charted a policy of détente with communist adversaries, the Soviet Union and China. In the first half of the 1970s, the United States concluded anti-ballistic treaties with the Soviets, normalized relations with China, and abandoned the Vietnam War. Soon after Nixon's reelection in 1973, the United States signaled a new attitude toward Cuba and signed an agreement to combat a rash of airline hijackings to the island usually carried out by disaffected American citizens.[64] The Ford Administration in 1974 pursued secret conversations with Cuba aimed at normalizing relations, and two U.S. Senators, Jacob Javits (a Republican from New York) and Claiborne Pell (a Democrat from Rhode Island), traveled to Cuba and met with Castro—the first visits by U.S. elected officials to Cuba since the break in diplomatic relations in 1961. The following year the administration acquiesced to a decision by the OAS to lift the hemispheric economic embargo on Cuba and modified the U.S. embargo, allowing subsidiaries of U.S. companies in third countries to trade with the island.

All further progress ceased, however, when Castro suddenly dispatched troops to Angola. Talks did not begin again until 1976, when the Carter administration expressed a renewed interest in normalizing relations. By early the next year, in lieu of formal diplomatic relations and presumably as a first step in that direction, the Carter administration and Castro negotiated the establishment of Interest Sections in third-party embassies in their respective capitals to handle diplomatic matters. Travel to Cuba from the United States became legal for the first time since the early 1960s, but diplomatic complications regarding Angola again stymied further progress.[65] During these years, the dominant exile leadership opposed lifting the embargo and normalizing diplomatic relations, but they also knew that they were on the defensive. If they did nothing, U.S. policy toward Cuba would proceed without reference to the exiles.[66] Still interested in maintaining a hostile U.S. policy toward Cuba and stemming the tide of international recognition of Castro, exiles worked to establish relationships and influence within the North American political system.

A Christian Democratic activist, Jorge Mas Canosa, became the most effective actor in this regard. Born in 1939 in Santiago de Cuba, Mas Canosa finished his last year of high school in North Carolina, where his father, a member of the Cuban military, had sent him to keep him out of politics. He returned in early January 1959, just after the triumph of the Revolution, for which he developed an immediate distaste. He entered law school at the University of Oriente in Santiago just as the government began the show trials against Batistianos, a process he considered unjust. Though apparently not connected with Catholic activism before the Revolution, later in the year he joined the MDC organized by Rasco, Ros, and others. He helped organize the youth section in Oriente province and in early 1960 entered university politics opposing the government. After several arrests, in July he went to Miami and helped organize the youth section of the FRD. He at first intended to volunteer for the invasion brigade training in Guatemala but instead joined a paramilitary group outside New Orleans that set out to establish a guerrilla operation in Oriente. They never landed on the heavily guarded coast and were picked up by an American destroyer as the general invasion floundered.[67]

On returning to Miami, Mas Canosa remained committed to exile activism and in 1964 was among a group elected to lead Representación Cubana del Exilio (RECE) and served as editor of its newspaper.[68] Initially funded by "Pepín" Bosch, of the wealthy Bacardí rum producing family, RECE worked to unite the exile community. Working with RECE in the early 1970s, Mas Canosa, like others, came to the conclusion that the paramilitary path on its own offered little chance of removing the regime in Cuba, but he also saw an alternative.[69] As Mas Canosa increasingly engaged the domestic political system in the United States, he learned to negotiate the world of Washington, DC, including influencing politicians and public opinion. His new career as a successful south Florida construction entrepreneur provided resources and leverage to continue his political work. In Washington he laid out the case of Cuban activists and sought congressional support for exiles.

Exiles often tended to see U.S. political views of Cuba as homogeneous and monolithic, interpreting policies of a given administration as "American opinion." Mas Canosa understood the nation's complex politics and sought opportunities for influencing different political sectors. In 1969, for example, as the Nixon administration took office and rumors of détente emerged, Mas Canosa traveled to Washington and met with congressional officials. He reported to Cubans in Miami the many in Congress who, despite the administration's policies, expressed great sympathy for the exile cause and supported legislation to allow them greater freedom of action to work against Castro.[70] In 1973, Mas Canosa condemned the hijacking agreement with Cuba but also expressed very clearly his intention to maintain ongoing conversations with U.S. government officials. "We live in the United States," he said, "[and I] understand that the government of the

United States exerts influence on the international politics of all the nations in the world, including the Soviet Union. It would be a blunder on our part not to maintain a channel of communication with the United States government." He went on to speculate that it was probably the Soviet Union that forced Cuba to negotiate the hijacking agreement with the United States, suggesting that U.S. pressure on international actors could play a critical role in undermining Castro.[71] Mas Canosa went beyond lobbying the State Department and established good relations with Dade County Congressman Dante Fascell along with other state and federal representatives willing to listen to the exiles' views.

In 1975 he conducted a frenzied lobbying campaign against the OAS's decision to lift the hemispheric embargo and normalize relations with Cuba. He traveled to the OAS meetings and appeared on conservative William F. Buckley's television program *Firing Line,* in which he debated U.S. policy toward Cuba with journalist Tad Szulc. Through the auspices of Senator James Buckley of New York, he also appeared on the NBC television program *The Today Show,* intending to debate Senator George McGovern, who had just returned from a visit to Cuba and supported normalizing relations. Though that debate never took place, Mas Canosa did participate with a panel of Cuban exiles who delivered testimony and fielded questions for three hours before a House of Representatives Subcommittee on International Trade, arguing for the maintenance of the economic and diplomatic sanctions on the Castro government. When asked what motivated his activist zeal, he said, "A faith that comes from an ideal, not reason." "The faith of a Christian," he went on, "the faith of a patriot, the faith of those who seek justice, not only because one is anxious to triumph, but because it is just to do so." At the time he believed that the United States would probably move to normalize relations with Cuba, which he thought reflected one of the country's great weaknesses, the propensity toward pragmatism and materialist values and forgetting its foundational spiritual and transcendent ideals.[72]

In time, Mas Canosa's ideas coalesced with those of North American conservatives. His nationalism and anti-communism remained intact, but if ever he embraced the social doctrines of the church, they were not evident in his discourses. During the decade his public political persona diverged from those who remained active with the Christian Democratic Party. While Rasco, for example, remained identified with traditional Christian

Democratic politics in Latin America and Europe, Mas Canosa became a Cuban-American politician adopting a much broader national political focus in the United States though still primarily driven by wanting to bring change in his homeland. He changed his frame of reference from Latin American Christian Democracy to U.S. Republican Party ideas. Through his newspaper, Mas Canosa managed during the 1970s to establish himself as a well-known voice in the Miami community, and in 1980, with the election of Ronald Reagan, who received the overwhelming Cuban vote, and with the support of Republican Party activists, he and a group of businessmen forged a new political enterprise called the Cuban American National Foundation (CANF).

Another successful entrepreneur, José "Pepe" Hernández, with strong ties to Catholic activism in Cuba in the 1950s, joined Mas Canosa in founding CANF. Inspired in his youth by the social concerns of the church, Hernández joined the youth section of Catholic Action at the age of twelve and eventually became a national secretary. Though his father was a military officer, Hernández joined in anti-Batista activism when he entered the University of Havana in 1954. With the triumph of the Revolution he returned to the university, but became distraught and joined a clandestine resistance group after his father suffered arrest and execution in a matter of days without due process. In summer 1960, Hernández left Cuba and joined the Bay of Pigs invasion, after which he joined the U.S. Marines. He became an intelligence officer and worked for a time with Alexander Haig at the Pentagon. In the mid-1970s, Hernández left the military and founded a successful agro-industrial business with a strong international orientation.

During the next twenty years, CANF became the leading voice of the hard-line element in Miami. Hernández shared Mas Canosa's beliefs that exile interests could be best served by engaging with the U.S. political system, lobbying, and gaining influence.[73] CANF's goals remained the same during the 1980s and 1990s: to promote a hard-line exile perspective dedicated to isolating Cuba internationally, maintaining the embargo, and cultivating conditions that might force the fall of the Castro regime.[74] After two decades in the United States, exiles had discovered how to maneuver within the political system of their adopted home. Mas Canosa and Hernández exemplified how Cubans adapted their exile politics within the U.S. political system, developing ethnic political strategies to advance not only the interests of their communities but their goals as exiles. Most exiles supported the shift in strategy from primarily advocating independent paramilitary activities to engaging in sophisticated political lobbying in Washington, DC, to ensure a hard-line intransigent stance by the United States, as well as a continuing economic embargo and constant political harassment of the Cuban government.

Though engaged and active, exiles had little overall success in undermining the Cuban Revolution. For all their efforts in Latin America, they did not succeed in convincing the region's leaders to support a military intervention and overthrow of Castro. International realities made direct U.S. or OAS intervention in Cuba unlikely, despite their incessant lobbying in Latin America, through the press, and in the U.S. Congress. Exiles also learned in the 1970s that the U.S. government increasingly viewed normalization with Castro as inevitable and that only they remained staunch advocates of a hard-line approach. Summing up the situation in 1969, José Ignacio Rasco concluded that exiles could expect little help in their struggle. Despite the embargo, Rasco pointed to the existing commercial relationships of Canada and Western Europe with Cuba and the lack of all recognition by the democratic nations for a Cuban government-in-exile or belligerency status for exiles. Indeed, he concluded, "international communist solidarity has functioned with greater effectiveness than the supposed alliances among democratic countries."[75]

In a speech at the inauguration of the Bay of Pigs memorial in April 1971, Catholic and Brigade veteran Carlos Allen offered a similar analysis. Cubans could only count on themselves to rid Cuba of communism. "We have just commemorated . . . the passion, death and resurrection of Our Lord Jesus Christ," he noted, "and . . . we have to be aware that our *patria* is on the painful road to Calvary but that it will resuscitate one glorious day, to be free over the ashes of its most deserving children."[76] Many disillusioned Cubans turned away from exile activism but certainly maintained their intransigent position against the Cuban Revolution, consistently supporting hard-line policies of isolating Cuba diplomatically, politically, and economically whenever possible.

During their first twenty years in exile Cuban Catholics participated in creating a strident exile community informed by a strong sense of faith, national identity, anti-communism, and political activism. Inspired by the traumatic experiences of displacement from their country of origin and undeterred by their faith's theological strictures on war, they and other exiles participated in military efforts to overthrow the Castro regime and return home. In many ways they were a very isolated community, hurt by the loss of their homes, resentful of the lack of solidarity from Latin America and Europe, and confused about the seeming contradictions in U.S. policy that on the one hand ranted against the Castro regime but on the other was unwilling to take effective action. They felt abandoned as well as politically isolated. As exiles they learned to rely on themselves and to expect little support from the outside world for their point of view. In the years following 1980, with a ferocity reignited by the Mariel exodus, hardened Cuban exiles aligned themselves with the harsh politics of the Reagan years, and the communities became even more conservative, ideological, and intransigent. Confrontation politics with Cuba increased within the context of the aggressive U.S. stance toward the Nicaraguan revolution and other leftist insurgencies, especially in Central America. A significant sector of exile opinion, Catholic and otherwise, remained committed to a violent overthrow of the Castro government.

Chapter Seven

ETHNICITY AND RIGHTS

What is important is the mental attitude: that [exiles] . . . see participation in two cultures as a positive thing and not as a tragedy that one cannot escape.

—José I. Lasaga (1969)

At first, to honor their origins and as an expression of defiance and a commitment to return, Cuban exiles hoped to live in single-minded isolation from the host society while they battled to free Cuba from communism, but this never really happened. Despite their great reluctance, they integrated into new societies. Exiles engaged societies with values different from their own—a world with a diversity of ideas that could not be ignored. Regardless of the intensity of their homeward gaze, they always contended with the realities of everyday life outside of Cuba. Their need to work and care for their families, or simply survive, forced engagement with the world around them. Cubans became pragmatic, recognizing the limitations of exile ideals, and they devised survival strategies and inevitably compromised somewhat with their traditional instincts that demanded a single-minded focus on Cuba. Advancing their economic interests demanded time, politics multiplied the issues they contended with, and social realities and tensions encouraged them to find ways to protect their interests in a new society.

By the late 1960s, Cuban exile observers already studied and commented on issues of Cuban adaptation and integration. Studies by exile scholars Alejandro Portes and Rafael J. Prohías, for example, argued that Cubans accommodated well into economic life in the United States and for the most part viewed the society as welcoming. Portes's examination of Cuban families in Milwaukee revealed strong emotional and psychological solidarity among Cubans but also characteristics leading toward "a fundamental shift from strong psychological attachments to the past to values and identities congruent with the new environment" that predicted eventual assimilation. Cubans well understood the relationship between assimilation and the socioeconomic rewards of life in the United States.[1] At the same time, Prohías pointed out that Cubans in Indianapolis tended to deemphasize social integration into U.S. life, preferring the relative insularity of their own family and Cuban community networks. The three hundred or so Cubans in that city resided relatively close to each other, met socially, and remained quite separate from the dominant Anglo society.[2] Many of these Cubans only reluctantly changed their citizenship for very practical reasons, but they held hard and fast to their language, culture, and religious traditions. In south Florida, these seemingly contradictory forces of ethnic solidarity and integration observed among Cubans in the heartland of the United States actually coexisted and complemented each other.

By the end of their first decade in the United States, Cubans found themselves in the crosscurrents of exile and ethnic experiences. In Dade County an unrepentant and strongly identified Cuban exile community produced sufficient economic resources to defend an emerging ethnic consciousness and make affirmative decisions about the nature of their integration process. A strong Cuban identity contributed to a powerful communitarian solidarity that not only defined their attitude toward Cuba but also influenced decisions within the United States itself. Living in the "Cuban capitol" of the United States, Miami Cubans believed they could have it both ways. They could gain the socioeconomic rewards of life in the United States and at the same time remain committed to their culture of origin, even to the point of considerably refashioning many of Dade County's communities in their own image.[3]

Ethnicity and Culture

Cubans across the country certainly recognized the inevitability of some kind of integration into life in the United States, but what did adjustment to this new society really mean, and on whose terms? Cubans instinctively maintained their ways, but they also had to consider how best to insert themselves into North American society. Catholics approached the problem while maintaining a strong hold on faith and national traditions. Their emergent and distinct Catholic communities offered a concrete space from which to engage the broader society with a sense of purpose, self-confidence, and security. Cuban Catholics quickly perceived that their daily commitment to protecting family, promoting culture, and maintaining identity simply could not exist independently of the society around them, especially a society ideologically predisposed to assimilating all newcomers on its own terms. They recognized that life in the United States would influence their children and that they would have to be affirmative actors on their own behalf to ensure their children retained the possibility of living in a community that reflected their traditions.

Cuban integration occurred precisely during an era of great transformation for the U.S. church and society. The attitudes of Cubans arriving in the United States during the first half of the 1960s came into direct contact with the nativist and assimilationist attitudes that dominated U.S. Catholicism and society during most of the century. The closing of the U.S. border through the National Origins Act in 1924 had inspired an assimilation ethic that Cubans encountered on arriving in 1960 and 1961. Immigrants had routinely passed through "Americanization" programs of various kinds, including the public schools, and the World Wars promoted a nationalist and often xenophobic mentality that created incentives for newcomers to shed their language and cultural traditions.[4]

Cubans, however, arrived during a period of radical change in identity politics when the Civil Rights Movement openly challenged traditional notions of what it meant to be "American." Within this new environment, during the 1960s Cubans in south Florida created faith communities with a strong sense of their national identity and in the 1970s turned to seeking a measure of power to defend their traditions and expand their opportunities. During that first decade, Cubans believed that, one way or another,

Castro would fall, but their confidence waned as their second decade in exile began. Over the next ten years Cubans recognized that the political conditions allowing for a return might never materialize; it also occurred to them that even if something dramatic changed in Cuba, they and their children were already deeply marked by their time in the United States. Though most Cubans who arrived in the 1960s would never have immigrated to the United States—they had no need, since they represented the established sectors of Cuban society—now, after ten years, it was possible that they would not return even if the possibility presented itself. Cuba would be a different place, and in the event of a return many wondered whether they might not be received by a hostile population with significantly different ideological perspectives resentful of exiles for leaving during that time of great hardship. Many turned more fully toward integration into the United States.

The Cuban journey toward empowerment was reflected in their participation in the electoral system that produced Cuban municipal elected officials in the 1970s, Cuban representatives in the Florida legislature in the 1980s, and Cuban members of the U.S. Congress in the 1990s. They also struggled for cultural rights, perhaps most evident on the linguistic front, which caused much distress among Anglo-Americans in south Florida in the early 1970s, when it became evident that Cubans intended to retain their language. Though Cuban youth certainly routinely learned English, this was obscured by the continuing use of Spanish by adults and their children. Increasingly negative attitudes toward Cubans led to the founding of the Spanish American League against Discrimination (SALAD), an organization that not only fought anti-Cuban attitudes but affirmatively proclaimed the value of Cuban traditions. SALAD questioned the idea of a "melting pot" and argued that Cubans had the right to maintain their language and culture, which they did.[5] In the mid-1980s, more than half of Cubans spoke Spanish at work, and more than 70 percent used it in social situations. Overwhelmingly, the home language remained Spanish.[6]

When Anglo-Americans responded with criticism, Cubans vigorously defended their interests. These kinds of experiences combined with their strong sense of national identity gave birth to the ethnic dimension of the Cuban exile communities. Though still deeply committed to their exile identity, which they never abandoned during the first two decades outside Cuba, their ethnic reality in the United States became clear. While they became generally conservative politically, they exhibited considerable militancy when issues focused on their culture and traditions. Among Catholics, preserving ethnic Cubanness (or *cubanidad*) became perhaps their central concern after their faith.

Cuban Catholics engaged the problem of adaptation not from a purely intellectual perspective but from the inevitable questions that arose in their daily engagement with life in exile and the church. At the third annual meeting of the Movimiento Familiar Cristiano (MFC) in November 1966, for example, more than one hundred couples convened to consider "The Problem of the Cuban Exile in Miami in the Light of the Vatican Ecumenical Council."[7] With Bishop Eduardo Boza Masvidal in attendance from Venezuela and offering opening remarks of orientation and encouraging a strong sense of national identity, participants spent a full afternoon and evening in wide-ranging discussions covering issues such as identity, assimilation, language, economics, family problems associated with adaptation, religious pluralism, and many others. Cuban lay Catholics recognized that life in Miami required accommodations and adjustments to the realities and expectations of the North American environment. They concluded that Cubans should find a place between the "ghetto" and assimilation, but in their own way and according to their own traditions. Alluding to the Vatican Councils' exhortations that "it is an urgent obligation to feel absolutely connected to all" people, Cubans at the gathering urged their fellow Catholics to "take what is good from this society but contribute what is good of ours." Also, taking from the thought of Boza Masvidal, they saw no conflict in maintaining a "warm and profound" *cubanía* and at the same time seeking a "healthy and just integration."[8]

José Ignacio Lasaga also explored the complexity of this careful balance between exile and ethnic identity and integration into North American life, and he articulated these ideas in the conceptual language of the times. Throughout the 1960s and 1970s, Cuban exiles in fact succeeded quite well in maintaining a vibrant and vital Cuban identity in the lives of their children and, furthermore, in transforming the entire cultural landscape in south Florida. Certainly their nationalist zeal, their economic resources, and their huge numbers played a critical part in this process, but so did the shifting attitudes in the United States itself. During these two decades, changes in the North American political and cultural environment gave Cubans the flexibility to fulfill their need to remain connected to their culture and simultaneously make political and socioeconomic demands on the larger society.

Initially Lasaga had lived in Miami but then moved to Maryland to work as a clinical psychologist. There, he watched the Civil Rights Movement closely and listened intently to the emerging ethnic discourses, which encouraged him to reflect on the relationship between his own exile identity and life experiences in the United States. Shortly after his return to Miami in 1975, he spoke publicly to Cubans about issues of cultural integration and acculturation.[9] He drew a sharp distinction between national identity (maintaining an allegiance to a political state) and acculturation (a process of cultural adaptation). Cubans could maintain their sense of exile nationality, he asserted, and at the same time undergo a process of accommodation in the United States, which would not imply relinquishing their basic cultural characteristics or a claim on their homeland identity.

Lasaga characterized the assimilation ideas of "Anglo-conformity" and "melting pot" as inimical to the survival of a basic Cuban cultural expression; both would suffocate Cuban culture and identity. Cubans should be thankful to Blacks, he said, "for the push they gave the Civil Rights movement in this country, which has contributed to changing the melting pot philosophy." In the 1970s, he observed, as a result of the work of Black activists, the United States had initiated a journey toward greater tolerance and diversity. Within this more flexible social context, Cubans could struggle to maintain their culture, respecting Lincoln and Jefferson and at the same time valuing the Cuban patriot figures Antonio Maceo and José Martí. Also, when necessary, Cubans could insist on their own ways and reject aspects of U.S. culture. Lasaga counseled his compatriots to reject assimilation— that is, abandoning Cuban identity and culture in favor of "American" culture. He advocated cultural pluralism, an approach he felt allowed Cubans to maintain an exile identity while at the same time integrating into U.S. society on their own terms. Lasaga did not see a contradiction; Cubans could be exiles as well as ethnic Cuban-Americans.[10] Cubans did not generally use the language of cultural pluralism and did not at this time often refer to themselves as Cuban-Americans, preferring to call themselves *exilidados* or *cubanos,* but their actions did reveal an appreciation for the importance of finding their place within U.S. society, not only as exiles but also as an ethnic community invested with legitimacy and access to power. "What is important is the mental attitude," Lasaga declared, "that [exiles] . . . see participation in two cultures as a positive thing and not as a tragedy that one cannot escape."[11]

The discourse of cultural pluralism, of course, reflected the emergence of a bicultural and bilingual community reality, a difficult phenomenon in itself, especially for children. Lasaga argued that the assimilative forces of the dominant society would especially influence the culture and identity of Cuban children. This was natural and not necessarily bad but did require the community itself to take an active role instilling their children with pride and commitment to their culture of origin. Only by actively and consciously promoting a bicultural ethic among children would *cubanidad* survive at all. Cubans were not helpless in the face of these assimilative pressures, though they had to approach the problem with caution and wisdom. He counseled Cuban families to be alert to the possible sense of marginalization a bicultural experience could create among children. It was important to be realistic and express a positive attitude toward the United States while at the same time constantly exposing them to their culture of origin, not as an imposition but as an ideal, and reinforcing their identity as exiles, not immigrants. This commitment to an exile identity would instill a sense of allegiance and commitment to their homeland in a way an immigrant mind-set would not. By remaining aware and accepting their children's inevitable embrace of many aspects of U.S. culture, parents would maintain a good relationship with their children, who in turn would maintain a positive attitude toward their culture of origin. In all of this, maintaining the Spanish language remained the central vehicle for ensuring authentic cultural vibrancy of everyday life. Children should of course learn English as native speakers, Lasaga argued, but Spanish should remain the language of the household, reinforced by formal language training in school or with private lessons after school.[12]

This concern about guiding children through a bicultural integrative process also received considerable attention in church organizations and the Catholic press. MFC, for example, always conducted their meetings in Spanish and discussed the complexities of language maintenance in their new environment, especially for their children. They advised Cubans to use Spanish with their children and send them to Spanish-language programs offered throughout the community by church and patriotic organizations. Using Spanish would not only enhance communication in the family but also provide the means for maintaining a strong sense of identity with Cuban culture and identity.[13]

Other lay organizations working with youth also took special care to keep them connected to their cultural origins. Encuentros Juveniles especially focused on this. At one meeting, "in the small living room there are some thirty young boys shouting and singing. One has an afro haircut, all wear their hair longish—but not too much—they are happy youngsters and a little crazy." Despite their "modern" expressions, characteristic of youth culture of the 1970s, the reporter concluded, all of those gathered, playing conga drums and communicating in the Spanish language, embraced Catholicism in an environment that was wholly Cuban.[14] Through these kinds of activities, Cuban Catholic youth remained in touch with their faith, culture, and language.

In the mid-1970s, the Spanish language insert of *The Voice* included a series, "Tú y tus hijos" (You and Your Children), by Dr. Elvira Dopico. Her ideas reminiscent of Lasaga's, she counseled parents on practical methods for adapting their children to the U.S. education system while at the same time instilling Cuban identity. As students became comfortable with English and engaged U.S. society and schools, she advised parents to keep them steeped in their own traditions while also demonstrating patience when they inevitably articulated concerns or even rejected aspects of their culture of origin. Inevitably, she cautioned, parents would perceive not necessarily a generation but rather a cultural gap that they would need to accept with maturity, openness, and dialogue, accepting their children's bicultural interpretations at the same time that they encouraged close ties to their culture of origin.[15]

Cuban seminarians and priests in the United States adapted to this bicultural reality and inevitably developed a Cuban-American ethnic identity. Initially, young seminarians viewed their activities as temporary, and most planned to return to a post-Castro Cuba that would need priests to re-create the nation on a firm Catholic foundation. As one priest noted, this was not the first time churches under communist regimes formed priests outside their country intending to return home. "I want to do something for Christ and for Cuba," said one, and certainly everyone expected the seminarians to return home at the appointed moment.[16] Present at the ordination of Daniel Sánchez in 1962, Bishop Boza Masvidal reminded the new priest that he must pray for Cuba and those still there, including his parents, and especially for those dying and suffering in jail, reinforcing the idea that in the end Cuba should remain his first priority. In time, however, seminarians and priests understood their work would not be in Cuba, but among Hispanics in the United States and more particularly in south Florida.

Recognizing this, the archdiocesan major seminary St. Vincent de Paul, in Boynton Beach, formally established a bilingual curriculum in 1972, and new seminarians brought with them a bicultural reality. Prominent Mexican American theologian Father Virgil Elizondo celebrated this development, the first of its kind, as "a source of hope and optimism in the church's efforts to meet the cultural and spiritual needs of the Spanish speaking people of the United States."[17] In 1980, at age thirty-four, Father Felipe Estevez became rector of the seminary. A Peter Pan child who arrived at age fifteen in 1961, Estevez grew up in Ft. Wayne, Indiana, and trained at Gregorian University in Rome. Still driven by the idea of going back to Cuba, Estevez requested permission to return and minister in his home province of Matanzas, only to be denied by Cuban authorities. Instead, Estevez ministered to Hispanics in the United States and as rector of the seminary promoted a multicultural environment that prepared seminarians to labor with the Latino population in the United States.[18] Though still deeply connected to their language and culture, seminarians also assumed characteristics of a "Cuban-American generation." As one observer noted, they want to make a reality of Bishop Boza Masvidal's thought to "love Cuba and integrate into the country in which we live."[19]

Cuban Catholics also looked to the theological traditions of their church for understanding and legitimacy of their strong claims to cultural rights and ethnic pluralism. Throughout the 1960s and 1970s, church documents supported the cultural diversity of Catholic expressions. In 1961, for example, Pope John XXIII's *Mater et Magistra* directly addressed the issue of national minorities, noting that while they should take care not to become overly ethnocentric and isolated from the society around them, government authorities should recognize "it is especially in keeping with the principles of justice that effective measures be taken by the civil authorities to improve the lot of the citizens of an ethnic minority." This included respecting "their language, the development of their natural gifts, their ancestral customs, and their accomplishments and endeavors in the economic order."[20]

Several years later, Vatican II document *Gaudium et Spes* reiterated the need to encourage Christian development within the context of particular cultures. "Culture, since it flows from man's rational and social nature, has continual need of rightful freedom of development and a legitimate possibility of autonomy according to its own principles. Quite rightly it demands respect and enjoys a certain inviolability, provided, of course, that the rights of the individual and the community, both particular and universal, are safeguarded within the limits of the common good."[21] Another Vatican II document, *Ad Gentes,* also addressed culture in its call for a renewal in the theoretical and practical approaches to missionary activity. In part, this document responded to the concerns of people around the world who increasingly resented the Vatican's historical and almost unquestioned colonialist proposition that genuine Christianity required a Western cultural overlay. Colonialist mentalities had to give way to an acceptance of the diversity of cultures and their Catholic expressions. In order to advance the universal church evangelization had to take into account and adapt to the specific cultural forms and expressions of particular societies.[22]

The Vatican's apostolic delegate to the U.S. church, Archbishop Jean Jadot, elaborated on the idea of pluralism in more concrete terms to a Cuban audience in *The Voice* in 1976. He emphasized the importance of the efforts by the church in the United States in recent years to be inclusive of Blacks, Hispanics, and others. "Perhaps for too long," he noted, the church in the United States had "remained under the pressure of the Anglo-American tradition, as if it were the only one." At the same time, extremism had to be avoided. "Pluralism is diversity in unity," he argued, not conformity or fragmentation. These ideas were central to the pope's conceptualization of evangelization, "which would lose all force and effectiveness if not expressed in the language, the signs and the symbols of those being evangelized." The Gospels had to respond to the particular questions of the faithful in order to truly impact their lives.[23]

Claiming Rights

Cuban Catholics brought with them into exile fully defined notions about how to organize their lives as well as a highly politicized consciousness about who they were and why they were in the United States. From the very start, Cubans informed their participation in U.S. life through their experience of exile and desire to return home. Catholics in Miami at first understood accommodation as re-creating as faithfully as possible the Cuban community they had known on the island: a community that reflected their faith traditions and material culture, a community that could offer a daily counterpoint and response to the situation at home. Defending the integrity of their community demanded a determined, indeed often militant *cubanidad* that guided their integration process into North American society as much as possible on their own terms.

Despite their own goals for accommodation, Cuban Catholics, much to their surprise, found that their idea of accommodation and integration differed considerably from the expectations of North American society, which, they soon learned, fully expected all newcomers to thoroughly assimilate. Indeed, the determination of Cubans to maintain their ways ran contrary to the expectations of the Irish-American–led church in Miami and quickly provoked tensions. Miami bishop Coleman Carroll and his staff worked hard and effectively for Cubans arriving in south Florida, but their basic assumptions about how best to accommodate the exiles immediately clashed with the Cubans' independent spirit and firm opposition to assimilation. The establishment by Cubans in 1961 of the Committee of Catholic Organizations in Exile (COCCE) to coordinate activities among exile Catholics immediately raised concerns. Bishop Carroll thought this and other similar Cuban Catholic organizations that formed spontaneously in exile without the sponsorship of the diocesan church could easily become a de facto ethnic church with a specific political agenda. An aide to the bishop, Msgr. John J. Fitzpatrick, argued that it would be a mistake to authorize the establishment in Miami of a large number of Cuban lay organizations, each with its own leadership. Cubans acted quite independently and demonstrated great loyalty to individual leaders, like the Protestants, he noted, a trait that would lead to disunity.[24]

Fitzpatrick nevertheless met with COCCE leadership in November 1961 and developed a plan for coordinating activities between the diocese and Cuban lay organizations.[25] All agreed to collaborate to develop plans to engage the mass of Cuban exiles arriving in Miami, resulting in February 1962 in the establishment of an office headed by Fitzpatrick to serve the needs of the Spanish-speaking Catholics in south Florida and to connect them directly to the church. His two assistants, Father Angel Vizcarra, a Spanish priest and vicar provincial of the Dominican Fathers of Santo Domingo, and Father Eugenio del Busto, a Cuban exile from the diocese of Matanzas, served as liaisons to the Cuban community.[26]

While the meeting served as a useful initial conversation between diocesan and Cuban Catholic leaders, it also made clear the bishop's opposition to the maintenance or creation of separate Cuban Catholic institutions. The bishop encouraged Cubans to carry out their activities within the structures of the diocesan church and avoid the creation of ethnic or national parishes or even Cuban lay organizations that would separate parishioners culturally and threaten divisions within the diocese. He counseled assimilation as the only way of maintaining conformity and unity in his diocese—a policy that reflected not only his own personal wishes but also the policies of the U.S. church.[27] The bishop did initially succeed in frustrating Cuban intentions to transfer their lay institutions intact from Cuba to Miami; the bishop's task was made easier by the differences in diocesan organizational tradition in the two countries. Once in Miami, Cuban lay leaders had to adjust to the centrality of the parishes, making it difficult for the independent-minded lay leaders to reestablish organizations as they had existed in Cuba.

The JEC offered one example of the difficulties Cubans faced in transferring their organizations directly from Cuba. An important and long-standing lay movement in Cuba during the 1940s and 1950s, JEC formed again in Miami in February 1961. Bishop Carroll hesitantly approved a request to establish the organization—and only with the stipulations that it would be responsible to the diocese, work through the parishes, avoid political activity, and refrain from identifying itself as "Cuban." Though JEC remained active for sometime, it often faced the outright opposition of North American priests, who apparently resented the encroachments on their own work with parish youth. In time JEC disappeared, unable to gain sufficient support in the parishes. The bishop's opposition to Cuban lay movements, except in the case of ACU, and the prominence of the parishes made the transplanting of Cuba's lay organizations intact all but impossible.[28] Cubans did nevertheless create new Cuban institutions in exile, and although they always held Bishop Carroll and local church officials in high esteem for their unwavering support of Cuban refugees throughout the 1960s and 1970s, they never accepted their assimilation policy.

Throughout the 1960s, Cuban and other Hispanic, mostly Spanish priests also felt uncomfortable with the bishop's openly stated assimilation policy. The Cubans in particular resented the hierarchy's unwillingness to tolerate their militant anti-communism, which the bishop no doubt thought fueled political nationalism and worked against unity within the diocese. In this regard, early talk of bringing the popular bishop and activist Boza Masvidal from Venezuela to work in Miami quickly diminished in the face of opposition among non-Cuban church leaders in Miami. "It wasn't accidental [that he remained in Venezuela]," remembered Msgr. Bryan Walsh.[29] Many Cuban priests felt marginal and dismissed. In a meeting with the diocesan clergy in 1962, Carroll went out of his way to assure the Cuban priests that he considered them an essential part of the operation of the dioceses and integral members of the parishes in which they worked. Nevertheless, as late as 1976, one North American parish priest writing to the Priests' Senate noted that Hispanic priests "should conduct themselves with the humility of gratitude rather than request prerogatives to which they have no right. With some exceptions they are refugees and completely dependent on the generosity of the archbishop and the priests of this archdiocese."[30] In the early years Carroll hoped to enhance assimilation by posting Spanish-speaking priests in as many parishes as possible to generally assist Anglo-American pastors, learn English, and become familiar with North American cultural practices. This policy was also apparently calculated to encourage Cubans to attend church in the parishes in which they lived and to ensure uniformity in liturgical practice so Cubans would not be drawn to a particular "Cuban" church with distinct worship practices.[31] Despite the fact that this policy actually helped institutionalize the use of Spanish across the diocese, many Cuban priests nevertheless interpreted the policy as part of the diocesan assimilation strategy and let the hierarchy know of their concerns.[32]

In 1966, perhaps in response, the Hispanic priests formed their own organization, separate from the Priest's Senate, called the Asociación Sacerdotal Hispana (ASH). Comprised of some twenty-nine priests, ASH elected Cuban Jorge Bez Chabebe president, José M. de La Paz (Spanish) secretary, and I. Pertika (Basque) treasurer. By 1980 the membership had increased to more than one hundred. Inspired by the Vatican Council's concern for issues of pluralism and ethnic minorities and to promote fraternity and solidarity among the Spanish-speaking priests, the group defined its work as supporting the spiritual welfare of Hispanics but also defending their culture, "which is a rich contribution to this country and the church." ASH spearheaded efforts among priests to resist efforts by the church, and society in general, to persuade Hispanics to embrace the dominant culture. They worked to implement liturgical reform, developing, for example, a special *misalito* and a repertoire of songs that provided liturgical unity for the diocese's Spanish-language masses. Published in 1968, the *misalito* was used in Spanish-language liturgies across the United States.[33]

By the late 1960s, ethnic tensions already were evident in Miami and language politics became a flashpoint. Intent on institutionalizing Spanish-language education in schools, Cubans took creative measures and pioneered bilingual education in Miami schools. In 1963, Coral Way Elementary School offered classes in English and Spanish. Receiving funds from the Cuban Refugee Program, Dade County public school bilingual instructional programs became prototypes for the national bilingual movement.[34] By 1968, the archdiocese had accepted bilingual programs in Miami's parochial schools for both English- and Spanish-speaking students, initiating the first effort at St. Michael's the Archangel School. In the morning, students learned in English and after lunch in Spanish.[35]

These developments caused considerable resentment among some, and anti-Cuban attitudes spilled onto the pages of *The Voice,* causing outrage among Cubans, Catholic and otherwise. In 1968, the newspaper published a letter to the editor that, among other things, declared Cubans to be "a dirty, lazy, filthy lot." "They got thrown out of Cuba and so now we have them," the letter declared. "We poor slobs have to pay taxes to give them free rides from Cuba, and then support them and their families." The writer, obviously reacting to the bilingual programs in the schools, continued: "We pay school taxes to teach their brats English, and they come out of school talking that yap yap yap of their own, and expect us to go to school to learn their language." The anonymous writer asked the church, "How would you like to see some damn Cubans who can't talk, telling the congregation to go to school to learn their language?" Though *The Voice's* editorial policy normally included editorial rebuttals immediately below the letters they disagreed with, no rebuttal appeared in this case. *The Voice* apologized for "the oversight," and the editor of the newspaper's Spanish-language insert engaged in damage control, reminding Cubans that the weekly had always supported the community and should not be condemned for one error. Cubans forgave, but many obviously felt betrayed and, given all of the tensions, perhaps wondered whether the "oversight" had actually been intended as a message for their community.[36]

The language issue continued to heighten ethnic tensions throughout the 1970s. In 1972, *The Voice's* Spanish-language editor, Gustavo Peña, expressed support for an initiative by two Cuban community leaders, Alfredo Durán and Luis Figueroa, recommending that the Dade County Commission ensure the hiring of bilingual personnel in county offices, especially telephone operators, workers in emergency centers, police, firefighters, and employees of Jackson Memorial Hospital. A letter to the editor protested bitterly, declaring that "English is our country's national language, the same language that millions of immigrants from all over the world learned." "Every conscious person," the writer added, "whatever his country of origin, who wants to be considered a citizen of this country, should make a special effort to learn our language."[37] A year after this exchange, the Dade County Commission approved an ordinance making the county officially bilingual, and in 1976 the *Miami Herald* began publishing a Spanish-language edition, further highlighting the growing influence of the Spanish-speaking in south Florida.

This Cuban commitment to bilingualism in 1980 provoked a strong backlash within the non-Hispanic community, resulting in a referendum that overturned the county's bilingual ordinance; 71 percent and 56 percent of non-Hispanic Whites and Blacks respectively voted to rescind the 1973 measure, while 85 percent of Hispanics voted to maintain official bilingualism.[38] This highly polarized referendum inspired the Cuban community to engage local politics more seriously, and by the end of the decade they dominated south Florida's electoral politics.[39]

While most North Americans, including some church leaders, seemed to resent the Cubans' insistence on maintaining their cultural ways and strong political views regarding Cuba, others recognized the need for accommodating the Cuban community. Irish-born Msgr. Bryan Walsh, who in 1968 became the director for the Spanish-speaking apostolate (replacing Fitzpatrick, who had headed the office since its creation in 1961), became a leader in this regard. Much attuned to the needs of the Cuban community, he initiated a shift in diocesan policy. He pushed for more Hispanic parish administrators, promoted Hispanic vocations by advocating for the bilingual seminary, opened the diocese to more Hispanic religious communities, and generally initiated a move away from the bishop's assimilation policy.[40] In addition, when Carroll became archbishop in 1968, many of the leaders of the Cuban apostolic movements received invitations to attend the installation ceremony—a first step toward the formal recognition of these movements by the diocese. Walsh served until 1973, when Orlando

Fernández replaced him; Fernández was the first Cuban to hold a significant diocesan office.[41]

All of this certainly represented progress for Cubans, but Archbishop Carroll continued to resist Cuban demands for greater freedom of cultural and political expression and more authority within the diocesan church, which was by now heavily Hispanic, including immigrants from Latin America. Disagreements over how to respond to the situation in Cuba also remained a source of friction between exiles and the church in Miami. Archbishop Carroll's concern about the political activism of Cuban exiles, for example, led him in August 1972 to prohibit Father Ramón O'Farrill, a popular and well-known Cuban priest, from delivering an invocation in Spanish at an ecumenical meeting during the 1972 Republican National Convention. Earlier, another popular and activist priest, Bez Chabebe, the first president of the Hispanic clergy's association, who had "carried out denunciations against communism and in support of the Cuban cause," was removed from his position as assistant at San Juan Bosco and transferred to New York. Pro-Castro in the late 1950s, Bez Chabebe remained an activist in exile but now denouncing the communist regime. In late 1961, for example, he published a series of articles in *The Voice* about the betrayal of the Cuban Revolution by Castro and his communist backers.[42] One Cuban newspaper complained of these slights, suggesting to the archbishop that "rather than persecuting those meritorious soldiers of Christ, Monsignor Carroll should discipline the many North American priests who are spreading doctrines contrary to the Church and the democratic system and who possess damaging attitudes toward the traditions and obligations of the priesthood."[43]

The Cuban clergy's conflicts with the archbishop arose not only in relation to Cuba politics but also with regard to their treatment within the diocese. The same newspaper article reporting the O'Farrill incident also pointed out that four other Cuban priests in conflict with Carroll had asked for a transfer out of the diocese or altogether abandoned the priesthood. Father Daniel Sánchez, the first Cuban ordained in exile in a much celebrated ordination in 1962, found himself ten years later pumping gas, "after he felt obligated to ask for a leave of absence, since Msgr. Carroll would not let him work [*dejarlo tranquilo*], transferring him constantly from parish to parish." Another "victim," according to the press report, was Father Eugenio del Busto, who had worked with Msgr. Fitzpatrick in the diocesan office for Hispanic affairs but was "removed without explanation" and later, while working at St. Robert Bellarmine Parish, had a run-in with the archbishop that caused him to leave his position and ultimately the priesthood. Yet another, Father Martínez, who worked with prisoners at the county jail, was expelled from Miami over the opposition of his Jesuit superiors. The article noted that the Cuban Christian Brothers running the La Salle School were also forced to leave the diocese.[44]

In 1975, disagreements between Cuban clergy and the diocese became even more aggravated and public. In June, a Cuban priest, Carlos M. Hernández, gave a sermon in which he criticized the hierarchy for not giving Hispanic priests a voice in the ecclesiastic policy-making process and for marginalizing them by constantly moving them from position to position within the diocese. He urged Latin parishioners to "organize and demand their rights," then resigned, and asked for a transfer out of the archdiocese. Hernández's concerns no doubt stemmed from the practical application of the archbishop's insistence on promoting Cuban assimilation in the diocese. In response to Hernández's resignation, the Hispanic clergy association issued a carefully worded declaration, signed by thirty-six priests, confirming the legitimacy of the complaints but denying that it represented a conscious strategy by the hierarchy to keep Cuban priests marginalized. At the same time, they appealed to the people to express their opinions on these issues, publicly or privately, but in the spirit of "truth, justice, love, and liberty."[45]

A newly formed Spanish-speaking lay pastoral coordinating group followed with a letter to the archbishop reiterating the grievances of the Cuban community and insisting that the Hispanic laity was perfectly capable of contributing to the church despite the hierarchy's lack of confidence. The letter called for the naming of a Hispanic auxiliary bishop and complained that the hierarchy and many North American priests failed to recognize the importance of the numerous Hispanic apostolic movements working among Spanish-speaking Catholics. The following month, tensions became even more public with the publication of an article in the *New York Times* reporting the large number of south Florida Hispanics leaving the church, citing estimates of forty to sixty thousand in recent years. Critics blamed this flight to Protestantism and Afro-Cuban traditions on a "breakdown in communication between the predominantly Irish hierarchy and the mass of Latin parishioners" and "frustration, disillusionment, and alienation felt by many Hispanic parishioners."[46]

An editorial in *The Voice* by Father Luís Oraa framed the problem and offered solutions that required paying attention to "the signs." Certain words and phrases, he noted, had to be buried, including "accommodation," "conformity," "that's the way it has always been done," and "nothing can be done." Many attitudes prevailed, including those who ignored the situation, those who violently repressed the problem, those who supported "Americanization," those who thought nothing could change, and those who saw in conflict a clear call by God for internal conversion and an external dedication. He called for the church to move from an administrative to a pastoral structure, from bureaucracy to community, and from an exclusively individual orientation to a collective vision. Moses, he reminded his readers, took Israel into the desert, but each time difficulties like hunger, uncertainty, and sand storms appeared, the Israelites were tempted to return to their slavery. "It's human to encounter difficult and dark times, and today everyone speaks of crisis, but hopefully we will never look back, like the Israelites in the desert, simply for wanting to overcome."[47]

In 1976, this conflict between Cuban Catholics and the diocese came to a culmination when the Vatican's apostolic delegate to the United States in Washington, DC, announced the appointment of Bishop Edward McCarthy of Phoenix as coadjutor archbishop of Miami with the right to succession to Archbishop Carroll.[48] Though neither the Vatican nor the diocese offered specific reasons for the measure, a local Miami Cuban newspaper reported that the Vatican had for some time been aware of the conflicts between the Cuban priests and laity and the archbishop, "who has for several years persecuted numerous Cuban priests and given little importance and consideration to Cuban and Latin Catholic militancy that at the moment is almost 60 percent of Catholics in the community, estimated at 689,300 persons." The newspaper also reported that "there is jubilation among Cuban priests and laity over the Pope's decision," reminding readers that Carroll had excluded "one of the most prestigious and beloved chiefs of the Cuban Catholic Church, Msgr. Eduardo Boza Masvidal, from all positions of importance in the Archdiocese of Miami."[49] The following year, the archbishop, who had been quite sick and deeply angered by events, died. His *New York Times* obituary offered a similar interpretation regarding his retirement. "Latin Catholics," the newspaper noted, "had complained that Archbishop Carroll showed little interest in establishing close contacts with Latin parishioners . . . [and] . . . that the chancery was trying to Anglicize the archdiocese by limiting Spanish-language education in parish schools and Spanish-language masses."[50]

Whatever the precise reasons for Carroll's removal, certainly it came at a time of considerable turmoil in south Florida and changing attitudes within the U.S. Catholic church. Responding to the Vatican Council's call for the recognition of Catholic diversity, the U.S. church spoke to the issue in a statement on the occasion of the bicentennial in 1976, recognizing that "our society is not a melting pot, but is composed of a rich diversity of ethnic, racial and cultural groups" and that the church leadership "recognizes and appreciates the right of diverse ethnic, racial and cultural groups to maintain and develop their traditional culture."[51] The new archbishop certainly embraced this attitude.

Installed on September 17, 1976, Archbishop Edward McCarthy seemed a good match for Miami and set out to heal the deep ethnic divisions in the community. One Cuban newspaper noted that he had carried out good work in Phoenix among Hispanics, was a modest man, and had even learned Spanish during his time in Arizona.[52] At his installation he told his audience that he had come to Miami to build bridges of comprehension, harmony, and mutual cooperation, and his message included two paragraphs in Spanish that offered special tribute to Cubans and all Hispanics in the archdiocese.[53] In addition he offered a special greeting to Hispanic Catholics, expressing his pride at being among them and his anticipation of getting to know them, including their culture and "that faith and devotion, so worthy of admiration, that characterizes them."[54] He also accepted a list of grievances from the Hispanic lay pastoral group, which asked that Hispanic priests be given greater consideration, Spanish use be openly accepted in majority Hispanic parishes, Spanish be taught more extensively in parochial schools, Hispanic churches be given names in Spanish, and more Hispanics be named to diocesan positions, including auxiliary bishop.[55]

Within ten days of his installation, McCarthy celebrated his first Spanish Mass at San Juan Bosco, in the heart of Little Havana. The day before, without notice, he visited the participants of an Encuentro Familiar meeting at the seminary where he resided, praising their work and meeting with their spiritual counselors—in effect, recognizing the Cuban apostolic movements that Carroll had maintained at arm's length. In December, the archbishop appeared on Spanish-language radio, La Fabulosa, for three consecutive days to speak about the church with local radio personality

Tomás Regalado. McCarthy again congratulated Cubans for their activism in creating apostolic organizations, which he saw not as a threat to the larger church but rather as complementary. "I think," he said, "that this does not present a threat to the larger community which is the parish." "They are the same people," he emphasized, "but I think they need both experiences. They need to participate in the liturgy of the larger community, and they need also the experience of being together in small groups." He promised to maintain a close relationship with the Hispanic community and work to increase their representation in diocesan offices. He made clear his intention to listen to Cubans and bring them closer to the diocesan church.[56]

New Perspectives

Cuban Catholics also struggled to better understand dimensions of their own cultural traditions that at home they had not often bothered to examine. Within the context of the ethnic pluralism they advocated for themselves in the United States, some turned their attention to the disturbing reports that exile Cubans were abandoning their Catholic faith in large numbers. Catholic leaders were particularly surprised and distressed to learn of the significant numbers of Cubans in this overwhelmingly white population that turned to Santería. The many *botánicas* (stores that sell plants and artifacts for Santería ceremonies) inspired much interest and considerable comment from the press.[57] Catholic leaders feared that Santería's historical relationship to Catholicism and use of Catholic saints as central symbols of faith "confused" many unchurched nominal Catholics who did not distinguish between the traditions. Some speculated that exile simply uncovered an already established devotion to Santería among white Cubans, even of the middle classes, that became apparent in Miami, where they felt freer to display their faith. Others argued that Vatican II's changes in the liturgy and the church generally during this time of particular vulnerability for exiles alienated many Catholics deeply tied to their traditional religious symbolism and rituals.[58]

Jesuit priest Luís Oraa attributed the growth of Santería and Protestantism alike to a failure of pastoral strategies, while Father Agustín Román pointed to a general lack of available information on the socio-religious reality in Miami that would guide the development of an effective evangelization plan. Father Bryan Walsh believed the numbers to be exaggerated but, in any case, speculated that those "converting" to the other traditions were probably nominal, unchurched Catholics, rather than those who already arrived in Miami as committed Catholics. "The issue then really is not one of active practical Spanish speaking Catholics leaving the church in Miami," Walsh noted, "but rather one of what the Church must do to evangelize the great mass of Spanish speaking people who have little more, if any, than a nominal relationship with the institutional Church." He believed that Cubans had faith but little understanding of the Catholic Church and that this presented a challenge.[59]

Whatever the reality, some thought that the church should work to counteract defections. In 1976, for example, Miguel Cabrera, lay leader of the *cursillo* movement in south Florida, cited the growth of "Santeria, spiritism, horoscopes and other religious deviations" as a sign of the need for greater evangelization and clarity about the faith.[60] While in agreement about the need for evangelization, others cautioned that this should proceed according to the new sensibilities. In Cuba, Catholics had generally viewed Santería as a remnant of nineteenth-century slavery to be dismissed as a primitive superstition that would eventually disappear. Certainly it was not to be taken seriously. In exile, however, some Catholics developed different attitudes inspired by the church itself. In general, Vatican II encouraged a greater spirit of tolerance for non-Catholic traditions, as did other papal documents. In 1975, for example, Pope Paul VI's encyclical *Evangelli Nuntiandi* asserted that particular cultural expressions in "search for God and for faith," often referred to as popular religiosity, if well oriented "manifests a thirst for God which only the simple and poor can know." While teaching Catholic orthodoxy, the church encouraged tolerance, respect, and sensitivity for their "undeniable value."[61] Influenced by this new thinking, some clergy encouraged exiles to engage Santería with new sensibilities, as a legitimate Cuban expression that, though not Catholic, was certainly tied to the development of Catholicism historically.

In 1976, Father Felipe Estevez, soon to be named rector of the seminary at Boynton Beach, thought about methods for approaching practitioners of Santería. He observed the attractiveness of the tradition among Cubans in south Florida, pointing to its many devotions and manifestations among Cubans in Miami, including devotions to San Lázaro ("not the one of the crutches"), Santa Bárbara (the Santería goddess), the *botánicas*, and relics of San Antonio María Claret (the Cuban saint). These kinds of popular traditions, he argued, were not new; they had existed since the Middle Ages, but what was different was the new interest among theologians and pastors about these practices. The Vatican Council documents, Estevez emphasized, called for a sympathetic approach to this phenomenon and the abandonment of the judgmental and elitist attitudes that generally predominated in the church. Evangelizing within the context of popular Catholicism required an open and flexible attitude, even perhaps encouraging a diversity of expressions beyond the Mass, which would reflect the folkloric cultural and religious traditions of the people. In this way the church would reveal a clearer testimonial of its universal nature. "For the people to become more Christian," Estevez concluded, "Christianity had to become more popular."[62]

Others looked at the issues from a theological point of view. Ordained in 1972, Father Juan Sosa began a serious study of Santería in the early 1970s, which he wrote about in *The Voice* and other Catholic publications, becoming the most prominent church voice on the topic. Inspired by changes in church attitudes toward non-Catholic traditions articulated in Vatican II documents, Sosa challenged Catholics to better understand Santería and encouraged those who practiced both traditions to understand the differences between the two. It was important to distinguish between Santería and Catholicism but recognize the former as a popular and legitimate community religious expression that Catholics should respect and understand. Even before Estevez, Sosa called on Catholics to recognize that Santería was not witchcraft (*brujería*), *vudú,* spiritism, or a satanic cult. Rather, Santería was an African religious tradition brought by slaves and wrapped in Catholic symbols and expressions. Viewing Santería with scorn and contempt served only to further distance its practitioners of this "primitive faith" from the Gospels. Santería revealed humankind's need for God, and this had to be respected. At the same time, he said that Santería reflected a truncated religion that did not believe in the possibility of a strong personal relationship between the individual and God. The task of the Catholic was not to judge and ridicule but to understand and evangelize everyone seeking God.[63] This evangelization included accompanying people searching for God within their own faith experiences.[64] Though still approaching Santería with a condescending attitude, exile Catholics began to see the Afro-Cuban religious tradition as a legitimate aspect of Cuban culture, something that only seemed relevant to them once they left home and engaged with what they viewed as an alien Protestant society.

Ethnicity and Social Activism

A growing Cuban-American ethnic consciousness also influenced the way Cubans practiced social activism, which for many remained firm as they sought ways to engage the realities of the United States. This impulse came not only from their tradition of social awareness in Cuba and the reinvigorated focus on social matters by the universal church but also as a result of the intense, ethnically based social movements in the United States itself.

In the early 1960s, Catholics in south Florida publicly restated their commitment to the social dimensions of their faith, most prominently through the Institute of Social Action. Even in the face of the trauma of exile, they dedicated time to teaching the traditional social encyclicals they had embraced and advocated in Cuba. Despite these initial efforts in the 1960s by former Catholic Action militants to convince their compatriots of the need to maintain social concerns, enthusiasm dissipated as they dealt with daily life in south Florida. While the church's social teachings still appealed to their sense of justice and continued to be articulated, the manner in which they had thought about the issues while in Cuba did not seem to fit their new environment. At home in Cuba, Catholics had begun to play a role in politics and advocated greater national attention to social problems. This changed in the United States, where they represented a tiny minority, marginal within the political system. Even if inclined to take part in reform movements, they did not really know how to proceed within the context of the United States, a highly decentralized nation with complex institutions dispersed throughout local, national, and federal governments. The exile communities as a whole became ambivalent at best, and in the late 1960s even ISA all but disappeared. Exiles not only acted more conservatively but in time articulated an ideological conservatism that reflected their anti-communism as well as their practical personal experiences within an entrepreneurial economic enclave.

In 1974, a report by Cuban Catholic lay leaders suggested this conservative orientation. It revealed, for example, that apostolic movements emphasized pastoral work with adults and especially the family at the expense of social ministries, including working with the aged, the sick, or the incarcerated. Also, these movements tended to be overwhelmingly middle class, with little representation among the workers and university students. With regard to faith, the report concluded that Miami reflected what

Medellín had expressed several years before about Latin America: "what exists is a pastoral of conservation, based on sacramental devotion with little emphasis on evangelization."[65] Rather than engaging the community, Catholics seemed content to practice their faith primarily through church attendance and participation in lay movements dedicated to strengthening personal conversion and national identity. The trauma of exile encouraged a lay activism dedicated to building a Catholic community committed to piety, family, traditional Cuban culture, and nostalgia for the homeland. Also, much of the Catholic intellectual leadership interested in social concerns that had originally gathered in south Florida ended up geographically dispersed, facing their own problems of economic survival. Cubans focused their energies on finding their place in a new society and promoting an anti-communist agenda.

This did not exclude, however, the reality that many Catholics remained influenced by the teachings of the church in these matters and, even if modestly, worked to ease the social difficulties faced by many, especially within their own communities. At first some Cubans organized informal networks to help each other. In New York, for example, UCE volunteers of Cuban Catholic Action origins identified and worked to resolve community needs. They opened an informal telephone line for information, referral, and consultation services, which was advertised in the organization's newsletter but also through word of mouth within the Cuban community. In 1973, volunteers received an average of two calls per day, mostly requesting assistance or information on matters of health, employment, cultural needs, social service and welfare problems, housing, immigration, and consumer problems. One of the most severe concerns expressed by callers was the lack of bilingual mental health services, especially among low- and middle-income people. In general, a lack of English-language skills proved to be a severe barrier to accessing social service resources, and UCE volunteers did what they could to help people resolve their needs, though their efforts were modest and voluntary.[66]

Cubans certainly recognized the many social problems existing in the United States, including racism, on which they often commented. The formal discriminatory and segregationist traditions of the South persuaded most Cubans of color to live in the north, especially New York and New Jersey. One Black Cuban exile, Sergio Carrillo, who had worked with ACU and the *comandos rurales* in Cuba, joined the Bay of Pigs invasion, and eventually became a priest in the United States, remembered leaving south

Florida because of the difficult economic situation and especially the "signs of 'no dogs, no blacks,' the segregated bathrooms and water fountains."[67] Valdespino, for example, wrote about the issue, characterizing race relations in the United States as "the Achilles heel of North American democracy." He argued that the United States could resolve the intolerable conditions in the South in only one of two ways: by continuing the path already begun, including federal congressional and judicial interventions, and supporting direct action by groups like the Freedom Riders and Black activist organizations leading sit-ins across the South; or, as many in the United States advocated, merely emphasizing education campaigns to fight ignorance among the White southern population, aimed at eventually eliminating prejudice, the basis of discrimination and segregation. The country had little choice but to take the first approach, he thought, since education would require several generations as well as a great deal of patience on the part of Blacks, which they certainly no longer possessed.

Besides the moral imperative to resolve the abusive conditions Blacks faced, Valdespino warned that lack of action offered fertile ground for communist propaganda and activism. He referred to published accusations by Mississippi's chief of highway patrol, T. B. Birdsong, that more than two hundred Freedom Riders had been trained in Cuba by Soviet agents. Though Valdespino thought that Birdsong had exaggerated, he did think it worth asking what role international communism might play in aggravating race relations in the United States. Valdespino confirmed that at least one of the young activists had indeed visited Cuba, but it should not surprise anyone that communists would offer training and indoctrination to these young North Americans and that they would accept. Marxists found the situation in the United States South, where in the middle of the twentieth century Blacks still had to struggle to attain basic rights, incalculably valuable in their propaganda campaigns against democracy. "If justice . . . and Christian charity . . . demand that these damaging discriminatory practices cease, and that all citizens of a country receive the same prerogatives, without reference to color of skin," he declared, "now we must add one more reason: that we are confronting an oppressive and unjust system—communism—and we are doing so precisely to defend the rights of all men to have their dignity recognized and respected."[68]

For the most part, however, the former Catholic Action activists from Cuba were out of their element when considering social matters in the United States. Their limited experience with reform politics in the United

States made a contribution difficult even if they had agreed to turn from their focus on Cuba. In reality, it took a younger cohort of the exile generation influenced by United States ethnic politics to refocus the social question, adapting their discourses and approaches to a new era and a new place. Unlike the majority of their elders, Cuban youth engaged a broad range of issues related to U.S. society, following developments in the Civil Rights and student movements of the 1960s.

Students associated with the newspaper *Nueva Generación* represented such a group. Influenced by social Christian ideas, they cut their teeth as social critics observing Latin American politics. The editors lived mostly in Miami and New York during the mid-1960s through the early 1970s, but contributions came from across the country, Latin America, and Europe. Articles in the newspaper explored the many political and social concerns of the day, including the radicalization of politics in Latin America, the international student movement, U.S. foreign policy, the dramatic changes in the Catholic Church, and the Cold War. Many had been associated with Catholic Action in Cuba and supported the changing attitudes of the Latin American church during the 1960s. Some embraced traditional Christian Democratic ideas, while others offered a more radical perspective.[69]

Though *Nueva Generación*'s relation to a journal with the same name edited by Angel del Cerro in Caracas beginning in 1963 is not exactly clear, their philosophies resonated with each other and were most certainly related. Cerro's *Nueva Generación* maintained a close relationship with CLASC (Confederación Latino Americano de Sindicalistas Cristianos), which in 1966 elected Cuban JOC activist Eduardo García Mouré, exiled in Venezuela, as the organization's undersecretary general.[70] The publication was promoted as a "social Christian magazine for Latin America," and Cerro's inaugural editorial in *Nueva Generación* declared, "We are Christians," revolutionary Christians dedicated to a system in which "our people can be authentically free of imperialist exploitation and capable of constructing economic and social democracy—not just political democracy—without converting each individual into a terrorized and powerless member of a large herd." "We reject equally," Cerro declared, "colonialism, dictatorship, capitalism, and paternalism."[71]

With a similar tone, *Nueva Generación* continued in Miami and New York led by José Prince, a former member of JOC and MRP and student at Florida Atlantic University, and Lourdes Casal, also of Catholic Action in

Cuba, who initially worked with DRE in the early 1960s. Casal, who received a doctoral degree from the New School of Social Research in New York in 1975, acted out of her particular experience in the United States through the lens of her Afro-Cuban heritage, provoking considerable rethinking on her part. During the 1960s, Casal's social thought moved from a social Christian perspective to an increasingly Marxist analysis, leading eventually to a reevaluation of the Cuban Revolution itself. Some contributors to the journal highlighted Catholic revolutionary voices in Latin America like that of Camilo Torres, the controversial Colombian priest who joined a guerrilla insurrection as an active combatant. They even formed a group called Vivero Camilo Torres in Miami.[72] In one issue of *Nueva Generación,* Prince declared that "Camilo Torres, like [Martin] Luther King, Ernesto Guevara, and others, are exemplars that should be known and studied." He noted that, "as a man Camilo Torres denounces the "Christian" world; he is an example of a man dedicated to his fellow man, and those who call themselves "Catholics" should find his testimony profoundly provoking."[73] Prince also worked with CLASC and its Cuban-exile affiliate, STC, a JOC-inspired group that advocated for a labor movement in Cuba free of government control.[74]

Nueva Generación's editors and many of its contributors believed that Cuba's future should be tied to a united Latin America independent of North American, European, or Soviet influence or control. Bringing an essentially Latin American, nationalist, and Christian sensitivity to their analysis, they called for radical socioeconomic—indeed, even revolutionary—change. As one article declared, revolution had to be accomplished in Latin America, "and to do that it is necessary that the revolutionary nationalist movements of all the Americas coordinate and project a revolutionary humanist thesis, and discard Marxist conceptions."[75]

As Christian revolutionaries, they opposed the system in Cuba. They opposed the Marxist-Leninist revolution but did not define themselves as anti-communists or counter-revolutionaries because their identity came from what they believed affirmatively, not what they opposed. They declared themselves to be revolutionaries, democrats, and humanists.[76] Communism had to be destroyed by making revolution—by definition, initially, an essentially spiritual exercise. "There is no revolution in society without changing man, without revolutionizing his spirit, and man cannot be changed without changing his society." The Christian revolution had to be free of theoretical dilettantism and driven by militancy and pragmatism, which made room for many strategies, depending on circumstances. When possible, peaceful methods were preferable, though at times, as in the case of Camilo Torres, peaceful revolutionaries had to be willing to endure a period of transitory defensive, not arbitrary violence, to defeat the oligarchs who could not be expected simply to accept revolutionary change. As *Nueva Generación* expressed it, "first the revolution must rip the whip from the hands of the oligarchs and then, with Christian spirit, invite him to a sincere supper of human confraternity."[77]

Casal and Prince applauded the 1970 election of Salvador Allende to the Chilean presidency. Though a Marxist, he had promised socialist reform through democratic procedure. Shortly after Allende's election, Prince traveled to the CLASC's twelfth Latin American congress in Santiago, which issued a statement of support for the new Chilean government, at the same time denouncing a host of Latin American military governments in Brazil, Guatemala, Haiti, and others. On his return to New York, Prince offered an optimistic assessment of the Chilean situation. Though Allende would certainly face difficult political and economic issues, Prince considered the Chilean president's plan for a peaceful and democratic path toward socialism viable and realistic. He did not see any similarities between Cuba and Chile, noting that Cuba's entire political system and military had collapsed with the departure of Batista, leaving a power vacuum filled by Castro. He believed that Allende's rejection of one-party rule, Chile's strong party system and electoral tradition, and the Chilean military's commitment to staying out of politics would ensure democratic procedure and peaceful change. Moreover, an important sector of Chile's Christian Democratic movement had embraced Allende. "The Chilean situation will be something very different and could signal a new path for Latin America."[78]

These activists also turned their attention to developments in their country of residence. As early as 1963, Casal published a lengthy analysis of the civil rights situation in the United States. Even though she dedicated considerable time to anti-Castro activism, even traveling to Africa with a DRE delegation in June 1962 to meet with student groups about the situation in Cuba, she also focused on the North American race situation. She had a special interest in the issue and offered a deeply critical review of race relations in the United States. Among other things she noted that North American Blacks would no longer tolerate the situation, meaning that radical steps had to be taken, including desegregation of schools, effective suffrage, and a general civil rights law. She also lambasted what she considered corrupt unions steeped in bourgeoisie values complicit with owners in denying Blacks access to employment. She hoped the Christian-inspired and nonviolent philosophy of Martin Luther King would prevail, but she also warned that the future was unpredictable and other more radical groups would have less patience.[79] In the late 1960s, numerous articles and letters to *Nueva Generación's* editors commented on the social and racial problems in the United States, arguing that racism, poverty, and violence represented some of the central problems in North American society.[80]

By the 1970s, many of the younger exiles who arrived in the United States in their teens and twenties became social activists, combining Cuban traditions with new influences. Though they did not view the old style Catholic Action as particularly relevant in the United States, consciously or not they certainly carried that tradition into their involvement with the new social movements emerging in their land of exile. Mostly educated outside of Cuba, or simply more thoroughly integrated in North American society, they learned that gaining rights in the United States often involved non-ideological often ethnically based local activism, indeed, what one might call entrepreneurial activism. The War on Poverty spearheaded by the Lyndon Johnson administration made resources available to the federal bureaucracy to fund local communities interested in resolving particular social problems. They also learned that local politics often organized around ethnic interests and identities. Without a doubt, this piecemeal and ethnically centered approach to social change was quite a different concept from the broad structural prescriptions social activists in Cuba had been used to and one that those Cubans trained in the United States with a social conscience learned to utilize.

In 1971 two Cuban employees of the federal Office of Health and Rehabilitation Services approached Father Mario Vizcaíno and urged him to take the lead in creating a Cuban social advocacy group similar to those run by Mexican Americans and Puerto Ricans. They told him of the numerous government grants available to study the social, educational, and psychological status of minority communities. He agreed and founded the Cuban National Planning Council (CNPC), recruiting a fourteen-member board of directors of Cubans from across the country and spearheading an important effort to evaluate the needs of the Cuban community. Having lived in Washington, DC, during the late 1960s until he moved to Miami in 1975, Vizcaíno became thoroughly familiar with the arena of U.S. ethnic politics and a leading voice in developing a social agenda for the needy in Cuban communities. Of working-class background himself, Vizcaíno brought diverse experience to his work. A Catholic Action militant during his youth in Cuba, he worked with the poor, taught catechism at Bishop Boza Masvidal's Caridad Church, and entered the novitiate. Vizcaíno's priestly vocation took him to study philosophy in Spain in 1953 and theology in Rome four years later. He became a Piarist priest in 1960. His stay in Rome coincided with the papacy of John XXIII and the opening of the Second Vatican Council, and in 1963 he traveled to the United States. In 1966, thirty-two-year-old Vizcaíno settled in Washington, DC, where for the next eight years he taught theology at Notre Dame of Mary College.[81]

Many Catholics influenced deeply by the social doctrines collaborated with Vizcaíno, including at least one UCE activist in New York.[82] Those recruited to collaborate with CNPC included Prince and Casal as well as Rafael Prohías, Andrés Hernández, and Guarione Díaz, all associated with *Nueva Generación* and trained social scientists who worked on the organization's first major research project. Based at Florida Atlantic University, Prohías initially led the research effort. He had already published a landmark article on Cubans in Indianapolis, but when he died prematurely in 1973, Casal became interim director of the research effort.[83] Eventually, Díaz, who had also studied the Cuban community, writing an important article on the emerging heterogeneity of the Cuban community by the late 1960s, became director of the organization's research initiatives and later the organization itself.[84] Another dozen or so Cubans across the country also participated. Besides New York and Miami, Cubans in Chicago, Washington, DC, and Los Angeles participated.[85]

"The fundamental objective of the Cuban Minority Study," these activists wrote in 1973, "is to gather all relevant data necessary to outline the multiplicity of social problems inherent in the high-speed transition of Cubans into our host society." The goal also involved "evaluating and restructuring the various systems presently engaged in providing for some of the most crucial needs" and finding creative ways to meet the concerns of Cubans in need.[86] CNCP produced the first profiles of the social needs of Cubans in the United States, ultimately challenging the prevailing view that the Cuban exile communities constituted an unqualified success story.

Their research revealed the many dimensions of these communities, including the elderly, Blacks, and others who had not fared so well and needed substantial social service support. Certainly, conventional wisdom held that Cubans as a whole fared better socioeconomically than most minority groups in the United States, especially given the educated, middle-class backgrounds of a significant number. Less well-known was that while Cubans achieved higher incomes than other Latinos in the U.S., they remained below average in income for the nation as a whole. "Even compared to the other ethnic groups in the [Miami] area," the report observed that Cubans "*have the highest percent of families in the poverty level and the lowest earning level*" (emphasis in original). The unemployment rate for Cubans represented "more than twice the rate for other whites in the area."[87]

Cubans faced problems on a number of fronts. Forced to enter the labor market in unprecedented numbers, Cuban women had to cope with lack of day care facilities and the cultural adjustments of working outside the home; working-class Cubans found barriers to participation in unions and apprenticeship programs, ending up in low-paying jobs; older Cubans became concentrated in low-income areas with few senior citizen day care centers, home services, and other alternatives to institutionalization; and Black Cubans, "the invisible Cubans," faced double discrimination at the hands of the dominant society as well as their own. The report questioned the widely expressed belief within the Cuban communities themselves that they did not discriminate against Black Cubans; it cited, for example, research demonstrating clear discrimination in housing within Cuban neighborhoods.[88] Certainly most Cubans objected to formal segregation, but they too came from a deeply racist society that also separated the races by economic reality and local custom, even if not by law. Black Cubans in Dade County often felt marginalized from their own community, evidenced by their residential setting between Cuban and U.S. Black communities.[89]

In 1976, the CNCP sponsored a conference in Miami Beach to introduce the south Florida Hispanic reality to federal officials in the social services field, including the undersecretary of the Department of Health, Education and Welfare. Vizcaíno, Lasaga, Ricardo Núñez (Cuban Refugee Program), Cecilia Alegre (Hispanic Coalition for Mental Health), and others represented a growing contingency of Cubans involved in raising social awareness among Cubans in south Florida.[90] By the end of the 1970s, CNPC, no longer headed by Vizcaíno, had also become a social services delivery organization. In December 1979, for example, the local office in Miami announced it had received federal funding for two programs to help Cubans and other Hispanics in Dade County. These included funding for work training and employment support programs and initiatives to help Hispanic youth facing problems in the criminal court system.[91]

The work of these Cubans reflected a practical commitment to promoting awareness of the socioeconomic needs of certain segments of the exile communities. Their activism combined the social Christian traditions so frequently articulated in Cuba during the late 1950s and clearly expressed in *Nueva Generación* during the 1960s with an emerging ethnic awareness reflecting their experiences in the United Sates. They thought Cuba had paid a heavy price for not resolving the grievances of the poor and thus supported Christian-inspired reform movements in Latin America as well as social activism in the United States. An emerging ethnic identity among especially younger exiles influenced how they thought about the social issues in the United States, and they practiced their activism within a secular, pragmatic, and relatively nonideological world. U.S.-trained Cuban social activists of the CNPC did not utilize the rhetoric of Catholic social doctrines; instead they relied on the secular language of the social movements in the United States as well as the discourse of ethnicity. At the same time, this commitment to social concerns among Catholics reflected their perspectives as exiles who understood the need for creating social justice in a post-Castro Cuba. Exiles had learned a hard lesson and recognized the need to ensure that Cuba's future reflected the social theology they so often espoused.

The strong exile identity and focus on return as well as the ability to establish an autonomous economic livelihood proved determining factors in how Cubans thought about integration into the United States. Those of the upper and middle classes, as well as many of the urban working classes, possessed the values, education, skills, and entrepreneurial ethic necessary to negotiate their way in the U.S. capitalist system. In the 1960s and 1970s, Cubans established their culture in Miami, permeating all aspects of daily life and making the south Florida region their own. Over time, those Cubans scattered across the United States by the Cuban refugee program adapted quite effectively, and many sooner or later migrated to Miami in search of a more familiar and comfortable cultural environment and climate, in the process reinforcing the south Florida economy.

In Miami, Cubans created an economic environment that allowed them to express their culture and heritage openly. As an economically stratified community with resources, Cubans in Miami possessed sufficient autonomy and power to create, maintain, and defend their culture and identity even in the face of considerable resistance and sometimes hostility. In so doing, Cubans converted an essentially Anglo-American dominated southern town into a multicultural, heavily Cuban, and increasingly Latino community. Exiles transformed south Florida into a Cuban cultural space with the Spanish language as evident in daily use as English, perhaps even more, which Cubans eventually have come to understand as part of their "American" identity.

Accepted and aided perhaps like no other immigrant group in the history of the United States, Cubans nevertheless rejected the idea of embracing this new society as a place of permanent transplantation. They cultivated their *cubanidad* and sought a manner of integration that served their needs while awaiting their eventual return. A very strong international perspective and identification with Latin America and Spain also strengthened their ethnic expression in the United States. They eventually shared U.S. nationality with the people to the north but maintained cultural affinity with people to the south. Whether fighting to overthrow Castro or offering more moderate solutions, Cubans remained in relationship and conversation with a Cuban diaspora scattered in many countries around the world. Though their commitment to integration into the United States on their own terms often challenged traditional expectations about immigrant assimilation, they remained unapologetic. They did not even consider becoming U.S. citizens a rupture with their Cuban national identity nor necessarily alter their intention of eventually returning home. Cubans came to terms with the reality of exile and gave birth to an ethnic consciousness that guided their integration into a new society.

Chapter Eight

U.S. HISPANIC CATHOLICISM

Beyond our own communities I am interested in our Chicano and Puerto Rican brothers. I collaborate with them here in Miami and in all parts of the United States.

—Father Mario Vizcaíno (1976)

The struggles of Cuban Catholics in south Florida during the 1970s for the right to participate in the U.S. church without shedding their own traditions brought them into contact with like-minded Hispanics across the country. Catholic activists of Latin American background in the United States demanded that the Euro-American dominated church respect their culture and religious practices and that they be given a place in the hierarchy and governance of the national institution. Latinos brought their own method to this endeavor, which many Cubans embraced and to which they also contributed. Though a cross-fertilization of Latin American and U.S. Latino experiences introduced Hispanic traditions to U.S. Catholicism, especially in the realms of devotional practices, pastoral strategies, and theology, the heterogeneous nature of Latino Catholics made the endeavor for a unified national movement in the 1960s and 1970s a difficult challenge.

Indeed, among Hispanics, social, economic, racial, and gender differences caused considerable tension and division. On the other hand, cultural affinities did prove sufficiently strong to build an effective national coalition of Latino Catholics. This time of innovation and new thought certainly inspired many Cuban exiles who looked beyond conforming to the established discourses in their own communities, considered new ideas and alternative perspectives, and participated in building a U.S. Latino Catholic identity.

Discovering U.S. Hispanic Catholics

In 1969, a young exile social activist, Guarioné Díaz, wrote about the increasing diversity (*pluralización*) of the Cuban population outside of Cuba. As more Cubans of various backgrounds left the island, congregating in numerous geographic spaces besides south Florida, including New York, Caracas, Madrid, San Juan, and many others, their political, social, and economic characteristics became more diverse than in earlier years.

In south Florida, refugees initially resided together in the Little Havana area of Miami, but residential patterns changed as they found jobs, gained income, and sought permanent homes. Wealthier Cubans, for example, eventually settled in Coral Gables or perhaps Miami Beach, while working-class Cubans moved to Westchester and Hialeah or remained in the Calle Ocho area. In the diaspora outside south Florida and areas of New Jersey, Cubans did not generally concentrate residentially in distinct neighborhoods. In these environments of greater political and social diversity, exiles— especially the youth—developed new attitudes and perspectives on many matters. Those raised and fully formed in Cuba tended to maintain a stronger and one-dimensional idea about themselves as Cubans, while younger exiles formed and educated outside their homeland necessarily engaged the world around them more fluidly and naturally.[1]

As Cubans struggled to define their own place in the United States during the 1970s, they became cognizant of a larger world of Latino activism with which they initially did not relate. At first, they did not know how to interpret the Chicano and Puerto Rican movement for political, cultural, and socioeconomic rights. They recoiled at how many activist Latino leaders in the United States celebrated the Cuban Revolution much in the same way as did leaders of the poor and marginalized in Latin America. Many Mexican American and Puerto Rican social activists, as well as other leftist leaders in the United States, viewed the Cuban Revolution as one acceptable alternative to the oppressive poverty in Latin America. Their admiration of the Cuban Revolution's social project as well as their militant and radical rhetoric seemed to exiles suspiciously like what they experienced in their homeland. Cubans condemned their uncritical support of the Revolution, accusing them of being fellow-travelers or just plain naïve.[2]

One Cuban priest, Raul Comesañas, a resident of New Jersey, for example, expressed skepticism about the motives of his Latino colleagues after attending a Liberation Theology workshop at Maryknoll, New York, in 1977. Organized by PADRES, an organization of Chicano priests, liberation theologians Gustavo Gutiérrez, Juan Luís Segundo, and Enrique Dussel led the discussions that obviously alienated the Cubans. In a critique published in Miami's Catholic magazine *Ideal,* Comesañas recognized the urgency of social problems needing concrete solutions in U.S. Latino and Latin American communities. As a matter of record, he cited his participation in the Civil Rights Movement and the War on Poverty and congratulated the work of PADRES and the Mexican American Cultural Center in San Antonio that did so much to advance the interests of Hispanics generally. He also lauded Latin American theologians like Gutiérrez because they all sought the betterment of the Americas, saying "there is no doubt that I respect and support my brothers' in Christ in their quest for liberty, rights and progress for all Latin America." On the other hand, "when this includes ignoring a sister nation that today suffers the worst oppressive domination, or when the existence of this situation is simply denied, it is time to doubt the sincerity of these brothers and the goals they seek." To be sure, he concluded, if they, "truly fight for the poor, for liberty, and against all oppression," they will garner the support of all Cubans, but he urged them not to support oppressive social systems, whether communist or otherwise, that in practice denied rights of evangelization and liberty.[3]

At the same time, the class framework emphasized in Liberation Theology did not necessarily translate easily into the Latino reality in the United States. Differences in class origin between the mostly working-class U.S. Latinos and heavily middle-class Cubans often caused divisiveness, but many focused on a unifying ethnic strategy for advancing the struggle based on cultural affirmation and pastoral methods. Culturally defined pastoral strategies challenged Hispanic marginalization, advanced evangelization, and at the same time confronted political, socioeconomic, racial grievances faced by Latino Catholics across the country.[4] The cultural approach proved less threatening, not only to the hierarchy of the United States Catholic Church but also to middle-class Cuban Catholics, who sympathized with the cultural and pastoral goals of Latinos, although not necessarily with their socioeconomic discourses or celebration of the Cuban Revolution.

Perhaps the most important theological advocate in the United States of this cultural and pastoral approach was Father Virgil Elizondo, a Mexican American priest from San Antonio, Texas, who challenged the U.S. church's "melting pot" mentality. His work reflected efforts by Latinos to gain acceptance, integration, and a voice within the U.S. Catholic Church, which began in earnest during 1960s in conjunction with the Chicano and Puerto Rican Civil Rights Movements that raised consciousness about their need to be actors on their own behalf. In 1972, Elizondo established a specialized pastoral institute, the Mexican American Cultural Center in San Antonio, to focus on theological education and promote a culturally specific mission to train laity, religious, priests, and seminarians in Hispanic ministry.[5] Three years later, Elizondo published an important theological reflection, *Christianity and Culture,* offering a practical application of pastoral theology in a minority setting. He argued that evangelizing the Mexican American community required a deep understanding of their historical roots in Spanish and Indigenous communities, mestizo reality, anthropological and psychological makeup, cultural traditions, historical and contemporary socioeconomic condition, and popular religion. Elizondo also spoke directly to matters of culture and pluralism that had emerged from the Vatican Council and found expression in a variety of papal documents.[6]

Cubans also took up many of these themes. Armed with a powerful sense of their cultural identity, the Vatican's theological support for cultural pluralism, and a growing awareness of the secular and Catholic minority discourses in the United States as manifested by Elizondo, Cuban exile activists joined in efforts to gain greater attention from the Catholic Church. While maintaining firm allegiance to their culture of origin, they began to see points of affinity with their Mexican American and Puerto Rican colleagues. During the 1970s, Elizondo received numerous invitations to speak in south Florida, beginning in October 1971 at a national convention on religious education. In subsequent years he spoke to seminarians at St.

Vincent de Paul Seminary at Boynton Beach and had a considerable influence on many future priests and theologians.[7]

In mid-November 1970, Bishop Patricio Flores of San Antonio—the first Hispanic (Mexican American) named bishop in the United States—also visited Miami. Appointed earlier in the year, Flores met with members of the Cuban Catholic community in south Florida, exposing them perhaps for the first time to a national church leader of Hispanic background. On a return trip from Latin America, where he visited several countries, Flores met in Miami with members of the Cuban MFC. He spoke about a national Hispanic agenda and called on them to collaborate, saying that their professional formation provided them with a great opportunity to participate as leaders and help others. Hispanics had not received much justice in the United States until they began to become political, and their power would only continue to grow if they joined in a unified effort. "I am the first [Hispanic] Bishop, but I do not want to be the last," he said, adding that he would like to see one of Miami's Cuban priests become a bishop as well. This work, he concluded, would need to come from unified Hispanic action because "no one else will have greater interest or do more than *hermanos de raza o de lengua* [brothers of race and tongue]." The bishop also asked Cubans to become aware of other Hispanics and their difficult socioeconomic conditions, especially the eighty thousand migrant families who every year crisscrossed the country following the crops. He challenged them to use their vacations to work among the migrants, to learn about them, to help them. At a recent national MFC congress, he said, forty families had agreed to participate in this kind of social work during their vacations; he hoped that Miami would likewise respond. "Communists do this frequently," he said, perhaps baiting the Cubans a bit, "but we Catholics never or seldom do."[8]

Though the specific Cuban response to the bishop is not known, Flores's visit symbolized the beginning of a process of mutual discovery Latino Catholics experienced during the 1970s. Some in Miami, like *cursillo* leader Miguel Cabrera, established relationships with Hispanics across the United States. After attending the first national Hispanic *cursillo* movement meeting in San Antonio with Father José L. Hernando, Cabrera expressed great enthusiasm for the benefits of Latino unity.[9] Cabrera characterized the meeting as a rich experience that brought together Hispanic brothers from across the country, noting the great interest Bishop Flores took in the Cuban community. "Once again we were able to prove," he said, "that this great [Hispanic] minority that we are . . . continues to awaken, not only to our rights, but also to our responsibilities to this great nation in which we live."[10] He argued that Hispanic Catholics in Miami had to become more aware of their gifts and contribute to the enrichment of the church. "We need to convince ourselves, this minority that we are," he said, "that God has permitted this exile for something more, and perhaps, until this something is accomplished, the return to Cuba will remain remote." This "something" he suggested was "our obligation . . . to convert ourselves into a real SPIRITUAL-RELIGIOUS INFLUENCE that helps not only to transform this materialist Miami which envelopes us and exert a transcending influence on other sectors and communities of this country, but at the same time makes us capable of preparing a dignified and responsible return to a free and Christian motherland"[11] (emphasis in original).

In addition to south Florida Cubans, many others from across the country perhaps even more rapidly developed a sense of solidarity with Mexican Americans, Puerto Ricans, and others of Latin American background. In late 1979, for example, Ada María Isasi-Díaz, a resident of Virginia who arrived in the United States at age eighteen, visited south Florida to encourage Cuban Catholic women to learn about Hermanas, an organization of activist Chicana religious formed in 1971. Working as a missionary in Lima, Peru, for three years in the late 1960s, she learned of poverty firsthand, inspiring her dedication to issues of social justice and ethnic equality within the U.S. Hispanic world. In the late 1970s, she attended a Roman Catholic women's conference that also raised her consciousness about gender inequalities in the church and society in general. She became active with Hermanas when the organization opened its ranks to lay women and Latinas of other than Mexican American origin in 1975. Acknowledging the organization's initially Chicana identity, Isasi-Díaz told Cubans in south Florida that Hermanas nevertheless "wants to represent the interests of all women, and we see that the voice of the Cuban women of the southeast is missing."[12]

María Teresa Gastón, who arrived from Cuba at age three and was raised in Milwaukee and New Berlin, Wisconsin, through eighth grade, grew up isolated from her extended family and the Cuban community. While her mother maintained a sense of Cuban culture at home, her father, Melchor Gastón, who had studied at Belén, joined ACU, and helped compose the pamphlet *¿Por qué la reforma agraria?* in 1958, encouraged the family to assimilate the best they could. Nevertheless, Gastón's connection to her heritage remained firm, and she "enjoyed telling people I was Cuban, even though I spoke Spanish haltingly and knew virtually no Cuban history, geography, or literature." During her college years at Marquette University she became active with the International Student Association and met other Hispanics through the Club Latino Estudiantil. Gastón's best friend was an articulate and militant Chicano, and through campus ministry Gastón became involved with the local Hispanic community, where she learned about the social realties of Mexican and Puerto Rican families. Her faith and commitment to social justice led to involvement in the Latino church movement that merged her identities as a Christian and a Hispanic. "I learned about [Paulo] Freire's liberating adult education, about small Christian communities, about cultural pluralism and international human rights. . . . The experience of fitting in, of belonging, of being called forth as a young Hispanic woman was wonderfully encouraging."[13]

Like Cabrera, Isasi-Díaz, and Gastón, Araceli Cantero also became an important interpreter of the Hispanic Catholic movement in the United States for south Florida Cubans.[14] Though a native of Spain, she established a close relationship with the Cuban community in which she lived. A reporter for *The Voice,* she took great interest in the emerging national Latino church movement and covered it closely in English and Spanish for her newspaper, which in 1980 became a separate Spanish-language diocesan newspaper, *La Voz Católica.* Through the efforts of activists like these, the south Florida Cuban Catholic community also became engaged with a national Hispanic church movement in the 1970s with the encouragement and guidance of the church itself.

Pastoral de Conjunto

In the midst of the controversies between Cuban Catholics and Miami diocesan officials in the 1960s, developments at the Vatican as well as Medellín encouraged Cubans to increase their activism as well as claim their role within the church. A central message from the Vatican Council, noted in *Gaudium et Spes* and *Lumen Gentium,* insisted that the church was for the world and that the laity occupied the heart of this world-serving character.[15] If the conciliar documents highlighted the need for greater involvement of the laity, the 1968 Latin American council of bishops (CELAM) at Medellín offered a concrete concept and strategy for implementing lay activism. Citing *Lumen Gentium,* Medellín documents on the lay movements noted that the "proper role of the layman consists, then, in his commitment to the world, understood as a framework of human solidarity, of significant accomplishments and facts, in a word, as history." To be effective this commitment to acting in the world through the lay apostolates had to be "promoted through teams or communities of faith, to whom Christ specifically promised his cohesive presence."[16]

On his return trip to Venezuela from the final meetings at the Vatican in December 1965, Bishop Eduardo Boza Masvidal stopped in Miami and described the conclusions as an internal and external renewal for the church. He described the liturgical reforms as encouraging more intense participation of the faithful with the interior world of the church, "making us one body within the temple" to enable a more effective projection outward to the world. This outward projection, he noted, required new responsibilities for the laity, including "transmitting to the world Christ's message and taking it to all the structures of society." Observing the burst of apostolic activism in Miami and what he interpreted as a resurgent spiritual life among Cubans in south Florida, he suggested that they had already begun Vatican II's work.[17] The Vatican Council's call for lay activism and engagement simply reinforced what Cubans had practiced in their homeland for three decades before the Revolution. The spirit of Catholic Action remained and in light of the Vatican Council's teachings translated quite easily into an equally vigorous or even more intense activism that helped them reorganize their lives in the United States after fleeing Cuba, reengage their faith and evangelize within the context of own traditions, and open themselves to a new world of Hispanic Catholicism as it emerged in the United States in the 1970s.

The Latin American bishops offered concrete strategies for encouraging and organizing the activities of the lay movements by introducing the idea of a *pastoral de conjunto* (joint pastoral work) through which the entire church would collaborate, plan, and implement common pastoral goals.[18] The *pastoral de conjunto* gave exiles a new way to think about their pastoral ministries, steeped in the grass roots of their community and in their own culture and way of life. In late November 1970, they heard directly from leaders of CELAM's *pastoral de conjunto* office who arrived in Miami to hold a workshop on pastoral theology. Archbishop Vicente Zaspe (Argentina) and Fathers Edgard Beltrán (Colombia) and Alfonso Gortaire (Ecuador) outlined for Miami's clergy and laity the new Latin American pastoral theology that had evolved from Vatican II. Beltrán spoke of the necessity of a pastoral strategy that took into account the realities of the world, of each community—a pastoral strategy that could adjust to the ever-changing and complex nature of the modern world. This required gathering concrete and detailed anthropological information about the social, economic, and cultural characteristics of the different communities to discover the nature of their families, social organization, religious practices, education levels, values, and other pertinent information. This, in turn, would inform the evangelical strategies of a unified pastoral plan based on church teachings.[19]

For Catholic religious and lay leaders alike this made a great deal of sense and coincided with their commitment to serving their community within the traditions of Cuban Catholicism. The idea slowly gained support with the help of the ASH and the urgings of Beltrán, who visited the community periodically. Composed of all Spanish-speaking priests, of various national origins, the association of priests met once a month to discuss pressing issues relating to their pastoral work, including liturgy, biblical, social, and cultural concerns.[20] During 1974, with the encouragement of Msgr. Orlando Fernández, vicar for the Hispanic apostolate, lay leaders in Miami, representing the *cursillos,* ACU, Knights of Columbus, MFC, Camino al Matrimonio, Encuentros Juveniles, Legión de María, and Impacto, also met and engaged in dialogue.[21] These activities gave birth to a joint pastoral coordinating team, Equipo Pastoral de Conjunto (EPC), composed of representatives of the apostolic movements, priests, and other religious. EPC established subcommittees to coordinate activities in the parishes and with the apostolic movements to investigate the creation of a pastoral institute and the development of a pastoral plan.[22]

During the 1970s, others of Latin American background in the Miami area joined in the initially Cuban lay movements and in time the term "Hispanic" (*Hispano*) began to be used, especially since a large number of Spanish priests served in the region. Hispanics gained greater standing within the church with the appointment of Archbishop McCarthy, who, at the end of 1977, consciously included them on a newly created diocesan lay council to advise the recently established archdiocesan office of lay ministries. At the first meeting designed to bring together Latino and Anglo-American

lay leaders, Roberto Hernández reviewed the history of Hispanic lay movements in Miami, noting that only recently had they been officially recognized by the archdiocese. Demonstrating a greater sensibility to Hispanics,
as well as to facilitate matters at the session, the archdiocese provided in-
stantaneous translation capabilities. Now that Hispanics were more fully
integrated into the diocesan structure, lay leaders looked forward to evangelizing the Hispanic community of south Florida.[23] The next year, more
than fifty representatives of the Hispanic lay movements met to discuss the
diocesan five-year evangelization plan; they not only made specific implementation recommendations and suggestions to the Hispanic lay movements but also offered specific critiques of the general pastoral plan itself.[24]
As a new decade began, the Cuban laity in south Florida had accomplished
their goal of being recognized by the church as Cubans and Hispanics and
ensuring their voice in the archdiocese.

Encuentro Movement

In addition to helping organize and guide the Cuban Catholic community
in south Florida, the *pastoral de conjunto* strategy inspired interaction and
engagement among Hispanic Catholics across the country. A month before
the CELAM workshop in November 1970, members of the United States
Catholic Conference (USCC) visited south Florida as part of an overall assessment of the condition of Hispanic Catholics in the United States. Hosted
by the Diocesan Hispanic vicar, Bryan Walsh, Father James Rausch (assistant
general secretary) and John Cosgrove (director of the department of social
development) met with leaders and toured the community, including the
migrant labor communities in the area. They discussed many of the problems plaguing Hispanic Catholics across the country, including discrimination, poverty, lack of education, and abuse of migrants, and they spoke of the
need of greater coordination among dioceses to deal with Hispanic issues.

This kind of attention to problems faced by Hispanics had first been
raised in the U.S. church in 1945 by San Antonio's Archbishop Robert Lucy,
when he established the Bishop's Committee for the Spanish-Speaking,
which in 1964 became the National Office of the U.S. Bishop's Committee for the Spanish-Speaking. Four years later, this office, still based in San
Antonio, became the Division for the Spanish-Speaking in the USCC's

Department of Social Development, which established regional offices in the Midwest (1965) and on the West Coast (1967). Now, the USCC delegation explained to their Miami audience, in a very symbolic as well as strategic move resulting from their visits across the country, the church's national office for the Spanish-speaking would be moved from San Antonio to Washington, DC, where it could more effectively coordinate the nationwide needs of Hispanic Catholics.[25]

The ongoing work among Latino Catholics to bring change to the U.S. church gained momentum at the National Catechetical Congress held in Miami in 1971, when more than one hundred Hispanics, including Puerto Ricans, Mexican Americans, and Cubans, officially requested the USCC to organize a congress specifically dedicated to creating a national Hispanic pastoral plan.[26] This first Encuentro Nacional took place at Trinity College in Washington, DC, in 1972, organized by the CELAM theologian Beltrán, who had visited Miami earlier, and raised for the national church some of the fundamental concerns of Latino Catholics.

Some 250 delegates responsible for the Hispanic apostolate, including nine bishops, made seventy-four recommendations emphasizing three themes. The delegates asked for greater respect, understanding, and legitimacy for Hispanic culture and the use of Spanish within the U.S. church. They called for Hispanic integration into the church based on equality and mutual respect. And they insisted on a greater participation of Hispanics in leadership and decision-making structures at all levels of the church and the creation of new institutions that would promote the formation of leaders within a self-determinist context. Though few Cubans participated in this 1972 Encuentro, the conclusions expressed the very same concerns they had dealt with throughout the 1960s.[27] As a result, the newly named Hispanic Secretariat of the USCC (formerly the Division of the Spanish-Speaking), headed by Paul Sedillo Jr. and assisted by Beltrán, worked to coordinate regional pastoral activities of Hispanic Catholics nationally and mobilize Latino Catholics across the country.

The USCC Hispanic Secretariat then issued a call for Hispanics to participate in the 41st International Eucharistic Congress to be held in Philadelphia in August 1976. A national Hispanic committee formed, headed by Sedillo, not only to coordinate activities at the congress but also to host a meeting several days before to discuss issues of particular concern to Latino Catholics. In a visit to Miami in February 1976, Sedillo explained that the now five Hispanic bishops of the U.S. church hoped the Philadelphia meeting would provide a platform from which to launch a spiritual renovation among Hispanics and respond to the pope's call for greater evangelization. They also sought to promote greater unity and coordination among Latino communities across the country and provide a framework for one day hosting a U.S. Hispanic "Medellín."[28]

The diocese of Miami named Father Fausto Fernández and Sister Florinda Bermúdez to coordinate local preparations, including distributing monthly study material to the parishes and lay movements forwarded by the national secretariat.[29] A diocesan assembly organized to reflect on the upcoming congress attracted more than one thousand participants, including representatives of all ten Hispanic apostolic movements, which included some five thousand congregants.[30] Agustín Román, who replaced Orlando Fernández as vicar for Hispanics and represented the community at the Philadelphia conversations, encouraged Hispanic laity to participate.[31] He held meetings once a month at the Ermita de la Caridad del Cobre with a coordinating team of lay leaders, Comité Coordinador del Apostolado Seglar (CCAS), inviting them to reflect on the apostolic priorities for south Florida and prepare suggestions on the theme of evangelization for the national Hispanic Secretariat in Washington. These local reports from across the country formed the basis of conversations among Hispanic bishops and leaders in Philadelphia.[32]

Shortly before the meeting in Philadelphia, Román met with more than forty lay leaders who late into the night developed priorities, including a pastoral plan advocating concrete research agendas, deeper communication among different social sectors, evangelizing among the masses rather than always working among the elites, and improving the use of the media for evangelization. They also pointed to obstacles to evangelization like the power of materialism and the scarcity of resources needed for the formation of laity.[33] On his return from Philadelphia, Román reported that Hispanic bishops and lay leaders had agreed on their pastoral agenda that included seeking "unity in pluralism"; emphasizing the idea of community and avoiding individualism; defending Hispanic culture and everything related to the dignity of Hispanic individuals, families, and communities; recognizing Hispanic contributions to social change; and supporting integral and political education in Hispanic communities. The conclusions were submitted to local communities for more study and discussion.[34]

By the end of 1976, Cuban Catholic activists in Miami had fully committed to the national Hispanic pastoral movement and found that they shared many of the values of other Latinos across the country, most importantly a deep abiding commitment to a unified defense of local Hispanic cultures and desire that the church in the United States embrace pluralism and open its doors to Hispanic Catholics. In November, Sedillo met with Román, the CCAS, and Archbishop McCarthy to update them on the activities of the national Hispanic Secretariat. At a consultation in October, during an ecclesial assembly in Detroit, the Hispanic bishops had announced a Segundo Encuentro Pastoral Hispano similar to the one held in Washington, DC, in 1972. This time, however, the bishops appealed not only to Hispanic leaders but to the communities themselves. Sedillo sought the cooperation of south Florida and asked the archbishop for support by encouraging the participation of CCAS, which in accordance with the strategies of *pastoral de conjunto* had successfully drawn together the many apostolic movements into coordinated action. "In no other place," Sedillo noted, "has a group of this caliber, representing so many diocesan organizations, been formed to undertake the work and reflection '*de conjunto.*'" He offered their experience as an excellent model for others. Meeting with the Hispanic lay group for the first time since taking office in September, the archbishop expressed great satisfaction on learning of their work, declaring that they would be of great help to him in the future. "I would like to be considered one of the group," he said.[35]

In February 1977, south Florida representatives Fathers Mario Vizcaíno and Felipe Estevez joined Hispanic leaders from across the country in Chicago for a four-day planning session for the second Encuentro, to be held in Washington, DC, in August. Professor at the Major Seminary at Boynton Beach, Florida, Estevez attended as the official delegate from the archdiocese, while Vizcaíno, professor of theology at Florida International University in Miami, attended at the request of the Hispanic bishops with whom he had been consulting. Vizcaíno became the Encuentro coordinator for the southeastern section of the country, an excellent choice since he had a deep appreciation for the importance of cooperation among the Latino groups, a stance he also advocated within the U.S. Catholic Church.[36] He took charge of organizing Latino Catholic communities in the Southeast region, including twenty dioceses in Florida, Louisiana, Alabama, Mississippi, North and South Carolina, and Tennessee, preaching to his compatriots the need to be cognizant of the larger world of Hispanics in the United States. "Beyond our own communities," Vizcaíno noted, "I am interested in our Chicano and Puerto Rican brothers. I collaborate with them here in Miami and in all parts of the United States."[37]

Estevez expressed similar ideas after the Chicago planning meeting. "I think the contribution of those from the Caribbean was interesting," Estevez noted. "Perhaps for the first time," he explained, "Puerto Ricans, Dominicans and Cubans gained consciousness regarding what unites us and what we should contribute to the national community." All agreed that an important theme would be "unity in pluralism" as a way of promoting respect for the diverse Hispanic cultures. Estevez also noted the delegates' general lack of knowledge about Cuban Miami, "perhaps because of our geographical situation and our tendency to remain on the margins of the national reality." But, "whatever we do not contribute, will not be contributed," suggesting that no one else could offer the south Florida perspective.[38]

In late March, Sedillo, representing the national secretariat, met with Latinos from six dioceses of the Southeast region, including Miami, at the Ermita de la Caridad to plan for the Encuentro. Sedillo provided a historical overview of the Encuentro movement and emphasized the Hispanic bishops' basic commitment to receiving direction from local communities. "The participatory model," he said, "will be what allows us to hear from the base." Focusing on the overall theme of evangelization, local communities would provide input to the national secretariat in charge of preparing discussion materials for the Encuentro.[39] During the next months, Román oversaw the structuring of the archdioceses' preparatory work for the Encuentro with the help of a CCAS organizing group that included Cabrera, José Figueras, and Araceli Luaces and later expanded to include clergy and women religious.[40] They organized reflection meetings on the ethnic experiences and realities of the diverse Hispanic groups in the archdiocese, accompanied by a community reconciliation service that became an integral aspect of the Encuentro process. The first reflection to consider the "Cuban reality" in late April included a talk on the history of the church in Cuba by Román, a lecture on the Cuban exile experience by sociologist Juan Clark, and a discussion on Cuban values led by Lasaga.[41] Various sectors of the community also organized meetings. Encuentros Familiares met throughout the summer to discuss each of the themes, as did Encuentros Juveniles, representatives of the Hispanic women religious, migrant workers in Del Rey, and others.[42]

Taking seriously the Encuentro movement's community and participatory spirit, some women religious sought to have their voices heard. In 1977, for example, they acknowledged the willingness of the archdiocese to include them in activities but complained that they were rarely asked to the organizing and planning meetings. At a 1979 meeting sponsored by the archdiocese to consider the role of women religious, a sister expressed similar concerns. She said that though sisters and nuns felt called to work with lay apostolic movements in the community, they also never received invitations to participate.[43] Despite these barriers to effective involvement, the women nevertheless persisted and contributed to discussions regarding the many problems facing Hispanic Catholics. At the 1977 meeting they called for the creation of a diocesan formation center to deal with issues of spirituality, liturgy, pastoral concerns, prayer, and reflection; the development of a pastoral on economic conditions; a diocesan office for women religious; a politics information center where Latinos could find orientation about political matters as well as information about federal assistance programs; and greater focus on the elderly and the ill.[44]

In early July 1977, the archdiocese announced its official delegation and held a mini Encuentro attended by more than one thousand to discuss their results; this was followed in early August by another meeting that brought together delegates from the entire Southeast region at the Our Lady of Charity shrine.[45] Until then, Cubans had mostly interacted only with each other, but the meeting of the entire region became a Latino gathering of people from New Orleans, Atlanta, Charlotte, Columbia, and many other cities, with ethnicities other than Cuban. At these meetings Latinos learned about each other, recognized the great potential of working together to advance their common goals, and produced a common pastoral vision they took with them to the national Encuentro in Washington.[46]

The Encuentro document produced by the southeast region included the concerns of a diverse constituency and considered evangelization from six perspectives following guidelines established by the national secretariat: evangelization, ministry, human rights, unity in pluralism, integral education, and political responsibility. To support evangelization in general, the document asked for the creation of a Hispanic Center that could cater to the religious needs of Latinos in the region and the development of joint community pastoral plans. It also urged the formation of base communities through which to conduct their work. In the area of ministries, they emphasized the special need to work with the young and agricultural migrant workers. With regards to human rights, they asked the church to raise its voice to protest violations in Latin America, especially in Cuba, Paraguay, Chile, and Bolivia, but also to actively advance the social teachings of the church, to support the human rights of migrant workers, and to create regional centers to form leaders among the agricultural workers. Under the theme of unity in pluralism, the document emphasized the need to evangelize within the cultural traditions and language of Latinos and urged the church to place the idea of integration, not assimilation, at the core of its evangelization method. In the area of education, the document stressed that Catholic, as well as public education, take into account the formation of the whole "integral" person and that special attention be given to developing bilingual and bicultural environments. As to political responsibility, the document encouraged Hispanics to be part of the national and local political process and asked the church to support efforts to inform, orient, and raise the political consciousness of Latinos.[47]

More than one thousand delegates representing more than one hundred thousand Latino Catholics met in Washington during August 18–21, 1977, to participate in the much-awaited Segundo Encuentro, including the Miami delegation, led by Archbishop McCarthy and Hispanic Vicar Román, as well as Bishop Boza Masvidal, who received a special invitation to address the convention. Cuban delegates joined Puerto Ricans, Mexicans, and others of diverse Latin American origin in several days of discussions, arguments, parliamentary procedure, and hurtful as well as heartfelt moments. One Cuban delegate came to tears when it seemed that a statement on the treatment of Cuban political prisoners would not be considered; later it was. As delegate Ada María Isasi-Díaz noted, "We have not solved differences or difficulties. But we know what we are—a people, the people of God that marches on. Recommendations that will be presented to the bishops have been agreed upon. But much more important is the courage for the struggle that our coming together gives us."[48]

Miguel Cabrera spoke positively of the Cuban contribution, imbued as it was with "balance and content," and urged a greater future presence at national meetings. "Perhaps we have shown that not all Cubans are reactionaries and that we have a sense of church and sensibility for the problems of Chicanos, Puerto Ricans, migrants," he noted. "What is still to be accomplished," he added, "is that we be better understood."[49] This was important because "unfortunately, we have to recognize that the Cuban is not often well understood by other Hispanic groups in the United States (and outside), perhaps because of Communist propaganda, and in many cases because of our own lack of prudence, apathy, and negative 'superiority' complex."[50]

Others had similar reactions. Youth delegate Adolfo Castañeda similarly noted that he had learned to see the needs of other groups, while Araceli Luaces said that it was good that Cubans had a chance to present their vision.[51] Juan Clark noted, "It is of great importance that we maintain contacts with the other Hispanic groups, especially Chicanos and Puerto Ricans." "This contact," he said, "was a very positive experience since it provided a way for us to know them better, their problems and their achievements."[52] Román also affirmed the importance of the coming together of all the Hispanic groups, saying, "We didn't really know each other," and he emphasized the imperative of pluralism. "We had to challenge the vision of assimilation," he declared, which goes against the doctrine of the church. Instead of listening to the Gospels, Román argued, the church had listened to sociologists who promoted the idea of a "melting pot."[53]

In line with this spirit, Latinos unfamiliar with the Cuban community also took away a favorable impression. As one Puerto Rican activist, Father Antonio Stevens Arroyo, noted in a reflection on the Encuentro, "A pleasant surprise was the positive effect of the Cuban presence." "Far from conforming to a stereotype as middle-class reactionary Catholics," he declared, "the Cuban delegation from Florida . . . enriched the Encounter by their presence. . . . The enthusiasm of their participation will surely be counted as one of the principal fruits."[54] Shortly after the Encuentro, a Cuban delegate, Sister María Luísa Gastón (sister of María Teresa), who had worked in Hispanic communities in Baltimore and Philadelphia, joined the national secretariat's youth ministry, further diversifying Latino representation in that office.[55]

Perhaps the highlight of the event for Cubans was the appearance of Bishop Eduardo Boza Masvidal and his message. Though not a resident of the United States, the Bishop's special address at the Encuentro, "Unity in Pluralism," reaffirmed to the congregated Hispanic delegates the advice he had given Cubans in 1962 to integrate into U.S. society without assimilating, especially emphasizing the importance of preserving their language.[56] Boza's advice to Cubans in 1962 was meant primarily as a formula for developing and maintaining an exile identity; fifteen years later, the same message to a larger Hispanic audience affirmed their struggle to forge a united Latino strategy for defending culture and identity within the United States. Having worked throughout the 1960s to preserve *cubanidad* and establish their own voice in the local church, many Cubans sympathized with Latino efforts during the 1970s to gain greater recognition. Indeed, it was precisely this emerging cultural consciousness among Hispanic Catholics across the country that inspired Cubans to participate in cross-ethnic activities and communication reflected in the themes of "Unity in Pluralism."

For Cuban Catholics attending the Encuentro, the underlying message was consistent with their almost twenty-year struggle to ensure the visibility of their cultural traditions in the local church. Embracing this larger Hispanic world was perhaps less difficult for Cubans than for others. From the early 1960s, Cubans had spent much time appealing to Latin American Catholics across the hemisphere for solidarity in their struggle against communism. They advocated a united Latin America that could effectively struggle for social justice and fight communism, without having to surrender to North American cultural domination. It was not difficult to articulate this same argument in support of cultural maintenance strategies within the United States.

Fruits of the Encuentro

The 1977 Encuentro accelerated the growth of Cuban and Hispanic influence in the Miami archdiocese during the next few years, confirming the value of working with the Latino movement nationally. Already more open to a pluralistic pastoral approach than his predecessor, Archbishop McCarthy could not have been other than deeply impressed by the Encuentro event in Washington, DC. If pluralism had not yet won the day in Miami, after the Encuentro a commitment to pluralism and diversity took its place as a guiding pastoral principle. While Cubans certainly did not achieve everything they wanted, they gained a great deal in the next two years. Perhaps most symbolically, Rome named Román auxiliary bishop in 1979, inserting a distinct Cuban voice within the local church and paving the way for a greater Hispanic presence in the leadership of the diocese.[57] The appointment also defused the great resentment many Cubans felt since the 1960s about the failure of the archdiocese to bring Bishop Boza Masvidal to Miami.

The ethnic cooperation among Latinos manifested in the Encuentro process also found institutional expression in Miami. After the Washington meeting the Southeast Regional Office of the Hispanic Secretariat became an official and permanent office headed by Father Vizcaíno. He continued visiting local communities, speaking about the Encuentro, collecting data and information about their needs, surveying existing resources, promoting communication between dioceses, and coordinating regional activities.[58] In south Florida Vizcaíno continued promoting the broad Hispanic message to Cuban lay and parish leaders, emphasizing the growing presence of Latinos across the country and reminding them that they would soon be a majority of the Catholic Church in the United States. Though Hispanics in general remained members of distinct groups, Vizcaíno pointed out similarities in their histories: they each carried deep wounds and grievances that had to be rectified. Mexican Americans in the southwest lost their lands and were subjected to the oppression of the dominant culture, Puerto Ricans lamented their neocolonial status, and Cubans denounced unjust and atheistic Marxist communism. Through these very different but related issues, Vizcaíno heard a prophetic Hispanic voice characterized by its objection to injustice, whether of the right or the left. Who would evangelize these many people from all over Latin America if not Hispanics themselves, with their own values, language, and culture? If Catholics did not do their work, he noted, others would, especially the Lutherans and the Baptists, who had recently announced plans to increase their evangelization among Latinos.[59]

Vizcaíno also created a pastoral institute called for in the conclusions of the Encuentro documents approved by all the bishops of the region. The Southeast Pastoral Institute (SEPI) opened in the summer of 1979 with two inaugural specialized pastoral courses in theology, including one on religion and culture offered by Father Elizondo, reflecting increasing relationships among Cubans and Mexican Americans. That fall, SEPI taught additional courses, initiating what would become its highly active pastoral and educational mission in south Florida and the southeastern United States following the general model of the Mexican American Cultural Center founded by Elizondo in 1972.[60]

The Encuentro movement and SEPI also contributed to reaffirming the social consciousness of many Cuban Catholics who felt comfortable expressing their social activism through a pastoral lens though not necessarily through more radical means. Overall, for example, Cubans did not respond very positively to the Mexican American migrant farm worker activism of the late 1960s and early 1970s, despite their sympathy for agrarian reform in Cuba during the 1940s and 1950s. Within the political context of the Civil Rights Movement and the War on Poverty, the plight of migrant farm workers in the United States became a topic of increasing national concern, discussion, and activism, shared by a significant sector of Catholic opinion. Despite the concerns of many Catholics regarding the agrarian situation in Cuba before the Revolution, once in exile enthusiasm for this issue waned. Anti-communist political activism, increasingly conservative socioeconomic ideas, and a need for spiritual and pastoral answers did not predispose exiles to sympathize with farm worker unions and their struggles to gain collective bargaining rights. By the early 1970s in California, organizers from United Farm Workers (UFW), led by Mexican American César Chávez, had won contracts for migrant workers, and efforts to organize workers spread to Texas and Florida. When UFW activists arrived in Florida, few Cubans offered their support, despite the union's strong symbolic attachments to Catholicism and staunch support by local archdiocesan leaders.

Under the direction of Msgr. Fitzpatrick, director of the diocesan Hispanic apostolate, the church accelerated pastoral services and material support for the mostly Mexican seasonal workers in the region. As early as 1960, for example, Father Bryan Walsh, head of Catholic Charities, encouraged by Bishop Carroll, asked the U.S. Senate to include migratory workers in the nation's minimum wage laws. By 1966, Father Martin A. Walsh had established a Coordinating Committee for Farm Workers to raise consciousness about the working conditions of farm workers, sponsor demonstrations, and organize support. Three years later, the archdiocese created the Rural Life Bureau under the direction of Father John R. McMahon, which worked to give the migrant worker a voice and coordinated material support especially during poor harvest seasons. In 1971, the church also established a series of community centers in the Florida towns of LaBelle, Delray, and Naranja designed to provide cultural and educational opportunities for migrant families.[61]

Despite this active support for farm workers by the archdiocese of Miami, with some exceptions Cubans did not at first demonstrate much solidarity with the rural poor. In 1963, an OCSHA priest who had worked five years in Cuba before arriving in the United States, Father Juan de la Calle, served as assistant pastor at Sacred Heart parish in Homestead, a Mexican American agricultural community in South Dade County on the road to the Florida Keys.[62] He tried to recruit Cuban priests and laity to help. For "Miami Latinos," he noted in February 1965, it would be "an unforgettable experience to contemplate the religious fervor of these men and women." He called on the members of ISA, the *cursillos,* MFC, and others to help these communities. "We need help, catechists, Catholics concerned about these brothers. . . . Come and share with them. . . . Help them in their cultural and material advancement."[63] Few responded.

The most conservative exile sectors actually campaigned against the farm worker movement and Chávez himself. In 1969, for example, exile activist Pedro Díaz Lanz accused the Mexican American labor leader of being a communist. "César Chávez is using the same techniques as the Communists," he said. "He has been trained by individuals highly trained in Communist indoctrination." Díaz Lanz pointed for evidence to Chávez's connections with the well-known "Marxist revolutionary" Saul Alinsky and the "Moscow-trained" Walter Reuther, the leader of the United Auto Workers Union.[64] Manuel Chávez, César's brother who headed organizing efforts in Florida, faced the same charges of being a communist. He denied that UFW had any links with communists, and when asked why the union flag included red, he asked impatiently why people did not educate themselves before speaking such nonsense. He wondered why people advanced such petty arguments to combat those interested in justice for campesinos.[65] The next year, at a press conference with Archbishop Carroll, when asked if he was a communist, Chávez replied sarcastically, "I'm not a Communist, I am a Mexican." "It's strange," he went on, "that when anyone tries to do something for the poor people they are thought to be a Communist. Can't Christians do things for poor people?"[66]

Even Cuban agricultural workers became targets of anti-communist Cubans. In March 1972, for example, Father Bryan Walsh and Nicolás Raymond, a Cuban labor leader of some 240 mostly Cuban workers attempting to organize a union at the Talisman sugar central in Belle Glade, north of Miami, joined César Chávez at a press conference announcing successful contract talks with Coca-Cola. Raymond's presence highlighted an ongoing strike at the Talisman operation, where a predominately Cuban workforce sought representation by the UFW. The Talisman workers gained not only the support of the UFW but also active backing from the archdiocese. Years later, volunteer organizers among the Talisman workers remembered the poor living conditions and harassment the striking workers faced at the hands of their Cuban overseers. Despite the fact that most of the workers living in these labor camps were Cuban, no Cuban clergy ever appeared to offer the strikers spiritual or material support.[67]

In fact, some clergy expressed their views on these issues in harsh and insensitive tones. OCSHA priest José Hernando, for example, very close to the Cuban community in Miami and leader of the *cursillo* movement, underestimated the plight of the farm workers despite the fact that he ministered to them in Homestead and Belle Glade. Reacting to a NBC network television documentary called "Migrant" that criticized conditions in the Florida migrant labor camps, Hernando insisted the film had exaggerated. Salaries (often only $10 per day), he said, actually varied, and workers could often earn more than suggested in the film. "These people are not starving," he said. "They may not be eating the right food, but they are not starving." He said medical clinics existed for workers and that social workers visited the camps regularly. "Mothers," he pointed out, "can have their babies delivered free at Jackson Memorial Hospital [in Miami]." He also said that migrant parents often chose not to send their children to school, which presumably could not be blamed on society. Despite Hernando's protestations, numerous others in the interview confirmed the difficult conditions, including seminarian Michael McNally and Father James Fetscher, who declared, "Perhaps a César Chávez in Florida is the only realistic way to deal with the problem."[68] This general reaction to farm worker activism within much of the south Florida Cuban community reflected its deep suspicions of what they perceived to be radical solutions to real social problems in the United States.

In time, as Cuban Catholics came into greater contact with other Latinos and their problems in the United States, many did slowly demonstrate solidarity with the rural poor. A few revealed their concerns early. In 1963, for example, Cuban Catholics working with ISA conducted a research project to document conditions among the rural migrant population, similar to the ACU survey in Cuba in 1958. The research revealed a mostly Catholic population of *tejanos*, *mexicanos*, and *puertorriquenos* with little English-language proficiency living in difficult circumstances.[69] In 1970, one seminarian, Orlando Espín, who worked among agricultural workers in Pompano, Florida, north of Miami, wrote in *The Voice* that it was a Christian duty to help the poorest and weakest in society. "In the face of the necessities of the people I serve," he noted, "I have only one alternative: work to bring oppression to an end." He judged that it was his duty to raise a voice in support of justice and apply his talents to help resolve marginality, suspicion, and hunger. Though he stated this forthrightly, tellingly he also rather defensively emphasized that his ideas were not communist. "This is NOT communism—although some would like to think so to satisfy their myopic vision—because IT IS CHRISTIANITY, solid and committed" (emphasis in original).[70]

By the end of the 1970s, Cubans with social Christian ideas, led and encouraged by Father Vizcaíno, committed themselves in practical ways to improving conditions of the disadvantaged farm workers. Though certainly not the kind of activism envisioned by Liberationist Latino Catholics, Vizcaíno's leadership in the early 1970s with CNPC prepared him and others, through SEPI, to work with Latino farm workers in the southeast United States. In preparation for this work, since the early 1970s Vizcaíno had been involved in taking Cuban youth to San Isidro Parish in Macuspana, Tabasco, in the mountains of southern Mexico, to participate in pastoral initiatives among the rural poor in some thirty communities. Work included helping with a variety of projects having to do with economic development, education, health, and religion. Besides raising the consciousness of young Catholics, Vizcaíno learned a great deal about working in difficult rural settings.[71]

Taking his cue from the conclusions of the regional Encuentro, Vizcaíno made evangelization among the farm workers a priority for the regional office from the very beginning. Already energized by their participation in the Encuentro, farm workers, for example, organized a "speakout" in the community of Lake Wales, Florida, in 1978. More than one hundred farm workers, religious, and clergy from the southeast United States, including over twenty from the archdiocese of Miami, attended the gathering coordinated by SEPI. The participants agreed on the need to establish small faith communities, improve pastoral outreach to migrants, create a national staff to coordinate farm worker interests, communicate the work of Encuentro to all farm workers, and develop migrant adult and youth leadership programs. Father Juan López, of St. Ann's Mission in Naranja, thought the meeting positive because of the awareness and communication it created.[72]

Another meeting later in the year, also coordinated by SEPI, brought leaders of farm worker communities together with church officials in Orlando. After listening to questions and concerns about evangelizing among farm workers, John J. Fitzpatrick, former auxiliary bishop of Miami and now Brownsville bishop, who oversaw a diocese with large numbers of migrants, spoke of the need for spiritual as well as material nourishment: "Before preaching about social justice we have to preach Christ and his Gospels and as a result we will become union organizers, reformers, and social workers." Vizcaíno, of course, emphasized the continuing importance of the sacramental but insisted that social justice for the workers needed equal attention. Others spoke about the history of farm worker unions and the attitude of the church toward organizing workers. Father Beltrán, from the national secretariat, talked about pastoral strategies, emphasizing the need to encourage workers to participate and gain the tools necessary to help themselves.[73]

The considerable focus on farm workers in the late 1970s, promoted by Vizcaíno and SEPI in conjunction with the national secretariat, created a better understanding among Cubans of the plight of farm laborers and their families. Among those attending the Orlando meeting, for example, was Alicia Marill, leader of a Miami-based apostolic movement, Amor en Acción. This lay organization's primarily social focus certainly lent itself to working among the migrants and others in need in south Florida.[74] In the early 1980s, María Teresa Gastón moved with her husband to Immokalee, Florida, to work in a farm worker community.[75] In late 1979, even Tomás Regalado, a well-known media personality in Miami, published an interview with César Chávez in *Ideal*, titled "Struggling against the System within the System," revealing a new sensitivity about a man who was quite controversial in Miami earlier in the decade. Though Regalado raised the question of communism again, this time it seemed calculated to give Chávez the opportunity to explain in some detail his ideas of nonviolent resistance and reform to a conservative Miami audience in one of their own publications. Certainly, Chávez did not have this opportunity earlier in the decade.[76] Though most Cuban exiles, Catholic and non-Catholic alike, no doubt remained suspicious of what they perceived to be radical social discourses throughout the 1960s and 1970s, they thoroughly committed themselves to cultural activism that for some in time translated into significant social action within the United States environment.

During the 1970s, Cuban Catholics became fully engaged in establishing their presence in the church. One of their own became a bishop; they established their cultural imprint in many south Florida parishes; they gained acceptance for their lay movements; they produced a bilingual and bicultural clergy dedicated to working in their communities; and they encouraged community-wide understanding for Hispanic forms of worship as well as tolerance of popular traditions like Santería. Cubans brought a spirit of pastoral diversity to the archdiocese of Miami, which was resisted by Archbishop Carroll but fully embraced by his successor, Archbishop McCarthy. At the same time, south Florida Cuban Catholics recognized that their pastoral movement and instinct for cultural preservation coincided with similar trends among Latinos of different nationalities across the United States. As Cubans struggled for their place in the south Florida church, they also established relationships with an emerging national Hispanic pastoral movement based in the Mexican American and Puerto Rican communities of the United States.

At first such a coalition seemed unlikely. In the 1960s, a national Latino Catholic movement, led by Chicanos and Puerto Ricans, emerged, demanding a greater recognition and voice not only in the local but also in the national Catholic Church. In general, the mostly conservative Cubans in Miami perceived the left-of-center Chicano and Puerto Rican activists as radicals with whom they had little in common. Hispanic Catholics, however, interacted in a variety of venues, including the Encuentro movement. Inevitably frictions emerged, but also mutual understanding and tolerance as they all worked to promote the inclusion of Latinos in the church. Despite often severe disagreements with Chicanos and Puerto Ricans about Cuba itself, Cubans appreciated the Mexican American and Puerto Rican struggle to defend their cultural traditions and social rights.

Cuban Catholics in Miami used the idea of the *pastoral de conjunto* as an effective tool not only for establishing a presence in the church but also for collaborating with other Hispanic groups in an ethnically inspired pastoral movement characterized by shared assumptions of cultural preservation and effective integration into church life in the United States. The movement promoted ethnic consciousness and pastoral practices and strategies aimed at eliciting sensitivity and respect for Latino identity and culture in the North American church as well as seeking social justice for the working poor. In sharing their experience with other Latinos, Cuban Catholics learned about the U.S. reality, leading to a deeper sense of belonging, especially within the Hispanic world. In subsequent decades, while developing a Cuban-American identity, exiles remained engaged with the larger world of Latino Catholicism that emerged with the Encuentro movement of the 1970s.

Chapter Nine

DIALOGUE

The Church continually invites us . . . [to dialogue].
                                        —Manolo Fernández (1969)

Despite integrating into new societies, Cubans remained deeply engaged with their homeland. For years the overwhelming majority of exiles agreed with the fundamental goal of dislodging the Cuban government from power by any means at their disposal. Slowly, however, some came to see this as unrealistic and began in the late 1960s to adjust their thinking and strategies when it became clear that Castro now enjoyed the full support of the Soviet Union and could not be overthrown without a large-scale assault by a major power.

Many exiles like Jorge Mas Canosa came to recognize that armed actions had little possibility of changing Cuba and instead turned to influencing the United States political system, mostly attempting to mobilize support for hard-line diplomatic positions toward the Cuban Revolution. Exile attitudes in this regard were not unanimous, however. Also by the late 1960s, a considerable number of exiles had grown weary of a constant climate of anger and violence. Almost a decade and a half of struggle against Castro, and Batista before, had caused much death, frustration, and confusion. Though clearly a minority, those with this perspective developed very different views, rejecting violence altogether and advocating dialogue and engagement with Cuba, which not only enjoyed a firm theological basis and Vatican backing but also reflected the ethnic experiences and educational formation of a new generation who learned to interpret the Cuban revolutionary experience from different vantage points. These were views not generally tolerated within the Cuban communities themselves. In response to this deeply controversial proposition, the majority community immediately condemned dialogue with the Cuban government as treachery and even denounced public discussion and debate of this alternative among exiles themselves. Throughout the 1970s, Catholics participated in these discussions and increasingly revealed diverse opinions, but, whatever their positions, they brought theological as well as practical political considerations to the debate, influenced by their experiences as exiles and ethnics.

Dialogue

The most enthusiastic promoters of dialogue and pragmatic approaches to the Cuban situation were those who left Cuba as children, adolescents, or young adults. What perhaps seemed so black and white in earlier years revealed different hues in light of complex world events, especially in Latin America. Many Cuban Catholics came to the conclusion that they needed to abandon aggressive stances and simplistic Cold War sloganeering and enter into the difficult realities of the Cuban problem with deeper analysis and informed argumentation. They lamented the deep intransigence of most exiles that ruled out anything but hostile approaches, and they condemned the hard-line voices that controlled the media and intimidated those with nonconformist political perspectives.

Certainly these new voices remained a minority opinion among exiles but did nevertheless advance an ethic of free discussion and diversity of perspectives that emerged slowly and painfully and not without considerable harshness of language and deed. Many, though not all, offering these alternative ideas came from Catholic families; they embraced the intellectual traditions of their faith, concern for their homeland, and concrete international realities. Their formative and educational experiences outside of Cuba molded their worldviews, which were quite distinct from their traumatized parents, who lost all they had worked for. They blazed their own path in a way that considered the local perspectives and realities of the communities in which they lived while simultaneously considering how they might reengage their homeland. Often living outside the south Florida region, they gained different perspectives difficult to see in Miami's highly politicized environment and controlled discourses. Experiences associated with their emerging ethnic identities and socialization in their new places of residence during a particularly turbulent period inspired many to think in new ways about the homeland they had departed as children, adolescents, and young adults.

Like their parents, they remained deeply marked by exile and focused on Cuba, but they differed in their instincts, which encouraged intellectual explorations, including options for dialogue and engagement rather than confrontation and intransigence. This certainly did not create consensus; indeed it led to divisions and even violence among exiles themselves. At the same time, this process did open a conversation among exiles that after the 1970s became more acceptable and even routine, though no less controversial. Opening the dialogue proved very difficult but necessary, and their commitment to civil discourse eventually gained a permanent backing even among exiles in south Florida. Many paid a fearful price for speaking out and acting from conviction, but they did carve out a space for Cuban exiles to express their thoughts.[1]

A group of students at the Catholic University of Louvain in Belgium, calling themselves "Grupo de Lovaina," illustrates the considerably different approaches of some young exiles in the late 1960s. They wrote about their views and experiences in *Nueva Generación* in 1966. Unlike their elders, who arrived in exile with well-formed identities and ideas, they departed in their teens and early twenties feeling displaced and disoriented. Their task, they thought, was to make sense of their experiences and find unity as a generation. Marked by revolution, they shared a geographically dispersed exile, suffered truncated educational trajectories, witnessed the economic distress of families they helped sustain, and shared a common love for their *patria*. They struggled to understand the nature of their obligations to family, to the nations that had accepted them, to their homeland, to themselves. In the short term they knew they had to make practical decisions about their education in order to realize "our most intimate vocations" and "associate ourselves with the real life of our times," to make a difference through communitarian service. Over the longer term this education would provide the "solid basis" for their own contributions to Cuba. Authenticity, they hoped, would be the shared legacy of their generation, which would itself be born of a lived Christianity that demanded local commitments but also (through "a flight of spirit") universal obligations. In this way they could live free of negative and sterile attitudes of constant "refutations," in favor of transcendent and constructive attitudes.[2] These young and idealistic Cuban Catholics sought an approach to life guided by Christian values of love rather than what they perceived to be the vindictiveness in the hearts of their elders. Certainly, this writing revealed an exile experience and engagement with contemporary Catholic ideas quite distinct from their Cold Warrior elders, though it did not necessarily reflect the views of most Cubans even of their generation.

Initially these new voices simply recognized the political and socioeconomic diversity of those who had left the homeland and encouraged free discussion about Cuba, Latin America, and other issues critical to exiles. In the mid-1960s, the group associated with the newspaper *Nueva Generación* led the way in expressing concerns about the quality and trajectory of political and intellectual discourse in their communities. One member of the group characterized his own community, Miami, as deeply marked by the trauma of exile, to the point of psychosis. The disturbing symptoms, he noted, included their feelings of persecution (communists cause all evil in their community), sentiments of grandiosity (Cuba was a paradise before the Revolution), and a propensity to blame others for their problems (Cuba fell to communism because of the Kennedy brothers). Another described Miami as a distortion of Cuban nationality, a place with an exile nationality he called "exilandia," which really had little to do with Cuba. The inhabitants of "exilandia" could not speak, just repeat. They suffered from mediocrity and an inability to discern. Citizens of "exilandia" abandoned all thought of living in the present or the future, preferring the past, and they possessed a threatening and violent vocabulary used to let everyone know that on their return to Cuba they would not only recover their property but "kill the *milicianos*." They were even oblivious to the obvious fact that, whatever happened, the Cuban people on the island would have to be consulted about their future. Though written tongue-in-cheek, the articles' meaning was clear. These young critics thought that the traditional leaders of their communities had lost all creative sense regarding how to deal with Cuba, leaving a legacy of frozen strategies, black-and-white thinking, intransigence, and inflexibility. This is why, they insisted, the diaspora needed a "new generation."[3]

In a 1968 reflection titled "Diálogo," *Nueva Generación's* editorial board declared that Cubans suffered from a crisis of understanding, of themselves as well as of their nationality. "We are a people divided territorially, ideologically, in our sentiments, and in our actions," the editors noted. And finding correct solutions to Cuba's socioeconomic, religious, ideological, philosophical, and political dilemmas required analyzing the grim landscape both on the island and in exile. Leaders in Cuba as well as in exile, they suggested, offered few solutions, and certainly neither group held the moral high ground. In Cuba a dramatic contradiction existed between rhetoric of human rights and dignity on the one hand and the bloody impositions that negated the very rights and dignity they claimed to provide on the other. How could one reach peace and justice through hate and force? At the same time, exiles lived with much emotion and confusion, heterogeneity, and considerable individual achievement but demonstrated little sense of renovation and even less creativity. How could people who embraced the challenge of beginning again in a new place not figure out how to collaborate to find solutions to national problems? The editors believed that solutions required everyone to reflect on Cuba's past and present and be willing to engage in dialogue, but they also lamented that Cubans on the island and in exile rejected dialogue, preferring to place their own interests above national interests. Whether supporters or opponents of the Revolution—inside or outside of Cuba—whether socialists, communists, democrats, capitalists, or Christians, those with power and influence preferred vengeance and hatred to exploring real solutions to Cuba's crisis. Rejecting this closed attitude of Cuban leaders on the island and in exile, *Nueva Generación* proclaimed 1968 the year of dialogue—to promote analysis of the Cuban reality and to engage in discussion on the one hundredth anniversary of the Grito de Yara (Yara Declaration), which launched the Cuban independence struggle from Spain.[4]

In addition to the *Nueva Generación* group, many well-known Catholic leaders also promoted discussion about the Cuban reality. In fact, the idea had gelled among several of the instructors who had taught at the ISA in Miami around 1965, including María Cristina Herrera, Carmelo Mesa Lago,

Fermín Peinado, and others.[5] With dialogue in mind, Catholics in Miami, New York, Washington, Caracas, San Juan, Madrid, Rome, and other places agreed to meet in Washington, DC, for the Primera Reunión de Estudios Cubanos (PREC). When the meeting finally took place in April 1969, after several false starts, it brought together the "cream of the crop" of Cuban Catholic thinkers in exile. The meeting gathered together a representative group of what one organizer, Herrera, called "the thinking and militant" Cuban Christian community in exile to engage conversations for several days.

Herrera herself had been the first president of Catholic Action at the University of Oriente in 1954 and was a member of MRP when she went into exile in 1961.[6] Others attending the first meeting included Bishop Boza Masvidal, José Ignacio Rasco, Laureano Batista and his brother Victor, Manuel "Manolo" Fernández, Andrés Valdespino, José Ignacio Lasaga, Lourdes Casal, Jorge Castellanos, and others, mostly Catholic Action activists and some from ACU. Organized as a symposium with written presentations, PREC in some ways represented—after a decade of exile—the first formal exile reflections on the legacy of the Cuban Revolution. Cubans attending PREC initiated a journey down an often harrowing path to understand the Revolution and its legacy on the island and in the diaspora.

According to Herrera, PREC's goal was to "think and rethink the Cuban process" through dialogue and negotiation, not violence or intimidation. The decision to reject violence, she said, came from blending theological and pragmatic concerns. "Conspiracies did not pay off. It was very self-defeating, very costly, the majority of our compatriots that had been with us in the underground were in jail or had been shot to death and we needed to find a way of relating to Cuba as a nation and as a people, and to Cuba as a process in a better and more nourishing way."[7] Many at the meeting agreed that a more fruitful approach to dealing with Cuba was necessary.

Just two years earlier, Valdespino had justified continuing armed action against the Cuban regime, saying that exiles felt conflicted "between their patriotic anxiety and their religious sentiments." How can we reconcile the clamor of the pope for peace with our own clamor to continue the fight against Castro? His answer was that Castro had unleashed a brutal and ongoing civil war in Cuba and the peace the pope yearned for could only be restored by removing the regime and creating a just society for all.[8] While certainly not changing their minds about the extent of devastation communism had brought to Cuba, or perhaps even the possibility of returning to arms if it seemed appropriate, Valdespino and the other participants nevertheless believed that as Catholics they had the obligation to analyze what had happened in their homeland and initiate discussions to consider an exile response.

So, for example, they asked, why had communists succeeded in coming to power in Cuba? Certainly, Catholics understood that though communism had always had a foothold in Cuban politics, which reflected the nation's socioeconomic stratification and inequities, its appeal had always been limited. Why had the mass of Cubans preferred Castro to the alternatives offered by the church? Some thought the Revolution simply reflected a betrayal foisted on the Cuban people by Castro and a handful of communists supported by the rebel army, while others believed that Cuba's social inequities gave communists the potent weapon they needed to gain mass support among Cubans. Whatever the case, after the initial years of reacting violently to the Revolution, some Cuban exiles recognized the value of reflection, analysis, and discussion. As Manolo Fernández, a former Catholic Action activist and resident of Madrid, noted, "The Church continually invites us . . . [to dialogue], to overcome ancient doctrinal and canonical fragmentation. The goals of this dialogue should not be to defend positions; it is not to point out mistakes or convince others of their errors; but to find points of convergence and find those strains of truth that have as their fruit human understanding. The church teaches and at the same time learns."[9]

Not all could agree with this approach however. Though initially involved as part of the PREC organizing committee, for example, José Illán, a Catholic lay activist, a former member of the first Cuban revolutionary government, and employee of the Inter-American Cooperative Bank, decided not to attend the meeting at all because of the group's decision that "objectivity" would be their guiding value. He rejected "that cold objectivity which does not want to accept the least bit of passion and sentiment." Illán feared that his presence would be disruptive given his "belligerent style" and commitment to "total struggle against that which I consider malignant." Reflecting the traditional views in Miami, he considered PREC's basic approach to be "unnecessarily and exaggeratedly respectful of our common enemy."[10] Most Cuban exile activists, particularly in Miami, shared Illán's views about this.

Despite the controversy, PREC participants did enjoy a successful meeting. They engaged in substantive discussions about exile, literature, religion, the church, economics, education, and international politics, among other things, in a respectful and tolerant way. Presentations and dialogue revealed a split between those with hard-line inclinations toward Cuba who characterized the Revolution as repressive and immutable, essentially black-and-white, and those inclined to study the situation closely and offer more complex and nuanced interpretations. The hard-liners who viewed the regime in Cuba as essentially defined, without any redeeming features at all, tended to offer presentations on the exile communities or pre-1959 Cuba, while the latter offered nuanced discussions on revolutionary Cuba, including literature, economics, and religion. Lourdes Casal's presentation on the Cuban novel during the first ten years of the Revolution, for example, concluded that "while it is not true that political conditions through 1968 have given the writer absolute liberty, it is also not true that conditions have impeded all possibility of creativity."[11] This certainly caused a reaction. Valdespino, Lasaga, and José Luís Díaz de Villegas all objected to what they considered Casal's benign interpretation of Cuba's reality. They recognized that perhaps artists could maintain a certain amount of personal freedom but emphasized that they could not utilize their art to challenge or criticize the system, which made their personal freedom irrelevant. On the other hand, when Mercedes García Tudurí offered a positive review of Cuban education before the Revolution, Casal sharply challenged her assessment as "exaggerated optimism." She also criticized García's wholesale condemnation of Cuba's socialized education system as "highly schematic, negative and politicized."[12]

Despite obvious differences of opinion and political instincts of those attending, the organizers managed a second meeting in 1971 that led to the formation of a permanent organization called the Instituto de Estudios Cubanos (IEC). In her mid-thirties, Herrera became IEC's guiding light and maintained the organization on a steady course, always reiterating that the enterprise would only survive if members maintained an atmosphere of openness and respect for all opinions. Manuel "Manolo" Fernández, a veteran journalist in his late forties, became the editor of *Reunión,* the IEC newsletter that kept members apprised of activities and maintained the active and controversial dialogue between gatherings. Fernández had edited the Catholic youth newspaper *Juventud* and cofounded and coedited *La*

Quincena with Biaín. Like other Catholic Action activists, Fernández initially supported the Revolution, working with the newly established film institute, but he also grew disillusioned and left.[13]

During the 1970s, IEC also attracted younger exiles, especially university students. The diversity in age and politics of IEC members ensured energetic debates and varying perspectives at the periodic meetings, sometimes leading to sharp disagreements and strains. Many, especially in Miami, felt deeply troubled by the conversations at IEC that would not be tolerated in exile public discourse. For many years, IEC offered the only safe "Cuban space" where differing ideas about Cuba could be expressed openly and respectfully without fear of personal attacks or accusations of being fascist, communist, or something else. IEC constantly instigated dialogue, bringing controversy but also new approaches to thinking about Cuba.

Among the most contentious debates for these Catholics involved the proper attitude of the Cuban church toward the Revolution or, more specifically, communism. At the inaugural IEC gathering two Cuban exiles offered theological approaches in line with the teachings of the Second Vatican Council. They asked their colleagues to reconsider conventional wisdom about Christianity in the world, its relationship to communism, and the role of the church in societies undergoing revolutionary transformation.[14] José R. Villalón, director of curriculum at Casa Generalicia of the La Salle Brothers in Rome, offered a dense discussion that questioned the theological basis for the hard-line confrontational strategies of most Cuban Catholics in exile and suggested new ways of thinking. He raised a series of questions, including how Cuban exiles might apply the new Vatican II teaching *Gaudium et Spes* to their homeland, pointing to aspects of the document relevant to Cubans on and off the island. Treating concerns about the place of the church in the modern secular world, *Gaudium et Spes* urged Catholics to be fully engaged. As one historian explained, the document placed the church "humbly at the service of humanity and points out how both church and world can find common ground in their mutual recognition of the dignity of the human person and the nobility of his vocation to build the human community."[15]

Villalón reviewed the document for those assembled, emphasizing the church's call to the faithful to be aware of the "signs of the times," including the great and profound changes affecting the modern world that required discernment and creative responses. According to the document, disruption and crisis throughout the world causing dramatic change had to be addressed by the church, including rapid economic growth, migration, a more unified and interdependent world threatened with dangerous and persistent tensions, the emerging centrality of science and technology, proliferation of industrialization and urbanization, information explosion, unprecedented population growth, and greater interaction of the social classes and individuals. Slow responses by the church, however, had caused many to abandon religion as irrelevant and unable to address everyday human problems. People sought solutions to their new realities through secular and often atheistic philosophies that promised dignity and a decent livelihood. Despite these difficulties and divisions, *Gaudium et Spes* offered positive responses. Declaring that the church was not tied to any particular political, economic, or social agenda, the new teachings promoted the essential concern for human dignity and solidarity in all its dimensions and called for the sincere collaboration of all, whether believers or not, for the achievement of this goal.

In light of these teachings, Villalón urged his colleagues to reassess their attitudes and explore options with regard to the Cuban Revolution. A greater sense of solidarity should inspire exiles not to want to provoke disturbances for Cuba, causing greater harm than good. Tolerance and a pluralistic outlook would lead exiles to a greater understanding of the complexity of the Cuban question and, without recriminations, to find common solutions. Recognizing that the Cuban church, as the church everywhere, had to live within a growing secular reality, Villalón suggested that it become a deeper church, accepting its role within the existing political context, not as a crusading voice, but one dedicated to faith and social criticism. A dynamic and active church in the socialist countries could help clarify not only the negative but also the possible positive aspects of communist societies.[16]

Fully in accord with Villalón, a second presentation by Mateo Jover took the issue a step further. A former leader of Catholic Action in Cuba and a student of Francois Houtart at the University of Louvain in Belgium, Jover suggested that the Cuban Revolution was, indeed, a "sign of the times" for Latin America, a "complex reality" that needed to be carefully studied. Using a highly theoretical and sociological approach reminiscent of his mentor and typical of the emerging Liberationist methodology, Jover offered ideas of how the church could not only find legitimacy within a communist society but influence it in ways that could lead to tolerance, more open-ness, and even possibilities for evangelization.

Jover clearly drew inspiration from the growing Latin American move-ments arguing for a revolutionary Christianity that could resolve the re-gion's pressing socioeconomic realities without resorting to communism, but the church had to accept that communism was already a concrete re-ality in Cuba. Open opposition by the church simply blocked its efforts to regain legitimacy within Cuban society and achieve space to work within the country. Rather than taking an oppositional political stance, the church should engage in dialogue and challenge the state in matters of ideological concern, not political theory. Dialogue, Villalón thought, provided the pos-sibility of allowing the church to move from a position of "pastoral preser-vation" to one of greater presence in society. In this way the church could manifest its faith where history was being made instead of on the margins.

Though this church dialogue could eventually engage government lead-ership and mid-level political organizations in society, discussions should commence at the base, where personal relationship could over time reduce tensions, suspicions, and animosities between Catholics and communists. With this methodology, the church could begin a pastoral reorientation among Catholics that could lead to more effective involvement and influ-ence with the revolutionary project.[17] Villalón and Jover both suggested that Cuban communism, like all political and social projects, could through its own internal dynamics change and become something different, not yet imaginable. "It is important to be conscious," Jover said, "that the road to total development (human development and orientation toward Christ) for the Cuban people is not completely in our hands. . . . God himself will de-fine this salvation."[18]

In fact, the ideas expressed by Villalón and Jover, both residents of Eu-rope and in all probability in contact with Cuban church officials, simply expressed ideas that had already been articulated in the church generally as well as in Cuba. Though also exiles, Jover and Villalón embraced the spirit of the new Latin American church and Medellín and, like the *Nueva Gen-eración* group, placed its understanding of the Cuban experience within a larger regional context. While problematic in many ways, especially the Revolution's atheism and intolerance toward religion and church, the Cuban drama did not seem any worse than the poverty, violence, and militarism ravaging Latin America generally. For this reason they did not refer to themselves as anti-communists but rather as Christian revolutionaries. Their analysis diverged from their elders, as did their strategies for dealing with the issues.

More conservative Catholic leaders attending PREC vigorously challenged the two. Not surprisingly, thinkers and activists like Valdespino, Rasco, Lasaga, Laureano Batista, and several others, steeped in their anti-communism and targets of Leslie Dewart's criticisms, expressed surprise at what they considered Jover and Villalón's naïveté about communism and criticized their presentations in no uncertain terms. Some questioned Vatican II theology outright, while others dissented from the theological interpretations offered by Villalón and Jover.

Victor Batista, for example, agreed that the church should be involved in the world but to promote the sacred rather than condone secularization, while Rasco seemed to distrust some aspects of Vatican II. Saying that he was raised in stable, solid, set in stone (*rocosas*) Catholic teachings, Rasco criticized the complicated intellectual environment of the 1960s as slippery (*movedizo*) and sandy. He criticized the tendency toward subjectivism or relativism, which he believed would eventually overtake the basic truths if not contradicted. Díaz de Villegas simply denied the usefulness of the notion of "signs of the times." For Villalón, he noted, the "signs" seemed to suggest a collectivist future, but could certain capitalist "signs" not be equally valid? Christians of good faith could interpret signs in divergent ways and implement subsequent actions differently despite the same circumstances. He added that Jover's interpretation of "signs" with regard to Cuba would lead to the conclusion that the Cuban Revolution actually had positive dimensions, an idea he could not accept. "Cuban totalitarianism," he noted, "has in ten years proven that it is not only incapable of achieving collective welfare, but, in addition, to stay in power has had to rely on the structures of a police state, systematically—not accidentally—abolishing the attributes Christians consider essential for dignified life and human development." These critics also reminded Jover that although dialogue among individual Christians and communists in Cuba would not hurt in principle, the fruits of such dialogue could never influence a totalitarian system unrelenting in its desire to control.

Valdespino observed that the danger of dialogue for the church was that it might become an instrument of the totalitarian regime with which it will eventually be forced to negotiate. "I think that the Church can provide testimony with its simple presence, with dignified silence, as has been the case with the [Cuban] Church of Silence." Jorge Castellanos, a former communist himself, advised Jover not to forget that the very nature of communism required the destruction of all opposing viewpoints. "Communism seeks, has to seek, the total control of man, each man. All opposition will be swept away." At the same time, he argued, the Bolsheviks used tactics, diverse postures, and manipulation to ensure control. These and similar responses by the old-guard Catholic intellectuals revealed that they had no intention of accepting the new flexible attitude of the church with regard to communism. "The Cuban Christian in Cuba or outside," declared Díaz de Villegas, "who interprets the idea of signs of the times currently in vogue as nothing more than a theory that smells of opportunism disguised as theological semantics is perfectly within his rights to passively or actively oppose the communist system, even through violence" without being considered a "counterrevolutionary, a reactionary, or caveman [*cavernícola*]." In the final comment of this enthusiastic and sometimes harsh but respectful exchange, Díaz reminded Jover and Villalón that tolerance is not always a virtue. In the end, Christ was not tolerant with "certain established orders, nor with hypocrisy, nor with lies, nor with evil."[19]

In further response, Victor Batista, who edited the exile literary journal *Exilio,* associated with writers of Christian inspiration and much influenced by the 1950s Cuban Christian-inspired literary magazine *Orígenes,* responded in a curious way with an article titled "Reflections on the History of Salvation." The article was "inspired by the Cuban Studies Meeting held in Washington, D.C." and dedicated to its participants. He recounted the history of the Protestant Reformation and pointed to parallels between that drama and the Cuban situation. Luther's ideas, which Batista argued eventually served as the intellectual source for Hegel and Marx, represented radical responses to the existing abuses within Catholicism. Though change was certainly necessary, the appropriate response was reform, not revolution. The church patiently dialogued with Luther, hoping to dissuade him and modify his positions, but when he refused, the church had no choice but to respond in kind. In the end, the repercussions of the Reformation were many and—from Batista's point of view—negative for humanity. Though he made no direct reference to the nature of the parallels he perceived, among other things he certainly implied that dialogue had already been attempted in 1960 and 1961 and Castro's response at the time was repression and violence. Perhaps his message was that exiles had no choice but to respond with violence, certainly justified in his mind through just war theory. To allow communism to persist and mold human society would be more harmful in the long-run than a short-term war of liberation and restoration of the faith. In any case, dialogue offered few possibilities, as the case of Luther demonstrated.[20]

Less than five years after the final Vatican II deliberations and only a few months after CELAM's gathering at Medellín, then, Cuban Catholics at PREC engaged the problem of Cuba within the context of the church's evolving post-conciliar theology. Having experienced the practical results of a harrowing communist revolution, the old-guard Catholic Action intellectuals and activists of the 1950s dedicated to the social thought of the church had a difficult time accepting many of the new teachings. It was bad enough that the new ideas seemed thoroughly permeated with relativism and secular methodologies, but most troubling was the backtracking on confronting communism and what seemed to be the church's legitimization of collectivist political schemes. Schooled in anti-communism in the 1930s and 1940s and chased from their country by a communist revolution, these Catholic leaders had little patience for the younger generation's application of post-conciliar theology to the Cuban case. The old-guard Catholics saw little option but to remain intransigent and do whatever possible to undermine and eventually depose the communist system, while many of the younger generation proposed that Catholics work within the communist system, maintaining and advancing a Christian voice and influencing the Revolution's future.

This discussion with its divergent visions and strategies proved to be a preview to what became a more generalized and heated debate in the exile communities when in 1969, encouraged by papal nuncio Msgr. Cesare Zacchi, the Cuban church hierarchy, which had been silent since the 1961 confrontations, issued two pastorals that stunned exiles. By this time, only Archbishop Díaz of Havana and Bishop Muller of Cienfuegos remained from the ecclesiastical hierarchy that had challenged Castro in 1960 and 1961, and they both resigned within the year. A new generation, following Zacchi's policies and led by Msgr. Francisco Oves Fernández, who replaced Díaz, now led the Cuban church.[21] Primary author of the first pastoral, "Christian Life," in April 1969, Oves Fernández had been deported in 1961 but returned in 1964 to continue serving the church. Drawing on Pope

Paul VI's speech at Medellín, which three Cuban bishops and Zacchi himself attended the previous year, the Cuban hierarchy emphasized the importance of themes of social morality and the problem of economic development. They began with quoting the pope: "Today, this visit [to Medellín] inaugurates a new period in ecclesiastical life . . . that requires effort, audacity and a sacrifice that provokes deep anxiety in the Church . . . a moment of total reflection." According to the Cuban bishops this new ecclesiastical period required incorporating ideas of social morality into the world of work and economic development, including new ways of thinking and acting. This work, however, was hindered by Cuba's internal problems, "men's deficiencies and sins," and by externally imposed isolation. Without much elaboration regarding the nature of the domestic limitations mentioned, the bishops very explicitly pointed to the especially harmful effects of the U.S. embargo, which they condemned.[22]

The second pastoral, issued in September, focused on "the problems of faith in a society in transition." Again drawing on post-conciliar ideas, after a conventional discussion of faith, the bishops raised the problem of atheism, which was a growing phenomenon in the contemporary world and could no longer be ignored. The time had arrived for Christians to approach atheists with respect and charity, and not question the honesty and sincerity of their ideas. Christians and atheists shared many common interests and goals, and there was no reason they could not cooperate to promote the welfare of humankind. The bishop also called for tolerance and openness toward "imperfect expressions of faith," alluding to the popular religious forms, like Santería, the church had traditionally excluded. Finally, the bishops called on Catholics to promote the faith through the liturgy, the Bible, and the catechism, despite the difficult circumstances. "We are confident," they concluded, "that our sincere and humble incarnation in this environment permits us to discover paths that help reveal the face of God to our brothers."[23] Together the pastorals suggested that Catholics in Cuba had an obligation to engage the society as it was and work to make it Christian without outside interference.

The pastorals shocked Cuban Catholics on and off the island. Certainly, exile Catholics did not expect the bishops, in their first pastorals since 1961, to advocate coexistence with communism and condemn the U.S. embargo without openly protesting the decade-long persecution of the church or referring to the many Catholics and others in Cuban prisons.

Nor did they expect, as in the second pastoral, that the bishops would urge Catholics to join atheists in their revolutionary process without pointing out the clear barriers Catholics faced in practicing their own religion, much less evangelizing. Though varied, exile criticisms of the Cuban bishops were informed by the deeply held conviction, expressed at PREC, that conversations, negotiations, or collaborations with communists were useless and only set Christians up for manipulation and treachery by the regime.[24]

Many exiles, Catholic and otherwise, and people on the island condemned the Cuban church leaders and the Vatican, criticizing their lack of courage to challenge the communist state. At their April 1969 meeting in Caracas, several hundred exile priests and lay leaders responded to the Cuban bishops with a sharp statement against the Cuban regime and a moderate rebuke of the first pastoral. Certainly, they pointed out, the church's role did not include promoting counterrevolution, but neither should it collaborate with a regime that most on the island rejected.[25] Animosity toward the Cuban church grew among many in exile in subsequent years, especially toward Archbishop Oves Fernández and the vicar of Havana, Father Carlos Manuel de Céspedes, who became a critical intermediary between the government and the church. On completing his studies in philosophy at San Carlos Seminary in Havana in 1959, Céspedes traveled to Rome to study theology, where he remained until 1963. On his return he embraced Zacchi's policies of constructively engaging the revolutionary process from a Catholic perspective. "I am not a Marxist," he said in 1966, "but neither am I a worm (*gusano*)," referring to the exiles.[26]

In 1971, the exile newspaper *Alerta* launched a harsh attack on Zacchi, the Vatican, the Cuban hierarchy (especially Oves and Céspedes), and the Cuban Studies group led by Herrera for secretly promoting coexistence with "the hated communist satrap in Cuba." These secret overtures, the newspaper argued, stemmed from the convergence of Christian humanism and atheist humanism (communism), which is the fruit of "seeds sewn by the subversive apparatus of international communism that with patient work over the years has infiltrated its agents among cadres of priests around the world, even penetrating the leadership of the powerful Vatican."[27] José A. Pantojan, a deacon in the archdiocese of Newark and an activist in matters having to do with political prisoners in Cuba, considered Oves and Céspedes unrepresentative of the Cuban church and merely pawns of the Cuban government. In his opinion they also fell into the category of the growing number of Catholic clergy in Latin America and the United States "allied with Marxists and liberation groups" instead of remaining loyal to "the doctrine of Christ their best ally."[28]

Nevertheless, some observers did recognize the need for a more pragmatic response to the Cuban church's situation. Manolo Fernández, for example, noted that while the exile community's negative response to "Christian Life" was understandable, given the pastoral's call for collaboration with the Revolution and the lifting of the U.S. and hemispheric embargo, two symbols of exile resistance, he also pointed out that the bishops' statement was well within the spirit of the post-conciliar church, following the ideas of Pope John XXIII and the Vatican Council. Though these same church documents also rejected the errors of atheism, including religious discrimination, attacks on human dignity, and the difficulties of dialogue with Marxists, Fernández noted that the bishops could not be expected to raise the full range of issues in one pastoral. It was unfair, he argued, to consider the bishops somehow "subversive," because they did not raise these concerns. Their communications had to be understood as theological and pastoral statements directed to a specific audience in Cuba for a specific social purpose and not as political documents from a particular pressure group.[29]

In Miami, another Catholic commentator, Brother Avelino Fernández, agreed on the need to consider the political reality but also pointed out the fact that the mere issuance of the pastoral, regardless of its specific content, initiated the construction of a public Christian position within the Cuban context. In some ways the pastoral *was* subversive, he noted, since it reminded the faithful that "the originality of the Christian message does not directly consist of affirming the necessity of structural changes, but on the insistence of the conversion of man, who will later demand that change." Fernández interpreted this to mean that only Christians, through conversion, were really capable of taking Cuba to that goal of economic development and social morality.[30] Though in the minority among exiles, certainly these commentators recognized the validity and importance of the pastorals that initiated what they considered to be a tenuous but nevertheless necessary move toward conversation between the church and the state.

In 1972, another exile observed that despite what exiles thought about religious repression in Cuba, in fact, Christian communities did maintain an active spiritual life. Relying on information from his sister, who had just arrived in exile from Pinar del Rio, Father Pablo Urquiaga, working in Venezuela, reported that small Christian communities had formed in Cuba, establishing great unity and brotherhood. Many of these activists, with the approval of the bishop, formed teams to go into the small towns, which were without churches and priests, to take the Christian message. In some towns local councils formed to represent the bishop in services. These communities helped each other with material goods, exchanging their state rations as needed to meet people's needs. "I think," noted Urquiaga, "this is sufficient for us to recognize that they are sincerely living a Christian life and without a doubt the Holy Spirit lives intensely within them, and they are living examples for many of our exile communities."[31] Earlier, Brother Fernández also reported on the intensity of Christian life among Cubans on the island, saying that the churches attracted not Sunday Christians but everyday Christians who went to church not "to show off their clothes" or "to adorn the parking lots with the latest model cars, or to cheaply comply with an obligation" but rather because, with their material life reduced to nothing, they realized their need of God. Cubans in Miami, he observed, could learn much from their coreligionists in Cuba.[32]

A young Cuban graduate student at Harvard University and member of IEC, Jorge Domínguez, was also interested in the Cuban church's new attitude and was among the first exile academics to comment on this topic. Representative of those exiles trained as scholars in the United States, Domínguez, who eventually became a leading authority on Latin American and Cuban affairs at Harvard University, offered a dispassionate and analytical approach that diverged from the emotional and intransigent tones typical of exile discourse. Though the church had to be careful not to "lose its soul to save its skin," Domínguez thought "that the wisdom of the basic decision [to engage the new society] is irrefutable." The church would not only benefit from ending its isolation but "*must* support those features of the revolution which are worth supporting" in order to gain political credibility in Cuba, as well supporting its own commitments to social justice (emphasis in original). Domínguez also questioned the U.S. policy of hostility and embargo, which he thought simply strengthened Castro's hand. "The current policy of the United States may be doing the opposite of what it intends," he explained. "International confrontation and internal confrontation have been linked. If one prop is removed, the other may slowly be removed too."[33]

Much of this debate took place within the context of growing discussions among Catholics generally about the possible common social interests between communism and Christianity, if not philosophically, then at least in practical terms. Several years after Medellín, with the new social activism among Latin American Catholics and the emergence of Liberation Theology, Castro encouraged and engaged an ongoing debate regarding potential intersections of interest. This became particularly public during a trip by Castro to Chile after the election of Salvador Allende. He met with the progressive Chilean Cardinal Raul Silva and made numerous statements to various audiences on the topic. Heartened by Castro's comments, many Catholics believed this signaled a possible warming of relations between communists and Catholics in Cuba. In April 1972, some of the priests who had spoken with Castro in Chile announced a meeting of Cristianos por el Socialismo, and a delegation of Cuban priests, seminarians, and laity participated.[34]

Nevertheless, despite Castro's rhetoric and the positive response by at least a small sector of Cuban Catholics, the regime itself did little during the 1970s to engage the Cuban church. Exiles quickly pointed out the discrepancy between Castro's comments to a Latin American audience and the reality in Cuba. Manolo Fernández questioned the long-term viability of devotional life in a country determined to erase it and concluded that the Cuban government's interest in collaboration with progressive Christians was a one-way affair. "If on the one hand the government seeks the support of Christians," he noted, "it seems clear that it offers nothing in return." Seemingly, he said, the Revolution's goal continued to be to transform religious faith into revolutionary faith, as dictated by the Marxist dialectic.[35] For most exiles, this was confirmed by the adoption of the Cuban Constitution in 1976, which reaffirmed Marxist-Leninist orthodoxy. While the constitutional document affirmed the right to practice religion, it also made clear that religion would be tolerated but not much more than that. How could Castro, Fernández wondered, speak of collaboration between Marxists and Christians in 1972 and subsequently oversee the writing of a constitution that defined the Cuban state as atheistic, institutionalizing an already generalized policy of hostility that made the open practice of religion possible only if the faithful willingly accepted the harmful consequences on their occupational and educational prospects.[36] The constitution virtually ensured that Christians would remain second- or third-class citizens, especially since the Revolution's goal remained to "overcome" the "ideological remnants of the past among which are mystical criteria and beliefs in the supernatural." Though individuals could certainly commit themselves to Christian life, they faced marginality and insignificance in Cuban life.[37] Fernández questioned the ability of Christianity under these conditions to find a legitimate place within Cuban society and survive in the long term, especially among subsequent generations deprived of all religious training and subject to Marxist indoctrination.

Villalón continued to challenge the church to become more creative and recognize that new political and socioeconomic realities in Cuba required new church structures and approaches to pastoral life. While Fernández lamented that lay movements no longer existed, Villalón pointed out that this was perhaps more because of the inaction of the bishops, with their traditional desire to control the church, than the lack of opportunities. Cuban priests and lay activists, he also noted, actually suffered less repression and violence than their colleagues in Brazil and other countries with military dictatorships as a result of their efforts to organize Christian communities dedicated to socioeconomic change among the poor.[38]

In the 1970s, this spirit of dialogue also influenced the exile clergy. At a three-day meeting of the international exile clergy gathering in September 1977, the priests also spoke openly and revealed differing perspectives that seemed influenced by the realities of the countries in which they lived. Those living in Latin America encouraged their colleagues to identify themselves with the whole region because "they suffer too." They criticized their colleagues in the United States for their obsessive focus on exile, to the exclusion of other concerns. "We should join our pain," said Father Sergio Cabrera, "to the pain and the misery of the whole world." Father Bazán, resident of Santo Domingo, agreed: "We cannot identify with a cheap anti-communism." "We need to know," he insisted, "that there are other Latin American nations that are oppressed, though they do not live with totalitarian regimes like Cuba." Father Urquiaga, resident of Venezuela, wondered what it meant to be anti-communist because one could identify that way and still be shameless and egotistical. "The exile communities are full of vacuous youth. What are we doing to create Catholic leadership for the future?" On the other hand, Msgr. Raul del Valle of New York said that many radicalized people who supported Cuba had no idea what the system was like, while Father Comesañas of New Jersey criticized those who believed that simply creating economic equality constituted a "Christian experience," without reference to freedom, an indispensable Christian value.[39]

Engaging Cuba

It did not take long for the spirit of dialogue to encourage some exiles toward the next logical step—finding ways to engage Cuban authorities directly. During the early 1970s, both Carmelo Mesa Lago and Lourdes Casal, for different reasons, traveled to Cuba. Certainly, as could have been expected, the traditional exile leadership condemned this travel and called them communists or Castro agents, but the two provoked disagreements even among exiles advocating dialogue. For some, open, frank, and respectful dialogue among themselves was one thing, but traveling to Cuba and engaging Cuban authorities directly was quite another. If most questioned this strategy by the church in Cuba, they certainly wondered whether it was prudent for exiles to do the same.

In 1966, Manolo Fernández had criticized the "intellectual tourism" that had become popular among left-wing intellectuals and even Christians, including priests, brothers, Catholic journalists, and others, who seemed to care little about the welfare of the Cuban people. He lamented that a week's travel in the country in an official government car seemed to provide sufficient legitimacy and authority to write definitively about the situation in Cuba.[40] In 1974, Fernández also raised concerns about the travel of exiles to Cuba. "Sooner or later," he noted, "those exiles with a certain level of sensibility will be attacked by an invincible nostalgia for the homeland," especially the youngest who arrived in exile with certain unformed impressions. Inevitably as they matured in exile and came into contact with diverse ideas, many of the youth questioned what they had been taught. They naturally became interested in traveling to Cuba, "with the generous goal of collaborating toward a positive evolution of a regime [they] understood as implementing practical measures for a just society." Unfortunately, Fernández lamented, the regime in the last fifteen years had not changed its unjustified rigidity, dogmatisms, and fundamental direction. Though the government now allowed some exiles to travel to the island, it limited and watched their movements in the Soviet way. It was something, but very little, and he thought it sad that one had to be a "directed visitor" in one's own country.[41]

Interpreting this criticism as directed toward him, Mesa Lago responded. An economics professor and assistant director of the Center for Latin American Studies at the University of Pittsburgh, Mesa Lago specialized in the economics of socialist Cuba. He would become the most recognized Cuban scholar in the United States on the Cuban Revolution, eventually establishing the Center for Cuban Studies at the University of Pittsburgh and *Cuban Studies/Estudios Cubanos,* the premier journal in what became the academic field of Cuban Studies. At PREC he had presented a paper on Cuba's economic situation, predicting that the economic failures of the 1960s would force policy toward either a Soviet or Yugoslav socialist model.[42] In 1970, after a decade of considerable economic chaos culminating in a sugar harvest that failed to reach expectations, Castro did indeed decide to adopt the Soviet socialist model. During this moment of great transition for the Revolution, Mesa Lago hoped to travel to Cuba for research and to see matters for himself. This trip led in 1974 to the publication of *Cuba in the 1970s: Pragmatism and Institutionalization,* a study of the Cuban economy that offered a scholarly criticism of the Cuban government's policies and rapidly became the work of record on the Cuban economy. Mesa Lago noted that traveling to Cuba did not imply bargaining with principles, accepting the Cuban system, or feeling constrained to speak the truth about the experience, but simply taking advantage of an opportunity to see firsthand what he had been studying in libraries for a decade.[43]

Casal also responded, but her motives were different, more complex. Unlike Mesa Lago, Casal expressed an openly political rationale driven by "a re-evaluation of the Cuban revolutionary process, a rethinking of the world situation and, simultaneously, a personal redefinition of my own relationship to these realities." Living in the United States throughout the 1960s had a decisive radicalizing effect on Casal, often expressed in *Nueva Generación.* As she placed events within the broader Latin American context, she became increasingly curious about the Revolution. When the possibility to travel appeared, Casal went to see for herself Cuba's national revolutionary project. It would have been unethical *not* to go, she said. Casal disagreed with Fernández's basic assumption, shared by most in exile, that the Revolution was immutable, unchanging. Since 1960, she argued, many changes had occurred, and Cuba continued to evolve, but it was also true that to expect the Cuban regime to change in the face of the constant hostility from the United States was unrealistic.

The overthrow of Chile's socialist president, Salvador Allende, whose fall and death occurred precisely the day after Casal's return from Cuba, affected her thinking decisively. She became convinced that in Latin America a peaceful path to a more just society was, in fact, an idealistic illusion. In ten years, Casal went from being a militant, socially conscious, anticommunist Catholic Action activist at Villanueva University to an exile in the United States more in tune with her African heritage, convinced that the social justice issues that attracted her to Catholicism in Cuba could only, in fact, be accomplished through a revolutionary experience.[44] She became a firm supporter of the Cuban Revolution, a path few of her own generation accepted, even her closest *Nueva Generación* collaborators. José Prince, who admired Casal and respected her journey, disagreed: "I could not accompany her on her journey under the circumstances and with the strategies she chose." Prince saw a substantive difference between Castro and what Allende had attempted through democratic means.[45]

On the other hand, some exiles who left Cuba at a young age and were raised in the United States did find Casal's trajectory compelling. They also became radicalized by the tumultuous 1960s and 1970s. "Change began," a group of these Cuban youth noted, "with a dual process of rejecting North American society and the Cuban exile community."[46] Many engaged the Civil Rights Movement, worked with Chicano and Puerto Rican activists, and supported the War on Poverty, while others participated in the counter-culture movement and opposition to the war in Vietnam. Ultimately, their alienation took them to the question of Cuba. One youth reconsidered the Revolution beginning in 1969 after having participated with the United Farm Workers' grape boycott in Miami and while studying at the University of Florida. Another underwent a similar process while taking a course on the Cuban Revolution at Indiana University. "The course challenged all of the myths that had been implanted in my head about prerevolutionary Cuba. Little by little all the reasons I opposed the revolution seemed to vanish."[47] Given these experiences in the United States, they, like Casal, saw the Cuban Revolution in a new light—not the perspective of their parents. Many interpreted the Revolution's commitment to social justice as not just rhetoric but concrete action.

During the early 1970s, radicalized Cuban youth published *Areíto* and *Joven Cuba* magazines, revealing socialist inclinations that took an openly sympathetic view of the Cuban Revolution. In October 1977, soon after President Carter renewed formal relations with Cuba and lifted the travel ban, Casal accompanied fifty-five Cuban youth known as the Grupo Areíto to the island for a month. They worked construction, got a firsthand look at the Revolution, and received an enthusiastic reception by Cubans. Subsequently, Casa de Las Americas, an important Cuban cultural institution in Havana, published their testimony, *Contra viento y marea,* and the Cuban film institute produced a documentary film, *Cincuenta y cinco hermanos,* celebrating their visit, which was shown across the island and in exile. The group also founded Brigada Antonio Maceo, an organization sympathetic with the Cuban Revolution that sponsored additional trips for Cuban youth interested in learning about the revolutionary reality.

But not only radicals questioned the hard-liners. Others of the same age cohort simply wanted to better understand what had happened. While studying at the University of Miami, one Cuban youth, Lisandro Pérez, said he participated in anti-Castro demonstrations and edited a strongly anti-Castro student publication, but by the time he graduated "it was clear that my relationship with Cuba would not be political, but rather one in which I would pursue the road of analysis and understanding."[48] Though all of this caused great scandal in Miami, especially among the dominant exile leadership, the many exiles who had grown tired of intransigence increasingly spoke their mind. Polls conducted by the *Miami Herald* revealed that a growing number of Cubans supported new ways of dealing with the Cuban problem; amazingly even 49.5 percent expressed an interest in visiting Cuba.[49]

The emergence of new voices among Cubans not only interested in understanding the reality of the Cuban Revolution but in some cases openly sympathizing with it was too much for some to bear. Though certainly committed to dialogue, Manolo Fernández, like many of the older Catholic leaders, was perplexed and disappointed that some Cuban youth seemed willing to go beyond dialogue to embrace the very ideology that had created their exile and radically altered their lives. Fernández acknowledged that most had been taken from Cuba by their parents and only later came to understand their situation and reached their own conclusions, but chided them for their support of the Revolution from a comfortable distance and in the safety of their university scholarships. "I think it is legitimate to ask—even as a reproach—why they do not take the definitive step, consistent with their pronouncements, of returning and inserting themselves into the revolution?"[50] Within a short time, this new generation, many of them graduate students and young professors, scholars, and researchers, became the dominant voice in IEC. Throughout the 1970s, IEC lost its original Catholic identity, becoming a clearly secular organization dedicated to the study of Cuba and the exile communities. Many of the old-guard Catholics like Rasco, Valdespino, the Batista brothers, and others stopped attending the meetings, though as editor of *Reunión,* Fernández maintained an ongoing discussion of religion and church in Cuba.

In addition to the relationship with the Areíto group, Cuban authorities opened conversations with other moderate sectors of the exile community. Among these was Bernardo Benes, a banker and member of the large Cuban Jewish community, who became a secret conduit between the Carter and Castro governments in 1977 and 1978. Benes's conversations led to an agreement that included the release of 3,600 Cuban prisoners, the reunification of separated families, and exile visits to Cuba.[51] In September 1978, Castro invited seventy-five exile Cubans to discuss a variety of issues.[52] Additional prisoners gained their freedom, and thousands of exiles began to visit the island. Among those prisoners freed in the late 1970s and early 1980s were many Catholics imprisoned in the 1960s, including Reinol González, Rodolfo Riesgo, Alberto Muller, and Polita Grau, the director of the clandestine program Operation Peter Pan in Cuba.[53]

Controversy and Violence

All of this did not unfold without considerable controversy, as the exile communities fell into bitter debates and recriminations, first about dialogue and later over travel to Cuba and conversations with the Cuban government. Unlike the frank and respectful disagreements among those committed to dialogue, those with intransigent views made a concerted effort to control the exile discourse through intimidation and violence. Mesa Lago had experienced a taste of exile wrath in February 1970, when he participated in a nationally televised debate held at the University of Miami to consider the usefulness of the U.S. embargo on Cuba. Mesa Lago, like Domínguez later, argued against the embargo because he considered it ineffective as an economic pressure and at the same time served the regime's propaganda needs well by allowing Cuba to characterize itself as a martyr nation confronting the North American Goliath. Threatened and insulted by exile leaders for his appearance and ideas expressed on the show, Mesa

Lago accused his detractors of refusing to reason objectively and consider the various alternatives. With all their intransigence and fanaticism, he asked, "What has the exile community done in eleven years to overthrow Castro, [and] save the prisoners from their suffering?"[54]

Throughout the decade, rhetoric escalated, and Cubans remained deeply divided. Some supported the total isolation of Cuba, rejecting all engagement. Others offered slightly different approaches. Former Catholic Action activist Amalio Fiallo, for example, in 1978 confirmed his opposition to dialogue with the Cuban government because he believed Castro would manipulate conversations to his own advantage, but he did support discussions with other sectors of Cuban society, including the armed forces, students, and workers, many of whom worked in the regime but did not necessarily support Fidel Castro.[55]

As divisions deepened, the most intransigent elements in exile responded with anger and violence. During these years militant paramilitary groups reorganized and carried out campaigns of intimidation and violence against Cuban and exile targets. Already in the late 1960s, as advocates of a new approach to dealing with Cuba began to raise their voices, remnants of the CIA-funded and trained paramilitary groups developed new strategies. Among other actions, militant exiles bombed Cuban diplomatic missions in Canada, Mexico, and Portugal, killing numerous employees; assassinated a Cuban United Nations diplomat in New York; and blew up a Cubana airliner carrying the Cuban national fencing team. They bombed travel agencies, shipping companies, and businesses that attempted to engage in business with Cuba. In Miami and other Cuban communities in New Jersey, Los Angeles, Puerto Rico, and elsewhere, those advocating coexistence suffered the consequences of their temerity to speak up. Supporting the lifting of the embargo in his newspaper and magazine, *Réplica,* for example, editor Max Lesnik faced constant threats, and eventually his office was bombed. Numerous others were assassinated. When radio commentator in Miami Emilio Milián raised his voice against these actions, a bomb planted in his car exploded leaving him close to death and without legs.[56] In 1979, well-known terrorist organization Omega 7 claimed responsibility for more than twenty bombings at the homes of those participating in the dialogue. They threatened to kill anyone who traveled to Cuba and in April assassinated Carlos Muñíz Varela, a member of the Brigada Antonio Maceo. In November they murdered another dialogue participant. During the next two years, an FBI task force finally managed to track down and arrest numerous members of Omega 7.[57]

Refusing to be intimidated, some Catholics openly condemned the terror and debated its sources. In 1976, Lasaga and Herrera both commented on the problem. Lasaga pointed out such actions had no ethical basis. While he had supported and participated in the organized armed military actions against Cuba in the early 1960s, this activity in the late 1970s went beyond the pale. It is not possible, he argued, to condemn repressive communist regimes and at the same time engage in similar actions of terror and repression. While absolute pacifism was also morally unjustified, any embrace of violence, according to Catholic theology, had to be proportional and effective in avoiding what would otherwise result in even greater harm and violence. The terror campaign in Miami not only failed to meet these requirements, and did nothing to undermine the regime in Cuba, but also damaged the reputation of Cubans in the United States who were increasingly seen as "a group of uncontrollable hot heads." This, he noted, only strengthened the Cuban regime. At the same time, Lasaga also wondered who really instigated the terror. He acknowledged the role of "anti-Castro fanatics," but he also suggested that the efficiency of the operations pointed to highly organized and funded groups possibly supported by the Castro regime itself.[58]

Perhaps in response to this and despite living in Miami, Herrera also condemned terrorist activities, wondering how Cubans could have lived in the United States for so long and still not have assimilated the idea that people should enjoy the right to express their views without fear of reprisals. As to who was behind these activities, Herrera disagreed with Lasaga, pointing out that the terrorists most certainly came out of the ranks of the paramilitary groups trained by the CIA to overthrow Castro in the 1960s and in reaction to changing politics of the United States and the emerging political heterogeneity within the exile communities. In any case, many of these people now made a living with these activities, raising funds with their title of "combatants for the freedom of Cuba." "The professional and economic reorientation of these Mafiosi elements," Herrera concluded, "could well explain part of the violence that affects our exile community."[59] She was not targeted at the time of her remarks, but in 1984 a bomb did explode in her garage. She was unharmed though the message of terror and intimidation was not lost on anyone.

Exile divisions energized the political opponents of the dialogue in 1979, reasserting the militant and intransigent (though non-terrorist) segments of the traditional exile communities. They formed the Junta Patriótica Cubana (JPC), which in April 1980 challenged the new openness among many exiles toward the Cuban Revolution, especially the Brigada Antonio Maceo. JPC welcomed all exiles into the new organization except "communists, fascists or nazis," or "pseudo-exiles that favor relations with the Havana regime in a blatant transgression and disregard for all our principles."[60] "There is a vacuum," declared Rasco, a JPC board member. "Exile organizations must renew their militance and develop new plans for struggle and action."[61] Coincidently, the Mariel exodus crisis erupted at this very moment, creating expectations in Miami that perhaps the regime had reached it limits. JPC not only denounced the Castro regime but also opposed allowing the Cuban government to dictate United States refugee policy and urged a quick termination of the exile flotilla. The Mariel exodus ignited fresh anger and provoked a new surge of anti-Castro activism and anti-communist rhetoric. For exiles, 1980 seemed to be a replay of twenty years earlier, when Cubans abandoned their homeland in mass.

Nevertheless, the initiative toward dialogue survived. Even as the Mariel crisis unfolded during the summer of 1980, members of IEC planned an already scheduled meeting of their organization in Cuba. For IEC, dialogue meant encouraging conversations not only among exiles but also with Cubans on the island. This commitment had inspired them in 1975 to invite Cubans to their meeting in Caracas, although the Cuban government did not approve. Several members of IEC attended the official dialogue with the Cuban government in 1978, leading to another invitation for island Cubans to attend their meeting the following year in Washington, DC. This time several Cubans attended, setting the stage for the 1980 meeting in Havana.[62] Even in the midst of the new refugee crisis, IEC met in Havana, a decision roundly denounced by many Cubans in the United States.

Responses to the IEC trajectory by the old-guard Catholics varied. Most no doubt objected, and during fall 1980 Lasaga very publicly resigned his membership and accused the organization of becoming an apologist for the Revolution. In his letter of resignation, which he asked *Reunión* to publish, Lasaga declared that given the recent Mariel exodus, it was clear to him that the Cuban regime had simply reaffirmed its repressive and opportunistic policies and had little interest in the welfare of the Cuban people.

Given the chaotic aftermath of the episode for the exile communities, with thousands of Cubans suffering in camps and prisons across the country, Lasaga wondered what IEC intended to do about it. He accused IEC of being nothing but a debating society, too often engaged in discussions about irrelevant details of one kind or another, without touching on the critical and central issues of the Cuban drama. He also accused IEC of having become a platform for sympathizers of the Revolution, no longer allowing critical voices. IEC had lost its pluralism, and as such he could no longer belong. In several responses, members pointed out that IEC was not a political organization and that its public persona merely reflected its membership. With the withdrawal of the older and more conservative members, naturally the tone of the meetings changed. They urged Lasaga to stay in the organization and encouraged others of his generation and ideas to rejoin in order to ensure pluralism.[63] Though expressed in civil terms, this exchange reflected deepening divisions even among those in exile willing to discuss the many complex issues associated with the Cuban question.

Herrera and Manolo Fernández had a different reaction to the path taken by IEC. Herrera recognized that the meeting in Havana proved difficult and certainly was not perfect, but it consolidated institutional links with Cuba.[64] Prior to the meeting, Fernández argued that those who considered themselves Christians had little choice but to participate. "A sense of transcendence encourages the continual search for ever more just and participatory ways of living together." At the same time, dialogue had to be real, not timid or obscured. Certainly, the government had its political motivations for agreeing to the meeting, but only by participating in discussion would exiles learn whether the Cubans simply intended to engage in political machinations that would lead to intellectual paralysis or sincerely sought an opening for substantive conversation and dialogue.[65] His experience in Havana, as well as his Christian convictions, convinced Fernández of the necessity of continuing the dialogue among Cubans, regardless of the risks. Only through a peaceful evolution would Cuba be able to overcome the lamentable contradictions created by the construction of socialism.[66]

Fernández also offered personal reflections about his trip to the island. After a nineteen-year absence he appreciated the opportunity to "recover" his memory about Cuba, the place and the people. He celebrated his immersion in what he perceived as a still cordial, communicative, and warm Cuban society and found that the superficial anecdotal criticisms about the

Revolution often heard in exile, emphasizing the lack of cars on the streets, deteriorating housing stock, and the lack of consumer goods, were of little consequence compared with the deeply entrenched difficult problems related to the regime's intransigent ideological pressure, the lack of popular participation, and the crisis in ethics among the youth. In reflecting on his experience, he lamented that the Revolution had not turned to Christianity for its doctrinal needs, which could have eventually resulted in the first concrete and empowered articulation of Liberation Theology in Latin America. Besieged and cornered, devoid of the necessary space to develop in that direction, the church in Cuba instead limited its struggle to mere preservation.[67]

Recognizing the dangers inherent in these deeply contentious divisions, during the decade the Cuban exile bishops raised their voice in a spirit of unity. They walked a fine line between the contending groups. Still considered the most important Catholic voice in exile by most, Bishop Boza Masvidal hoped to calm emotions by appealing to Christian ethics. During 1974, the bishop did recognize the general necessity of establishing ongoing conversations with communist regimes, but this had to be done with caution so that efforts at reducing tensions were not misinterpreted as providing moral legitimacy to systems that systematically repressed their people. This was also true for Cuba. He supported the Cuban church's policies because of the moral obligation to work in all environments, to ensure its presence. But, he warned, this had to be done with the spirit of "calling bread, bread and wine, wine." "The Church," he concluded, "does not impose governments but undertakes a spiritual mission, and should work to soften frictions, seek peace, and promote the best conditions to be able to do its work, but always maintaining a dignified and clear position, avoiding policies that imply complicity, and without cowardice or opportunism."[68]

In 1979, in referring to the practical politics of dialogue with Castro, the bishop pointed out that except for a few, most exiles opposed the regime whether supporting dialogue and travel to Cuba or not. He also noted that the debates had actually benefited political prisoners by reminding the world of their plight and leading to their release. Both sides, pro- and anti-engagement with the Cuban government, made legitimate and sincere arguments that had to be respected. Individuals had to make their own decisions, and his only counsel was to respect these decisions. "This teaches us to live in democracy," he noted. He also took the opportunity to remind Cubans "to watch our language." "We are passionate by temperament," he noted, " . . . easily offended and insulted." But, "we have to make an effort toward mutual respect, and discuss with argument, which is more powerful than insults."[69] Boza Masvidal also issued a joint statement with Bishop Román, condemning all terror, whatever its origins, asking God to "illuminate everyone to end the causes of violence and the acts of terrorism that sow pain, division and hatred, when what we need is unity, and fertile and constructive efforts."[70]

In 1983, the two bishops again felt compelled to issue a message on reconciliation within the exile community. In the quite lengthy statement, among other things they called on exiles to accept diversity of opinion and practice mutual respect and comprehension. Within the secular realm, exiles should act from conscience but with "maximum respect for the ethical principles that God has taught us."[71]

The constant call by the old political leaders for unity behind a hard-line agenda really reflected the militant ethic they had brought from Cuba— also expressed by the Revolution itself. But this could not survive as the exclusive approach, especially among the young, raised as they were in a pluralistic society. Despite the controversy and terror, those interested in dialogue persisted. In time, the terror subsided, or at least lessened, as did much of the violent rhetoric. Certainly, deep differences remained, but after 1980 voices never heard publicly in the 1960s took their place permanently in the exile discourse. Many sectors of exile opinion struggled for and welcomed this dialogue, as did many Catholic leaders, who played a significant role in challenging the dominant political voices who, like Castro in Cuba, had little use for diversity of opinion.

EPILOGUE

From the time Cubans arrived in the early 1960s, exile and ethnic identities interacted like a dancing couple seeking to meld two impulses into one motion. Their impulses sought return but, simultaneously, belonging in their new space. Everyday life for Cubans in the United States during the 1960s and 1970s involved an intimate interaction between commitment to exile and return on the one hand and the reluctant, inevitable integration into a new society on the other. Engagement with U.S. society did not represent a linear movement from exile to ethnic, but rather manifested itself as a parallel process, sometimes pregnant with tension but also mutually supportive and lasting, evolving together with complexity in the lives of the exile generation.

Self-consciously dedicated to cultural survival and return, many Cubans cultivated their exile identity by relying on religious and other traditions as an enduring bridge to the homeland. This strong commitment to tradition, in turn, gave rise to an ethnic identity as refugees inevitably engaged their new society and recognized the challenges to their cultural integrity. Exile identity looked to Cuba, and ethnic identity existed in relation to their adopted land, but both strove for cultural maintenance and remained inextricably connected. Exile identity served as the basis for ethnic consciousness, and experiences associated with integration influenced attitudes about exile and return. As theologian Ada María Isasi-Díaz noted, "During those years in *el exilio,* as we Cubans continue to refer to our lives away from the island . . . I struggled to find a way of being committed to what I was doing, at the same time always being ready to go back to Cuba as soon as it was possible. 'If I forget you, O Jerusalem, may my right hand wither! May my tongue cleave to my palate if I forget you!'"[1]

Whether or not the long-term integration experience ultimately results in a substantively different outcome for Cuban exiles than has been the case in immigrant trajectories of assimilation so common in United States history, this book does reveal a rather different process. During the 1960s and 1970s, Cuban Catholics established trends that persisted into the future, casting a long shadow over the daily lives of Cuban Catholic exiles.

As long as Castro and communism remained in Cuba, frames of reference remained substantially unchanged after the 1980s. Exile kept Cubans focused on the homeland even after it became clear most would not necessarily return home even if they could. This in turn fueled their determination to retain their heritage and develop relationships with the broader Hispanic world in the United States, Latin America, and Spain. They remained sensitive to international matters, engaged Cubans in other countries, and continued to espouse the social teachings of the church, which they believed provided ideal guidelines for the reconstruction of Cuba after communism. At the same time, integration into the United States proceeded, inevitably influenced by their deep sense of obligation to their homeland—a dynamic that will cease only when exile sensibilities pass or the communist regime disappears.

Exile

As a practical matter, Cuban refugees became exiles when they made the affirmative decision to remain committed to Cuba, insisting on their eventual return. Although they certainly had the option of acting as immigrants, identifying with the United States, and embracing a new society and culture, most initially embraced an exile perspective. Exile Catholics expressed a deep grounding in nationalism, anti-communism, and a social consciousness rooted in the teachings of their faith; while forging their lives within the world of exile, some revealed attitudes of rigidity and intransigence on the one hand, while others embraced flexibility and dialogue on the other.

In the early years, exile leaders, Catholic and otherwise, acted from a revolutionary ethic cultivated for years in Cuba's unruly political climate and without hesitation used armed and violent actions to achieve political goals. They participated in the struggle of the broader community to overthrow the Castro government and return home, where they hoped to build Cuba anew based on Christian traditions and principles. The events associated with departure produced a life-long trauma that remained an open wound, colored worldviews, and provided the emotional fuel for an exile frame of reference, an essentially psychological predisposition defining Cuban identity. Driven by their anger, many exiles continued to pepper their intransigence with a taste for vengeance. Their anger also encouraged an ongoing tendency toward a one-dimensional analysis of the Cuban Revolution that emphasized the system's oppression of civil society and the church.

The anti-communism of most Cuban Catholics actually hardened as the Vatican urged a more reflective and tolerant approach. It also became more militant at a time when a greater social consciousness appeared throughout the Americas and when sometimes violent and brutal military dictatorships seemed a greater danger to most in Latin America than the Cuban Revolution or communism in general. Raised in the tradition of *Divini Redemptoris,* the exiles concurred with Pope Pius XI's analysis that communism by its very nature repressed all possibility of individual spiritual growth and certainly did not offer a solution to the world's social problems. They fully embraced the traditional Catholic view that communism struck at the heart of human dignity and freedom, by definition negating its claims to justice. Deeply affected by their experience, the majority of exiles also rejected the more pragmatic attitude toward communist nations articulated in the Vatican Council and resented the church for attempting to establish dialogue with the Cuban government in the 1970s. They spoke out against what they considered to be benign interpretations of the Revolution by Catholic leaders in Latin America and the United States and even among Vatican officials. As Lasaga said in 1977, those Catholic leaders displaying sympathy for the Revolution "lack the necessary human sensibility to feel in their own beings the suffering of those persecuted by leftist regimes simply because of their personal sympathies for those governments."[2]

At the same time that many exile Cuban Catholics remained intransigently committed to pre-Vatican formulations about communism, many others in the 1970s embraced the Second Vatican Council's call to the faithful to pay attention to the "signs of the times." Certainly a minority, and mostly young, those advocating new perspectives, often inspired by matters of faith, softened their intransigence and called on the majority to consider the changing realities inside and outside Cuba. Though thoroughly rejecting communism for its atheism, neglect of the religious spirit, human rights violations, and practical inability to resolve concrete political and socioeconomic problems, these exiles accepted the need to be realistic in the "modern world," engage in dialogue, be present among the faithful, and proceed with an attitude of reconciliation, in exile and with their homeland. The new teachings encouraged greater discernment about the realities in Cuba and a much needed moderating influence in the exile communities.

Though few in number at first, these new voices called the faithful to conversion and a release of anger and pessimism, and they appealed to a spirit of tolerance and reconciliation so that their desire to return could be expressed fruitfully and with optimism.[3] These voices promoted a new sense of responsibility, called for tolerance and dialogue, and challenged the use of violence as fruitless, a point of view Catholics could hardly ignore. Only slowly did this approach spread among exiles, but spread it did. This optimism and openness became more pronounced by 1980s, though anger and intransigence remained pervasive among the majority.

Regardless of its precise expression, whether intransigent or tolerant, exile identity and an ongoing concern for the homeland remained at the heart of community consciousness after the 1970s. The differing instincts among Cubans also persisted in their politics of return, with the majority of exiles reaffirming an unyielding quality evidenced in the activities of the Cuban American National Foundation and Cuban-American elected officials throughout the 1980s and much of the 1990s. This continued to be defined by confrontational strategies, which remain intact among many to this day. This quality was even evident when Pope John Paul II visited Cuba in 1998, prompting many exile Catholics to visit the island, including Bishop Boza Masvidal, but provoking among others a strong opposition.[4] Indeed, Bishop Román and perhaps most exile priests remained in exile to offer pastoral support for those who absolutely refused to visit Cuba as long as Castro remained in power, though offering daily masses in support of the pope's mission. Exiles also demonstrated the enduring nature of their intransigence in 2000, when they vigorously resisted and condemned the U.S. government's return of a refugee boy, Elián González, to his father in Cuba after he was rescued at sea, where his mother drowned. As the drama played out over several months, many Cubans appealed to their religious traditions and symbols to justify confrontation and refusal to comply with U.S. law.[5]

Minority approaches, however, also persisted after the 1970s and increasingly questioned the intransigence of the exile majority. CRECED's call in the early 1990s "to practically show and demonstrate, with simplicity and humility, our fundamental belonging with each other" represented a changing tone.[6] Those with an instinct for reengaging the Cuban church responded to the initiatives of their island coreligionists, who called for greater tolerance and communication between island and diaspora, expressed in 1986 in the Encuentro Nacional Eclesial Cubano (ENEC). A consultation of the Cuban church that took place during the first half of the 1980s, ENEC outlined a pastoral strategy for the future, including affirming its intention to be present among the Cuban people by critically accepting the Cuban situation and evangelizing within that reality, a strategy traditionally detested by most exiles. It also encouraged contacts with Catholic Cubans abroad, which "helped us discover each other, as well as the ample horizons of the Church and how the Church and our singular faith in Jesus Christ and devotion to the Virgin are privileged factors toward uniting Cubans despite the geographic distance and diverse political and social options."[7]

Though the majority of Catholics in exile had consistently resisted the Cuban church's turn to realism and dialogue in its relations with the Cuban communist state, CRECED did acknowledge the importance of ENEC, especially given the crisis faced by Cuba in the aftermath of the collapse of the Soviet bloc. While continuing to insist on the essential evil of the communist regime in Cuba, CRECED responded to their colleagues on the island and urged exiles also to cultivate a spirit of dialogue, tolerance, and reconciliation. Eventually, Catholic leaders in exile encouraged their people to foster communication and even personal encounters with Cubans on the island, as well as to provide material aid and religious support and to "recognize, in our attitudes, that nobody has a monopoly on truth or error."[8] This meant not abandoning the traditional objective of working to change Cuba toward a democratic society but urging that it be a "peaceful and popular transition."[9] Though still permeated with a measure of arrogance and self-righteousness, certainly this attitude toward reconciliation reflected a process of exile maturation rooted in the dialogue process of the 1970s. In the 1990s, south Florida Cuban Catholics engaged in ongoing dialogue with Catholics in Cuba, creating fruitful exchanges that have continued despite growing tensions (encouraged by Cuban-American politicians) between the United States and Cuban governments.[10]

Integration

Despite the retention by Cubans in the United States of a powerful attachment to exile identity, their failure to overthrow Castro left them with little choice but to engage the practical aspects of being outside of Cuba and dealing with day-to-day life and realities. Many Catholics found answers to the dilemmas of integrating into a new society through the church itself. Certainly, the tensions inherent in their instinctive need to remain connected to Cuba and their culture and identity while attempting to resettle in an alien culture became clear to them quite quickly. Though not without resistance from the church in the United States, Catholics who settled in communities with a large concentration of Cubans found ways to practice their faith as Cubans and to engage their rights as ethnic citizens. Catholics utilized their political activism, strong faith traditions, and economic influence to combat the assimilation attitudes of the diocesan church hierarchy and society in general. Their economic self-sufficiency allowed for a certain cultural autonomy that became an ethnic consciousness expressed not only politically but also in everyday life, including language, culture, and religion. They saw no contradiction between their condition as exile Cuban Catholics hoping eventually to go home and as ethnic Americans obtaining a measure of influence and authority within the Anglo-dominated diocesan church. Cubans self-consciously fought assimilation in favor of a pluralistic understanding of their eventual citizenship. They recognized themselves as just one of many permanent cultural expressions that diverged from the so-called melting pot model of U.S. society and culture. During the 1960s and 1970s, the Civil Rights Movement and other political and social developments provided space for the appearance of ethnic movements among African Americans, Mexican Americans, Native Americans, and others. Arriving at this very moment, Cubans naturally embraced the ideas of ethnic pluralism as perfectly compatible with their clearly articulated sense of exile identity.

Homeland traditions provided Cuban exiles with the basic values for defining a new sense of belonging in an initially alien place, creating an ethnic reality and perspective—combining the old and the new—that guided exile communities along the path toward integration. While waiting to return, they journeyed, inevitably losing connection to the changing reality of their place of origin as they themselves changed in their new environment. As the waiting continued, exiles urged fidelity to their culture and ways, even as their children accommodated themselves to their new country, and they evolved increasingly intricate reflections about the nature of their experience.

This pattern certainly persisted during the next two decades. In the early 1990s, CRECED, for example, projected on Cuban children this commitment to Cuban identity. While recognizing the importance for children to adopt the nationality of the country in which they were born, CRECED continued to believe that "the main problem" faced by the new generation was "the danger that their parents' language and culture may become for them a foreign language and culture, of which they only have some basic notions." Consistent with their Babylonian exile model, integration for Catholics still meant rejecting assimilation or loss of culture and historical memory. Their own idea of integration and adjustment rooted in exile perspectives remained the preferred approach because it "refers to the dialogue between renewed fidelity to the original identity . . . and the culture in which the immigrant is inserted," and because it seeks "to be faithful to one's own traditions, at the same time that it is innovative and open as to the new system of life." Therefore, they urged "initiatives to keep and develop programs of Spanish teaching for children and grandchildren of exiles . . . not only as a strategy of preservation and defense, but above all an expression of cultural promotion and a social and civilizing service to the beneficiaries and the community at large."[11]

In some ways, Bishop Román's role in the community symbolized the coexistence between this inevitable integration and the commitment to the homeland. With his appointment as auxiliary bishop of the archdiocese of Miami in 1979, Román assumed a post many felt should have been given to Boza Masvidal in the 1960s. As a popular religious leader and teacher Román engaged exile and integration as one. He spoke to the specific concerns of Cubans with regard to Cuba but also in relation to the events in the United States.

During the 1980s, in the aftermath of the Mariel exodus, a prisoner fiasco unfolded under intense national scrutiny. Román's post in the church hierarchy provided him with a prestigious forum from which to denounce the dramatic events that unfolded in Havana but also demand humanitarian support and just treatment for those arriving from Cuba. He acted as an exile leader in 1980, when thousands crowded onto the grounds of the Peruvian embassy in Cuba, affirming for him, once again, Cuba's disregard for human rights. He called on international organizations to take some action and remembered the pleas of the bishops at the CELAM meeting at Puebla the year before, urging the nations of the world to strengthen the right of asylum and increase the quotas for immigrants and refugees. He later said a Mass for Cuba, with thousands gathered at the Ermita de la Caridad.[12] Besides pointing to the deficiencies of Marxism in Cuba, Román offered a local pastoral response to the situation, advising Hispanic laity and priests in the archdiocese to offer special care to the waves of new arrivals from Cuba.[13]

Simultaneously, the United States government faced the task of accommodating a brand-new exile population with very different characteristics from earlier Cuban arrivals. Rather than being greeted with open arms, the heavily working-class, mulatto, and Black *marielitos* were viewed by North American society and the many Cubans of earlier waves with considerable suspicion. Not only did they not receive the significant aid extended to the refugees of the 1960s and early 1970s, but tens of thousands of new refugees landed initially in detention camps, and many remained indefinitely in prisons for breaking the law in the United States or under suspicion of being hardened criminals or people with criminal potential. Thousands remained in prison for years without access to due process, eventually provoking anger among many in the Cuban communities, including Román, who now became an ethnic leader in a campaign to defend the prisoners.[14]

For the first time, Román found himself expressing concerns about the human rights of Cuban refugees in the United States, many probably held without cause.[15] This problem of incarcerated Cuban refugees persisted throughout the 1980s, and Román, along with Bishop Enrique San Pedro of the archdiocese of Galveston-Houston (appointed in 1986), led efforts first to seek their release and later to block their possible repatriation when the United States and Cuba signed a new immigration agreement. Román then took on national visibility in 1987, when he negotiated the end of two prison revolts in which Cuban prisoners took hostages to protest their possible deportation.[16]

Román, as well as San Pedro and Boza Masvidal, provided important moral leadership for the Cuban community in the face of the immigration crisis of 1980 and its aftermath. They condemned the Cuban government, asked the local community to embrace the latest refugees, and engaged domestic authorities, questioning their goal of returning refugees to Cuba as well as for holding them in prison indefinitely and violating their rights to due process. Twenty years earlier, this kind of advocacy had been carried out by U.S. authorities, including clergy like Archbishop Carroll and Msgr.

Walsh. Even in the face of antagonistic North American public opinion, reacting, among other things, to rioting Cubans in detention camps and prisons while authorities processed the arrivals, the bishops appealed to the legal and humanitarian traditions of their adopted land to defend the rights and privileges of the newest members of their ethnic community. They acted as exiles but also as empowered ethnic citizens and residents of their adopted land.

International Diaspora

The integration of Cubans into the United States as ethnics proceeded in an almost inevitable manner, given the circumstances, but their exile experience also contributed to another important dimension of their reality. The communities of Cuban exiles that formed not only in the United States but in many other regions, including Puerto Rico, Venezuela, Mexico, and Spain—to name the most important—created an international diasporic reality.[17] On the one hand Cubans often lived in insular communities, but on the other the exile dimension kept the scattered communities in touch, encouraging an international solidarity, with Miami at its heart. Cubans in the diaspora adapted to the realities of their respective places of residence but also maintained strong relations with each other based on their exile interests.

During the 1960s and 1970s, Cubans especially in south Florida cultivated relations with the rest of Latin America and Spain, to which they were drawn by cultural affinity, economic possibilities, and political necessity. The politics of exile tied U.S. Cubans to compatriots in various places through their participation in the Christian Democratic movement, the Unión de Cubanos en el Exilio, and many other organizations. In traveling to Latin America, Catholic leaders spoke to individuals, intellectuals, government leaders, and all who would listen about the "realities of communism" and the devastation they felt it brought their homeland, but they found leaders in the region fundamentally unresponsive. Their experiences nevertheless proved valuable as they established lasting contacts and relationships not only with other Cubans scattered in the region but among Latin Americans themselves. Their principle Catholic pastoral leader, Bishop Boza Masvidal, actually lived in Venezuela, where he offered his religious perspective to Cubans throughout the diaspora. Boza Masvidal, Román, and other Catholic leaders continually emphasized the need for Cuban Catholics to maintain consciousness about their Latin American origins. Younger Cubans of the *Nueva Generación* group also found inspiration in Latin American attitudes and views about current events, reform, and other matters. In time, south Florida Cubans established strong economic and cultural ties to Latin America and Spain generally.

These characteristics remained an important dimension of life for Cubans in the United States into the 1990s. CRECED, for example, reaffirmed "our friendship and openness towards all peoples," and emphasized "that Cuba, because of its history, its culture, its language and its Catholic experience, is an integral part of Latin America, with which we wish to maintain the utmost unity in the expression of our faith, in the struggle for justice and in the historical destiny of the integration of all our peoples, in order to become, in reality, 'the continent of hope.'"[18] After so many years, exiles remained committed to a Cuba rooted in its historical links with Latin America and its Catholic traditions. The universal nature of the church itself and its doctrines certainly encouraged this dimension, but so did political and social activism and theological exploration. Whether working to overthrow the regime or cultivate dialogue and change on the island peacefully, exiles in the United States, Spain, Venezuela, and other places remained in conversation with each other.

At the same time, however, the maintenance of relationships among Cubans in different regions did not mean they experienced uniform trajectories. Those living in Latin America, for example, often came to very different conclusions about how exiles should deal with Cuba from those living in the United States, but they all engaged the debates. Even those living in the United States but outside south Florida often exhibited quite different attitudes. With all these forces at work, exile discourses inevitably became heterogeneous, causing divisions and resentment but also shifting perspectives and encouraging reflection and reevaluation within the overall context of their exile identity.

Hispanicism

Two final aspects of the Cuban Catholic experience that are perhaps not generally thought of as characteristic of the broader community in the

United States relate to U.S. Hispanicism and concern for issues of social justice. Though most Cuban exiles perhaps did not see themselves in solidarity with other Latino immigrants to the United States during the 1960s and 1970s, the particular concerns of Catholics led many to develop cooperative relationships with Mexican American and Puerto Rican Catholics. Engaged in sometimes contentious struggles with local church officials in south Florida who insisted on their assimilation, Cuban Catholics recognized that other Latinos across the country contended with similar issues. The Catholic Church's traditional encouragement of universality threatened Hispanic ways of worship and language within the United States, but that same universality at another level encouraged Hispanics of different backgrounds to work together to promote attitudes about diversity and tolerance within the church. Throughout the 1970s, Cuban Catholics discovered the Hispanic reality of the United States outside of Florida, which prompted them to support the Encuentro movement's demands for a greater Latino presence in the North American church.

This engagement with U.S. Hispanic Catholicism also persisted into the future, especially as south Florida received immigrants from throughout Latin America. In 1980s and 1990s, hundreds of thousands of mostly—at least nominally—Catholic immigrants from other Latin American countries found Cuban south Florida a receptive environment. Latin Americans entered and shared a geographic space with a traditionally Cuban community proud of its culture, committed to their language and traditions, and unapologetic about their exile and ethnic identity, which became institutionalized and predominant in many ways. Colombians, Puerto Ricans, Mexicans, Salvadorans, Nicaraguans, Argentines, and many other Hispanic immigrants also engaged the enclave economy created initially by Cubans and established their own Spanish-language communities that deepened the Hispanic nature of the region. Though they certainly did not translate their experience into the kind of political and socioeconomic power Cubans attained, they did embrace Cuban attitudes about language and cultural maintenance.[19] Cuban religious spaces like the shrine at Our Lady of Charity and San Juan Bosco Church received the newest immigrants and encouraged their participation.

This experience in the 1970s prepared Cubans for a continuing participation in the Latino church of the United States. In 1983, the U.S. Bishops approved a pastoral letter, *The Hispanic Presence: Challenge and Commitment,* which called for a third national Encuentro, held in 1985 with the particular goal of reaching out to the alienated and nonpracticing nominal Latino Catholics.[20] Cubans joined with U.S. Hispanic Catholics in defending their ways, even engaging those aspects of Latin American theological trends useful for their reality while challenging others. As the creed formulated at the third Encuentro proclaimed, "We believe that the waters of the Rio Grande and the Caribbean Sea are a unifying source, for as we cross them to come here, they allow us to become instruments of God for fertilizing and enriching the land that received us."[21]

In the process of engaging other Latinos, Cuban Catholic scholars in the 1980s and 1990s contributed intellectual muscle to the Hispanic theological movement launched by Virgil Elizondo in the 1970s. As the various Hispanic groups in the United States interacted and collaborated during the 1960s and 1970s, scholars explored what it meant to be Hispanic Catholics, providing a critical theological grounding for Latino Catholicism. Hispanic theologians made a case for understanding Catholicism from the Hispanic point of view, creating a formal U.S. Latino theology in the 1980s and 1990s. Cubans contributed to these theological reflections, inspired by the realities of their own communities.

The heavily middle-class and educated Cuban Catholics arriving in the United States possessed a strong background in traditional European— especially Spanish and French—intellectual and theological currents, but their ethnic experience in exile brought new concerns, perspectives, and sensibilities. Their experience in the United States and in particular with other Hispanics, along with post-Vatican theological developments in Latin America, produced another layer of complexity to their worldviews that contributed to the landscape of U.S. Latino theology. In south Florida, for example, Cuban Catholics had engaged the complex issue of popular religiosity, a tradition of worship that became a conceptual centerpiece of Latino theology in the 1980s and 1990s.

The discussion of Santería among south Florida Cuban Catholics fore-shadowed a growing interest in popular religion among Latino Catholics generally and was further developed by Orlando Espín, who spent much of the 1970s in Brazil and the Dominican Republic and eventually wrote prolifically about the topic. Espín broadened the discussion, arguing for the centrality of popular religious expression in the Hispanic tradition generally. "It is practically impossible," Espín noted, "to study any Hispanic community in the United States, regardless of disciplinary point of departure or methodology, without encountering popular religion." "Whether it be to denigrate it or lament its omnipresence in the Hispanic milieu," he continued, "or to encourage and defend it as a sign of cultural affirmation, scholars sooner or later have to take a stand vis-à-vis popular religious beliefs, practices, and worldviews."[22] In effect, popular religion was one of the distinguishing features of Hispanic Catholicism.

Lo popular also provoked a journey of theological exploration for another exile, Ada María Isasi-Díaz, who in subsequent years developed a *mujerista* theology that struggled with the problems of gender, class, and ethnic discrimination faced by Hispanic women, emphasizing also the need for women of the dominant society to incorporate the perspectives and ideas of women of color. Her experiences with the feminist and Chicana movements of the 1970s led her toward an activist stance reflected in her writings in the 1980s and 1990s. Also, as an activist of the Encuentro movement, she participated in promoting greater representation of Hispanics in the church hierarchy. Isasi-Díaz always reminded Catholics of the gender and social dimensions, contributing to placing these issues at the heart of the emerging Latino theology.[23]

Another influential scholar engaged the issue of Catholic Hispanicity itself and its relation to the dominant society. Roberto Goizueta in the late 1980s and early 1990s examined the idea of Hispanic Catholicism and drew together many strands into a comprehensive Latino theology. Born in Cuba, raised in the southeast United States in the 1960s and 1970s, and cognizant of the emerging Hispanic Catholic activism, Goizueta wrote eloquently about the specific character of a Latino religiosity and its relationship to mainstream Western theology. Besides the obvious history of oppression, Goizueta also considered praxis and aesthetics necessary elements for understanding Latino theology. Certainly, the Encuentro movement evolved from a practical need for Hispanics to defend their ways while breaking down barriers to participation in the U.S. Catholic Church, but according to Goizueta, Hispanics also needed a theological foundation for what they were doing. "U.S. Hispanic theology is itself challenged to embrace the responsibility of bringing the historical praxis of U.S. Hispanic communities into critical relationship with the dominant culture and its institutions, thereby helping to forge a truly liberative pluralism."[24]

In some ways, these and other Cuban exile theologians were the intellectual descendents of activists like Valdespino, Rumbaut, Cerro, and others who in the 1950s spoke to a Cuban national audience of reform and social justice. Unlike their elders, of whom they may or may not have been aware, Espín, Isasi-Díaz, Goizueta, and many others experienced their formation in the United States; they shared with their predecessors, however, a desire for a world shaped by a Catholic vision.[25] Though certainly aware of themselves as exiles, they focused their attention on their realities in the United States and especially in relation to the Hispanic world they encountered. They drew from their life experiences to speak to a national theological community about the Hispanic experience, hoping to change the minds of a North American world fundamentally disinterested in these "alien" people, except to express fear about their growing cultural impact on the country. Also like their elders, who called on Catholics in Cuba to be true to their faith and bring reform to their country, these Cuban exile theologians in the United States encouraged Latinos to be activists while challenging the dominant society to adopt new attitudes and perspectives. They combined exile sensibilities, ethnic experiences, and a strong affinity with Latin America—inspired by experience in the region or simply an understanding of their origins—to develop sophisticated theological reflections on the reality of Latinos in the United States.

The Social Question

Although somewhat counterintuitive in the face of the increasingly conservative character of the Cuban community, many Catholics also remained engaged with the church's social doctrines, both as exiles and as ethnics. Cuban Catholics had developed a strong commitment to the church's social teachings in the 1940s and 1950s, which inspired many to support the Revolution. Drawn from the social traditions of corporatist Spanish Catholicism as well as the more liberal-minded thought of the French philosopher and theologian Jacques Maritain, Cuban Catholic social ideas emphasized economic justice within a socioeconomic system that avoided socialism (i.e., communism) and exaggerated liberal capitalism. They insisted that the social vision they had advocated in Cuba in the 1940s and 1950s had been distorted by Marxism under Castro but encouraged the faithful to remain dedicated to this aspect of Catholic teaching. Despite the deception and confusion exiles felt in the early 1960s, they did retain the social discourse. While the increasingly conservative exile community mostly lost interest in social matters, many Cuban Catholics remained cognizant of the injustices across Latin America and also discovered the social and racial inequities of North American society especially affecting Hispanics and African Americans, provoking them to speak about these realities. Cuban apostolic movements in the United States encouraged spirituality and individual piety but also reaffirmed concern for the community's social welfare and attitudes of openness to other Catholics in the United States, especially Hispanics.

As exiles Cuban Catholics continually relied on the traditional writings of intellectual activists like Foyaca and Maritain, but as ethnic people within the United States they learned new approaches in the 1960s and 1970s. Their social instinct remained, but their frameworks of action changed. The theoretical visions of Catholic social thought gave way to practical local social activism that was not necessarily framed in the theological language to which they were accustomed in Cuba. Exiles who mostly arrived as young adults, adolescents, and children and who experienced educational formation in the United States joined in the spirit of reform and change of the era. They worked for the improvement of their communities and learned strategies for accessing the necessary federal, state, and local funding opportunities to address problems among the urban and rural poor in south Florida.

This too persisted beyond the 1970s. In the early 1990s, CRECED reaffirmed this commitment to Catholic social concern. Pope John Paul II, the document noted, "does not hesitate in using the expression 'preferential option for the poor' . . . as a special manner of primacy in the practice of Christian charity." In light of the teachings of the popes on the subject, CRECED further stated, "it is incumbent upon the Cuban Diaspora to maintain a consciousness of the duties and rights that are ours as Catholics," and ensure the "primacy of the worker over capital, that of the human being over the machine and matter, and that of solidarity over profit." The document added, among other things, that justice also included fair wages; the right of private property within a clear social dimension; sensitivity to demands for solidarity at all levels, including in international development; the value of social property; attention to the relationship between the market and the state in the economic process; and the existence of authority to promote the common good. "We must recognize," CRECED insisted, "that the social doctrine of the Church . . . is basically Biblical, and that is why it encompasses a number of issues that are essential for the clear and correct interpretation of human existence, both individual and social or collective.[26] While José Ignacio Lasaga and other Cuban Catholics acknowledged the poverty and misery of millions in Latin America and the church's right and obligation to raise its voice with a message of social justice, they also rejected theological ideas defined with the conceptual language of class division and other Marxist ideas. Lasaga believed that liberation theologians offered many valuable insights regarding the clear biblical condemnation of "poor use of wealth," but they erred in attempting to "compare the teachings of Christ about the poor and rich with the Marxist thesis of the irreconcilable enmity between proletariats and the bourgeoisie."[27]

In general, Cuban Catholics' traditional concern with the social doctrines, as well as the constant citing of their importance by exile church leaders, imprinted them into the consciousness of south Florida Catholics. In the late 1980s, for example, research among parishioners, members of apostolic movements, employees of the archdiocese, and clients of church-based programs determined that a majority of south Florida Cuban Catholics were familiar with the doctrines. Though not necessarily conversant with the texts themselves, they did express support for the inherent values and principles of Catholic social thought, no doubt learned through tradition and word of mouth, school, church, or perhaps the apostolic movements. In one particularly strongly worded statement in the research questionnaire, for example, 66 percent of respondents agreed with the proposition that since private property is not an absolute right, "I do not have the right to use my property for extraordinary luxuries while others lack the basic necessities." The report nevertheless concluded that there was no reason why any Catholic in Miami should lack knowledge or sensibility in matters of social justice.[28]

Catholicism

Though Cuban exiles are often thought of as a mostly secular community, Catholicism did affect the way many thought about their experiences. In recreating their community in exile, which they at first considered merely temporary, Catholics linked faith and nationality as inseparable aspects of their identity and viewed Christianity generally as the obvious ideological counterpoint to the communist regime on the island. Catholics joined and formed parishes and founded numerous lay organizations designed to meet their specific needs. They established newspapers, magazines, radio stations, cultural organizations of various kinds, schools, monuments, and even a shrine to the Cuban patroness to maintain their traditional ways of worship, their identity as Cubans, their language, and a fierce anti-communism. Religion did not set Catholics off radically from the rest of the Cuban community but did provide a particular filter through which to analyze and understand their experiences of exile and integration. The over-all themes they contended with did not differ that much from their secular, Protestant, and Jewish compatriots, or for that matter from those who prac-ticed Santería. Indeed, Catholicism did not define the Cuban exile commu-nity's major themes of experience but did influence the weight given to particular issues and their interpretation. Cuban Catholics interpreted their experiences of displacement, resettlement, and integration through their particular spiritual, theological, and intellectual frameworks; church and faith provided the essential ideas, beliefs, and practices for understanding their dilemma.

During this historical moment of great change and considerable inten-sity, exiles contended not only with the consequences of Cuba's Revolution but also with significant reform in their church and an era of turbulence in the United States and Latin America. These changes certainly made theo-logical, political, or social consensus among Catholics even more difficult than ordinarily would be the case, but Catholicism nevertheless did often provide sufficient common ground to encourage conversation within shared parameters of thought and experience. Whether they agreed with church orientations or not, Cubans did not ignore them; they read, reflected, and acted. Even if church teachings often caused some Catholic exiles much confusion and even resentment, Catholicism offered the exiles a commu-nity of faith; a place to gather; networks; a sense of legitimacy as a people, even if displaced; and a bridge to others, which influenced their beliefs and actions as they integrated into different societies and tried to make sense of events in their homeland.

NOTES

Introduction

1. On historical communities before 1959, see Gerald E. Poyo, *"With All, and For the Good of All": The Emergence of Popular Nationalism in the Cuban Communities of the United States, 1848–1898* (Durham, NC: Duke University Press, 1989); Gary Mormino and George Pozzetta, *The Immigrant World of Ybor City: Italians and Their Latin Neighbors in Tampa, 1885–1985* (Urbana: University of Illinois Press, 1987); Susan Greenbaum, *More Than Black: Afro-Cubans in Tampa* (Gainesville: University Presses of Florida, 2002). For an overview of the Cuban experience in the United States, see Gerald E. Poyo and Mariano Díaz-Miranda, "Cubans in the United States," in *Handbook of Hispanics Cultures in the United States: History,* ed. Alfredo Jiménez (Houston: Arte Público Press, 1994), 302–320.

2. "En misión y con Cuba en el corazón," *La Voz Católica,* August 21, 1992. Meeting participants included the three exile bishops (Boza Masvidal, Román, and San Pedro); *cursillo* activists Roglio de la Torre and Miguel Cabrera, Instituto de Estudios Cubanos leaders María Cristina Herrera and Manolo Fernández, youth leader Manny Alvarez, former members of Cuban Catholic Action Natalia Casamayor and Alberto Pérez, and exile clergy Mario Vizcaíno, Felipe Estevez, Raul Comesaña, and many others. Also, representatives of the Cuban church— Auxiliary Bishop Alfredo Petit, Vicar of Havana, and Father José Conrado from the diocese of Santiago de Cuba—participated actively.

3. Comunidades de Reflexión Eclesial Cubana en la Diaspora, *CRECED: Final Document,* English edition (Hato Rey, PR: Ramallo Brothers Printing, 1996), 84–85, 102–103. See also "Dios con los hombres: Los exiliados," *The Voice,* December 4, 1970, the earliest reference I found to the Babylonian exile as applied to the Cuban exile experience.

4. *CRECED: Final Document,* 121–122.

5. Ibid., 118.

6. Ibid., 171.

7. For a rather emphatic argument regarding the secular nature of Cuban society, see Guillermo J. Grenier and Lisandro Pérez, *The Legacy of Exile: Cubans in the United States* (Boston: Allyn & Bacon, 2003), 40–42.

8. See Miguel A. De La Torre, *La Lucha for Cuba: Religion and Politics on the Streets of Miami* (Berkeley: University of California Press, 2003), and María de los Angeles Torres, *In the Land of Mirrors: Cuban Exile Politics in the United States* (Ann Arbor: University of Michigan Press, 1999).

9. Fernando F. Segovia, "In the World But Not Of It: Exile as Locus for a Theology of the Diaspora," in *Hispanic/Latino Theology: Challenge and Promise,* ed. Ada María Isasi-Díaz and Fernando F. Segovia (Minneapolis: Fortress Press, 1996), 214.

10. See Alejandro Portes and Robert L. Bach, *Latin Journey: Cuban and Mexican Immigrants in the United States* (Berkeley: University of California Press, 1985). See also Silvia Pedraza-Bailey, *Political and Economic Migrants in America: Cubans and Mexicans* (Austin: University of Texas Press, 1985), and Grenier and Pérez, *The Legacy of Exile.*

11. See María Cristina García, *Havana, USA: Cuban Exiles and Cuban Americans in South Florida, 1959–1994* (Berkeley: University of California Press, 1996), and Miguel González-Pando, *The Cuban Americans* (Westport, CT: Greenwood Press, 1998).

12. See Thomas A. Tweed, *Our Lady of the Exile: Diasporic Religion at a Cuban Catholic Shrine in Miami* (New York: Oxford University Press, 1997), and Lisandro Pérez, "Cuban Catholics in the United States," in *Puerto Rican and Cuban Catholics in the U.S.: 1900–1965,* ed. Jay P. Dolan and Jaime R. Vidal (Notre Dame, IN: University of Notre Dame Press, 1994), 147–209.

13. For an overview of the national Hispanic church, see Moises Sandoval, *On the Move: A History of the Hispanic Church in the United States* (Maryknoll, NY: Orbis Books, 1990). See also Timothy Matovina and Gerald E. Poyo, eds., *Presente! U.S. Latino Catholics from Colonial Origins to the Present* (Maryknoll, NY: Orbis Books, 2000).

Chapter One.   Reform and Revolution

1. Marifeli Pérez-Stable, *The Cuban Revolution: Origins, Course and Legacy* (Oxford: Oxford University Press, 1993), 36–60.

2. John Kirk, *Between God and the Party: Religion and Politics in Revolutionary Cuba* (Tampa: University of South Florida Press, 1989), 1–31. For details of the history of the Catholic Church in Cuba, see Ramón Suárez Polcari, *Historia de Iglesia Católica en Cuba,* 2 vols. (Miami: Ediciones Universal, 2003).

3. Manuel P. Maza, "The Cuban Catholic Church: True Struggles and False Dilemmas: The Historical Characteristics of the Cuban Catholic Church and Their Impact on the 1959–1960 Episcopal Documents" (master's thesis, Georgetown University, 1982), 56–57.

4. For a survey of Catholic education in Cuba, see Teresa Fernández Soneira, *Cuba: Historia de la educación católica,* 2 vols. (Miami: Ediciones Universal, 1997).

5. Kirk, *Between God and the Party,* 41.

6. Universidad de Santo Tomás de Villanueva, *Contribución a la historia de sus diez primeros años* (Havana: UCAR, García, S.A., 1956), 20–26.

7. For background on Latin American Catholic Action, see Enrique Dussel, *A History of the Church in Latin America: Colonialism to Liberation, 1492–1979* (Grand

Rapids, MI: William B. Eerdmans Publishing, 1981), 106–108; Rosa María Martínez de Codes, *La iglesia en la América independiente: Siglo XIX* (Madrid: MAPFRE America, 1992), 287–295.

8. "Deliberaciones de los Sres. Arzobispos y Obispos de Cuba," in *La voz de la iglesia en Cuba: 100 documentos espiscopales* (Mexico City: Obra Nacional de la Buena Presna, 1995), 23–25.

9. Teresa Fernández Soneira, *Cuba: Historia de la educación católica, 1582–1961,* 2 vols. (Miami: Ediciones Universal, 1997), 1:426; Andrés Valdespino, "El legado espiritual del Hno. Victorino," in *Cuba Diáspora 1976: Anuario de la Iglesia Católica* (Miami: Unión de Cubanos en el Exilio, 1976), 81; "El Hermano Victorino, DLS," in *Cuba Diáspora 1978: Anuario de la Iglesia Católica* (Miami: Unión de Cubanos en el Exilio, 1978), 41–42; Raul Zayas-Bazán, "Bodas de Oro. Juventud Católica Cubana," in *Cuba Diáspora 1979: Anuario de la Iglesia Católica* (Miami: Unión de Cubanos en el Exilio, 1979), 29–31; Rubén D. Rumbaut, "Julio Morales Gómez (1913–1979)," in *Cuba Diáspora 1981: Anuario de la Iglesia Católica* (Miami: Unión de Cubanos en el Exilio, 1981), 79–81; José M. Hernández, *ACU: Agrupación Católica Universitaria: Los primeros cincuenta años* (Miami: Agrupación Católica Cubana, 1981), 5; Richard Pattee, *Catholic Life in the West Indies* (Washington, DC: Catholic Association for International Peace, 1946), 25.

10. Pattee, *Catholic Life in the West Indies,* 23–24; Hernández, *ACU,* 5.

11. See Miguel Figueroa y Miranda, *Historia de la Agrupación Católica Universitaria, 1931–1956* (Havana, 1956), and Hernández, *ACU.*

12. "Historia de veinticinco años," in Juventudes de Acción Católica Cubana, *Bodas de Plata, 1928–1953* (Hato Rey, PR: Ramallo Brothers Printing, 1978; facsimile of 1953 Havana edition); Pattee, *Catholic Life in the West Indies,* 25–26; Gustavo Amigó Jansen, "Cuba," in *El catolicismo contemporaneo en hispanoamerica,* ed. Richard Pattee (Buenos Aires: Editorial FIDES, 1951), 79; Raul del Valle, *El Cardenal Arteaga: Resplandores de la púrpura cubana* (La Habana, 1954), 77–80.

13. Kirk, *Between God and the Party,* 41.

14. For details on the ideological formation of the reformist generation of the 1930s, see Inés Segura Bustamante, *Cuba: Siglo XX y la Generación de 1930* (Santo Domingo: Editora Corripio, 1984).

15. Edward A. Lynch, *Religion and Politics in Latin America: Liberation Theology and Christian Democracy* (New York: Praeger, 1991), 35–38; Mary E. Hobgood, *Catholic Social Teaching and Economic Theory: Paradigms in Conflict* (Philadelphia: Temple University Press, 1991), 96–123; Charles E. Curran, *Catholic Social Teaching: A Historical, Theological and Ethical Analysis* (Washington, DC: Georgetown University Press, 2002).

16. Hernández, *ACU,* 1–61.

17. José Ignacio Lasaga, "Que es el catolicismo social?" *Esto Vir* 3, no. 25 (September 17, 1933) in *Dr. José Ignacio Lasaga: Recuerdos, escritos, publicaciones, conferencias* (26 vols.), vol. 3, Belén School Library, Miami. See also José Ignacio Lasaga,

"El estudiantado no debe inmiscuirse en el conflico español: Carta abierta a Camilo García Sierra," in *Dr. José Ignacio Lasaga,* vol. 1.

18. Stanley G. Payne, *Fascism in Spain, 1923–1977* (Madison: University of Wisconsin Press, 1999), 144–158.

19. Ibid., chapters 8–11.

20. Ibid., 285–286. For an excellent treatment of the corporatist tradition in Latin America, see Howard J. Wiarda, *The Soul of Latin America: The Cultural and Political Tradition* (New Haven, CT: Yale University Press, 2001), 246–280.

21. Stanley G. Payne, *Spanish Catholicism: An Historical Overview* (Madison: University of Wisconsin Press, 1984), 177.

22. Allan Chase, *Falange: The Axis Secret Army in the Americas* (New York: G. P. Putnam's Sons, 1943), 55–61.

23. Ibid., 63.

24. Michael Campbell-Johnson, "Evolución de la cuestión social en la Compañía de Jesús: Breve historia" (June 1984) (Internet article in possession of author).

25. Foyaca's work *Un nuevo orden economico-social* (Havana: Compañía Editora de Libros y Folletos, 1941) relied heavily on the work of Joaquín Azpiazu, including *El derecho de propiedad* (Madrid: Razón y Fe, 1930), *Patronos y obreros* (Madrid: Razón y Fe, n.d.), *Problemas sociales de actualidad* (Madrid: Razón y Fe, n.d.), *El Estado Corporativo* (Madrid: Biblioteca Fomento Social, n.d.), and *La Encíclica "Quadragesimo Anno"* (Burgos: Biblioteca Fomento Social, 1938).

26. Pattee, *Catholic Life in the West Indies,* 28–29.

27. Figueroa y Miranda, *Historia de la Agrupación Católica Universitaria,* 177–178; Pattee, *Catholic Life in the West Indies,* 26–27, 29; interview with José M. Hernández, Miami, August 2001.

28. Democracia Social Cristiana, *Discurso-programa: Pronunciado por el Dr. Manuel Foyaca, en la gran asamblea del Teatro Auditorium, 22 Noviembre de 1942* (Havana, 1942).

29. See Jacques Maritain, *Integral Humanism: Temporal and Spiritual Problems of a New Christendom,* trans. Joseph W. Evans (Notre Dame, IN: University of Notre Dame Press, 1968).

30. Thomas Bokenkotter, *Church and Revolution: Catholics in the Struggle for Democracy and Social Justice* (New York: Image Books, 1998), 381–389.

31. Ernst Halperin, *Nationalism and Communism in Chile* (Cambridge, MA: MIT Press, 1965), 182–183.

32. Lynch, *Religion and Politics in Latin America,* 35–54, 57–58, 67–86.

33. José M. Hernández and José Ignacio Rasco explain that Foyaca also admired Maritain, while Rubén D. Rumbaut believed that Foyaca and the Cuban Jesuits generally were critics of Maritain. According to Rumbaut, "Maritain's popularity made them nervous and suspicious that his ideas would not be sufficiently orthodox." From personal interviews with Hernández and Rasco (Miami, August 2001)

and written responses to questions submitted to Rumbaut (April 2002) shortly before his death in March 2003.

34. Rubén D. Rumbaut, "El Humanismo y La Revolución," *La Quincena* 5, no. 8 (April 1959): 16–17.

35. "Declaración de principios del 'movimiento humanista' de Cuba," *Política y Espíritu* (Chile), 7, no. 66 (December 1951): 533, 555–560.

36. Rumbaut vita in folder "Cuba-Consejo Revolucionario," box 19, Bureau of Inter-American Affairs, Office of the Deputy Assistant Secretary of Inter-American Affairs, General Records of the Department of State, National Archives and Records Administration, Washington, DC.

37. Rubén D. Rumbaut, "El Humanismo y La Revolución," *La Quincena* 5, no. 8 (April 1959): 16.

38. Cerro's vita in folder "Cuba-Consejo Revolucionario," box 19, Bureau of Inter-American Affairs, Office of the Deputy Assistant Secretary of Inter-American Affairs, General Records of the Department of State, National Archives and Records Administration, Washington, DC.

39. Angel del Cerro, "El Humanismo de Maritain: En busca de una tercera posición," *Bohemia* 51, no. 23 (June 7, 1959): 75, 96.

40. Andrés Valdespino, "Al Comunismo no se le destruye por decreto (1953)," 74–77, and "Lo histérico y lo histórico en el anticomunismo (1954)," 81, in *Valdespino: Cuba como pasión* (Hato Rey, PR: Ramallo Brothers Printing, n.d.).

41. "Circular para la diócesis de La Habana acerca de la precaria situación de los obreros: Mons. Severiano Sainz, Gobernador Eclesiástico, 2 de septiembre de 1914," in *La voz de la Iglesia en Cuba,* 21–22.

42. "Deliberaciones de los Sres. Arzobispos y Obispos de Cuba, Diciembre 1922," in *La voz de la Iglesia en Cuba,* 23–25.

43. Pérez-Stable, *The Cuban Revolution,* 42.

44. "La voz de la iglesia," in *La voz de la iglesia en Cuba,* 151–158.

45. José Ignacio Lasaga, "Agrupación Católica Universitaria: Informe de los trabajos realizados en el reparto de 'Las Yaguas,'" in *Dr. José Ignacio Lasaga,* vol. 4; Hernández, *ACU,* 7–28.

46. Juventudes de Acción Católica Cubana, *Bodas de Plata, 1928–1953.*

47. Junta Nacional de la Acción Católica Cubana, *Primer catálogo de las obras sociales católicas de Cuba* (La Habana, 1953), 5–22.

48. Gilberto García Valencia, "Juventud Obrera Católica," *Cuba Diáspora 1972: Anuario de la Iglesia Católica* (Miami: Unión de Cubanos en el Exilio, 1972), 113; Teresa Fernández Soneira, *Con la estrella y la cruz: Historia de la Federación de las Juventudes de Acción Católica Cubana* (Miami: Ediciones Universal, 2002), 302–303, 311, 340–346.

49. José Ignacio Lasaga, "El pensamiento social católico y los derechos económicos de la persona humana," in *Dr. José Ignacio Lasaga,* vol. 11.

50. Fernández Soneira, *Con la estrella y la cruz,* 322–323, 328–330.

51. "Semanas Sociales," *Cuba y su Iglesia Católica* (CD-ROM), 1999. In author's possession.

52. Melchor Gastón et. al., *¿Por qué reforma agraria?* (Habana: ACU; BIP, 1958), 5–6, 62–63; Alfred L. Padula Jr., "The Fall of the Bourgeoisie: Cuba, 1959–1961" (PhD dissertation, University of New Mexico, 1974), 449.

53. Angel del Cerro, "Cuarenta casos de injusticia social," *Bohemia* 51, no. 17 (April 26, 1959): 72–73, 95. Salvador de Freixedo's book was titled *Cuarenta casos de injusticia social: Examen de conciencia por cristianos distraidos.*

54. "Exposición del episcopado cubano a los delegados a la asamblea constituyente," in *La voz de la iglesia en Cuba,* 30–31.

55. Hugh Thomas, *Cuba: The Pursuit of Freedom* (New York: Harper & Row, 1971), 733–734; Nestor Carbonell Cortina, ed., *Grandes debates de la constituyente cubana de 1940* (Miami: Ediciones Universal, 2001), 258–275.

56. Hernández, *ACU,* 44; *CRECED: Final Document* (Hato Rey, PR: Ramallo Brothers Printing, 1996), 46.

57. See Carbonell Cortina, ed., *Grandes debates.*

58. Hernández, *ACU,* 47–52; José Ignacio Rasco, "La Democracia Cristiana en Cuba: Un poco de historia," Laureano Batista Archive, box 3 (green three-ring binder), Cuban Heritage Collection, University of Miami Library.

59. Ramón L. Bonachea and Marta San Martín, *The Cuban Insurrection, 1952–1959,* 2nd ed. (New Brunswick, NJ: Transactions Publishers, 1995), 27–28. See also Thomas, *Cuba,* 848–850.

60. José Ignacio Lasaga, "La actuación de los católicos en la política cubana," in *Dr. José Ignacio Lasaga,* vol. 10.

61. "Los católicos cubanos y el gobierno de estado de Batista," *Política y Espíritu* 8, no. 71 (May 1952), 152–153.

62. Angel de Jesús Piñera, "Hablan para 'Avance' politicos del futuro," *Avance Criollo,* October 20, 1961, 14; interview with José Ignacio Rasco, Miami, August 2001.

63. "Catolicismo: La cruz y el diablo," *Bohemia* 51, no. 3 (January 1959): 99.

64. For discussion of the strike see Bonachea and San Martín, *The Cuban Insurrection, 1952–1959,* 211–215.

65. Rodolfo Riesgo, "El marzato y la JOC," *La Quincena* 5, nos. 1–2 (January 1959): 22–24.

66. Lasaga, "La actuación de los católicos en la política cubana," in *Dr. José Ignacio Lasaga,* vol. 10.

67. Ibid.

68. Hernández, *ACU,* 93–94.

69. "Catolicismo: La cruz y el diablo," 98–100.

70. "En favor de la paz," in *La voz de la iglesia en Cuba,* 40–41.

71. Manuel Fernández, "Presencia de los católicos en la revolución triunfante," *La Quincena* 5, nos. 1–2 (January 1959): 10–16, 94; Kirk, *Between God and the Party,* 48–53; "Catolicismo: La cruz y el diablo," 98–100.

72. "Catolicismo: La cruz y el diablo," 100.

73. Fernández, "Presencia de los católicos de la revolución triunfante," 16.

74. "Catolicismo: La cruz y el diablo," 100.

75. "Queremos la paz," in *La voz de la iglesia en Cuba,* 42–43.

76. "Vida nueva," in *La voz de la iglesia en Cuba,* 53–59.

77. Ignacio Biaín, "Balance del marcismo y destinos de una revolución," *La Quincena* 5, nos. 1–2 (January 1959): 51.

78. "Cambios en la Iglesia Católica de Cuba," *Prensa Libre,* March 10, 1959.

79. "Ratificación de fé católica y reafirmación revolucionaria se efectuó ayer," *Avance,* January 26, 1959.

80. "Con brillantez y entusiasmo celebró la Juventud Obrera Católica su XII aniversario," *Diario de la Marina,* February 22, 1959.

81. "Confederación de sindicalistas cristianos: Exiliado cubano es líder sindical continental," *The Voice,* January 13, 1967.

82. Gerhard Wahlers, *Nace una alternativa* (Miami: SAETA Ediciones, 1991), 92–99.

83. Gilberto García Valencia, "II Semana de Estudios Sociales y Jocistas para sacerdotes y religiosos," *La Quincena* 5, no. 18 (September 30, 1959): 22–23, 46–47.

84. "Valores cristianos de la revolución," *Avance,* March 10, 1959.

85. "La batalla que aún nos falta," in *Valdespino: Cuba Como Pasión* (Hato Rey, PR: Ramallo Brothers Printing, n.d.), 118–119.

86. Andrés Valdespino, "Carta a los ricos," *Bohemia* 51, no. 21 (May 24, 1959).

87. Andrés Valdespino, "El cristianismo de los sepulcros blanqueados," *Bohemia* 51, no. 22 (May 31, 1959): 61, 97.

88. Angel Del Cerro, "La iglesia tiene que resusitar," *Bohemia* 51, no. 14 (April 5, 1959): 78–79.

89. Thomas, *Cuba,* 1198–1214.

90. Padula, "The Fall of the Bourgeoisie: Cuba, 1959–1961," 128–129.

91. "La ley agraria del gobierno revolucionario contempla el interés supremo de la sociedad," *La Quincena* 5, no. 3 (February 1959): 12–14.

92. "El manifiesto de las Asociaciones Católicas," *La Quincena* 5, no. 3 (February 1959): 30.

93. Thomas, *Cuba,* 1083.

94. Manuel Artime, *Traicion! Gritan 20,000 tumbas cubanas* (Mexico: Editorial Jus, 1960), 169.

95. Thomas, *Cuba,* 1215–1216.

96. Padula, "The Fall of the Bourgeoisie: Cuba, 1959–1961," 132–133, 136.

97. "Entrevista con Mon. Evelio Díaz," in *La voz de la iglesia en Cuba,* 76.

98. "La Iglesia Católica y la nueva Cuba," in *La voz de la iglesia en Cuba,* 77, 79.

99. Ignacio Biaín, "El espíritu de la reforma agraria," *La Quincena* 5, no. 11 (June 15, 1959): 30–32.

100. See Alberto Martín Villaverde, "La reforma agraria cubana y la Iglesia Católica," *Bohemia* (July 5, 1959), and Enrique, Arzobispo de Santiago de Cuba,

"La reforma agraria y el Arzobispado de Santiago de Cuba. Aclaraciones, July 21, 1959," in *La voz de la iglesia en Cuba*, 80–86.

Chapter 2.   Betrayal and Dissent

1. Andres Valdespino, "La revolución que hay que salvar," *Bohemia Libre* 52, no. 5 (November 6, 1960): 42. See also Rubén Rumbaut, *Revolucion traicionada* (Miami: Frente Revolucionario Democrático, 1962). The role of the church during 1959–1961 has been the subject of considerable controversy. For a survey of competing views on the church's conduct, see John C. Super, "Interpretations of Church and State in Cuba, 1959–1961," *The Catholic Historical Review* 89, no. 3 (July 2003): 511–535.

2. See *Información Católica Cubana*, 1 (July 1, 1961); 2 (July 15, 1961). During August 1961, Andrés Suárez wrote the U.S. State Department inquiring about funds to continue the bulletin. It is not clear whether funds were provided, but the bulletin continued publishing through at least 1965.

3. See José Ignacio Rasco, "La generación traicionada," *Bohemia Libre* 53, no. 18 (February 5, 1961): 48–49, 59; Angel del Cerro, "Radiografía de una traición," *Bohemia Libre* 52, no. 3 (October 23, 1960): 36–37, 66; Rubén Darío Rumbaut, "Intrínsecamente perverso!" *Bohemia Libre* 53, no. 13 (January 1, 1961): 41, 58, 64.

4. Hugh Thomas, *Cuba: The Pursuit of Freedom* (New York: Harper & Row, 1971), 1003.

5. For an excellent review of the first three years of the revolutionary experience, see Marifeli Pérez-Stable, *The Cuban Revolution: Origins, Course, and Legacy* (Oxford: Oxford University Press, 1993), 61–81.

6. Thomas, *Cuba*, 1196–1198.

7. Alfred L. Padula Jr. "The Fall of the Bourgeoisie: Cuba, 1959–1961" (PhD dissertation, University of New Mexico, 1974), 156, 163. Padula's study details the process of collectivization during 1959–1961.

8. See Jesús Arboleya Cervera, *La contrarevolución cubana* (Havana: Editorial Ciencias Sociales, 1997), 57–64, for details on these developments.

9. Boris Goldenberg, *The Cuban Revolution and Latin America* (New York: Praeger, 1966), 185–192.

10. Rodolfo Riesgo, "No tiene carácter político el Congreso Católico Nacional," *La Quincena* 5, nos. 21–22 (November 1959): 22.

11. Ignacio Biaín, "El Congreso Católico de Noviembre," *La Quincena* 5, no. 20 (October 31, 1959): 34.

12. Padre Aldeaseca, "Mons. Evelio Díaz en la television," *La Quincena* 5, nos. 21–22 (November 1959): 51.

13. "Religion Part of Cubans' Nature—Castro," *The Voice*, December 4, 1959.

14. Mariano Errasti, "Reportaje del Congreso Católico Nacional: La noche mas luminosa de la historia," *La Quincena* 5, nos. 23–24 (December 1959), 45.

15. The description of the congress is from Errasti, "Reportaje del Congreso Católico Nacional," and "Gran demonstración de fe popular, el Congreso Católico," *Bohemia* 51, no. 49 (December 6, 1959).

16. Comité Organizador del Congreso Nacional, *Temas del Congreso Católico Nacional*, Havana, November 29, 1959, 10.

17. Ibid.

18. "Una declaración conjunta hacen los católicos de Cuba," *The Voice*, April 22, 1960.

19. Rodolfo Riesgo, "15 dias en la nación," *La Quincena* 5, no. 4 (February 1959): 19. Many additional articles in *La Quincena* warned of the dangers of communism.

20. Manuel Artime, *Traición! Gritan 20,000 tumbas cubanas* (Mexico: Ediciones Jus, 1960), 170–182.

21. Artime, *Traición!*, 57–72.

22. Leslie Dewart, *Christianity and Revolution* (New York: Herder & Herder, 1963), 144–145; Teresita Rodríguez de Molina, "Mártir: Rogelio González Corzo (Francisco)," *Tridente* 1, no. 2 (April 1981): 7, in box 3 (green three-ring binder), Laureano Batista Archive, Cuban Heritage Collection, University of Miami Library.

23. "Comentando los puntos basicos del MRR," *Tridente* 1, no. 1 (January 1, 1965): 12, in box 3 (green three-ring binder), Laureano Batista Archive, Cuban Heritage Collection, University of Miami Library.

24. Thomas, *Cuba*, 1325–1328.

25. José Ignacio Rasco, *La libertad en San Agustín* (La Habana: Ediciones Insula, S.A., 1958), 20–24.

26. José Ignacio Rasco, "La Democracia Cristiana en Cuba: Un poco de historia," box 3 (green three-ring binder), Laureano Batista Archive, Cuban Heritage Collection, University of Miami Library.

27. Interview with José Ignacio Rasco, Miami, March 24, 1998. For more details on Rasco's relations with Castro when they were students, see José Ignacio Rasco, *Semblanza de Fidel Castro* (Miami: Cuban Center for Cultural, Social and Strategic Studies, 1999).

28. Thomas, *Cuba*, 1198.

29. Ibid., 1203.

30. "Chronology 1961," Subject Files, 1960–1963, box 12, Office of the Coordinator of Cuban Affairs, Bureau of Inter-American Affairs, General Records of the Department of State, National Archives and Records Administration, Washington, DC.

31. Thomas, *Cuba*, 1085–1086.

32. See José Ignacio Rasco, *Cuba 1959: Artículos de combate* (Buenos Aires: Ediciones Diagrama, 1962).

33. "Cuba Christian Democrats Answer Castro," *The Voice,* January 22, 1960.

34. Rasco, "La Democracia Cristiana en Cuba." This document includes a list of the founding members of the Christian Democratic Movement. See also "Cuba Christian Democrats Answer Castro."

35. Ignacio Biaín, "'El Movimiento Democrata Cristiano," *La Quincena* 6, no. 2 (January 30, 1960): 32–33.

36. José Vilasuso Rivero, "Es oportuno un partido demócrata de inspiración cristiana?" *La Quincena* 5, no. 11 (June 15, 1959).

37. "Cuban Party Ends Activity Until Free Speech Returns," *The Voice,* June 10, 1960.

38. Enrique Ros, *Playa Girón: La historia verdadera* (Miami: Ediciones Universal, 1994), 22–26, 35–41, and "Informe 1963: MDC-Militar," box 13, folder 305, Laureano Batista Archive, Cuban Heritage Collection, University of Miami Library.

39. Enrique Ros, *Playa Girón,* 24–28, 37–40.

40. "Three Cuban Exile Groups Call Castro Regime Red," *The Voice,* July 1, 1960.

41. Ros, *Playa Girón,* 35–36.

42. "Memorandum: El Movimiento Demócrata Cristiano de Cuba," n.d., box 6, folder 86, Laureano Batista Archive, Cuban Heritage Collection, University of Miami Library.

43. "Laureano Batista Falla," box 1, folder 5, Laureano Batista Archive, Cuban Heritage Collection, University of Miami Library.

44. Cuban Student Directorate, *Those Who Rebel and Those Who Submit* (n.d.), 15–16.

45. Directorio Revolucionario Estudiantil, *La cruz sigue en pie: Biografía y escritos de Alberto Muller: Ideario de una nueva generación cubana* (Caracas: Tipografía Lincoln, n.d.), 27–28.

46. Ibid., 9.

47. Ibid., 13–15. For a detailed review of MRR's ideas see *Tridente* 1, nos. 1–18 (1965).

48. "Directorio Estudiantil del Frente Revolucionario Democratico: Primer pleno en el exilio," box 9, folder 5, Bureau of Inter-American Affairs, Office of the Deputy Assistant Secretary of Inter-American Affairs, General Records of the Department of State, National Archives and Records Administration, Washington, DC.

49. Directorio Revolucionario Estudiantil, "Reunión celebrada en el local del D.R.E. . . . el día 26 de septiembre de 1961 de 91/2 p.m. a 4 a.m. para tratar sobre las líneas, tesis y metas específicas y generales del D.R.E."; and "Esencia; principios; fines u objetivos; medios del Directorio Revolucionario Estudiantil," box 6, folder 100 ("ideología"), Directorio Revolucionario Estudiantil Archive, Cuban Heritage Collection, University of Miami Library.

50. Interview with María Cristina Herrera, Miami, May 11, 1998.

51. Rodolfo Riesgo, *Cuba: El movimiento obrero y su entorno socio-politico, 1865–1983* (Miami: Saeta Ediciones, 1985), 77–100.

52. See Reinol González, *Y Fidel creo el punto x* (Miami: Saeta Ediciones, 1987), a memoir written after his release from prison that includes his activities as member of the executive committee of the CTC during 1959 as well as his disillusionment with Castro and the Revolution.

53. "La enseñanza privada," in *La voz de la iglesia en Cuba: 100 documentos episcopales* (Mexico City: Obra Nacional de la Buena Prensa, A.C., 1995), 64–69.

54. "Current Intelligence Weekly Review," July 21, 1960, box 2, folder 8, Records Relating to the Paramilitary Invasion at the Bay of Pigs, April 1961, Records of the Central Intelligence Agency, National Archives and Records Administration, Washington, DC.

55. "Por Dios y por Cuba," in *La voz de la iglesia en Cuba,* 107–114.

56. Ismael Testé, *Historia eclesiástica de Cuba,* 5 vols. (Burgos, Spain: Imprenta El Monte Carmelo and Artes Gráficas Medinaceli, 1969–1975), 5:617–618.

57. "Circular colectiva del espicopado cubano," in *La voz de la iglesia en Cuba,* 115–118.

58. "Ni traidores ni parías," and "Roma o Moscú," in *La voz de la iglesia en Cuba,* 126–130, 135–141.

59. Dewart, *Christianity and Revolution,* 112–113, 157, 159.

60. Directorio Revolucionario Estudiantil, *La persecución de la iglesia católica en Cuba* (Quito, Ecuador, 1962[?]), 7–8; "Cuba Bishops Blast Reds, Demand Religious Rights," *The Voice,* August 12, 1960.

61. José Duarte Oropesa, *Historiología cubana, 1959–1980,* 5 vols. (Miami: Ediciones Universal, 1993), 4:255.

62. "Agentes castristas incitan a los campesinos contra la iglesia," *The Voice,* July 1, 1960.

63. "Violence Mounts as Red Curtain Falls on Cuba," *The Voice,* August 26, 1960.

64. "Cuba Bishops Blast Reds, Demand Religious Rights."

65. "Violence Mounts as Red Curtain Falls on Cuba."

66. "Cuba Bishops Blast Reds, Demand Religious Rights."

67. "Reds Lashing out at Cuban Clergy, Laity," *The Voice,* August 19, 1960.

68. Ibid. For background on Lence and his activities, see Juan Clark, *Cuba: Mito y realidad: Testimonios de un pueblo* (Miami: SAETA Ediciones, 1990), 324–327; "Por la unidad de la iglesia," in *La voz de la iglesia de Cuba,* 124–125. See the interesting pamphlet on Chinese strategies for creating a nationalist Catholic Church independent of the Vatican: Li Wei Han, *La Iglesia Católica y Cuba: Programa de acción* (Pekin: Ediciones en Lenguas Extranjeras, 1959).

69. "Suprimidos en La Habana todos los programas católicos de radio y TV," *The Voice,* October 14, 1960; Angel Aparicio Laurencio, *"Donde está el cadaver? . . . Se reunen los buitres" (crónicas de la persecución religiosa en Cuba)* (Santiago de Chile, 1963), 128–129.

70. "Castro Makes Move to Seize Control of Catholic Schools," *The Voice,* November 4, 1960; "Témese en La Habana el control absoluto de la educación privada," *The Voice,* November 11, 1960.

71. "Juventud católica reafirma lealtad a la iglesia," *The Voice,* September 9, 1960.

72. "Cubans Rally to Church's Defense," *The Voice,* October 28, 1960.

73. Ros, *Playa Girón,* 99, 115.

74. Directorio Revolucionario Estudiantil-Cuba, *Porfirio R. Ramírez: Mártir del estudiantado cubano,* box 9, notebook 180, Directorio Revolucionario Estudiantil Archive, Cuban Heritage Collection, University of Miami Library.

75. "Fight Communism, Archbishop Again Tells Cubans," *The Voice,* November 18, 1960.

76. "'Revolución' ataca a la iglesia en Cuba," *The Voice,* November 25, 1960.

77. Benito Novas, "Existe una quinta columna en los colegios católicos," *Bohemia* 52, no. 48 (November 27, 1960).

78. "Three Churches in Havana Bombed," *The Voice,* December 16, 1960.

79. "Bishops Send Letter to Castro," *The Voice,* December 9, 1960.

80. "Con Cristo o contra Cristo," in *La voz de la iglesia de cuba,* 159–166.

81. "Castro insulta al cardenal, ataca al clero y a los jueces," *The Voice,* December 30, 1960.

82. Thomas, *Cuba,* 1297–1298.

83. "Clausurada 'La Quincena' por milicias de Castro," *The Voice,* January 20, 1961; Directorio Revolucionario Estudiantial, *La persecución de la iglesia católica en Cuba,* 15.

84. "Anti-Castro Students Strike in Catholic Schools in Cuba," *The Voice,* February 17, 1961.

85. Ibid.; Teresa Fernández Soneira, *Cuba: Historia de la educación católica, 1582–1961,* 2 vols. (Miami: Ediciones Universal, 1997), 1:447–449; Aparicio Laurencio, *"Donde esta el cadaver?"* 134–142.

86. "Castro Agents Hunt Trouble, Schools Warned," *The Voice,* March 17, 1961; "More Priests Terrorized by Castro Mobs, Militia," *The Voice,* March 24, 1961; "Catholic Priest Reported Executed in Cuba," *The Voice,* March 31, 1961.

87. "Castro Troops Mar Good Friday Rites," *The Voice,* April 7, 1961.

88. Thomas, *Cuba,* 1360–1370.

89. Clark, *Cuba,* 329–334, and "La persecución religiosa," *Información Católica Cubana* 1 (July 1, 1961), in box 19, folder "Cuba-Consejo Revolucionario," Office of the Deputy Assistant Secretary of Inter-American Affairs, Bureau of Inter-American Affairs, General Records of the Department of State, National Archives and Records Administration.

90. Thomas, *Cuba,* 1349.

91. See flyers published by the Directorio Revolucionario Estudiantil–Cuba: "Alberto Tapia Ruano: Mártir del estudiantado cubano," and "Virgilio Campanería Angel: Estudiante mártir de Cuba," in DRE Collection, box 9, folder no. 180, Di-

rectorio Revolucionario Estudiantil Archive, Cuban Heritage Collection, University of Miami Library.

92. Thomas, *Cuba,* 1371.

93. "Reds Seize All Cuban Schools," *The Voice,* June 16, 1961.

94. "Primeros americanos evacuados de Cuba," *Avance Criollo,* June 2, 1961.

95. "Cuba Reds Stifling Church in 'Bloodless Purge,'" *The Voice,* July 21, 1961.

96. "En sus puestos prelados y sacerdotes," *The Voice,* August 4, 1961. For examples of Boza Masvidal's writings in the parish bulletin of Caridad Church, see Mons. Eduardo Boza Masvidal, *Voz en el destierro* (Miami: Revista Ideal, 1997), 29–67.

97. Directorio Revolucionario Estudiantil, *La persecución de la iglesia católica en Cuba,* 24–25; Aparicio Laurencio, *"Donde está el cadaver?"* 145–146; Clark, *Cuba,* 335; Kirk, *Between God and the Party,* 103. For a government version of these events, see *El Mundo,* September 12, 1961.

98. "Pope Grieves for Persecuted Cuba; Bishop and Priests Deported by Castro," *The Voice,* September 22, 1961; "Expulsión de 131 religiosos de Cuba," *Diario Las Americas,* January 7, 1982; Kirk, *Between God and the Party,* 109.

99. "Exiled Bishop Declares," *The Voice,* October 6, 1991.

Chapter Three.   Faith Community

1. For an overview of this early refugee experience, see María Cristina García, *Havana, USA: Cuban Exiles and Cuban Americans in South Florida, 1959–1994* (Berkeley: University of California Press, 1996), 13–19.

2. Manolo Reyes, "The Great Cuban Exodus: Every Four Hours Someone Risks Life to Make Escape," *The Voice,* September 11, 1964.

3. Silvia Pedraza-Bailey, *Political and Economic Migrants in America: Cubans and Mexicans* (Austin: University of Texas Press, 1985), 23–25.

4. García, *Havana, USA,* 47–74.

5. Pedraza-Bailey, *Political and Economic Migrants in America,* 29–40.

6. Thomas D. Boswell and James R. Curtis, *The Cuban-American Experience: Culture, Images, and Perspectives* (Totowa, NJ: Rowman and Allanheld, 1983), 66; Pedraza-Bailey, *Political and Economic Migrants in America,* 40–43. See also Eleanor M. Rogg and Rosemary Santana Cooney, *Adaptation and Adjustment of Cubans: West New York, New Jersey* (Monograph 5; New York: Fordham University Hispanic Research Center, 1980).

7. García, *Havana, USA,* 19.

8. "200,000 Latin Americans Here No Problem but Asset," *The Voice,* August 9, 1963.

9. Interview with Msgr. Bryan O. Walsh, Miami, April 1, 1998.

10. For a detailed account of Operation Peter Pan, see Yvonne M. Conde, *Operation Pedro Pan: The Untold Story of 14,048 Cuban Children* (New York: Routledge,

1999), and María de los Angeles Torres, *The Lost Apple: Operation Pedro Pan, Cuban Children in the U.S., and the Promise of a Better Future* (Boston: Beacon Press, 2003).

11. García, *Havana, USA*, 23–26; Conde, *Operation Pedro Pan,* and Torres, *The Lost Apple.*

12. "Catholic Relief Shows U.S. Aid to Cubans Inadequate," *The Voice,* December 15, 1961.

13. Bryan O. Walsh, "The Spanish Impact Here: How the Archdiocese Is Meeting the Challenge," *The Voice,* July 18, 1975.

14. "Cuban Refugees Receive Church, U.S., Private Aid," *The Voice,* December 9, 1960.

15. "Cuban Women Give $10,000 to Assist Refugees at Centro," *The Voice,* November 18, 1960.

16. Michael J. McNally, *Catholicism in South Florida, 1868–1968* (Gainesville: University Presses of Florida, 1984), 147.

17. "Many Cuban Refugees Going Hungry," *The Voice,* January 20, 1961.

18. García, *Havana, USA,* 19–23; Félix Roberto Masud-Piloto, *From Welcomed Exiles to Illegal Immigrants: Cuban Migration to the U.S., 1959–1995* (Lanham, MD: Rowman & Littlefield, 1996), 47–51.

19. Alejandro Portes and Robert L. Bach, *Latin Journey: Cuban and Mexican Immigrants in the United States* (Berkeley: University of California Press, 1985), 88.

20. Sasha Rumbaut, "The Banana Boat Story," manuscript of family remembrances by Carmen and Rubén Rumbaut's granddaughter, which also includes Carmen Rumbaut's diary entries (in author's possession).

21. Alejandro Portes, "Dilemmas of a Golden Exile: Integration of Cuban Refugee Families in Milwaukee," *American Sociological Review* 34 (1969): 505–518. See also Pedraza-Bailey, *Political and Economic Migrants in America,* and Guillermo Grenier and Lisandro Pérez, *The Legacy of Exile: Cubans in the United States* (Boston: Allyn & Bacon, 2003).

22. Gustavo Peña and Skip Flynn, "The Spiritual Impact of an Exiled People," *The Voice,* September 22, 1967.

23. "Exiled Bishop Boza Coming to Miami for Religious Rally," *The Voice,* January 12, 1962.

24. "Exiled Bishop Boza on Radio to Cuba," *The Voice,* January 6, 1962; "Unite in God to Halt Communism, Bishop Boza Tells Latin America," *The Voice,* February 2, 1962; "Conferencia de prensa del obispo cubano Eduardo Boza Masvidal," *The Voice,* February 2, 1962; "Vatican Relations with Cuba no Approval of Red Regime," *The Voice,* February 2, 1962.

25. "Bishop Boza Uniting Exiles," *The Voice,* March 23, 1962.

26. "Normas generales de la U.C.E.," in *Cuba Diáspora 1978: Anuario de la Iglesia Católica* (Miami: Unión de Cubanos en el Exilio, 1978), 17.

27. "Deben inscribirse los hispanos en sus respectivas parróquias," *The Voice,* March 30, 1962. This was not unique to Cuba. In Latin America Catholics generally relied less on the parish than U.S. Catholics did. Allan Figueroa Deck, *The Sec-*

ond Wave: Hispanic Ministry and the Evangelization of Cultures (New York: Paulist Press, 1989), 58–59.

28. Guillermina Damas, "Panorama histórico-pastoral de la dimensión hispana de la Archidiocesis de Miami, 1958–1983" (master's thesis, Southeast Pastoral Institute and Barry University, 1983), 35.

29. "St. Dominic Church Blessed; Bishop Praises New Parish," *The Voice*, December 20, 1963.

30. "Intensa vida parroquial en St. Robert Bellarmine," *The Voice*, May 9, 1969.

31. "Los sacerdotes de la OCSHA: Pioneros de la misión apostólica en la colonia latina del sur de la Florida," *The Voice*, March 22, 1963; "OCSHA: 25 años de generosidad y entrega ilusionado," *The Voice*, December 13, 1974.

32. "Deben inscribirse los hispanos en sus respectivas parróquias," *The Voice*, March 30, 1962; conversation with Father Jorge Perales, San Juan Bosco Parish, Miami, Florida, March 9, 2002.

33. "Misas dominicales en español," *The Voice*, March 23, 1962.

34. "Archidiocesis de Miami," in *Cuba Diáspora 1975: Anuario de la Iglesia Católica* (Miami: Unión de Cubanos en el Exilio, 1975), 108–109; Walsh, "The Spanish Impact Here: How the Archdiocese Is Meeting the Challenge," *The Voice*, July 18, 1975.

35. "Un llamado a la vocación sacerdotal en el exilio," *The Voice*, July 6, 1962; "Primera misa del Padre Francisco Dorta Duque: Cuba necesita mas de diez mil sacerdotes," *The Voice*, June 22, 1962.

36. Marjorie L. Fillyaw, "Largest Group Ever to Witness an Ordination in Florida," *The Voice*, September 7, 1962; "Ordination Sunday Symbol of Hope to Cuban Refugees," *The Voice*, August 31, 1962. Sánchez remained in Miami and ministered until 1976, when he died of cancer. See *The Voice*, April 9, 1976; McNally, *Catholicism in South Florida*, 157, 268.

37. José Jorge Vila and Guillermo Zalamea Arenas, *Exilio* (Miami, 1967), 377.

38. "Open-door parish: St. John Bosco marks 25 years of welcoming immigrants of all nationalities," *The Voice*, May 27, 1988; "Nuevo local para la misión de San Juan Bosco," *The Voice*, January 10, 1964; "St. John Bosco Church Dedicated by Bishop Carroll," *The Voice*, August 27, 1965; McNally, *Catholicism in South Florida*, 153–154.

39. "Festival de verano en San Juan Bosco," *The Voice*, July 25, 1969.

40. Vila and Zalamea Arenas, *Exilio*, 378–380. See *San Juan Bosco Church Silver Jubilee, 1963–1988* (Miami, San Juan Bosco Church, 1988).

41. "Zona por zona misionarán la parróquia del Corpus Christi," *The Voice*, September 25, 1964; "Aumenta la asistencia a misa y sacramentos," *The Voice*, October 2, 1964.

42. "Intensa vida parroquial en St. Robert Bellarmine," *The Voice*, May 9, 1969.

43. "La Pasión según . . . varias parróquias de Miami," *The Voice*, March 29, 1965.

44. Lisandro Pérez, "Cuban Catholics in the United States," in *Puerto Rican and Cuban Catholics in the U.S., 1900–1965,* ed. Jay P. Dolan and Jaime R. Vidal (Notre Dame, IN: University of Notre Dame Press, 1994), 201–206.

45. "Pagina del Padre Llorente," *Esto Vir* 31, no. 2 (September–October, 1962).

46. Vila and Zalamea Arenas, *Exilio*, 368–372.

47. Ibid.

48. See *The Voice*, 1965–1969, and Ana Rodríguez-Soto, "Miles de fieles lloran la pérdida del P. Villaronga," *La Voz Católica* (January–March 2005).

49. "Matrimonios cristianos advierten su responsabilidad apostólica," *The Voice*, November 13, 1964; "Estudiarán problemas de la familia exiliada," *The Voice*, October 21, 1966.

50. Damas, "Panorama histórico-pastoral de la dimensión hispana."

51. "Amor en Acción: History and Theology," Amor en Acción Web site, http:// amorenaccion.com/e_html/history/history.html.

52. Miguel Cabrera, "Cristo en las calles de Miami," *Cuba Diáspora 1976: Anuario de la Iglesia Católica* (Miami: Unión de Cubanos en el Exilio, 1976), 33–36. See also Damas, "Panorama histórico-pastoral de la dimensión hispana."

53. Figueroa Deck, *The Second Wave*, 67–69.

54. "Preparan Cursillo de Cristiandad para hombres," *The Voice*, February 16, 1962, and "Inícianse con exito en Miami los Cursillos de Cristiandad," *The Voice*, March 16, 1962.

55. "Ultiman detalles del cursillo," *The Voice*, June 1, 1962, and "Clausurado el II Cursillo de Cristiandad," *The Voice*, June 15, 1962.

56. Ibid.

57. "Secretariado de Cursillos de Cristiandad," *The Voice*, September 14, 1962.

58. "Efectúan el primer Cursillo de Cristiandad para mujeres," *The Voice*, June 7, 1963.

59. "'El cursillo en Miami, lleno de vida va creciendo en madurez cada dia'— Habla el nuevo director arquidiocesano de cursillos," *The Voice*, November 21, 1969.

60. Carlos H. Obregón, "Cursillo de Cristiandad: Mi mejor recomendación a un hombre," *The Voice*, November 2, 1962.

61. Vila and Zalamea Arenas, *Exilio*, 395–398.

62. "Organizan CDC para latinos de la diócesis," *The Voice*, July 13, 1962; "Spanish CCD Meeting Set," *The Voice*, September 28, 1962; "Fecunda labor de la rama latina de la CCD," *The Voice*, September 20, 1963.

63. "High School at Centro for Teenagers," *The Voice*, January 20, 1961. For a detailed first-person account of the activities of the CHC in the early 1960s by its first director, see Sister Miriam Strong, O.P., "Refugees from Castro's Cuba: 'Of Fish and Freedom': An Historical Account of the Cuban Refugees Received and Relieved by His Excellency, Bishop Coleman F. Carroll, in the Catholic Diocese of Miami, Florida, 1959–1964" (master's thesis, Fordham University, New York, 1964). "23 Students Were Graduated from Bachillerato," *The Voice*, June 23, 1961.

64. "Miami's Cuban Refugee Tragedy," *The Voice*, December 8, 1961.

65. Boswell and Curtis, *The Cuban-American Experience*, 127.

66. "Brothers on La Salle High Staff Once Studied in U.S.," *The Voice*, June 16, 1961.

67. "A Tribute to Belen in Exile," *The Voice,* February 9, 1962.

68. "Celebra el Colegio de Belén la fiesta de su patrona," *The Voice,* February 8, 1963.

69. "Jesuit Preparatory School Blessed by Bishop Carroll," *The Voice,* October 5, 1962.

70. Pérez, "Cuban Catholics in the U.S.," 198–201.

71. "Graduación del Jesuit Preparatory School," *The Voice,* June 22, 1962.

72. "Abrirán en el exilio los colegios católicos cubanos," *The Voice,* August 18, 1961.

73. María Cristina Herrera, "The Cuban Ecclesial Enclave in Miami: A Critical Profile," *U.S. Catholic Historian* 9, nos.1–2 (Winter/Spring 1990), 211.

74. Vila and Zalamea Arenas, *Exilio,* 365.

75. Lorenzo de Toro, "Despúes de cuatro años, que pretende Ideal?" in *Cuba Diáspora 1976,* 42.

76. José L. Hernando, "Una parróquia en el aire," in *Cuba Diáspora 1976,* 37–40; "Enfoque en Miami," *Ideal* 4, no. 38 (October 15, 1974): 39.

77. "La pelea está planteada," *Avance Criollo,* September 22, 1961.

78. "Bishop Makes Proposal at Lady of El Cobre Mass," *The Voice,* September 16, 1966.

79. "Significado de la celebración del cincuentenario," *The Voice,* September 9, 1966.

80. "New Cuban Shrine Plan Announced," *The Voice,* September 30, 1966. For additional detail about how the idea developed and was implemented, see Thomas A. Tweed, *Our Lady of Exile: Diasporic Religion at a Cuban Catholic Shrine in Miami* (New York: Oxford University Press, 1997), 32–37.

81. "Unese WMIE y WFAB para triudo a la Virgen del Cobre," *The Voice,* August 25, 1967, and "Miles de cubanos honrarán a su patrona," *The Voice,* September 1, 1967.

82. Araceli Cantero, "Misionero y obispo pero campesino de corazón," *The Voice,* March 23, 1979.

83. "La Capilla de la Caridad, lugar de cubanía y cristianismo," *The Voice,* September 22, 1967.

84. Interview with Bishop Agustín Román, Miami, March 31, 1998; Tweed, *Our Lady of the Exile,* 31–37.

Chapter Four. Identity and Ideology

1. Comité Organizador del Congreso Católico Nacional, *Temas del Congreso Católico Nacional,* Havana, November 29, 1959, 20–30.

2. Eduardo Boza Masvidal, "Comunidades cristianas cubanas," in *Cuba Diáspora 1976: Anuario de la Iglesia Católica* (Miami: Unión de Cubanos en el Exilio, 1976), 31–32.

3. UCE Internacional, "Normas generales de la U.C.E.," in *Cuba Diáspora 1978: Anuario de la Iglesia Católica* (Miami: Unión de Cubanos en el Exilio, 1978), 17. See also "Comité Católico Cubano-Unión de Cubanos en el Exilio," *Boletín* 7, no. 83 (May 1969), in Truth About Cuba Committee (TACC) Archive, box 56, folder 24 in Cuban Heritage Collection, University of Miami Library, and "UCE," in *Cuba Diáspora 1978,* 18.

4. See Eduardo Boza Masvidal, *Voz en el destierro* (Miami: Revista Ideal, 1997).

5. Ibid.

6. Obispos Mons. Eduardo Boza Masvidal and Mons. Agustín Román, "Cuba ayer, hoy y siempre, exilio, 20 de Mayo de 1982." Made available to the author by the archdiocese of Miami.

7. Jay P. Dolan, *The Immigrant Church: New York's Irish and German Catholics, 1815–1865* (Notre Dame, IN: University of Notre Dame Press, 1975), 45–67.

8. Boza Masvidal and Román, "Cuba ayer, hoy y siempre." See also "De Varela a Martí," *Ideal* 1, no. 10 (June 15, 1972): 33–34.

9. Antonio Calatayud, "Monumento en el exilio para los caidos en Girón," *Diario Las Américas,* April 18, 1968.

10. Gustavo Peña Monte, "Misa y monumento en memoria de los mártires de Girón, mañana," *The Voice,* April 16, 1971.

11. For a full description of the unveiling ceremony, see "Develación del monumento a los mártires," *Girón,* April–May 1972. Carlos Allen, "Yo vi a Dios en Girón," *Ideal* 1, no. 8 (April 15, 1972): 5–7. For the twenty-year commemoration, see "Honor a nuestros muertos," *Girón* (March–April 1981).

12. "De la historia de Cuba," *Ideal* 4, no. 37 (September 8, 1974): 49.

13. Teok Carrasco, "El mural de la Ermita," *Ideal* 4, no. 49 (September/October 1975): 9, 11–12.

14. "Virgen de la Caridad, salve Cuba," *The Voice,* September 14, 1962.

15. "Ofrecieron ramillete espiritual al Papa," *The Voice,* September 13, 1963.

16. "Cubanos observarán 20 de Mayo orando," *The Voice,* May 19, 1967. The participating priests included: Daniel Sánchez, Pinar del Rio; Emilio Vallina, Habana; Eugenio del Busto, Matanzas; Ramón O'Farrill, Las Villas; Ignacio Hualde, Camaguey; and Jorge Bez Chabebe, Oriente.

17. "Refugees Pray at Shrine Site," *The Voice,* May 26, 1967.

18. "127 peregrinaciones a la Ermita de la Caridad," *The Voice,* January 17, 1969.

19. Interview with Msgr. Agustín Román, Miami, March 31, 1998; Thomas A. Tweed, *Our Lady of the Exile: Diasporic Religion at a Cuban Catholic Shrine in Miami* (New York: Oxford University Press, 1997), 121–125; "Habla el Padre Román: Actos para el Dia de la Caridad," *The Voice,* August 15, 1969.

20. "Romería Pinareña," *The Voice,* May 9, 1969.

21. "Habla el Padre Román." For more on these activities, see Tweed, *Our Lady of the Exile,* 121–131.

22. "Estudiarán problemas de la familia exiliada," *The Voice,* October 21, 1966; "Presentarán mañana conclusiones sobre la familia cubana exiliada," *The Voice,* No-

vember 11, 1966; "Familia exiliada a la luz del concilio," *The Voice,* November 18, 1966; "Dilema de nuestros hijos: cubanía o americanización," *The Voice,* December 23, 1966.

23. "Dirigentes del MFC latinoamericano en Miami," *The Voice,* June 28, 1963. For background on this movement in Latin America, see John J. Considine, *The Church in the New Latin America* (Notre Dame, IN: Fides Publishers, 1964), 86–89.

24. "Exito del festival folklórico de la parróquia de la Inmaculada," *The Voice,* May 8, 1964.

25. Gustavo Peña Monte, "Nuevo exito del festival folklórico cubano," *The Voice,* July 3, 1964.

26. "Celebra el Colegio de Belén la fiesta de su patrona," *The Voice,* February 8, 1963.

27. "Escuela cívico religiosa crean en San Juan Bosco," *The Voice,* October 7, 1967; "Escuela cívico religiosa de San Juan Bosco," *The Voice,* February 9, 1968.

28. "Posición de la iglesia ante el comunismo," *Ideal* 1, no. 9 (May 15, 1972), 14–17. See also "Austeridad, responsabilidad y unión" and "Vietnam: Un cubano testigo," *Ideal* 1, no. 11 (July 15, 1972): 6–9, 29.

29. Diana Montané, "Manuel Salvat pasó de la política a los libros," *Exito* 3, no. 13 (March 31, 1993): 70. Vertical Files, Cuban Heritage Collection, University of Miami Library.

30. Teresa Fernández Soneira, *Con la estrella y la cruz: Historia de la Federación de las Juventudes de Acción Católica Cubana,* 2 vols. (Miami: Ediciones Universal, 2002), 2:8–17, 23–39; La Juventud Católica Cubana cumple 50 años," *Cuba Diáspora 1978,* 40–42.

31. Fernández Soneira, *Con la estrella y la cruz,* 2:11.

32. Ibid., 2:13.

33. "Dirigentes del MFC latinoamericano en Miami," *The Voice,* June 28, 1963.

34. "Encuentro de matrimonios cristianos proyecta cruzada del rosario familiar," *The Voice,* December 10, 1965.

35. Humberto y María López, "Presencia de Cuba en el congreso familiar continental," *The Voice,* September 30, 1966.

36. Rubén Darío Rumbaut, "Silueta psicológica de Fidel Castro Ruz," *Cuba Nueva* 2, no. 4 (November 1, 1962): 15–21.

37. Anne Femantle, ed., *The Papal Encyclicals in Their Historical Context* (New York: G. P. Putnam's Sons, 1956), 220–262.

38. José Ignacio Lasaga, "Meditación roja" (Habana, 1934), in *Dr. José Ignacio Lasaga: Recuerdos, escritos, publicaciones, conferencias* (26 vols.), vol. 5., Belén School Library, Miami.

39. Gerald Brenan, *The Spanish Labyrinth: An Account of the Social and Political Background of the Spanish Civil War* (Cambridge: Cambridge University Press, 1969), 188–192.

40. Hugh Thomas, *Cuba: The Pursuit of Freedom* (New York: Harper & Row, 1971), 846; Andrés Valdespino, "Al comunismo no se le destruye por decreto"

(1953) and "Lo histérico y lo histórico en el anticomunismo" (1954), *Valdespino: Cuba como pasión* (Hato Rey, PR: Ramallo Brothers Printing, n.d.), 71–84.

41. See Lourdes Casal, "Nosotros y el comunismo," *La Quincena* 5, no. 3 (February 1959): 38–39; "El materialismo de izquierda y de derecha," *La Quincena* 5, nos. 5–6 (March 1959): 37, 78, 84; and "Democracia y liberalismo," *La Quincena* 5, no. 7 (April 1959): 26, 46.

42. Letter from Dr. Angel del Cerro (Miami) to Carlos McCormick (Department of State, Washington, DC), November 18, 1961, box 19, folder "Cuban-Consejo Revolucionario," Office of the Deputy Assistant Secretary of Inter-American Affairs, Bureau of Inter-American Affairs, General Records of the Department of State, National Archives and Records Administration, Washington, DC.

43. Angel del Cerro, "Un año del boletín," *Boletín Semanal Informativo,* 2, October 9, 1961, box 19, Folder "Cuba-Consejo Revolucionario," Office of the Deputy Assistant Secretary of Inter-American Affairs, Bureau of Inter-American Affairs, General Records of the Department of State, National Archives and Records Administration, Washington, DC.

44. Letter from Cerro to McCormick.

45. "El tercer aniversario de la reforma agraria cubana," *Cuba Nueva* 1, no. 7 (June 15, 1962): 9–15.

46. "El movimiento obrero cubano bajo la hoz y el martillo," *Cuba Nueva* 1, no. 4 (May 1, 1962): 11–15.

47. Carmelo Mesa Lago, "Seguridad social o inseguridad socialista?" *Cuba Nueva* 2, no. 1 (September 1, 1962); Andrés Valdespino, "Como cayo bajo el comunismo La Universidad de la Habana," *Cuba Nueva* 1, no. 2 (April 1, 1962); Edilberto Marbán, "Como se apoderó el comunismo de la enseñanza secundaria en Cuba," *Cuba Nueva* 2, no. 2 (October 1, 1962); Efrén Córdova, "La legislación laboral del castrismo," *Cuba Nueva* 1, no. 4 (May 1, 1962).

48. For an account of repression and political prisoners in Cuba, see Juan Clark, *Cuba: Mito y realidad: Testimonios de un pueblo* (Miami: Saeta Ediciones, 1990), 131–202.

49. Manuel Maza, "Editorial: Hasta cuando?" *Mundo Nuevo* 3 (June–July 1962): 1–3.

50. Boza Masvidal and Román, "Mensajes: Cuba ayer, hoy y siempre."

51. Ibid., 23.

52. Ibid., 24.

Chapter Five.   The Social Question

1. For background on this movement see Frederick B. Pike, *Hispanismo, 1898–1936* (Notre Dame, IN: University of Notre Dame Press, 1971).

2. Manuel Artime, *Traición! Gritan 20,000 tumbas cubanas* (Mexico City: Editorial Jus, 1960), 245–246.

3. "Memorandum: R. A. Hurwitch to G. P. Lamberty; Derogatory Comment on Manuel Artime," April 11, 1961, 1960–1963, box 15, folder "Counter-Revolutionary Acts-Cuba, 1961," Subject Files, Office of the Coordinator of Cuban Affairs, Bureau of Inter-American Affairs, General Records of the Department of State, National Archives and Records Administration, Washington, DC.

4. Artime, *Traición!*, 245–246.

5. After *Traición!*, Artime does not seem to have written anything more reflecting his ideological stances, though he was generally viewed as connected to corporatist thought. Catholics in Miami often characterized Artime as charismatic, authoritarian, and very close to the pro-Franco spiritual leader of ACU, Jesuit priest Armando Llorente. Artime died of cancer in 1977.

6. Andrés Valdespino, "La revolución que hay que salvar," *Bohemia Libre* 52, no. 5 (November 6, 1960), 42. See also Rubén Rumbaut, *Revolución traicionada* (Miami: Frente Revolucionario Democrático, 1962).

7. "Urgencia de reformas, America debe aprender la lección de Cuba," *The Voice,* September 29, 1961.

8. Ali Presalde, "Reflexiones de un deterrrado," *Unión,* August 1965.

9. Andrés Valdespino, "Los peligros que hay que evitar a tiempo (apuntes sobre el futuro cubano)," *Bohemia Libre* 53, no. 26 (April 2, 1961): 30–32, 78.

10. Quoted in "Editoriales: Nuestra posición," *Cuba Nueva* 1, no. 10 (August 1, 1962): 3.

11. Ibid., 3–9.

12. Luís Aguilar León, "Raíces del futuro," *Cuba Nueva* 1, no. 3 (April 15, 1962): 13–16.

13. Andrés Valdespino, "Imagen de una Cuba distinta," *Cuba Nueva* 1, no. 4 (May 1, 1962): 23–27.

14. Fermín Peinado, "Imagen de la Cuba posible y deseable," *Cuba Nueva* 1, no. 5 (May 15, 1962):16–22.

15. Angel del Cerro, "No reincidamos," *Cuba Nueva* 1, no. 6 (June 1, 1962): 12–15.

16. "Exiled Bishop Boza on Radio to Cuba," *The Voice,* January 6, 1962; "Unite in God to Halt Communism Bishop Boza Tells Latin America," *The Voice,* February 2, 1962; "Conferencia de prensa del obispo cubano Eduardo Boza Masvidal," *The Voice,* February 2, 1962; "Vatican Relations with Cuba No Approval of Red Regime," *The Voice,* February 2, 1962.

17. Eduardo Boza Masvidal, *Revolución cristiana en latinoamerica* (Santiago, Chile: Editorial del Pacifico, 1963).

18. Mary E. Hobgood, *Catholic Social Teaching and Economic Theory: Paradigms in Conflict* (Philadelphia: Temple University Press, 1991), 130–154.

19. Ibid.

20. Francois Houtart and Emile Pin, *The Church and the Latin American Revolution* (New York: Sheed & Ward, 1965), 99–100.

21. Ibid., 214–218.

22. Edward L. Cleary, *Crisis and Change: The Church in Latin America Today* (Maryknoll, NY: Orbis Books, 1985), 44–50.

23. "Obispo Boza habla del concilio y exodo cubano," *The Voice,* December 31, 1965.

24. Andrés Valdespino, "Que ha significado para la iglesia el Pontificado de Juan XXIII [1963]," in *Valdespino: Cuba como pasión,* Fundación Andrés Valdespino (Hato Rey, PR: Ramallo Brothers Printing, n.d.), 47–53.

25. Andrés Valdespino, "La voz de la Iglesia en un mundo en crisis: La encíclica social de Juan XXIII," *Bohemia Libre* 53, no. 43 (July 30, 1961): 50–51, 58, 62, 64. See also Valdespino, "Que ha significado para la iglesia el Pontificado de Juan XXIII," 47–53.

26. See *Boletín Informativo Demócrata Cristiano* (New York), box 16, folder 375, and *Conciencia* (Organo Oficial del Movimiento Demócrata Cristiano de Cuba, Caracas), box 16, folder 377, Laureano Batista Archive, Cuban Heritage Collection, University of Miami Library.

27. Enrique Ros, "Un congreso y dos documentos," *Conciencia* 13 (April–May 1964): 2.

28. José Ignacio Rasco, *Cuba 1959: Artículos de combate* (Buenos Aires: Ediciones Diagrama, 1962). This book includes articles published by Rasco in the Cuban newspaper *Información* during 1959.

29. See José Ignacio Rasco, *Jacques Maritain y la Democracia Cristiana* (Miami: Ediciones Universal, 1980). See also Rasco's *La Libertad en San Agustín* (Havana: Ediciones Insula, S.A., 1958), and "La Democracia Cristiana en Cuba: Un poco de historia," Laureano Batista Archive, box 3 (green three-ring binder), Cuban Heritage Collection, University of Miami Library.

30. José Ignacio Rasco, "La tesis de sub-desarrollo," *Conciencia,* April 1963.

31. José Ignacio Rasco, "Inter-Americanism," in *Integration of Man and Society in Latin America,* ed. Samuel Shapiro (Notre Dame, IN: University of Notre Dame Press, 1967), 270–280; Arthur Southwood, "Church Helping to Turn Tide in Latin America," *The Voice,* February 5, 1965.

32. Salvador de Cistierna, *Doctrina social pontificia* (Havana: Instituto Social Pio XII, Universidad Católica de Santo Tomás Villanueva, 1960), 29.

33. Manuel Foyaca, *Crisis en nuestra America* (Miami: Instituto de Acción Social, 1963).

34. Oscar A. Echevarría Salvat, *Democracia y bienestar* (Miami: Ediciones Universal, 1968), 89–91.

35. "Inauguración del I.A.S.," *The Voice,* September 7, 1962.

36. "New Social Action Institute to Aid Latin American Unity," *The Voice,* August 3, 1962. Institute instructors included Antonio Fernández Rubio, Oscar Echevarría, Lourdes Yero, Ignacio Pleitas, Fermín Peinado, Ofelia Tabares, José Illán, José de Jesús Planas, María Cristina Herrera, and Carmelo Mesa Lago, among others.

37. José Jorge Vila and Guillermo Zalamea Arenas, *Exilio* (Miami, 1967), 376.

38. "Apertura del Insituto de Acción Social," *The Voice,* August 31, 1962.

39. "Hombres de empresa estudian la doctrina social cristiana," *The Voice,* February 1, 1963.

40. "Nuevas actividades del Instituto de Acción Social," *The Voice,* February 15, 1963; "Trabajadores migratorios: una preocupación de la iglesia," *The Voice,* October 26, 1962.

41. "El plan del IAS a nivel parroquial," *The Voice,* December 13, 1963; "Clausuró el IAS el primer curso parroquial de formación social," *The Voice,* March 20, 1964; "Formación social curso parroquial," *The Voice,* December 4, 1964; "Clausuran hoy curso de formación social," *The Voice,* February 19, 1965.

42. "Primer año de cooperativismo en Miami," *The Voice,* March 29, 1968.

43. "Curso de temas sociales en el Barry College," *The Voice,* January 10, 1964.

44. Padre Salvador de Cistierna, "Cinco lecciones necesarias para una reforma social," *The Voice,* April 3, 1964.

45. See "Derecho de la iglesia a intervenir en lo social," *The Voice,* June 26, 1964; José A. Moreno, "Qué es la doctrina social cristina?" *The Voice,* July 3, 1964; Carmelo Mesa Lago, "La Iglesia Católica y la reforma de la empresa," *The Voice,* July 24, 1964; "El derecho de propiedad y la doctrina social cristiana," *The Voice,* August 7, 1964; Humberto Pérez Herrera, "La respuesta cristiana al problema agraria," *The Voice,* August 28, 1964; Gustavo Peña Monte, "Interés popular en vivir la doctrina social cristiana," *The Voice,* August 21, 1964; Humberto Peña, "La seguridad social y las enseñanzas potificias," *The Voice,* September 25, 1964.

46. "Editors Told of Red Threat to Latin American Nations," *The Voice,* May 10, 1963.

47. Gustavo Peña Monte, "Pide Obispo Carroll a jóvenes dominicanos que difundan doctrina social católica," *The Voice,* December 18, 1964.

48. "Crean Instituto de Acción Social en Miami," *The Voice,* July 27, 1962; "Dejamos al enemigo sembrar la cizaña en el campo economico social," *The Voice,* August 3, 1962.

49. Gustavo Peña Monte, "61 líderes dominicanos y puertorriqueños reciben preparación social cristiana aquí," *The Voice,* November 6, 1964; Gustavo Peña Monte, "Coopertativistas de 7 paises reciben formación en Miami," *The Voice,* February 12, 1965.

50. Gustavo Peña Monte, "Pide Obispo Carroll a jóvenes dominicanos que difundan doctrina social católica," *The Voice,* December 18, 1964.

51. Araceli Cantero, "El dilemma marxismo-capitalismo es falso y paralizante, dice el Dr. Fiallo," *The Voice,* August 28, 1978.

52. "Pastoral Constitution on the Church in the Modern World, Vatican II, Gaudium Et Spes, 7 December 1965," in *Vatican Council II, Volume 1: The Conciliar and Postconciliar Documents,* ed. Austin Flannery (Northport, NY: Costello, 1998), 922.

53. François Houtart, *The Challenge to Change: The Church Confronts the Future* (New York: Sheed & Ward, 1964), 159–166.

54. Enrique Oslé, Antonio Fernández Nuevo, and Alfredo Cepero, eds., *Recorrido por suramerica: Informe, junio-agosto, 1961* (n.p./n.d.), 19.

55. Ibid., 67.

56. Ibid., 26.

57. Ibid., 51–52.

58. "Entrevista con el Señor José Fernández Badue (Lucas)," *Cuba Nueva* 2, no. 7 (December 15, 1962).

59. Leslie Dewart, *Christianity and Revolution: The Lesson of Cuba* (New York: Herder & Herder, 1963), 216–217.

60. Edward L. Cleary, ed. *Born of the Poor: The Latin American Church Since Medellín* (Notre Dame, IN: University of Notre Dame Press, 1990), 9–41.

61. Charles E. Curran, *Catholic Social Teaching, 1891–Present: A Historical, Theological, and Ethical Analysis* (Washington, DC: Georgetown University, 2002), 23–25.

62. Cleary, *Crisis and Change*, 84–87.

63. José Ignacio Lasaga, "Memorandum sobre problemas relacionados con la iglesia en Cuba," Letter to S. E. Rma. Mons. Dell' Acqua, Secretaria de Estado de Su Santidad, 1964, in *José Ignacio Lasaga: Recuerdos, escritos, publicaciones, conferencias* (26 vols.), vol. 11, Belén School Library, Miami.

64. "No hay libertad religiosa en Cuba afirma el Obispo Boza Masvidal," *The Voice*, August 9, 1963.

65. "Una denuncia del Obispo Boza sobre la tragedia cubana," *The Voice*, November 9, 1973.

66. "Encuentro de sacerdotes cubanos," *Ideal* (October 1978); "Exile Priests feel Unrepresented," *The Voice*, July 14, 1978; For a similar statement by Bishop Boza Masvidal see "Una iglesia que avanza," *Unión* 16, no. 88 (October–November, 1978).

67. "Mensaje del Movimiento Demócrata Cristiano de Cuba a la III Conferencia Episcopal Latinoamericana, Puebla, Enero de 1979," *Ideal* 92 (February 1979): 20–21.

Chapter Six.   "Just and Necessary War"

1. José Ignacio Rasco, "Sociologia del exilio," *Exilio* (Spring 1970): 48.

2. "Los profesionales," *Esto Vir* 31 (March–April 1962). Translated version available in Timothy Matovina and Gerald E. Poyo, eds., *Presente! U.S. Latino Catholics from Colonial Origins to the Present* (Maryknoll, NY: Orbis Books, 2000), 176–178.

3. José Ignacio Lasaga, Letter to Bishop Agustín Román, October 30, 1982, José Ignacio Lasaga Papers, Belén School Library, Miami.

4. See Enrique Ros, *Playa Girón: La verdadera historia* (Miami: Ediciones Universal, 1994).

5. Haynes Johnson, *The Bay of Pigs: The Leaders' Story of Brigade 2506* (New York: W. W. Norton, 1964), 32–39.

6. Jesús Arboleya Cervera, *La contrarevolución cubana* (Havana: Editorial Ciencias Sociales, 1997).

7. Grayston L. Lynch, *Decision for Disaster: Betrayal at the Bay of Pigs* (Washington, DC: Brassey's, 1998), 19–20.

8. Ros, *Playa Girón,* 16–17, 54–56, 88.

9. James Blight and Peter Kornbluh, *Politics of Illusion: The Bay of Pigs Invasion Reexamined* (Boulder: Lynne Rienner Publishers, 1998), 176–177.

10. Andrés Valdespino, "Detras de esas bombas," *Bohemia Libre* 52, no. 12 (December 25, 1960): 49. See Arboleya Cervera, *La contrarevolución cubana,* 82–85.

11. Johnson, *The Bay of Pigs,* 32–39; Peter Kornbluh, ed., *Bay of Pigs Declassified: The Secret CIA Report on the Invasion of Cuba* (New York: New Press, 1998), 271.

12. Trumbull Higgins, *The Perfect Failure: Kennedy, Eisenhower and the CIA at the Bay of Pigs* (New York: W. W. Norton., 1989), 46, 49–51, 57, 63–64; author's conversation in 1998 with Salvador Miranda, an ACU member and Bay of Pigs combatant. See also Arboleya Cervera, *La contrarevolución cubana,* 89, who says the majority of brigade members were recruited by Catholic organizations.

13. Enrique Ros, *De Girón a la crisis de los cohetes: La segunda derrota* (Miami: Ediciones Universal, 1995), 50. See also interviews by Bejamín de la Vega, "Grafoentrevista con Manuel Ray," and "Habla Ignacio Mendoza: Ray olvidó sus deberes para con los miembros del comité clandestino," *Avance Criollo,* August 16, 1961.

14. "Secret Memorandum: Recent Cuban Developments. March 16, 1961," box 9, folder 3, Office of the Deputy Assistant of Inter-American Affairs, Bureau of Inter-American Affairs. General Records of the Department of State, National Archives and Records Administration, Washington, DC.

15. "Informe 1963. MDC-D. Militar," box 13, folder 305, and "MDC," box 3 (green three-ring binder), Laureano Batista Archive, Cuban Heritage Collection, University of Miami Library.

16. Hans Tanner, *Counter-Revolutionary Agent: Diary of Events Which Occurred in Cuba Between January and July, 1961* (London: G. T. Foulis,1962), 1–2.

17. "MDC-Exile Military High Command: Record of Military Activities," box 13, folder 308, Laureano Batista Archive, Cuban Heritage Collection, University of Miami Library.

18. Tanner, *Counter-Revolutionary Agent,* 54–62; Ros, *Playa Girón,* 195–202.

19. Ros, *De Girón a la crisis de los cohetes,* 86–89.

20. "Prayers for Liberation: Refugees Fill Churches Here," *The Voice,* April 28, 1961.

21. John M. Kirk, *Between God and the Party: Religion and Politics in Revolutionary Cuba* (Tampa: University of South Florida Press, 1989), 85–96.

22. Ros, *De Girón a la crisis de los cohetes,* 193n; "Combatiremos hasta erradicar del mundo el comunismo internacional, dice M.R.R.," *Avance Criollo* (April 28, 1961), 5, 58.

23. Enrique Encinosa, *Cuba: The Unfinished Revolution* (Miami: Endowment for Cuban American Studies, Cuban American National Foundation, 1994), 160–165.

24. José Angel Bufill, *Manuel Guillot Castellano: Presente! (bosquejo biográfico de un héroe, de un mártir)* (Central America: Movimiento de Recuperación Revolucionaria, Secretaría de Información, 1964); Ros, *De Girón a la crisis de los cohetes,* 133–134.

25. *Guerra revolucionaria* (Miami: Movimiento Demócrata Cristiano de Cuba, 1966), box 16, folder 361, Laureano Batista Archive, Cuban Heritage Collection, University of Miami Library. See the Batista Archive for information on the military activities of the MDC during the 1960s.

26. Ros, *De Girón a la crisis de los cohetes,* 158–162. See also Al Burt, "El ataque comando de Manuel Salvat," *El Nuevo Herald,* June 11, 1980.

27. See Luís Fernández Rocha et al., Letter to hermano del D.R.E., Miami, January 10, 1964, box 1, Directorio Revolucionario Estudiantil Archive, Cuban Heritage Collection, University of Miami Library.

28. Enrique Ros, *Cubanos combatientes: Peleando en distintos frentes* (Miami: Ediciones Universal, 1998), 17–34.

29. Manuel Salvat, Letter to René Pérez, Juan G. De León, and Jorge Lamerán, April 28, 1965, box 6, folder no. 67 (Estados Unidos, Salida), Directorio Revolucionario Estudiantil Archive, Cuban Heritage Collection, University of Miami Library.

30. Laureano Batista, Letter to Ernesto Aguilar, June 28, 1965, box 1, folder 13, Laureano Batista Archive, Cuban Heritage Collection, University of Miami Library.

31. MDC's military department protested the organization's decision to abandon armed actions in favor of political strategies. "Proposición de Resolución No. 1 del Departamento Militar al XI Congreso," box 9, folder 58, Laureano Batista Archive, Cuban Heritage Collection, University of Miami Library.

32. "Comparecencia del Dr. Manuel Artime en el programa 'Pan Americana' transmitido por el Canal 10-TV en Miami del Dia 13 de Febrero de 1966," *Tridente* 2, no. 24, February 18, 1965.

33. For a good discussion of how the exile militants reorganized themselves, see Arboleya Cervera, *La contrarevolución cubana,* 154–167.

34. *Historia de una agresión* (Habana: Ediciones Venceremos, 1962), 89–92.

35. "Se infiltra el MDC en el ejercito rebelde," *Avance,* September 30, 1960; Ros, *Playa Girón,* 80–81; "Declaraciones del mercenario Manuel Artime Buesa," in *Historia de una agresión,* 109–110.

36. Ros, *Playa Girón,* 71

37. Nestor T. Carbonell, *And the Russians Stayed: The Sovietization of Cuba* (New York: William Morrow, 1989), 191–208. See this book for details on the diplomatic activities of exiles.

38. Fermín Peinado, "La II Declaración de La Habana: Un manifiesto comunista para la America Latina," *Cuba Nueva* 1, no. 1 (March 15, 1962): 17–23.

39. Andrés Valdespino, "America ante la intervención comunista: No podrá haber 'Alianza para el Progreso' sin 'Alianza para la Libertad,'" *Bohemia Libre* 53, no. 34 (May 28, 1961): 38–40, 61; Andrés Valdespino, "El viaje de Stevenson: Triunfo o fracaso de una misión?" *Bohemia Libre* 53, no. 39 (July 2, 1961), 54–56, 64; Angel del Cerro, "Un aniversario de la Alianza para el Progreso," *Cuba Nueva* 1, no. 2 (April 1962): 15–18; "Editoriales: Un año de Alianza para el Progreso," *Cuba Nueva* 1, no. 12 (September 1, 1962): 3–4; Valentín Arenas Amigó, "Tad Szulc en la pantalla: Nota sobre la concepción de la Alianza para el Progreso," *Cuba Nueva* 2, no. 2 (October 1, 1962): 6–8; "Editorial: America ante las dos alianzas," 2, no. 10 (February 1, 1963): 3–5.

40. Sheldon B. Liss, *Diplomacy and Dependency: Venezuela, the United States, and the Americas* (Salisbury, NC: Documentary Publications, 1978), 225–230.

41. Batista, Letter to Aguilar, June 28, 1965; Enrique Oslé, Antonio Fernández Nuevo, Alfredo Cepero, eds., *Recorrido por suramerica: Informe, junio-agosto 1961* (n.p./n.d.), 14–15.

42. Ros, *Playa Girón,* 71.

43. Andrés Valdespino, Antonio Fernández Nuevo, and Angel del Cerro, "Respuesta al Congreso de la Juventud Demócrata Cristiana," *Cuba Nueva* 1, no. 2 (June 15, 1962): 23–30; "Los delegados de la Juventud Demócrata Cristiana al II Congreso Latinoamericano de Juventudes, D.C.," *Cuba Nueva* 1, no. 8 (July 1, 1962): 11–14.

44. "Pope Grieves for Persecuted Cuba: Bishop and Priests Deported by Castro," *The Voice,* September 22, 1961.

45. Cuban Lay Leaders, Letter to Pope John XXIII, "A Su Santidad Juan XXIII, Pontifice gloriosamente reinante de la Santa Iglesia Católica," October 4, 1961, José Ignacio Lasaga Papers, Belén School Library, Miami.

46. Kirk, *Between God and the Party,* 110–126.

47. José Ignacio Lasaga, Letter to S. E. Rma. Mons. Dell' Acqua, Secretaria de Estado de Su Santidad, "Memorandum sobre problemas relacionados con la iglesia en Cuba," 1964, in *Dr. José Ignacio Lasaga: Recuerdos, escritos, publicaciones, conferencias* (26 vols.) vol. 11, Belén School Library, Miami.

48. Manuel Fernández, *Religión y revolución en Cuba: Veinticinco años de lucha ateista* (Miami: SAETA Ediciones, 1984), 124–125.

49. "Absurdo decir que Castro es 'eticamente cristiano,'" *The Voice,* June 7, 1968.

50. "En torno a la visita de Mons. Casaroli a Cuba," *The Voice,* April 12, 1974.

51. "Ayuda para los presos en Cuba pide Mons. Boza al dejar Miami," *The Voice,* February 9, 1962.

52. Humberto Medrano, "Porfirio Remberto Ramírez: No lo busquen en la tumba," *Bohemia Libre* 53, no. 27 (April 9, 1961): 24–25.

53. Directorio Revolucionario Estudiantil, "Alberto Muller: Lider del estudi-antado cubano," box 2, envelope 5, Directorio Revolucionario Estudiantil Archive, Cuban Heritage Collection, University of Miami Library.

54. Juan Clark, *Cuba: Mito y realidad: Testimonio de un pueblo* (Miami: Saeta Edi-ciones, 1990), 200–201.

55. "Comité Mundial 'Pedro Luís Boitel': Pro-Presos Politicos Cubanos," 12, *Asociación de Cubanos de Long Beach* (October 1972), box 130, folder 9, Truth About Cuba Committee Archive, Cuban Heritage Collection, University of Miami Library. See also Consejo Asesor y Junta de Gobierno del Comité Mundial "Pedro Luís Boitel" Pro-Presos Politicos Cubanos, *Pedro Luis Boitel: Diario de un mártir* (Hoboken, 1978).

56. Agustín Villegas, "Francisco," *Ideal* 4, no. 45 (May 15, 1975): 19–22.

57. José Prince, "Carta desde una celda en Cuba," *Nueva Generación* 11, no. 14 (September–October 1967), 14–15.

58. "Periodista cubano revela horrors del presidio," *The Voice,* November 12, 1971.

59. María Cristina García, *Havana USA* (Berkeley: University of California Press, 1996), 157.

60. David A. Badillo, "Catholicism and the Search for Nationhood in Miami's Cuban Community," *U.S. Catholic Historian* 20, no. 4 (Fall 2002): 82–83.

61. See, for example, files for California (box 30, folder 9); Indiana (box 41, folder 6); Chicago (box 38, folder 9); Houston (box 65, folder 4); Cleveland (box 62, folder 1), in Truth About Cuba Committee Archive, Cuban Heritage Collection, University of Miami Library.

62. "For American Public Opinion: Letter to Archbishop Humberto Medeiros (of Boston)," *Abdala,* June 1972.

63. "Bishops to Eye Cuban Jails," *The Voice,* June 14, 1974; Bob O'Steen, "He's Waging Human Rights War on Castro Jails," *The Voice,* June 14, 1974; "Comité es-tudia situación de los presos políticos en Cuba," *The Voice,* August 2, 1974.

64. "Fidel & Uncle Sam: Some See Possibility U.S., Cuba May Restore Diplo-matic Ties," *The Wall Street Journal,* February 13, 1969.

65. Ann Louise Bardach, *Cuba Confidential: Love and Vengeance in Miami and Havana* (New York: Random House, 2002), 257–261.

66. See, for example, "Runión secreta en Washington por coexistencia con Castro," *Alerta,* April 30, 1971; "Posición de Abdala," *Abdala* 19 (March 1973); "Kissinger y sus narices," *El Triunfo,* February 16, 1973; "Una encuesta sobre la 'coexistencia' y una pregunta 'de contra,'" *Réplica,* February 14, 1973.

67. Alvaro Varga Llosa, *El exilio indomable: Historia de la disidencia cubana en el destierro* (Spain: Editorial Espasa, 1998), 15–34.

68. Ibid., 51–74.

69. Despite his focus on lobbying, Mas Canosa did remain supportive of vio-lent approaches. See Arboleya Cervera, *La contrarevolución cubana,* 150–151.

70. Benjamín de la Vega, "Rechazan coexistencia con F. Castro senadores norte-americanos declara Mas Canosa," *Rece* 5, no. 53 (April 1969).

71. "El entendimiento de los Estados Unidos y Cuba comunista: Fragmentos de la comparecencia de Jorge Mas Canosa . . . en el programa 'Ante el 23' del Canal 23 de television de Miami, Florida, el domingo dia 18 de Febrero de 1973, a las 5:30 de la tarde," box 29, folder 2, Truth About Cuba Committee Archive, Cuban Heritage Collection, University of Miami Library. In fact, Che Guevara had suggested a hijacking agreement to the United States in 1961. See Maurice Halperin, *The Rise and Decline of Fidel Castro: An Essay in Contemporary History* (Berkeley: University of California Press, 1972), 119.

72. "Jorge Mas Canosa," *Ideal* 46 (June 15, 1975), 13–15.

73. On Mas Canosa's and Hernández's careers, see Varga Llosa, *El exilio indomable*.

74. For a discussion on the origins and activities of the Cuban American National Foundation, see María de los Angeles Torres, *In the Land of Mirrors: Cuban Exile Politics in the United States* (Ann Arbor: University of Michigan Press, 1999), 115–120.

75. Rasco, "Sociologia del exilio," *Exilio,* 42.

76. Gustavo Peña Monte, "Misa y monumento en memoria de los mártires de Girón, mañana," *The Voice,* April 16, 1971.

Chapter Seven.   Ethnicity and Rights

1. Alejandro Portes, "Dilemmas of a Golden Exile: Integration of Cuban Refugee Families in Milwaukee," *American Sociological Review* 34 (1969): 505–518.

2. Rafael J. Prohías, "Cubanos en Indianapolis: Un ejemplo de acomodación," *Nueva Generación* 14 (1967[?]): 7–8.

3. Alejandro Portes and Robert L. Bach, *Latin Journey: Cuban and Mexican Immigrants in the United States* (Berkeley: University of California Press, 1985), 89, 200–205. For details on the various dimensions of the growth of the Cuban-American enclave, see the following: Silvia Pedraza-Bailey, *Political and Economic Migrants in America: Cubans and Mexicans* (Austin: University of Texas Press, 1985); Miguel González-Pando, *The Cuban Americans* (Westport, CT: Greenwood Press, 1998); Guillermo J. Grenier and Lisandro Pérez, *The Legacy of Exile: Cubans in the United States* (Boston: Allyn & Bacon, 2003).

4. Jay P. Dolan, *The American Catholic Experience: A History from Colonial Times to the Present* (Garden City, NY: Doubleday, 1985), 349–383, and Jay P. Dolan, *In Search of an American Catholicism: A History of Religion and Culture in Transition* (Oxford: Oxford University Press, 2002), 211–213.

5. González-Pando, *The Cuban Americans,* 155–157.

6. María Cristina García, *Havana, USA: Cuban Exiles and Cuban Americans in South Florida, 1959–1994* (Berkeley: University of California Press, 1996), 89.

7. "Estudiarán problemas de la familia exiliada," *The Voice,* October 21, 1966.

8. "Presentarán mañana conclusiones sobre la familia cubana exiliada," *The Voice,* November 11, 1966; "Familia exiliada a la luz del Concilio," *The Voice,* November 18, 1966; "Dilema de nuestros hijos: cubanía o americanización," *The Voice,* December 23, 1966; "Conclusiones del encuentro del MFC de Miami," *Unión* 50 (February–March 1967): 3–6 and (April–May 1967): 3–6.

9. "Datos y fechas para una biografía de José Ignacio Lasaga y Travieso," in *Dr. José Ignacio Lasaga: Recuerdos, escritos, publicaciones, conferencias* (26 vols.), vol. 1, Belén School Library, Miami.

10. José I. Lasaga, "La juventud del exilio y la tradición nacional cubana," *Exilio* (Winter/Spring 1970): 52–81; Araceli Cantero, "El pluralismo cultural: Es posible?" *The Voice,* May 13, 1977.

11. Lasaga, "La juventud del exilio y la tradición nacional cubana," 73.

12. Ibid., 15–50.

13. "Rompiendo la barrera del idioma," *The Voice,* October 24, 1969.

14. Loló Acosta de Villalta, "Perdóname Mamá! Los encuentros juveniles de los muchachos cubanos católicos de las parroquias de Miami," *Réplica* (magazine) 5, no. 189 (May 15, 1974): 29–32.

15. "Adaptación del niño exiliado al sistema escolar de E.U.," *The Voice,* August 6–13, 1971.

16. "Seminaristas de Cuba y Colombia en Miami," *The Voice,* October 12, 1962; Enrique Rubiola, "Seminaristas cubanos en Miami: Alegría, estudio y oración," *The Voice,* March 19, 1965.

17. "Vocaciones en un seminario bilingüe y bicultural," *The Voice,* April 21, 1972.

18. "Nombrado P. Felipe Estevez rector del seminario," *La Voz Católica,* August 2, 1980; "Instalado Padre Estevez rector del Seminario St. Vincent," *La Voz Católica,* October 3, 1960. Estevez went on to be pastor at St. Agatha Parish in Miami, and in 2003 he was named auxiliary bishop of the archdiocese of Miami.

19. "Los futuros sacerdotes del exilio," in *Cuba Diáspora 1977: Anuario de la Iglesia de Cuba* (Miami: Unión de Cubans en el Exilio, 1977), 101–104.

20. "Mater et Magistra," in *Official Catholic Teachings: Social Justice,* ed. Vincent P. Mainelli (Wilmington, NC: Consortium Books, 1978), 84.

21. "Pastoral Constitution on the Church in the Modern World: Gaudium Et Spes, 7 December 1965," in *Vatican Council II: The Conciliar and Post Conciliar Documents,* vol. 1, ed. Austin Flannery (Northport, NY: Costello Publishing, 1998), 963.

22. Adrian Hastings, ed., *A Concise Guide to the Documents of the Second Vatican Council,* vol. 1 (London: Darton, Longman & Todd, 1968), 204–206, 242–243.

23. "Pluralismo, sí; pero atención a la unidad, Arz. Jadot," *The Voice,* September 24, 1976; "Delegado Apostólico señala prioridades, problemas: 'Buscad nuevas soluciones pastorales,'" *The Voice,* November 12, 1976.

24. Guillermina Damas, "Panorama histórico-pastoral de la dimensión hispana de la Archidiocesis de Miami, 1958–1983" (master's thesis, Barry University and Instituto Pastoral Del Suroeste, 1983), 90.

25. "Discuten planes apostólicos dirigentes católicos cubanos," *The Voice,* November 24, 1961.

26. "Chancery for Spanish Opens," *The Voice,* February 9, 1962.

27. Michael McNally, *Catholicism in South Florida, 1868–1968* (Gainesville: University of South Florida Press, 1982), 151.

28. Guillermina Damas, "Panorama histórico-pastoral de la dimensión hispana," 40–42.

29. Interview with Msgr. Bryan Walsh, April 1, 1998.

30. Letter from Priest of St. Pius Church to the Senate, May 21, 1976, quoted in Damas, "Panorama histórico-pastoral de la dimensión hispana," 69.

31. McNally, *Catholicism in South Florida,* 151, 153.

32. Ibid., 156–157; Damas, "Panorama histórico-pastoral de la dimensión hispana," 71–72.

33. "Nueva directiva a Asociación Sacerdotal Hispana-ASH," *The Voice,* November 18, 1977; "La Asociación Sacerdotal Hispana cumple 15 años," *Ideal* 157 (November 1981): 31; McNally, *Catholicism in South Florida,* 156–157; Damas, "Panorama histórico-pastoral de la dimensión hispana," 71–72.

34. James S. Olson and Judith E. Olson, *Cuban Americans: From Trauma to Triumph* (New York: Twayne Publishers, 1995), 98–99.

35. "Rompiendo la barrera del idioma," *The Voice,* October 24, 1969.

36. "Voice of the People," *The Voice,* October 18, 1968.

37. "En torno a la petición de personal bilingüe," *The Voice,* June 16, 1972.

38. Adolfo Leyva de Varona, "The Political Impact of Cuban Americans in Florida," in *Cuban Exiles in Florida: Their Presence and Contributions,* ed. Antonio Jorge, Jaime Suchlicki and Adolfo Leyva de Varona (Miami: North-South Center, University of Miami, 1991), 83–85.

39. Humberto López Morales, *Los cubanos de Miami: Lengua y sociedad* (Miami: Ediciones Universal, 2003), 61–67.

40. McNally, *Catholicism in South Florida,* 224.

41. "Msgr. Bryan Walsh Gives Views: Urges Latins to Preserve Image," *The Voice,* November 14, 1969.

42. See Father Jorge Bez Chabebe, "Cubans Defying Death for Faith," and "Catolicismo, Blanco de Fidel," *The Voice,* October 27, 1961; "Oppressed Cubans Look to Free, Democratic Future," and "Tradición anticomunista en Cuba," *The Voice,* November 10, 1961.

43. "Conflicto en la iglesia miamense," *Alerta,* September 1, 1972.

44. Ibid. According to one source the brothers were removed from the school because they taught in Spanish and did not run the school according to U.S. standards or diocesan policy. The Cuban brothers were replaced in 1962 by North

American brothers and later by diocesan administrators. Eventually the Cuban Christian Brothers left the diocese. McNally, *Catholicism in South Florida,* 158.

45. "Latin Catholics Quitting Church: Many Become Protestants or Join Afro-Cuban Cults," *New York Times,* July 1, 1975. See also "Sigue la crisis católica local: Mas de 70 mil feligreses latinos de Miami han abandonado la iglesia: Denuncia el dirigente Reinaldo Pico al Arzobispo Coleman Carroll," *Réplica* (newspaper), August 28, 1976.

46. Damas, "Panorama histórico-pastoral de la dimensión hispana," 80–83.

47. Luis Oraa, "Compromiso cristiano: Miami," *The Voice,* April 23, 1975.

48. "Bp. McCarthy Named Coadjutor Archbishop," *The Voice,* July 9, 1976.

49. "Sustituirán a Carroll," *Alerta,* July 9–11, 1976.

50. "Archbishop Carroll; Was Florida Leader," *The New York Times,* July 27, 1977.

51. Dolan, *In Search of an American Catholicism,* 219.

52. "Sustituirán a Carroll."

53. "Vengo como 'Pontífice'—a construir puentes de comprensión," *The Voice,* September 17, 1976.

54. "Arzobispo McCarthy saluda a hispanos," *The Voice,* September 17, 1976.

55. Damas, "Panorama histórico-pastoral de la dimensión hispana," 84.

56. "Estrechando lazos," *The Voice,* October 1, 1976, and "Arz. McCarthy habló a hispanos por radio," *The Voice,* December 17, 1976.

57. Thomas A. Tweed, *Our Lady of Exile: Diasporic Religion at a Cuban Catholic Shrine in Miami* (New York: Oxford University Press, 1997), 52–53. See also Armando Couto, "Revelaciones de Carlos Canet: El que mas sabe dice todo lo que sabe de la religión Lucumí," *Réplica* (magazine) 4, no. 152 (August 29, 1973): 14–17.

58. Juan M. Sosa, "Santería," in *Cuba Diáspora 1974: Anuario de la Iglesia Católica* (Miami: Unión de Cubans en el Exilio, 1974), 74–75.

59. Araceli M. Cantero, "Miami hispano," *The Voice,* April 25, 1975, and Bryan O. Walsh, "The Spanish Impact Here: How the Archdiocese Is Meeting the Challenge," *The Voice,* July 18, 1975.

60. Miguel Cabrera, "Cristo en las calles de Miami," in *Cuba Diáspora 1976: Anuario de la Iglesia Católica* (Miami: Unión de Cubans en el Exilio, 1976), 33–36.

61. "Evangelli Nuntiandi," in Mainelli, ed., *Official Catholic Teachings,* 403–404.

62. Felipe Estevez, "El catolicismo popular," *Ideal* 56 (April 1976): 41.

63. Juan M. Sosa, "Santería," in *Cuba Diáspora 1974,* 66–78. See also the following articles by Sosa in *The Voice:* "Santería: What Is It; How It Came to Florida," May 17, 1974; "The Influence Behind the Spread of Santería," May 24, 1974; "Santería: Includes Many Symbols, Statues of Saints, 'Gods'"; "Santería: Spawned in Impersonal Society," June 7, 1974; "Santería—Is It a Form of Superstition?" June 14, 1974; "Santería: Delicate Problem for Christian Leaders," June 31, 1974.

64. "La piedad popular: El desafío de la iglesia actual," *The Voice,* September 14, 21, 1979.

65. Araceli M. Cantero, "Comunidad hispana reflexiona unida," *The Voice,* May 2, 1975; Araceli M. Cantero, "Miami hispano: Union=Efectividad," *The Voice,* May 9, 1975.

66. Rafael J. Prohías and Lourdes Casal, eds., *The Cuban Minority in the U.S.: Preliminary Report on Need Identification and Program Evaluation* (Cuban National Planning Council, 1974), 94–97.

67. "De Playa Girón al seminario," *Ideal* 60 (August 1976): 30–31.

68. Andrés Valdespino, "El talón de aquiles de una democracia: Conflictos raciales en los Estados Unidos: También está detras la mano del comunismo?" *Bohemia Libre* 53, no. 42 (July 23, 1961): 32–34, 67.

69. Grupo Areíto, *Contra viento y marea* (Havana: Casa de las Americas, 1978), 12.

70. For information on CLASC, see Gerhard Wahlers, *Nace una alternativa* (Miami: Saeta Ediciones, 1991).

71. "Comenzamos," *Nueva Generación* (September 1963): 3–4.

72. Grupo Areíto, *Contra viento y marea,* 12–13; interview with María Cristina Herrera, May 11, 1998.

73. "Un testimonio," *Nueva Generación* 17, n.d. [1968?].

74. For information on STC, see Eduardo García Moure, *Cuba: Un proyecto para la nación* (Caracas: Editorial Torino, 1994).

75. Manuel Fernández García, "Apuntes del pensamiento revolucionario," *Nueva Generación* 16 (February–March 1968).

76. "Alternativas," *Nueva Generación* 12 (March–April 1967).

77. J. Xiquez, "El valor y la revolución pacifica," *Nueva Generación* 14 (n.d.).

78. "Chile, Octubre 1970: Entrevista con José Prince," *Nueva Generación* 20 (1970).

79. Lourdes Casal, "La revolución negra en los Estados Unidos," *Nueva Generación* (October 1963): 11–21; See also "Africa ante el problema cubano," *Cuba Nueva* 1, no. 10 (August 1, 1962): 11–17.

80. See, for example, M. Miranda, "Violencia negra en los EE.UU.," *Nueva Generación* 14 (September–October 1967), and R. Rodríguez, "En torno a la cuestión racial," *Nueva Generación* 16 (February–March 1968).

81. Interview with Father Mario Vizcaíno, Miami, March 6, 2002.

82. Ibid.

83. Rafael J. Prohías, "Cubanos en Indianapolis: Un ejemplo de acomodación," *Nueva Generación* 14 (n.d.).

84. Guarioné Díaz, "El proceso de pluralización del exilio cubano," *Nueva Generación* 20 (1970).

85. Prohías and Casal, *The Cuban Minority in the U.S.,* iii.

86. Ibid., 8.

87. Ibid., 84–85.

88. Ibid., 84–101.

89. See series on Black Cubans in *El Miami Herald* beginning with "Negros cubanos se enfrentan al racismo en E.U.," August 1, 1976, available in the Vertical File of the Cuban Heritage Collection, University of Miami Library. See also "Prejudice Felt by Latin Blacks: Darker Hispanics Say White Countrymen Discriminate," *The Miami Herald,* June 30, 1991, 1b–2b.

90. "Estudian servicios humanos para los hispanos," *The Voice,* February 6, 1976; Araceli Cantero, "Queremos saber sus problems—dignatarios federales a conferencia hispana," *The Voice,* February 13, 1976.

91. "Investigan las necesidades de los cubanos en EE.UU.: Aplicarán programas de ayuda federal," *Réplica* (newspaper), December 6, 1979; "Proponen dos programas federales para ayudar a los cubanos necesitados," *Réplica* (newspaper), December 13, 1979.

Chapter Eight. U.S. Hispanic Catholicism

1. Guarioné Díaz, "El proceso de pluralización del exilio cubano," *Nueva Generación* 20 (1970): 16–27.

2. For a good review of Latino Catholic activism in the 1960s and 1970s, see Moises Sandoval, *On the Move: A History of the Hispanic Church in the United States* (Maryknoll, NY: Orbis Books, 1990).

3. Raul E. L. Comesañas, "Silencio incomodo," *Ideal,* April 1977.

4. See Sandoval, *On the Move,* 61–87; María Pilar Aquino, "Theological Method in U.S. Latino/a Theology: Toward an Intercultural Theology for the Third Millennium," in *From the Heart of Our People: Latino/a Explorations in Catholic Systematic Theology,* ed. Orlando Espín and Miguel H. Díaz (Maryknoll, NY: Orbis Books, 1999), 16.

5. María Teresa Gastón Witchger, "Recent History of Hispanic Ministry in the United States," in *Prophetic Vision: Pastoral Reflection on the National Pastoral Plan for Hispanic Ministry,* eds. Soledad Galerón, Rosa María Icaza, Rosendo Urrabazo (Kansas City, MO: Sheed & Ward, 1992), 183–188.

6. Virgilio P. Elizondo, *Christianity and Culture: An Introduction to Pastoral Theology and Ministry* (San Antonio: Mexican American Cultural Center, 1975).

7. "Mas de 7,000 delegados en congreso de educación religiosa," *The Voice,* October 29, 1971.

8. "Los cubanos deben cooperar al desarrollo de hispanos en U.S.," *The Voice,* November 13, 1970.

9. "Organizan secretariado de cursillos en español de E.U.," *The Voice,* July 11, 1975.

10. Miguel Cabrera, "Cursillos hispanos en E.U.A.: Primer encuentro nacional celebrado en San Antonio, Texas," *Ideal* 47 (July 1975): 43–44.

11. Miguel Cabrera, "Cristo en las calles de Miami," in *Cuba Diáspora 1976: Anuario de la Iglesia Catolica* (Miami: Unión de Cubanos en el Exilio, 1976), 33–36.

12. Araceli Cantero, "Grupo nacional Hermanas busca promover el liderazgo entre la mujer hispana en USA," *The Voice,* March 2, 1979.

13. Arturo Pérez, Consuelo Covarrúbias, and Edward Foley, eds., *Así Es: Stories of Hispanic Spirituality* (Collegeville, MN: Liturgical Press, 1994), 39–44.

14. "Destaca el 'New York Times' influencia cubana en Miami," *The Voice,* July 24, 1970.

15. Adrian Hastings, ed., *A Concise Guide to the Documents of the Second Vatican Council* vol. 1 (London: Darton, Longman & Todd, 1968), 1:49–51.

16. Second General Conference of Latin American Bishops, *The Church in the Present-Day Transformation of Latin America in the Light of the Council: II Conclusions,* 2nd ed. (Washington, DC: Division for Latin America, USCC, 1973), 142–143.

17. "Obispo Boza habla del concilio y exodo cubano," *The Voice,* December 31, 1965.

18. CELAM offered the following definition of *pastoral de conjunto:* "An action of the whole Church, acting as an organic body, with the hierarchical integration of all its ecclesial activities and of the different pastoral agents, toward common goals, under the coordination of the hierarchy and in reference to persons within their own concrete and historical situations." Cited in Sr. Dominga M. Zapata, "The Being and Doing of the Church: *Pastoral de Conjunto,*" in Galerón et al., eds., *Prophetic Vision,* 268. See also Latin American Conference of Bishops, *Pastoral de Conjunto* (Bogotá: CELAM, 1971), 31.

19. "Teólogos vienen a Miami," *The Voice,* November 20, 1970; "Sacerdotes de habla hispana estudian métodos de pastoral," *The Voice,* December 4, 1970; "Estimulan aplicación de nuevas normas de pastoral en español," *The Voice,* December 11, 1970.

20. Araceli M. Cantero, "Miami hispano: Hacia una pastoral de conjunto," *The Voice,* April 23, 1975; "Sacerdotes hispanos estudian, reflexionan y trabajan unidos," *The Voice,* April 18, 1975.

21. "Coordinan su acción movimientos hispanos de apostolado seglar," *The Voice,* November 15, 1974.

22. Araceli M. Cantero, "Comunidad hispana reflexiona unida," *The Voice,* May 2, 1975.

23. "A establecerse consejo para el laicado," *The Voice,* December 16, 1977.

24. "Estudia realidad de Miami el apostolado hispano," *La Voz Católica,* December 12, 1980.

25. "Estudian situación de la población hispana de E.U.," *The Voice,* October 30, 1970. See also Sandoval, *On the Move,* 69–71.

26. Araceli M. Cantero, "Miami hispano: Hacia una pastoral de conjunto," *The Voice,* April 23, 1975.

27. Sandoval, *On the Move,* 79–81. See also María Teresa Gastón Witchger, "Recent History of Hispanic Ministry in the United States," in Galerón et al., eds., *Prophetic Vision,* 188–189.

28. Araceli Cantero, "Congreso Eucarístico: Nuestro pueblo tiene hambre de evangelización," *The Voice,* February 6, 1976.

29. "Preparan asamblea diocesana," *The Voice,* April 23, 1976.

30. Araceli Cantero, "Hispanos preparan Congreso Eucarístico: Hemos de ser evangelizadores," *The Voice,* May 21, 1976.

31. "Habla el nuevo vicario, Mons. Román: Ha madurado mucho la población hispana," *The Voice,* March 5, 1976.

32. "Dirigentes evaluan, planean apostolado," *The Voice,* June 11, 1976.

33. "Pastoral hispana busca prioridades," *The Voice,* June 25, 1976.

34. "Hispanos planifican pastoral," *The Voice,* August 13, 1976.

35. Araceli Cantero, "Secretariado nacional a apsotolado seglar local: 'Este es un grupo único en el país,'" *The Voice,* November 26, 1976.

36. Interview with Father Mario Vizcaíno, Miami, March 2002.

37. "El Padre Vizcaíno habla para 'Ideal,'" *Ideal* 62 (October 1976), 43–45.

38. "Líderes hispanos de la nación: Preparan Segundo Encuentro Nacional," *The Voice,* February 18, 1977; "Planifican participación del pueblo en II Encuentro Nacional Hispano," *The Voice,* March 4, 1977.

39. "Respondiendo mandato de obispos USA," *The Voice,* April 1, 1977.

40. In addition to the lay leaders, the committee included Sisters M. Elena Rodríguez, Ernestina Hernández, and Ana Luísa Céspedes and Fathers Francisco Villaverde, Luís Casabón, and José Luís Hernando; "Aspostolado seglar elige comité pro-encuentro," *The Voice,* April 22, 1977; "Comité nombrado," *The Voice,* June 3, 1977.

41. "Hispanos celebrarán noche penitencial en preparación a II Encuentro Nacional," *The Voice,* March 11, 1977.

42. See "Jovenes pro-Encuentro Nacional," and "Tambien los trabajadores agrícolas," *The Voice,* June 3, 1977; "Jovenes reflexionan," *The Voice,* June 18, 1977.

43. "La religiosa hispana," *The Voice,* January 26, 1979.

44. A. Cantero, "Religiosas piden parte en planificación," *The Voice,* June 17, 1977.

45. Araceli Cantero, "We Want a Poor, United, Missionary Church . . . ," *The Voice,* July 15, 22, 1977. The archdiocese announced the official delegates. Elected: Miguel Cabrera, Juan Figueras, Araceli Luaces, Cecilia Alegre, and Juan Clark; youth representatives: Adolfo Castañeda, Clementina García; rural missions (migrants): Mary Maldonado, Julián Cortés, and Milagros Rivera; ex-officio delegates: Archbishop Edward A. McCarthy, Msgr. John McMahon (coordinator of rural apostolate), Msgr. Agustín Román (Hispanic vicar), Father Mario Vizcaíno (regional coordinator for Encuentro Nacional); regional representatives: Father Luís Casabón, Father Francisco Villaverde; observers: Sisters Ernestina Hernández, Modesta Domínguez, Soledad Galerón. The official southeast region delegation included thirty-three elected delegates, thirteen diocesan directors, thirteen bishops, and five migrant workers. All participants in the reflections were welcome to attend the Encuentro

as observers. "Representantes regionales ultimaron planes," *The Voice,* May 20, 1977; "Delegados y observadores de la arquidiocesis al II Encuentro Nacional," *The Voice,* August 5, 1977.

46. "Spanish Meet Facing Issues," *The Voice,* August 5, 1977; "P. Frank Ponce a mini-Encuentro del Sureste: II Encuentro será festival de la fe," *The Voice,* August 5, 1977.

47. Official text of southeast region *conclusiones* are found in *The Voice,* August 12, 18, 1977.

48. Ada María Isasi-Díaz, "The People of God on the Move: Chronicle of a History," in *Prophets Denied Honor: An Anthology on the Hispano Church of the United States,* ed. Antonio M. Stevens Arroyo (Maryknoll, NY: Orbis Books, 1980), 333.

49. "Delegados de Miami, contentos de aportación al Encuentro," *The Voice,* August 26, 1977.

50. "II Encuentro Hispano Nacional de Pastoral," *Ideal,* August 1977, 10–12.

51. "Delegados de Miami, contentos de aportación al Encuentro."

52. "II Encuentro Hispano Nacional de Pastoral," 10–12.

53. "Latin Vicar: Booted by Castro, He Now Looks After Latin People Here," *The Voice,* July 21, 1978.

54. Arroyo, ed., *Prophets Denied Honor,* 314.

55. "Religiosa hispana a equipo nacional hispano," *The Voice,* May 26, 1978.

56. Most Rev. Eduardo Boza Masvidal, Cuban Bishop-in-Exile, "Unity in Pluralism," in *Pueblo de Dios en Marcha: Proceedings of the II Encuentro Nacional Hispano de Pastoral,* Secretariat for Hispanic Affairs, National Conference of Catholic Bishops/United States Catholic Conference (Trinity College, Washington, DC, August 8–21, 1977), 58–59.

57. Guillermina Damas, "Panorama histórico-pastoral de la dimensión hispana de la Archidiocesis de Miami, 1958–1983" (master's thesis, Barry University and Instituto Pastoral del Sureste, 1983), 76–79.

58. Araceli Cantero, "Encuentro II continúa su impacto," *The Voice,* August 25, 1978; Araceli Cantero, "Hispanos estan creando modelo ecclesial propio," *The Voice,* April 27, 1979.

59. "Pueblo hispano en USA es voz profética," *The Voice,* March 2, 1979.

60. "Oficina regional hispana para enero," *The Voice,* November 11, 1977; "Instituto Pastoral del Sureste se abre con dos cursos," *The Voice,* March 30, 1979; "Inaugurado Instituto Pastoral con Padre Virgilio Elizondo," *The Voice,* June 15, 1979; "They'll Learn Spanish in 3 Weeks," *The Voice,* August 3, 1979.

61. Damas, "Panorama histórico-pastoral de la dimensión hispana," 50–56.

62. "Church Speeds Migrant Aid," *The Voice,* January 16, 1963.

63. Martin A. Walsh and Paul Randall, "Churches Work to Improve Migrants' Conditions," *The Voice,* April 29, 1966.

64. Maurice Labelle, "Former Castro Aide Talks Communism, Grape Boycott," unidentified newspaper clipping, December 22, 1969, in box 16, folder 21, Truth About Cuba Archive, Cuban Heritage Collection, University of Miami Library.

65. "Firman acuerdo Coca Cola y los obreros agrícolas de la Florida," *The Voice,* March 3, 1972.

66. "Abp. Carroll Talks with Chávez, Backs Migrants," *The Voice,* June 22, 1973.

67. See "Denuncian comunismo en Talisman," *Triunfo,* February 3, 1972; "Terror en Talisman," *Impacto,* February 1, 1972; "Huelga en Talisman," Impacto, February 17, 1972. For other articles on the Talisman strike, see *Impacto,* March 11, April 4, May 20, June 6, 1972. Present at this strike, former United Farm Workers organizers Larry and Linda Hufford said they saw no Cuban religious on the scene helping the Cuban workers (author's conversation with the Huffords, San Antonio, Texas, June 2003).

68. Father Donald F. X. Connolly, "Migrants, In-Depth Report," *The Voice,* July 24, 1970.

69. Damas, "Panorama histórico-pastoral de la dimensión hispana," 54.

70. Orlando O. Espín, "El exilio, el cristiano y la acción social," *The Voice,* October 2, 1970.

71. "Jóvenes vivieron con los indios de Mexico," *The Voice,* July 28, 1978.

72. Araceli Cantero, "Farmworkers 'Speakout' in Lake Wales," and "Piden más información, educación y obsipo para migrantes," *The Voice,* January 20, 1978.

73. Araceli Cantero, "Buscan pastoral nacional para trabajadores agrícolos," *The Voice,* October 27, 1978.

74. "Formar comunidad," *The Voice,* March 14, 1975.

75. Galerón et al., eds., *Prophetic Vision,* 360.

76. Tomas Regalado, "César Chávez: Luchar contra el sistema dentro del sistema," *Ideal* 112 (December 1979): 22–23.

Chapter Nine. **Dialogue**

1. Guarioné Díaz, "El proceso de pluralización del exilio cubano," *Nueva Generación* 20 (1970). See also Lourdes Casal, "Cubans in the U.S.," *Nueva Generación* 24-25-26 (197?).

2. Grupo de Lovaina, "El universitario cubano ante las realidades del momento," *Nueva Generación* 10 (October 1966): 8–11.

3. R. Rodríguez, "Los medios de difusión, los estados psicóticos y la colonia de Miami," and J. M. Xiques, "Exilandia y la nueva generación," *Nueva Generación* 12 (March–April 1967).

4. "Diálogo: 1968," *Nueva Generación* 15 (1968).

5. María Cristina Herrera, "Las cuatro grandes encíclicas sociales," *The Voice,* July 13, 17, 1964.

6. Interview with María Cristina Herrera, May 11, 1998.

7. María Cristina Herrera, "Prólogo," *Exilio* (Winter 1969/Spring 1970): 11–14. Interview with María Cristina Herrera, May 11, 1998.

8. Andrés Valdespino, "La paz cristiana y el caso de Cuba," *Unión* 41 (March 1966).

9. Manuel Fernández, "El diálogo, el silencio y la palabra," *Reunión* 3–4 (July–August 1969).

10. "José M. Illán to María Cristina Herrera, 9 de Octubre de 1968," box 33, folder 735, Laureano Batista Archive, Cuban Heritage Collection, University of Miami Library.

11. See Lourdes Casal, "La novela en Cuba, 1959–1967: Una introducción," and "Comentarios a la ponencia . . . de Lourdes Casal," *Exilio* (Winter 1969/Spring 1970): 184–217; 294–301.

12. See Mercedes García Tudurí, "Resumen de la historia de la educación en Cuba; su evaluación: problemas y soluciones del futuro," and "Comentarios a la ponencia de . . . Mercedes García Tudurí," *Exilio* (Winter 1969/Spring 1970): 108–142; 293–294.

13. See Manuel Fernández, *Religión y revolución en Cuba: Veinticinco años de lucha ateista* (Miami: SAETA Ediciones, 1984).

14. "Relación de los participantes que han asegurado su asistencia a la Primera Reunión de Estudios Cubanos a celebrarse en New York de Noviembre 27 a Diciembre 1 de 1968," box 33, folder 736, Laureano Batista Archive, Cuban Heritage Collection, University of Miami Library.

15. Thomas Bokenkotter, *Concise History of the Catholic Church* (rev. and exp. ed.; New York: Doubleday, 2004), 408. See "Pastoral Constitution on the Church in the Modern World, Vatican II, Gaudium et Spes, 7 December 1965," in *Vatican Council II: The Conciliar and Post Conciliar Documents,* vol. 1, ed. Austin Flannery (Northport, NY: Costello Publishing, 1998), 903–1001.

16. José Villalón, "El camino del exiliado cubano," *Exilio* (Winter 1969/Spring 1970): 255–277.

17. Mateo Jover, "Presencia de la iglesia en una sociedad en transformación revolucionaria: la experiencia cubana: Ensayo de análisis prospectivo," *Exilio* (Spring 1970): 219–253.

18. José Villalón, "El camino del exiliado cubano," *Exilio* (Spring 1970): 266.

19. See "Comentarios a la ponencia . . . de Mateo Jover," and "Comentarios a la ponencia . . . de José Ramón Villalón," *Exilio* (Winter 1969/Spring 1970): 302–318.

20. La Redacción, "Reflexiones en torno a la historia de la salvación," *Exilio* (Spring 1969): 3–8.

21. Fernández, *Religión y revolución en Cuba,* 131–138.

22. "Vida cristiana," in *La voz de la iglesia en Cuba: 100 documentos episcopales* (Mexico City: Obra Nacional de la Buena Prensa, 1995), 171–176.

23. "A nuestros sacerdotes y fieles," in *La voz de la iglesia en Cuba,* 177–186.

24. Fernández, *Religión y revolución en Cuba,* 134.

25. "Valiente denuncia de sacerdotes cubanos desterrados," *RECE* 5, no. 53 (April 1969).

26. Miguel Gómez Treto, *La Iglesia Católica durante la construcción del socialismo en Cuba* (San José, Costa Rica: Editorial Departamento Ecumenico de Investigaciones, 1987), 81.

27. "Reunión secreta en Washington pro coexistencia con Castro," *Alerta,* April 30, 1971.

28. "Entrevista a José A. Pontojan: 'Yo no concibo obispos aliados a marxistas,'" *Ideal* 127 (August 1980): 21–23.

29. Manolo Fernández, "Una opinion sobre la pastoral de los obispos cubanos," *The Voice,* June 6, 1969.

30. Hno. Avelino Fernández, "Reflexiones sobre la carta pastoral," *The Voice,* May 9, 1969.

31. Pablo Urquiaga, "Comunidades cristianas en mi Cuba," in *Cuba Diáspora 1972: Anuario de la Iglesia Católica* (Miami: Unión de Cubanos en el Exilio, 1972), 125–127.

32. Hno. Avelino Fernández, "Vocación de regreso," *The Voice,* February 14, 1969.

33. Jorge I. Domínguez, "Cuban Catholics and Castro," *Worldview* 15, no. 2 (1972): 29.

34. Gómez Treto, *La Iglesia Católica,* 80.

35. Manuel Fernández, "Fidel Castro: Tiende la mano a los cristianos?" *Reunión* 35–36 (March–April 1972).

36. Manuel Fernández, "Dios ha muerto (constitucionalmente) en Cuba," *Reunión* 75–77 (July–September 1975). For a thorough critique of the Cuban Constitution of 1976 from an exile Catholic perspective, see José Ignacio Lasaga, "La iglesia cubana en el marco de la constitución socialista de 1976," in *Dr. José Ignacio Lasaga: Recuerdos, escritos, publicaciones, conferencias* (26 vols.), vol. 16, Belén School Library, Miami.

37. Manuel Fernández, "La crisis actual del catolicismo en Cuba," *Reunión* 93–94 (January–February 1977); "El futuro de la evangelización en Cuba," in *Cuba Diáspora 1978: Anuario de la Iglesia Católica* (Miami: Unión de Cubanos en el Exilio, 1978), 43–46; "Verdad y verdades sobre la religión en Cuba," *Reunión* 137–138 (September–October 1980). The third article reflected Fernández's views after a trip to Cuba.

38. José Ramón Villalón, "Otra visión de la crisis actual del catolicismo en Cuba," *Reunión* 95–96 (March–April 1977).

39. Araceli Cantero, "Enfoquemos nuestro dolor junto al del mundo entero," *The Voice,* September 23, 1977.

40. Manuel Fernández, "Cuba, paraiso de los turistas?" *Unión* 45 (July 1966).

41. Manuel Fernández, "El 'Retorno de los Brujos,'" *Reunión* 57–58 (January–February 1974).

42. Carmelo Mesa Lago, "Evaluación de las técnicas socialistas como via para resolver problemas estructurales de la economía de Cuba: 1959–1968," *Exilio* (Winter 1969/Spring 1970): 143–183.

43. Carmelo Mesa Lago, "Carta sobre 'El Retorno de los Brujos,'" *Reunión* 61–62 (May–June, 1974).

44. Lourdes Casal, "Mas sobre los brujos," *Reunión* 63–64 (July–August 1974). For a more detailed review of her intellectual journey, see "El IEC o los estrechos limites del pluralismo," *Reunión* 158 (August 1984), and María Cristina Herrera and Leonel Antonio de la Cuesta, *Itinerario ideológico: Antología de Lourdes Casal* (Miami, 1982). Casal traveled to Cuba in December 1979, where she became gravely ill and died in February 1981.

45. Herrera and de la Cuesta, *Itinerario ideológico,* 11.

46. Grupo Areíto, *Contra viento y marea* (Havana: Casa de las Americas, 1978), 74–76.

47. Ibid.

48. Guillermo J. Genier and Lisandro Pérez, *The Legacy of Exile: Cubans in the United States* (Boston: Allyn & Bacon, 2003), 8–10.

49. Maria Cristina García, *Havana, USA: Cuban Exiles and Cuban Americans in South Florida, 1959–1994* (Berkeley: University of California Press, 1996), 138–139.

50. Manuel Fernández, "Los revolucionarios ausentistas," *Reunión* 83–84 (March–April 1976).

51. Ann Louise Bardach, *Cuba Confidential: Love and Vengeance in Miami and Havana* (New York: Random House, 2002), 260–261.

52. Robert M. Levine, *Secret Missions to Cuba: Fidel Castro, Bernardo Benes, and Cuban Miami* (New York: Palgrave, 2001), 88–91.

53. María de los Angeles Torres, *In the Land of Mirrors: Cuban Exile Politics in the United States* (Ann Arbor: University of Michigan Press, 1999), 94–95.

54. Carmelo Mesa Lago, "El embargo, el dialogo, y el exilio," *Reunión* 12 (April 1970).

55. "Amalio Fiallo ratifíca su opinión sobre El Diálogo," *Ideal* 8, no. 87 (November 1978): 29.

56. García, *Havana, USA,* 140–141. See also Jesús Arboleya Cervera, *La contrarevolución cubana* (Havana: Editorial de Ciencias Sociales, 1997).

57. Torres, *In the Land of Mirrors,* 100–102.

58. José Ignacio Lasaga, "El terrorismo en Miami," *Krisis* 1, no. 4 (1976): 23, 30. See also José Ignacio Lasaga, Letter to Agustín Román, October 30, 1982, José Ignacio Lasaga Papers, Belén School Library, Miami.

59. María Cristina Herrera, "El terrorismo en Miami y otras cosas," *Reunión* 91–92 (November–December 1976).

60. Junta Patriotica Cubana, "Resolución Final," and "What Is the Cuban Patriotic Council? Its Origins, Composition and Purposes (1982)," Vertical Files, Cuban Heritage Collection, University of Miami Library.

61. "En Miami: Congreso de organizaciones anticastristas en febrero del '80," *Réplica* (newspaper), December 13, 1979.

62. "El I.E.C. y el diálogo: Una tradición y una política," *Reunión* 143–144 (March–April 1981).

63. See José Ignacio Lasaga, "Carta de renuncia: Las alternativas del I.E.C.," "Suplemento al no. 137–138: Dos respuestas a José Ignacio Lasaga," and "Letter, Enrique Baloyra to José Ignacio Lasaga, Chapel Hill, September 22, 1980," *Reunión* 137–138 (September–October 1980).

64. María Cristina Herrera, "El I.E.C. y Cuba: Un hito en el diálogo," *Reunión* 139–140 (November–December 1980).

65. Manuel Fernández, "Significado de una cita en La Habana," *Reunión* 133–134 (May–June 1980).

66. Manuel Fernández, "En Cuba: la recuperación de la memoria," *Reunión* 135–136 (July–August 1980).

67. Manuel Fernández, "Ideas y creencias en Cuba," *Reunión* 139–140 (November–December 1980).

68. Reinaldo Pico, "Los cristianos debemos buscar la paz pero no a costo de nuestros principios," *Réplica* (magazine) 5, no. 201 (August 7, 1974): 24–26.

69. Mons. Boza Masvidal, "A proposito del diálogo Cuba-Exilio," *Ideal* 8, no. 89 (January 1979): 7–8. See also "Pide Mons. Boza al exilio respeto al pluralismo," *The Voice,* October 13, 1978.

70. Eduardo Boza Masvidal and Agustín A. Román, "Mensaje a todos nuestros hermanos del destierro," *Unión* 91 (1979).

71. Eduardo Boza Masvidal and Agustín Román, "La reconciliación en nuestro pueblo: Mensaje 1983," September 1, 1983. Given to author by the archdiocese of Miami.

Epilogue

1. Ada María Isasi-Díaz, *Mujerista Theology: A Theology for the Twenty-First Century* (Maryknoll, NY: Orbis Books, 1996), 36.

2. "Apuntes Encuentro: Responsibilidad política y derechos humanos," *The Voice,* July 29, 1977.

3. Comunidades de Reflexión Eclesial Cubana en la Diaspora, *CRECED: Final Document* (English ed.; Hato Rey, PR: Ramallo Brothers Printing. 1996), 198–200.

4. For examples of the controversy, see Cynthia Corzo, "Crucero a la isla levanta olas entre iglesia y exiliados," *El Nuevo Herald,* August 26, 1997; Fabiola Santiago, "Exiliados continúan divididos por crucero papal," *El Nuevo Herald,* December 14, 1997; Miguel Pérez, "Bishop's Vow to Return to Cuba Stirs Controversy among Exiles, *The Record* (Bergen County, New Jersey), October 15, 1997.

5. This incident frames the book by Miguel A. De La Torre, *La Lucha for Cuba: Religion and Politics on the Streets of Miami* (Berkeley: University of California Press, 2003).

6. *CRECED: Final Document,* 190.

7. Manuel Fernández Santalices, *Presencia en Cuba del Catolicismo: Apuntes históricos del siglo veinte* (Caracas: Fundación Adenauer, ODCA, 1998), 85–93;

Conferencia Episcopal Cubana, *Encuentro Nacional Eclesial Cubano: Documento final e instrucción pastoral a los obispos* (Havana, 1988), 57.

8. *CRECED: Final Document,* 192.

9. Ibid.

10. Bibi Hidalgo-Caporizzo, "The Archdiocese of Miami and the Cuban-American Community: Creating a Safe Space for Discussion on the Community's Relationship with the People of Cuba" (Policy Analysis Exercise, Master of Public Policy, John F. Kennedy School of Government, Harvard University, June 2000). See Ana Rodríguez-Soto, "Group seeks unity among Cubans," *La Voz Católica* (2004). Calling themselves Comunión, the group formed in 2004 to embark on seeking reconciliation between exile and island Catholics. The group includes priests, religious, and laity who work and live in the archdiocese of Miami.

11. *CRECED: Final Document,* 89–91.

12. "Y la iglesia . . . que dice?" *Ideal* 121 (May 1980): 31.

13. "Mons. Román a los sacerdotes," *The Voice,* August 15, 1980; "Carta de Mons. Román a seglares," *The Voice,* August 22, 1980.

14. For a detailed story of these prisoners, see Mark S. Hamm, *The Abandoned Ones: The Imprisonment and Uprising of the Mariel Boat People* (Boston: Northeastern University Press, 1995).

15. "Los presos y los obispos," *Ideal* 136 (October 1980), 23.

16. See Hamm, *The Abandoned Ones;* Félix Roberto Masud-Piloto, *From Welcomed Exiles to Illegal Immigrants: Cuban Migration to the U.S., 1959–1995* (Boston: Rowman & Littlefield, 1996), 92–110. See also "Declaración de Monseñor Agustín A. Román, Obispo Auxiliar, Arquidiócesis de Miami y Monseñor Enrique San Pedro, Obispo Auxiliar, Arquidiócesis de Galveston-Houston, 21 de Diciember de 1986," *New York Times,* November 23–24, 1987, and "Declaración conjunta de los Obispos Monseñor Enrique San Pedro, S.J. y Agustín A. Román, 25 Noviembre de 1987," *New York Times,* December 2–4, 1987 (trans. and made available to the author by the archdiocese of Miami); "Si hoy no fuera cubano, pagaría por serlo," *Diario Las Americas,* December 1, 1987.

17. See Thomas Tweed, *Our Lady of Exile: Diasporic Religion at a Cuban Catholic Shrine in Miami* (New York: Oxford University Press, 1997), 84. Tweed defines "diaspora" as "a group with some shared culture which lives outside the territory that it considers its native place, and whose continuing bonds with that land are crucial for its collective identity." Also, they "share a language, even if some members of the group also speak another tongue as well, and they appeal to common symbols (such as flags, heroes, or parades), even if they struggle among themselves over their meaning. Most important, these migrants symbolically construct a common past and future, and their shared symbols bridge the homeland and the new land."

18. *CRECED: Final Document,* 199–200.

19. For background on the complexity of Miami's ethnic mix, see Alejandro Portes and Alex Stepick, *City on the Edge: The Transformation of Miami* (Berkeley: University of California Press, 1993), especially chapter 7 on Nicaraguans.

20. Moises Sandoval, "The Organization of a Hispanic Church," in *Hispanic Catholic Culture in the U.S.: Issues and Concerns,* ed. Jay P. Dolan and Allan Figueroa Deck (Notre Dame, IN: University of Notre Dame Press, 1994), 141–146; Soledad Galerón, Rosa María Icaza, and Rosendo Urrabazo, eds., *Prophetic Vision: Pastoral Reflections on the National Plan for Hispanic Ministry* (Kansas City, MO: Sheed & Ward, 1992), 206.

21. Galerón et al., eds., *Prophetic Vision,* 198.

22. Orlando O. Espín, "Tradition and Popular Religion: An Understanding of the *Sensus Fidelium,*" in *Frontiers of Hispanic Theology in the United States,* ed. Allan Figueroa Deck (Maryknoll, NY: Orbis Books, 1992), 62. Perhaps his earliest contribution on this topic is "Religiosidad popular: Un aporte para su definición y hermenéutica," *Estudios Sociales* 17, no. 58 (October–December, 1984): 41–56.

23. Araceli Cantero, "Hispanos USA presentaron necesidades," *The Voice,* February 18, 1978. See Isasi-Díaz, *Mujerista Theology.*

24. Roberto S. Goizueta, "United States Hispanic Theology and the Challenge of Pluralism," in Figueroa Deck, ed., *Frontiers of Hispanic Theology,* 19. See also Roberto S. Goizueta, ed., *We Are a People! Initiatives in Hispanic American Theology in the United States* (Minneapolis: Fortress Press, 1992).

25. Like Sixto García, Alicia Marill, Fernando Segovia, and Alex García Rivera. For an excellent overview on the development of U.S. Hispanic theology, see Eduardo C. Fernández, *La Cosecha: Harvesting Contemporary United States Hispanic Theology, 1972–1998* (Collegeville, MN: Liturgical Press, 2000). See especially discussions of contributions by Espín, Goizueta, Alex García Rivera, and Isasi-Díaz, 43–71.

26. *CRECED: Final Document,* 112–117.

27. José Ignacio Lasaga, "Que es la Teología de la Liberación?" in *Dr. José Ignacio Lasaga: Recuerdos, escritos, publicaciones, conferencias* (26 vols.), vol. 20, Belén School Library, Miami.

28. Margarita Gavaldá Romagosa, "Estudio del conocimiento y actitudes de los católicos cubanos de Miami sobre la enseñanza social de la iglesia" (master's thesis, Southeast Pastoral Institute and Barry University, 1988), 119–120.

BIBLIOGRAPHY

Archives

Cuban Heritage Collection, University of Miami Library
- Bernardo Benes Archive
- Directorio Revolucionario Estudiantil Archive
- Laureano Batista Archive
- Truth About Cuba Committee Archive
- Vertical Files (newspaper clippings, pamphlets, and miscellaneous materials)

National Archives and Records Administration, Washington, DC
- Records of the U.S. Department of State
- Records of the Central Intelligence Agency

Belén School Library, Miami
- *Dr. José Ignacio Lasaga: Recuerdos, escritos, publicaciones, conferencias* (26 vols.). Bound (unpublished) volumes of speeches and lectures, newspaper clippings, and other materials
- José Ignacio Lasaga Papers—additional materials not included in above collection

La Voz Católica Archive, Archdiocese of Miami
- Newspaper clippings and miscellaneous materials

Newspapers, Magazines, and Newsletters

Abdala (Washington, DC)
Alerta (Miami)
Avance (Havana)
Avance Criollo (Miami)
Bohemia (Havana)
Bohemia Libre (Miami)
Boletín (Union de Cubanos en el Exilio, New York)
Boletín Informativo Demócrata Cristiano (New York)
Boletín Semanal Informativo (Consejo Revolucionario Cubano, Miami)
Conciencia (Organo Oficial del Movimiento Demócrata Cristiano de Cuba, Caracas)
Cuba Diáspora: Anuario de la Iglesia Católica (Unión de Cubanos en el Exilio, Caracas)

Cuba Nueva (Consejo Revolucionario Cubano, Miami)
Diario de la Marina (Havana)
Diario las Americas (Miami)
Esto Vir (Agrupación Católica Universitaria, Miami)
Girón (Miami)
Ideal (Miami)
Información Católica Cubana (Miami)
The Miami Herald (Miami)
El Mundo (Havana)
Impacto (Miami)
Mundo Nuevo (Agrupación Católica Universitaria, Miami)
Nueva Generación (Venezuela-Miami-New York)
El Nuevo Herald (Miami)
Política y Espíritu (Chile)
Prensa Libre (Havana)
RECE (Miami)
The Record (Bergen County, NJ)
Réplica (newspaper) (Miami)
Réplica (magazine) (Miami)
Reunión (Instituto de Estudios Cubanos newsletter)
Triunfo (Miami)
Tridente (Miami)
Unión (Unión de Cubanos en el Exilio, Caracas)
The Voice (Archdiocese of Miami)
La Quincena (Havana)
La Voz Católica (Archidiocesis de Miami)

Oral Histories, Conversations, and Communications

Uva de Aragón
Bernardo Benes
Araceli Cantero
José M. Hernández
María Cristina Herrera
Larry and Linda Hufford
Max Lesnik
Alicia Marill
Ondina Menocal
Salvador Miranda
Father Jorge Perales
Lisandro Pérez

Jorge Poyo
José Poyo
Sergio Poyo
José Ignacio Rasco
Rubén Darío Rumbaut
Father Emilio Vallina
Antonio Veciana
Father Mario Vizcaíno
Monsignor Bryan Walsh

Books

Ameringer, Charles D. *The Cuban Democratic Experience: The Auténtico Years, 1944–1952.* Gainesville: University Press of Florida, 2000.

Aparicio Laurencio, Angel. *"Donde está el cadaver? . . . Se reunen los buitres": Crónicas de la persecución religiosa en Cuba.* Santiago, Chile, 1963.

Arboleya Cervera, Jesús. *La contrarevolución cubana.* Havana: Editorial de Ciencias Sociales, 1997.

Artime, Manuel. *Traición! Gritan 20,000 tumbas cubanas.* Mexico: Editorial Jus, 1960.

Azpiazu, Joaquín. *El estado corporativo.* Madrid: Biblioteca Fomento Social, n.d.

———. *El derecho de propiedad.* Madrid: Razón y Fe, 1930.

———. *Patronos y obreros.* Madrid: Razón y Fe, n.d.

———. *Problemas sociales de actualidad.* Madrid: Razón y Fe, n.d.

———. *La Enciclica "Quadragesimo Anno."* Burgos: Biblioteca Fomento Social, 1938.

———. *Manual de Acción Católica.* Madrid: Editorial Razón y Fe, 1933.

Bardach, Ann Louise. *Cuba Confidential: Love and Vengeance in Miami and Havana.* New York: Random House, 2002.

Barquín, Ramón M. *Las luchas guerrilleras en Cuba: De la colonia a la Sierra Maestra.* 2 vols. Madrid: Playor, S.A., 1975.

Blight, James, and Peter Kornbluh. *Politics of Illusion: The Bay of Pigs Invasion Re-examined.* Boulder: Lynne Rienner Publishers, 1998.

Bokenkotter, Thomas. *Church and Revolution: Catholics in the Struggle for Democracy and Social Justice.* New York: Image Books, 1998.

———. *Concise History of the Catholic Church.* Rev. and exp. ed. New York: Doubleday, 2004.

Bonachea, Ramón L., and Marta San Martin. *The Cuban Insurrection, 1952–1959.* 2nd ed. New Brunswick, NJ: Transactions Publishers, 1995.

Boswell, Thomas D., and James R. Curtis. *The Cuban-American Experience: Culture, Images and Perspectives.* Totowa, NJ: Rowman & Allanheld, 1983.

Boza Masvidal, Eduardo. *Revolución cristiana en latinoamerica.* Santiago, Chile: Editorial del Pacifico,1963.

———. *Voz en el destierro.* Miami: Revista Ideal, 1977.

Brenan, Gerald. *The Spanish Labyrinth: An Account of the Social and Political Background of the Spanish Civil War.* Cambridge: Cambridge University Press, 1969.

Carbonell, Néstor T. *And the Russians Stayed: The Sovietization of Cuba: A Personal Portrait.* New York: William Morrow, 1989.

Carbonell Cortina, Néstor, ed. *Grandes debates de la constituyente cubana de 1940.* Miami: Ediciones Universal, 2001.

Cárdenas, Eduardo. *La iglesia hispanoamericana en el siglo XX (1890–1990).* Madrid: MAPRE, 1992.

Chase, Allen. *Falange: The Axis Secret Army in the Americas.* New York: G. P. Putnam's Sons, 1943.

Cistierna, Salvador. *Doctrina social pontificia.* Havana: Instituto Social Pio XII, Universidad Católica de Santo Tomás Villanueva, 1960.

Clark, Juan. *Cuba: Mito y realidad: Testimonios de un pueblo.* Miami: Saeta Ediciones, 1990.

———. *Why? The Cuban Exodus: Background, Evolution and Impact in U.S.A.* Miami: Union of Cubans in Exile, 1977.

———. *Religious Repression in Cuba.* Miami: Institute of Inter-American Studies, University of Miami, 1985.

Cleary, Edward L. *Crisis and Change: The Church in Latin America Today.* Maryknoll, NY: Orbis Books, 1985.

———, ed. *Born of the Poor: The Latin American Church Since Medellín.* Notre Dame, IN: University of Notre Dame Press, 1990.

Comunidades de Reflexión Eclesial Cubana de la Diáspora. *CRECED: Final Document.* Hato Rey, PR: Ramallo Brothers Printing, 1996.

Conde, Yvonne M. *Operation Pedro Pan: The Untold Story of 14,048 Cuban Children.* New York: Routledge, 1999.

Conferencia Episcopal Cubana. *Encuentro Nacional Eclesial Cubano: Documento final e instrucción pastoral a los obispos.* Havana: Conferencia Episcopal Cubana, 1988.

Congreso Católico Nacional. Havana: Ponciano, 1960.

Considine, John J. *The Church in the New Latin America.* Notre Dame, IN: Fides Publishers, 1964.

Cortés, Carlos E., ed. *Cuban Exiles in the United States.* New York: Arno Press, 1980.

Costello, Gerald M. *Mission to Latin America: The Successes and Failures of a Twentieth-Century Crusade.* Maryknoll, NY: Orbis Books, 1979.

Curran, Charles E. *Catholic Social Teaching: A Historical, Theological and Ethical Analysis.* Washington, DC: Georgetown University Press, 2002.

Deck, Allan Figueroa. *The Second Wave: Hispanic Ministry and the Evangelization of Cultures.* New York: Paulist Press, 1989.

De La Torre, Miguel A. *La Lucha for Cuba: Religion and Politics on the Streets of Miami.* Berkeley: University of California Press, 2003.

De Varona, Esperanza B. *Cuban Exile Periodicals at the University of Miami Library: An Annotated Bibliography.* Madison: SALAM, 1987.

Dewart, Leslie. *Christianity and Revolution: The Lesson of Cuba.* New York: Herder and Herder, 1963.

Dolan, Jay P. *The American Catholic Experience: A History from Colonial Times to the Present.* Garden City, NY: Doubleday, 1985.

———. *The Immigrant Church: New York's Irish and German Catholics, 1815–1865.* Notre Dame, IN: University of Notre Dame Press, 1983.

———. *In Search of an American Catholicism: A History of Religion and Culture in Transition.* Oxford: Oxford University Press, 2002.

Duarte Oropesa, José. *Historiología Cubana.* 5 vols. Miami: Ediciones Universal, 1993.

Dussel, Enrique. *A History of the Church in Latin America: Colonialism to Liberation, 1492–1979.* Grand Rapids, MI: William B. Eerdmans Publishing, 1981.

Echevarría Salvat, Oscar A. *Democracia y bienestar.* Miami: Ediciones Universal, 1968.

Eckstein, Susan, ed. *Power and Popular Protest: Latin American Social Movements.* Berkeley: University of California Press, 1989.

Elizondo, Virgilio P. *Christianity and Culture: An Introduction to Pastoral Theology and Ministry.* San Antonio: Mexican American Cultural Center, 1975.

Encinosa, Enrique. *Cuba: The Unfinished Revolution.* Miami: Endowment for Cuban American Studies, Cuban American National Foundation, 1994.

———. *Escambray: La guerra olvidada.* Miami: Editorial SIBI, 1998.

Fagen, Richard, Richard A. Brody, Thomas J. O'Leary. *Cubans in Exile: Disaffection and the Revolution.* Stanford, CA: Stanford University Press, 1968.

Femantle, Anne, ed. *The Papal Encyclicals in their Historical Context.* New York: G. P. Putnam's Sons, 1956.

Fernández, Eduardo C. *La Cosecha: Harvesting Contemporary United States Hispanic Theology, 1972–1998.* Collegeville, MN: Liturgical Press, 2000.

Fernández Santalices, Manuel. *Presencia en Cuba del catolicismo: Apuntes históricos del siglo veinte.* Caracas: Fundación Adenauer, ODCA, 1998.

———. *Religión y revolución en Cuba: Veinticinco años de lucha ateista.* Miami: SAETA Ediciones, 1984.

Fernández Soneira, Teresa. *Con la estrella y la cruz: Historia de la Federación de las Juventudes de Acción Católica Cubana.* Miami: Ediciones Universal, 2002.

———. *Cuba. Historia de la educación católica.* 2 vols. Miami: Ediciones Universal, 1997.

Figueroa y Miranda, Miguel. *Historia de la Agrupación Católica Universitaria, 1931–1956.* Havana, 1956.

Flannery, Austin, general ed. *Vatican Council II, Volume 1: The Conciliar and Postconciliar Documents.* Northport, NY: Costello Publishing, 1998.

Floridi, A., and A. Stiefbold. *The Uncertain Alliance: The Catholic Church and Labor in Latin America.* Miami: University of Miami, Center for Advanced International Studies, 1973.

Foyaca, Manuel. *Crisis en nuestra America.* Miami: Instituto de Acción Social, 1963.

————. *Un nuevo orden economico-social.* Havana: Compañia Editora de Libros y Folletos, 1941.

Fundación Andrés Valdespino. *Valdespino: Cuba como pasión.* Hato Rey, PR: Ramallo Brothers Printing, n.d.

Galerón, Soledad, Rosa María Icaza, and Rosendo Urrabazo, eds. *Prophetic Vision: Pastoral Reflections on the National Pastoral Plan for Hispanic Ministry.* Kansas City: Sheed & Ward, 1992.

Gallegos, José Andrés. *Pensamiento y acción social de la iglesia en España.* Madrid: Espasa-Calpe, S.A., 1984.

García, María Cristina. *Havana, USA: Cuban Exiles and Cuban Americans in South Florida, 1959–1994.* Berkeley: University of California Press, 1996.

García Olivares, Julio A. *José Antonio Echeverría: La lucha estudiantil contra Batista.* Havana: Editora Política, 1980.

García-Pérez, Gladys Marel. *Insurrection & Revolution: Armed Struggle in Cuba, 1952–1959.* Trans. Juan Ortega. Boulder: Lynne Rienner Publishers, 1998.

Goizueta, Roberto S., ed. *We Are a People! Initiatives in Hispanic American Theology in the United States.* Minneapolis: Fortress Press, 1992.

Goldenberg, Boris. *The Cuban Revolution and Latin America.* New York: Praeger, 1966.

Gómez Treto, Raul. *La Iglesia Católica durante la construcción del socialismo en Cuba.* San José, Costa Rica: Editorial DEI, 1987.

Gonzalez, Reinol. *Y Fidel creo el Punto X.* Miami: Saeta Ediciones, 1987.

González-Pando, Miguel. *The Cuban Americans.* Westport, CT: Greenwood Press, 1998.

Greenbaum, Susan. *More Than Black: Afro-Cubans in Tampa.* Gainesville: University Press of Florida, 2002.

Grenier, Guillermo J., and Lisandro Pérez. *The Legacy of Exile: Cubans in the United States.* Boston: Allyn & Bacon, 2003.

Grupo Areíto. *Contra viento y marea.* Havana: Casa de las Americas, 1978.

Halperin, Ernst. *Nationalism and Communism in Chile.* Cambridge, MA: MIT Press, 1965.

Halperin, Maurice. *The Rise and Decline of Fidel Castro: An Essay in Contemporary History.* Berkeley: University of California Press, 1972.

Hamm, Mark S. *The Abandoned Ones: The Imprisonment and Uprising of the Mariel Boat People.* Boston: Northeastern University Press, 1995.

Hastings, Adrian, ed. *A Concise Guide to the Documents of the Second Vatican Council.* Vol. 1. London: Darton, Longman & Todd, 1968.

Hernández, José M. *ACU: Agrupación Católica Universitaria: Los primeros cincuenta años.* Miami: Agrupación Católica Cubana, 1981.

Herrera, María Cristina, and Leonel Antonio de la Cuesta. *Itinerario ideológico: Antología de Lourdes Casal.* Miami, 1982.

Higgins, Trumball. *The Perfect Failure: Kennedy, Eisenhower and the CIA at the Bay of Pigs.* New York: W. W. Norton, 1989.

Historia de una agresión: Declaraciones y documentos del juicio seguido a la brigada mercenaria organizada por los imperialistas yanquis que invadió a Cuba el 17 de abril de 1961. Havana: Ediciones Venceremos, 1962.

Hobgood, Mary E. *Catholic Social Teaching and Economic Theory: Paradigms in Conflict.* Philadelphia: Temple University Press, 1991.

Houtart, Francois. *The Challenge to Change: The Church Confronts the Future.* New York: Sheed & Ward, 1964.

———, and Emile Pin. *The Church and the Latin American Revolution.* Trans. Gilbert Barth. New York: Sheed and Ward, 1965.

Isasi-Díaz, Ada María. *Mujerista Theology: A Theology for the Twenty-First Century.* Maryknoll, NY: Orbis Books, 1996.

Johnson, Haynes. *The Bay of Pigs: The Leaders' Story of Brigade 2506.* New York: W. W. Norton, 1964.

Jorge, Antonio, Jaime Suchlicki, and Adolfo Leyva de Varona, eds. *Cuban Exiles in Florida: Their Presence and Contributions.* Miami: North-South Center, University of Miami, 1991.

Julien, Claude. *La Revolución Cubana.* Montevideo: Ediciones Marcha, 1961.

Junta Nacional de Acción Católica. *Cuba Católica.* Havana, 1951.

Junta Nacional de la Acción Católica Cubana. *Primer catálogo de las obras sociales católicas de Cuba.* Havana, 1953.

Juventudes de Acción Católica Cubana. *Bodas de Plata, 1928–1953.* San Juan, PR: Ramallo Brothers Printing, 1978. Facsimile of 1953 Havana edition.

Kelly, J. J. *La Cuba del Padre Spirale.* Madrid: Ediciones Fe Católica, 1971.

Keogh, Dermot, ed. *Church and Politics in Latin America.* New York: St. Martin's Press, 1990.

Kirk, John. *Between God and the Party: Religion and Politics in Revolutionary Cuba.* Tampa: University of South Florida Press, 1989.

Kornbluh, Peter, ed. *Bay of Pigs Declassified: The Secret CIA Report on the Invasion of Cuba.* New York: New Press, 1998.

Lannon, Frances. *Privilege, Persecution and Prophecy: The Catholic Church in Spain, 1875–1975.* Oxford: Clarendon Press, 1987.

Latin American Conference of Bishops. *Pastoral de Conjunto.* Bogotá: CELAM, 1971.

Leiseca, Juan Martín. *Apuntes para la historia eclesiástica de Cuba.* Havana: Carasa y Cia, 1938.

Levine, Robert M. *Secret Missions to Cuba: Fidel Castro, Bernardo Benes, and Cuban Miami.* New York: Palgrave, 2001.

Liss, Sheldon B. *Diplomacy & Dependency: Venezuela, The United States, and the Americas.* Salisbury, NC: Documentary Publications, 1978.

López Morales, Humberto. *Los cubanos de Miami: Lengua y sociedad.* Miami: Ediciones Universal, 2003.

Lynch, Edward A. *Religion and Politics in Latin America: Liberation Theology and Christian Democracy.* New York: Praeger, 1991.

Lynch, Grayston L. *Decision for Disaster: Betrayal at the Bay of Pigs.* Washington, DC: Brassey's, 1998.

Mainelli, Vincent P., ed. *Official Catholic Teachings: Social Justice.* Wilmington, NC: Consortium Books, 1978.

Mainwaring, Scott. *The Catholic Church and Politics in Brazil, 1916–1985.* Stanford, CA: Stanford University Press, 1986.

Maritain, Jacques. *Integral Humanism: Temporal and Spiritual Problems of a New Christendom.* Trans. Joseph W. Evans. Notre Dame, IN: University of Notre Dame Press, 1968.

Martínez de Codes, Rosa María. *La Iglesia Católica en la América independiente: Siglo XIX.* Madrid: Editorial MAPFRE, 1992.

Masud-Piloto, Félix Roberto. *From Welcomed Exiles to Illegal Immigrants: Cuban Migration to the U.S., 1959–1995.* Lanham, MD: Rowman and Littlefield Publishers, 1996.

Matovina, Timothy, and Gerald E. Poyo, eds. *Presente! U.S. Latino Catholics from Colonial Origins to the Present.* Maryknoll, NY: Orbis Books, 2000.

McNally, Michael J. *Catholicism in South Florida, 1868–1968.* Gainesville: University Presses of Florida, 1982.

Medrano, Humberto. *Sin patria pero sin amo.* Miami: Service Offset Printers, 1963.

Moody, Joseph N., and Justus George Lawler. *The Challenge of Mater et Magistra.* New York: Herder & Herder, 1963.

Mormino, Gary, and George Pozzetta. *The Immigrant World of Ybor City: Italians and Their Latin Neighbors in Tampa, 1885–1985.* Urbana: University of Illinois Press, 1987.

Murray, J. P. *The Second Revolution in Cuba.* New York: M R Press, 1962.

Pattee, Richard. *Catholic Life in the West Indies.* Washington, DC: Catholic Association for International Peace, 1946.

———, ed. *El catolicismo contemporaneo en Hispanoamerica.* Buenos Aires: Editorial FIDES, 1951.

Payne, Stanley G. *Fascism in Spain, 1923–1977.* Madison: University of Wisconsin Press, 1999.

———. *Spanish Catholicism: An Historical Overview.* Madison: University of Wisconsin Press, 1984.

Paz-Sánchez, Manuel de. *Zona rebelde: La diplomacia española ante la Revolución Cubana (1957–1960).* Santa Cruz de Tenerife: Litografía Romero, S.A., 1997.

Pedraza-Bailey, Silvia. *Political and Economic Migrants in America: Cubans and Mexicans.* Austin: University of Texas Press, 1985.

Penabaz, Manuel. *Girón 1961: Anatomía de una traición.* Miami, 1979.

Pérez, Arturo, Consuelo Covarrúbias, and Edward Foley, eds. *Así Es: Stories of Hispanic Spirituality.* Collegeville, MN: Liturgical Press, 1994.

Pérez-Stable, Marifeli. *The Cuban Revolution: Origins, Course, and Legacy.* Oxford: Oxford University Press, 1993.

Pike, Fredrick B. *Hispanismo, 1898–1936.* Notre Dame, IN: University of Notre Dame Press, 1971.

Portes, Alejandro, and Alex Stepick. *City on the Edge: The Transformation of Miami.* Berkeley: University of California Press, 1993.

Portes, Alejandro, and Robert L. Bach. *Latin Journey: Cuban and Mexican Immigrants in the United States.* Berkeley: University of California Press, 1985.

Portuondo, Yolanda. *Guillermo Sardiñas: El sacerdote comandante. Testimonio.* Habana: Editorial Cultura Popular. 1987.

Poyo, Gerald E. *"With All, and For the Good of All": The Emergence of Popular Nationalism in the Cuban Communities of the United States, 1848–1898.* Durham, NC: Duke University Press, 1989.

Prohías, Rafael J., and Lourdes Casal, eds. *The Cuban Minority in the U.S.: Preliminary Report on Need Identification and Program Evaluation.* Cuban National Planning Council, 1974.

Rasco, José Ignacio. *Cuba 1959: Artículos de combate.* Buenos Aires: Ediciones Diagrama, 1962.

———. *La libertad de San Agustín.* Havana: Ediciones Insula, S.A., 1958.

———. *Jacques Maritain y la Democracia Cristiana.* Miami: Ediciones Universal, 1980.

Riesgo, Rodolfo. *Cuba: El movimiento obrero y su entorno socio-político, 1865–1983.* Miami: Saeta Ediciones, 1985.

Rogg, Eleanor M., and Rosemary Santana Cooney. *Adaptation and Adjustment of Cubans: West New York, New Jersey.* Monograph 5. New York: Fordham University Hispanic Research Center, 1980.

Ros, Enrique. *Cubanos combatientes: Peleando en distintos frentes.* Miami: Ediciones Universal, 1998.

———. *De Girón a la crisis de los cohetes: La segunda derrota.* Miami: Ediciones Universal, 1995.

———. *Playa Girón: La verdadera historia.* Miami: Ediciones Universale, 1994.

Sandoval, Moises. *On the Move: A History of the Hispanic Church in the United States* Maryknoll, NY: Orbis Books, 1990.

San Juan Bosco Church Silver Jubilee, 1963–1988. Miami, 1988.

Second General Conference of Latin American Bishops. *The Church in the Present-Day Transformation of Latin America in the Light of the Council: II. Conclusions,* 2nd ed. Washington, DC: Division for Latin America, USCC, 1973.

Segura Bustamante, Inés. *Cuba: Siglo XX y la generación de 1930.* Santo Domingo: Editora Corripio, 1984.

Shapiro, Samuel, ed. *Cultural Factors in Inter-American Relations.* Notre Dame, IN: University of Notre Dame Press, 1968.

———, ed. *Integration of Man and Society in Latin America.* Notre Dame, IN: University of Notre Dame Press, 1967.

Suárez, Andrés. *Cuba: Castroism and Communism, 1959–1966.* Cambridge, MA: MIT Press, 1967.

Suárez Policari, Ramón. *Historia de la Iglesia Católica en Cuba*. 2 vols. Miami: Ediciones Universal, 2003.

Tanner, Hans. *Counter-Revolutionary Agent: Diary of Events which Occurred in Cuba between January and July 1961*. London: G. T. Foulis, 1962.

Testé, Ismael. *Historia Eclesiastica de Cuba*. 5 vols. Burgos and Barcelona, Spain: El Monte Carmelo and Artes Gráficas Medinaceli, 1969–1975.

Thomas, Hugh. *Cuba: The Pursuit of Freedom*. New York: Harper & Row, 1971.

Torres, María de los Angeles. *In the Land of Mirrors: Cuban Exile Politics in the United States* Ann Arbor: University of Michigan Press, 1999.

———. *The Lost Apple: Operation Pedro Pan, Cuban Children in the U.S., and the Promise of a Better Future*. Boston: Beacon Press, 2003.

Tweed, Thomas A. *Our Lady of the Exile: Diasporic Religion at a Cuban Catholic Shrine in Miami*. New York: Oxford University Press, 1997.

Universidad de Santo Tomás de Villanueva. *Contribución a la historia de sus diez primeros años*. Havana: UCAR, García, S.A., 1956.

Urrutia-Lleó, Manuel. *Fidel Castro & Company, Inc.: Communist Tyranny in Cuba*. New York: Praeger, 1964.

Valle, Raul del. *El Cardinal Arteaga: Resplandores de la purpura cubana*. Havana: Impreso Ramallo, 1957.

Vargas Llosa, Alvaro. *El exilio indomable: Historia de la disidencia cubana en el destierro*. Spain: Editorial Espasa, 1998.

Vila, José Jorge, and Guillermo Zalamea Arenas. *Exilio*. Miami, 1967.

La voz de la Iglesia en Cuba: 100 documentos episcopales. Mexico City: Obra Nacional de la Buena Prensa, 1995.

Wahlers, Gerhard. *Nace una alternativa*. Miami: SAETA Ediciones, 1991.

Wiarda, Howard J. *The Soul of Latin America: The Cultural and Political Tradition*. New Haven, CT: Yale University Press, 2001.

Wright, Thomas C. *Latin America in the Era of the Cuban Revolution*. Westport, CT: Praeger, 2001.

Book Chapters, and Journal and Magazine Articles

Acosta de Villalta, Loló. "Perdóname Mamá! Los encuentros juveniles de los muchachos cubanos católicos de las parroquias de Miami." *Réplica* (magazine) 5, no. 189 (May 15, 1974): 29–32.

Aguilar León, Luís. "Raíces del futuro." *Cuba Nueva* 1, no. 3 (April 15, 1962): 13–16.

Aldeaseca, Padre. "Mons. Evelio Díaz en la television." *La Quincena* 5, nos. 21–22 (November 1959): 51.

"Amalio Fiallo ratifíca su opinión sobre El Diálogo." *Ideal* 8, no. 87 (November 1978): 29.

Amigó Jansen, Gustavo. "Cuba." In *El catolicismo contemporaneo en hispanoamerica,* ed. Richard Pattee, 79. Buenos Aires: Editorial FIDES, 1951.

Aquino, María Pilar. "Theological Method in U.S. Latino/a Theology: Toward an Intercultural Theology for the Third Millennium." In *From the Heart of Our People: Latino/a Explorations in Catholic Systematic Theology,* ed. Orlando Espín and Miguel H. Díaz. 6–48. Maryknoll, NY: Orbis Books, 1999.

"Archidiocesis de Miami." In *Cuba Diáspora 1975: Anuario de la Iglesia Católica,* 108–109. Miami: Unión de Cubanos en el Exilio, 1975.

Arenas Amigó, Valentín. "Tad Szulc en la pantalla: Nota sobre la concepción de la Alianza para el Progreso." *Cuba Nueva* 2, no. 2 (October 1, 1962): 6–8.

"La Asociación Sacerdotal Hispana cumple 15 años." *Ideal* 157 (November 1981): 31.

"Austeridad, responsabilidad y unión." *Ideal* 1, no. 11 (July 15, 1972): 6–9.

Badillo, David A. "Catholicism and the Search for Nationhood in Miami's Cuban Community." *U.S. Catholic Historian* 20, no. 4 (Fall 2002): 75–90.

Biaín, Ignacio. "Balance del marcismo y destinos de una revolución." *La Quincena* 5, nos. 1–2 (January 1959): 51.

———. "El Congreso Católico de Noviembre." *La Quincena* 5, no. 20 (October 31, 1959): 34.

———. "El espíritu de la reforma agraria." *La Quincena* 5, no. 11 (June 15, 1959): 30–32.

———. "El Movimiento Demócrata Cristiano." *La Quincena* 6, no. 2 (January 30, 1960): 32–33.

Boza Masvidal, Eduardo. "A proposito del diálogo Cuba-Exilio." *Ideal* 8, no. 89 (January 1979): 7–8.

———. "Comunidades cristianas cubanas." *Cuba Diáspora 1976: Anuario de la Iglesia Católica,* 31–32. Miami: Unión de Cubanos en el Exilio, 1976.

———. "Unity in Pluralism." In *Pueblo de Dios en Marcha: Proceedings of the II Encuentro Nacional Hispano de Pastoral,* 58–59. National Conference of Catholic Bishops/United States Catholic Conference, Washington, DC, August 8–21, 1977.

Cabrera, Miguel. "Cristo en las calles de Miami." *Cuba Diáspora 1976: Anuario de la Iglesia Católica,* 33–36.

———. "Cursillos hispanos en E.U.A.: Primer encuentro nacional celebrado en San Antonio, Texas." *Ideal* 47 (July 1975): 43–44.

Carrasco, Teok. "El mural de la Ermita." *Ideal* 4, no. 49 (September/October 1975): 9, 11–12.

Casal, Lourdes. "Africa ante el problema cubano." *Cuba Nueva* 1, no. 10 (August 1, 1962): 11–17.

———. "La novela en Cuba, 1959–1967: Una introducción." *Exilio* (Winter 1969/ Spring 1970): 184–217.

"Catolicismo: La cruz y el diablo." *Bohemia* 51, no. 3 (January 18, 1959): 98–100.

"Los católicos cubanos y el gobierno de estado de Batista." *Política y Espíritu* 8, no. 71 (May 1952) : 152–153.

Cerro, Angel del. "Un aniversario de la Alianza para el Progreso." *Cuba Nueva* 1, no. 2 (April 1962): 15–18.

———. "Ante el Congreso Católico Nacional." *Bohemia* 51, no. 47 (November 22, 1959): 54–55, 90–91.

———. "En busca de una tercera posición." *Bohemia* 51, no. 23 (June 7, 1959): 75, 96.

———. "Cuarenta casos de injusticia social." *Bohemia* 51, no. 17 (April 26, 1959): 72–73, 95.

———. "Los curas son reaccionarios." *Bohemia* 51, no. 16 (April 19, 1959): 68–69, 97.

———. "El Humanismo de Maritain: En busca de una tercera posición." *Bohemia* 51, no. 23 (June 7, 1959): 75, 96.

———. "La Iglesia tiene que resucitar." *Bohemia* 51, no. 14 (April 5, 1959): 78–79.

———. "Radiografía de una traición." *Bohemia Libre* 52, no. 3 (October 23, 1960): 36–37, 66.

———. "No reincidamos." *Cuba Nueva* 1, no. 6 (June 1, 1962): 12–15.

———. "Un mar de fe." *Bohemia* 51, no. 49 (December 6, 1959): 98–99, 112–113.

———, ed. "Cuba, 1961." *Cuadernos* 47 (supplement) (March–April 1961).

Chaurrondo, Hilario. "Fidel Castro, de rodillas ante un sacerdote." *La Quincena* 5, nos. 1–2 (January 1959): 21.

———. "Operación suburbios: La corona de espinas de La Habana Católica." *La Quincena* 6, no. 7 (April 15, 1960): 20–21.

"Comentarios a la ponencia . . . de José Ramón Villalón." *Exilio* (Winter 1969/Spring 1970): 302–318.

"Comentarios a la ponencia . . . de Lourdes Casal." *Exilio* (Winter 1969/Spring 1970): 294–301.

"Comentarios a la ponencia . . . de Maeto Jover." *Exilio* (Winter 1969/Spring 1970): 302–318.

"Comentarios a la ponencia . . . de Mercedes García Tudurí." *Exilio* (Winter 1969/Spring 1970): 293–294.

Comesañas, Raul E. L. "Silencio incomodo." *Ideal* 68 (April 1977): 27–28.

Cordoba, Efrén. "La legislación laboral del castrismo." *Cuba Nueva* 1, no. 4 (May 1, 1962): 16–22.

Couto, Armando. "Revelaciones de Carlos Canet: El que mas sabe dice todo lo que sabe de la religión Lucumí." *Réplica* (magazine) 4, no. 152 (August 29, 1973): 14–17.

"Declaración de principios del 'movimiento humanista' de Cuba." *Política y Espíritu* 7, no. 66 (December 1951): 533, 555–560.

De Kadt, Emmanuel. "Paternalism and Populism: Catholicism in Latin America." *Journal of Contemporary History* 2, no. 4 (October 1967): 89–106.

"De la historia de Cuba." *Ideal* 4, no. 37 (September 8, 1974): 49.

"Los delegados de la Juventud Demócrata Cristiana al II Congreso Latinoamericano de Juventudes, D.C." *Cuba Nueva* 1, no. 8 (July 1, 1962): 11–14.

"Democracia y liberalismo." *La Quincena* 5, no. 7 (April 1959): 26, 46.

"De Playa Girón al seminario." *Ideal* 60 (August 1976): 30–31.

De Toro, Lorenzo. "Despúes de cuatro años, que pretende Ideal?" In *Cuba Diáspora 1976: Anuario de la Iglesia Católica*, 42.

"De Varela a Martí." *Ideal* 1, no. 10 (June 15, 1972): 33–34.

Domínguez, Jorge I. "Cuban Catholics and Castro." *Worldview* 15, no. 2 (1972): 24–29.

"Editorial: America ante las dos alianzas" *Cuba Nueva* 2, no. 10 (February 1, 1963), 3–5.

"Editoriales: Nuestra posición." *Cuba Nueva* 1, no. 10 (August 1, 1962): 3–9.

"Editoriales: Un año de Alianza para el Progreso." *Cuba Nueva* 1, no. 12 (September 1, 1962): 3–4.

"Encuentro de sacerdotes cubanos." *Ideal,* October 1978.

"Enfoque en Miami." *Ideal* 4, no. 38 (October 15, 1974): 39.

"En misión y con Cuba en el corazón." *La Voz Católica,* August 21, 1992.

"Entrevista a José A. Pontojan: 'Yo no concibo obispos aliados a marxistas.'" *Ideal* 127 (August 1980): 21–23.

"Entrevista con el Señor José Fernández Badue (Lucas)." *Cuba Nueva* 2, no. 7 (December 15, 1962): 5–9.

Errasti, Mariano. "Reportaje del Congreso Católico Nacional. La noche mas luminosa de la historia." *La Quincena* 5, nos. 23–24 (December 1959): 42–47.

Espín, Orlando O. "Religiosidad popular: Un aporte para su definición y hermenéutica." *Estudios Sociales* 17, no. 58 (October–December 1984): 41–56.

———. "Tradition and Popular Religion: An Understanding of the *Sensus Fidelium.*" In *Frontiers of Hispanic Theology in the United States,* ed. Allan Figueroa Deck, 62–87. Maryknoll, NY: Orbis Books, 1992.

Estevez, Felipe. "El catolicismo popular." *Ideal* 56 (April 1976): 41.

Fernández, Manuel. "Presencia de los católicos en la revolución triunfante." *La Quincena* 5, nos. 1–2 (January 1959): 10–16, 94.

Fiallo, Amalio. "Amalio Fiallo ratifica su opinion sobre el diálogo." *Ideal* 87 (November 1978): 29.

"Los futuros sacerdotes del exilio." In *Cuba Diáspora 1977: Anuario de la Iglesia de Cuba,* 101–104. Miami: Unión de Cubanos en el Exilio, 1977.

García Tudurí, Mercedes. "Resumen de la historia de la educación en Cuba: Su evaluación, problemas y soluciones del futuro." *Exilio* (Winter 1969/Spring 1970): 108–142, 293–294.

García Valencia, Gilberto. "Juventud Obrera Católica." In *Cuba Diáspora 1972: Anuario de la Iglesia Católica,* 113. Miami: Unión de Cubanos en el Exilio, 1972.

Gastón Witchger, María Teresa. "Recent History of Hispanic Ministry in the United States." In *Prophetic Vision: Pastoral Reflection on the National Pastoral Plan for Hispanic Ministry,* ed. Soledad Galerón, Rosa María Icaza, and Rosendo Urrabazo, 183–188. Kansas City, MO: Sheed & Ward, 1992.

Goizueta, Roberto S. "United States Hispanic Theology and the Challenge of Pluralism." In *Frontiers of Hispanic Theology in the United States,* ed. Alan Figueroa Deck, 1–22. Maryknoll, NY: Orbis Books, 1992.

"Gran demonstración de fe popular, el Congreso Católico." *Bohemia* 51, no. 49 (December 6, 1959).

"El Hermano Victorino, DLS." *Cuba Diáspora 1978: Anuario del a Iglesia Católica,* 41–42. Miami: Unión de Cubanos en el Exilio, 1978.

Hernando, José L. "Una parróquia en el aire." In *Cuba Diáspora 1976: Anuario de la Iglesia Católica,* 37–40.

Herrera, María Cristina. "The Cuban Ecclesial Enclave in Miami: A Critical Profile." *U.S. Catholic Historian* 9, no. 1–2 (Winter/Spring 1990): 209–221.

Herrera, María Cristina. "Prólogo." *Exilio* (Winter 1969/Spring 1970): 11–14.

"Historia de veinticinco años." In *1928–1953 Bodas de Plata,* Juventudes de Acción Católica Cubana, 1–13. Hato Rey, PR: Impreso Ramallo, 1978. Facsimile of 1953 Havana edition.

Isasi-Díaz, Ada María. "The People of God on the Move: Chronicle of a History." In *Prophets Denied Honor: An Anthology on the Hispano Church of the United States,* ed. Antonio M. Stevens Arroyo, 330–333. Maryknoll, NY: Orbis Books, 1980.

"Jorge Mas Canosa." *Ideal* 46 (June 15, 1975): 13–15.

Jover, Mateo. "Presencia de la iglesia en una sociedad en transformación revolucionaria: la experiencia cubana. Ensayo de análisis prospectivo." *Exilio* (Spring 1970): 219–253.

La Juventud Católica Cubana cumple 50 años." *Cuba Diáspora 1978: Anuario de la Iglesia Católica,* 40–42.

Lasaga, José Ignacio. "La actual ley agraria cubana y el comunismo." *La Quincena* 5, no. 12 (June 30, 1959): 17–19, 30.

———. "La caridad y la justicia social." *Cuba Diáspora 1975: Anuario de la Iglesia Católica,* 68–72.

———. "La Iglesia Cubana en el marco de la constitución socialista de 1976." *Cuba Diáspora 1977: Anuario de la Iglesia Católica,* 11–17.

———. "La juventud del exilio y la tradición nacional cubana." *Exilio* (Winter/Spring 1970): 51–81.

———. "Que es el catolicismo social?" *Esto Vir* 3, no. 25 (September 17, 1933): 1–2.

Lebroc, Gerardo. "Sintesis histórica de la iglesia católica." *Cuba Diáspora 1972: Anuario de la Iglesia Catolico,* 7–29.

"La ley agraria del gobierno revolucionario contempla el interés supremo de la sociedad." *La Quincena* 5, no. 3 (February 1959): 12–14.

Leyva de Varona, Adolfo. "The Political Impact of Cuban Americans in Florida." In *Cuban Exiles in Florida: Their Presence and Contributions,* ed. Antonio Jorge, Jaime Suchlicki and Adolfo Leyva de Varona, 63–109. Miami: North-South Center, University of Miami, 1991.

"El manifiesto de las Asociaciones Católicas." *La Quincena* 5, no. 3 (February 1959): 30.

Marbán, Edilberto. "Como se apoderó el comunismo de la enseñanza secundaria en Cuba?" *Cuba Nueva* 1, no. 4 (May 1, 1962).

"El materialismo de izquierda y de derecha." *La Quincena* 5, nos. 5–6 (March 1959): 37, 78, 84.

Maza, Manuel. "Editorial: Hasta cuando?" *Mundo Nuevo* 3 (June–July 1962): 1–3.

Medrano, Humberto. "Porfirio Remberto Ramírez: No lo busquen en la tumba." *Bohemia Libre* 53, no. 27 (April 9, 1961): 24–25.

"Mensaje del Movimiento Demócrata Cristiano de Cuba a la III Conferencia Episcopal Latinoamericana, Puebla, Enero de 1979." *Ideal* 92 (February 1979): 20–21.

Mesa Lago, Carmelo. "Evaluación de las técnicas socialistas como via para resolver problemas estructurales de la economía de Cuba: 1959–1968." *Exilio* (Winter 1969/Spring 1970): 143–183.

———. "Seguridad social o inseguridad socialista?" *Cuba Nueva* 2, no. 1 (September 1, 1962): 18–22.

"El Movimiento obrero cubano bajo la hoz y el martillo." *Cuba Nueva* 1, no. 4 (May 1, 1962): 11–15.

"Normas generales de la U.C.E." *Cuba Diáspora 1978: Anuario de la Iglesia Católica,* 17.

Novas, Benito. "'Existe una quinta columna en los colegios católicos,' denuncian los alumnos expulsados de Villanueva." *Bohemia* 52, no. 48 (November 27, 1960): 48–49, 71–72.

"El Padre Vizcaíno habla para 'Ideal.'" *Ideal* 62 (October 1976): 43–45.

Peinado, Fermin. "Imagen de la Cuba posible y deseable." *Cuba Nueva* 1, no. 5 (May 15, 1962): 16–22.

Peinado, Fermín. "La II Declaración de La Habana: Un manifiesto comunista para la America Latina." *Cuba Nueva* 1, no. 1 (March 15, 1962): 17–23.

Pérez, Lisandro. "Cuban Catholics in the United States." In *Puerto Rican and Cuban Catholics in the U.S.: 1900–1965,* ed. Jay P. Dolan and Jaime R. Vidal, 147–209. Notre Dame, IN: University of Notre Dame Press, 1994.

Pico, Reinaldo. "Los cristianos debemos buscar la paz pero no a costa de nuestro principios." *Réplica* (magazine) 5, no. 201 (August 7, 1974): 24–26.

"Posición de la iglesia ante el comunismo." *Ideal* 1, no. 9 (May 15, 1972): 14–17.

Portes, Alejandro. "Dilemmas of a Golden Exile: Integration of the Cuban Refugee Families in Milwaukee." *American Sociological Review* 34 (1969): 505–518.

Poyo, Gerald E. "'Integration Without Assimilation': Cuban Catholics in Miami, 1968–1980." *U.S. Catholic Historian* 20, no. 4 (Fall 2002): 91–109.

———, and Mariano Díaz-Miranda. "Cubans in the United States." In *Handbook of Hispanics Cultures in the United States: History,* ed. Alfredo Jiménez, 302–320. Houston: Arte Público Press, 1994.

"Los presos y los obispos." *Ideal* 136 (October 1980): 23.

Rasco, José Ignacio. "La generación traicionada." *Bohemia Libre* 53, no. 18 (February 5, 1961): 48–49, 59.

————. "Inter-Americanism." In *Integration of Man and Society in Latin America,* ed. Samuel Shapiro, 270–280. Notre Dame, IN: University of Notre Dame Press, 1967.

————. "Sociologia del exilio." *Exilio* (Spring 1970): 15–50.

La Redacción. "Reflexiones en torno a la historia de la salvación." *Exilio* (Spring 1969): 3–8.

Regalado, Tomás. "César Chávez: Luchar contra el sistema dentro del sistema." *Ideal* 112 (December 1979): 22–23.

Riesgo, Rodolfo. "El marzato y la JOC." *La Quincena* 5, nos. 1–3 (January 1959): 22–24.

————. "15 dias en la nación." *La Quincena* 5, no. 4 (February 1959): 19.

————. "No tiene carácter político el Congreso Católico Nacional." *La Quincena* 5, nos. 21–22 (November 1959): 22.

Rumbaut, Rubén D. "El Humanismo y La Revolución." *La Quincena* 5, no. 8 (April 1959), 16–18, 29–32.

————. "Julio Morales Gómez (1913–1979)." *Cuba Diáspora 1981: Anuario de la Iglesia Católica,* 79–81. Miami: Unión de Cubanos en el Exilio, 1981.

————. "Intrínsecamente perverso!" *Bohemia Libre* 53, no. 13 (January 1, 1961): 41, 58, 64.

————. "Silueta psicológica de Fidel Castro Rúz." *Cuba Nueva* 2, no. 4 (November 1, 1962): 15–21.

Sandoval, Moises. "The Organization of a Hispanic Church." In *Hispanic Catholic Culture in the U.S.: Issues and Concerns,* ed. Jay P. Dolan and Allan Figueroa Deck, 136–165. Notre Dame, IN: University of Notre Dame Press, 1994.

"II Encuentro Hispano Nacional de Pastoral." *Ideal* 84 (August 1977): 10–12.

Segovia, Fernando F. "In the World But Not Of It: Exile as Locus for a Theology of the Diaspora." In *Hispanic/Latino Theology: Challenge and Promise,* ed. Ada María Isasi-Díaz and Fernando F. Segovia, 195–217. Minneapolis: Fortress Press, 1996.

"Semanas Sociales." In *Cuba y su Iglesia Católica* (CD-ROM). 1999.

Sosa, Juan M. "Santería." *Cuba Diáspora 1974: Anuario de la Iglesia Católica,* 74–75. Miami: Unión de Cubanos en el Exilio, 1974.

Super, John C. "Interpretations of Church and State in Cuba, 1959–1961." *The Catholic Historical Review* 89, no. 3 (July 2003): 511–535.

"El tercer aniversario de la reforma agraria cubana." *Cuba Nueva* 1, no. 7 (June 15, 1962): 9–15.

"UCE." In *Cuba Diáspora 1978: Anuario de la Iglesia Católica,* 18.

Urquiaga, Pablo. "Comunidades cristianas en mi Cuba." In *Cuba Diáspora 1972: Anuario de la Iglesia Católica,* 125–127.

Valdespino, Andrés. "America ante la intervención comunista: No podrá haber 'Alianza para el Progreso' sin 'Alianza para la Libertad." *Bohemia Libre* 53, no. 34 (May 28, 1961): 38–40, 61.

————. "Como cayó bajo el comunismo La Universidad de la Habana." *Cuba Nueva* 1, no. 2 (April 1, 1962): 19–24.

————. "Al comunismo no se le destruye por decreto (1953)." In *Valdespino: Cuba como pasión,* Fundación Andrés Valdespino, 74–77. Hato Rey, PR: Ramallo Brothers Printing, n.d.

————. "El cristianismo de los sepulcros blanqueados." *Bohemia* 51, no. 22 (May 31, 1959): 61, 97.

————. "Detras de esas bombas." *Bohemia Libre* 52, no. 12 (December 25, 1960): 48–50, 98.

————. "Lo histérico y lo histórico en el anticomunismo (1954)." In *Valdespino: Cuba como pasión,* Fundación Andrés Valdespino, 79–84. Hato Rey, PR: Ramallo Brothers Printing, n.d.

————. "Imagen de una Cuba distinta." *Cuba Nueva* 1, no. 4 (May 1, 1962): 23–27.

————. "El legado espiritual del Hno. Victorino." *Cuba Diáspora 1976: Anuario de la Iglesia Católica,* 81.

————. "Los peligros que hay que evitar a tiempo (apuntes sobre el futuro cubano)." *Bohemia Libre* 53, no. 26 (April 2, 1961): 30–32, 78.

————. "Que ha significado para la iglesia el Pontificado de Juan XXIII (1963)." In *Valdespino: Cuba como passion,* Fundación Andrés Valdespino, 47–53. Hato Rey, PR: Ramallo Brothers Printing, n.d.

————. "La revolución no necesita del comunismo." *Bohemia,* February 22, 1959.

————. "La revolución que hay que salvar" *Bohemia Libre* 52, no. 5 (November 6, 1960): 40–42.

————. "El talón de aquiles de una democracia. Conflictos raciales en los Estados Unidos: También está detras la mano del comunismo?" *Bohemia Libre* 53, no. 42 (July 23, 1961): 32–34, 67.

————. "El viaje de Stevenson: Triunfo o fracaso de una misión?" *Bohemia Libre* 53, no. 39 (July 2, 1961): 54–56, 64.

————. "La voz de la Iglesia en un mundo en crisis: La encíclica social de Juan XXIII." *Bohemia Libre* 53, no. 43 (July 30, 1961): 50–51, 58, 62, 64.

————, Antonio Fernández Nuevo, and Angel del Cerro. "Respuesta al Congreso de la Juventud Demócrata Cristiana." *Cuba Nueva* 1, no. 2 (June 15, 1962): 23–30.

Vega, Benjamín de la. "Grafo-entrevista con Manuel Ray." *Avance Criollo,* August 16, 1961, 6.

————. "Habla Ignacio Mendoza: Ray olvidó sus deberes para con los miembros del comité clandestino." *Avance Criollo,* August 16, 1961, 7, 48.

"Vietnam: Un cubano testigo." *Ideal* 1, no. 11 (July 15, 1972): 29.

Vilasuso Rivero, José. "Es oportuno un partido demócrata de inspiración cristiana?" *La Quincena* 5, no. 11 (June 15, 1959): 18, 44.

Villalón, José. "El camino del exiliado cubano." *Exilio* (Winter 1969/Spring 1970): 255–277.

Villegas, Agustín. "Francisco." *Ideal* 45 (May 15, 1975): 19–22.

"Y la iglesia . . . que dice?" *Ideal* 121 (May 1980): 31.

"Yo vi a Dios en Girón." *Ideal* 1, no. 8 (April 15, 1972): 5–7.

Zapata, Dominga M. "The Being and Doing of the Church: *Pastoral de Conjunto.*" In *Prophetic Vision: Pastoral Reflections on the National Pastoral Plan for Hispanic Ministry,* ed. Soledad Galerón, Rosa Maria Icaza, and Rosendo Urrabazo, 267–276. Kansas City, MO: Sheed & Ward, 1992.

Zayas-Bazán, Raul. "Bodas de Oro. Juventud Católica Cubana." *Cuba Diáspora 1979: Anuario de la Iglesia Católica,* 29–31. Miami: Unión de Cubanos en el Exilio, 1979.

Working Papers, Theses, and Dissertations

Bidegain, Ana María. "From Catholic Action to Liberation Theology: The Historical Process of the Laity in Latin America in the Twentieth Century." Working Paper #48, University of Notre Dame, Helen Kellogg Institute for International Studies, November 1985.

Campbell-Johnson, Michael. "Evolución de la cuestión social en la Compañía de Jesus: Breve historia" (unpublished). June 1984.

Damas, Guillermina. "Panorama histórico-pastoral de la dimension hispana de la Archidiocesis de Miami, 1958–1983." Master's thesis, Southeast Pastoral Institute and Barry University, 1983.

Gavaldá Romagosa, Margarita. "Estudio del conocimiento y actitudes de los católicos cubanos de Miami sobre la enseñanza social de la iglesia." Master's thesis, Southeast Pastoral Institute and Barry University, 1988.

Hidalgo-Caporizzo, Bibi. "The Archdiocese of Miami and the Cuban-American Community: Creating a Safe Space for Discussion on the Community's Relationship with the People of Cuba." Policy Analysis Exercise, Master of Public Policy, John F. Kennedy School of Government, Harvard University, June 2000.

Maza, Manuel P. "The Cuban Catholic Church: True Struggles and False Dilemmas: The Historical Characteristics of the Cuban Catholic Church and Their Impact on the 1959–1960 Episcopal Documents." Master's thesis, Georgetown University, 1982.

Padula, Alfred L., Jr. "The Fall of the Bourgeoisie: Cuba, 1959–1961." PhD dissertation, University of New Mexico, 1974.

Rosado, Caleb. "Sect and Party: Religion under the Revolution in Cuba." PhD dissertation, Northwestern University, 1985.

Strong, Sister Miriam, O.P. "Refugees from Castro's Cuba—'Of Fish and Freedom': An Historical Account of the Cuban Refugees Received and Relieved by his Excellency Bishop Coleman F. Carroll, in the Diocese of Miami, Florida, 1959–1964." Master's thesis, Fordham University, New York, 1964.

Published and Unpublished Pamphlets

Boza Masvidal, Eduardo, and Agustín Román. *Mensajes: Cuba ayer, hoy y siempre.* Miami, May 20, 1982.

Bufill, José Angel. *Manuel Guillot Castellano: Presente! (bosquejo biográfico de un héroe, de un mártir).* Centro America: Movimiento de Recuperación Revolucionaria, Secretaría de Información, March 1964.

Comité Organizador del Congreso Católico Nacional. *Temas del Congreso Católico Nacional.* Havana, November 29, 1959.

Consejo Asesor y Junta de Gobierno del Comité Mundial "Pedro Luís Boitel" Pro-Presos Políticos Cubanos. *Pedro Luís Boitel: Diario de un mártir.* Hoboken, New Jersey, 1978.

Cuban Student Directorate. *Those Who Rebel and Those Who Submit* (n.d.).

Directorio Revolucionario Estudiantil. *La cruz sigue en pie: Biografía y escritos de Alberto Muller. Ideario de una nueva generación cubana.* Caracas: Tipografía Lincoln, n.d.

———. *La persecución de la Iglesia Católica en Cuba.* Quito, Ecuador, 1962 (?).

———. *Porfirio R. Ramírez : Mártir del estudiantado cubano.* Miami, 1962 (?).

Foyaca, Manuel. *Democracia Social Cristiana: Discurso-programa: Pronunciado por el Dr. Manuel Foyaca, en la gran asamblea del Teatro Auditorium, 22 Noviembre de 1942.* Havana, 1942.

———. *La iglesia frente al comunismo.* Havana: Editorial Lex, 1960.

Freixedo, Salvador de. *Cuarenta casos de injusticia social; examen de conciencia por cristianos distraidos.* Havana: Centro de Informaciones y Acción Social, 1958.

García Moure, Eduardo. *Cuba: Un proyecto para la nación.* Caracas: Editorial Torino, 1994.

Gastón, Melchor, et al. *¿Por qué reforma agraria?* Havana: ACU; BIP, 1958.

Li Wei Han. *La Iglesia Católica y Cuba: Programa de acción.* Pekin: Ediciones en Lenguas Extranjeras, 1959.

Movimiento Demócrata Cristiano de Cuba. *Guerra revolucionaria.* Miami, 1966.

Oslé, Enrique, Antonio Fernández Nuevo, and Alfredo Cepero, eds. *Recorrido por suramerica: Informe, junio-agosto, 1961.* N.p./n.d.

Rumbaut, Rubén D. *Revolución traicionada.* Miami: Frente Revolucionario Democrático, 1962.

INDEX

Sánchez Arango, Aureliano, FRD leader, 159
Santamaría, Primitivo, priest and cursillo leader, 100
Santería, 12, 200, 201–202, 238, 254, 282, 287
Santiago de Cuba, 12, 34, 37–38, 40, 55, 75, 125, 175
Sardiñas, Guillermo, priest and revolutionary leader, 38, 41
schools, escuelitas cubanas, 103. *See* Catholic schools
Second Declaration of Havana, 167
Second Vatican Council: *Ad Gentes*, 190; on apostolic activism, 221–222; on cultural diversity and pluralism, 189–190, 200–202; effect on Latin American views of the Cuban revolution, 136, 139, 147, 169, 248–251, 251, 253; *Gaudium et Spes*, 137, 147, 189, 220, 248–249; on liturgical reforms, 95, 221; *Lumen Gentium*, 220–221; mentioned, 3, 129, 210, 273
Sedillo, Paul, Jr., priest and USCC leader, 224, 226–227
Segovia, Fernando, theologian, 5
Segundo, Juan Luís, priest and theologian, 216
semana social, 31
Semanario Católico, Havana, newspaper, 35
SEPI. *See* Southeast Pastoral Institute
Shrine of Our Lady of Charity. *See* Ermita de Nuestra Señora de la Caridad del Cobre
silenced church. *See* church of silence
Silva, Raul, archbishop and cardinal, 258
social Catholicism: in Cuba, 15–32; in exile, 129–155, 203–213, 232–238
Sociedad Interamericana de Hombres de Empresa, Miami, 143

Solidaridad de Trabajadores Cubanos. *See* labor organizations
Solzano de Villalón, Elordio, Catholic Action leader, 77
Sorí Marín, Humberto, revolutionary leader, 46, 59, 77
Sosa, Juan, priest and theologian, 202
Sotus, Jorge, exile paramilitary leader, 161
Southeast Pastoral Institute, Miami, 232–233, 236–237
Southeast Regional Office, Hispanic Secretariat, USCC, 226–228, 232
Soviet Union and Soviets, 52, 72, 86, 120, 127, 164, 174–175, 177, 240
Spanish American League against Discrimination, 184
Spanish Civil War, 19, 23, 79, 123
Spanish language: Anglo reactions to, 194–195; archbishops use of, 103, 199; at devotional spaces, 105–106; at home, work and social situations, 184, 187–189, 213; literary production in, 119; loss of, 220, 277; maintenance of, 6; in masses, rituals, and programs, 94–97, 117; media outlets and, 103–105, 118, 220; at meetings of lay organizations, 98–100, 117, 197, 223; at parishes, 193; priests use of, 222; at schools, 85, 101–103, 117–118. *See also* bilingual and bilingualism
Spanish Republic, 18
Spellman, Francis, archbishop and cardinal, 95
Spirali, Lorenzo, priest and founder of Villanueva University, 13, 78
St. John Vianney Seminary, Miami, 92, 95
St. Vincent de Paul Seminary, Boynton Beach, Florida, 189, 201, 218, 226
STC. *See* labor organizations

GERALD E. POYO

is professor of history at St. Mary's University. He is the author
and editor of a number of books, including *With All, and for the
Good of All* and *¡Presente!: U.S. Latino Catholics from Colonial
Origins to the Present.*